OH WHAT A MOVE!

To my friend, Bob Pollack,
with all my best wishes —
Howie Grunblatt

Oh What A Move!
Profiles of Hartford Basketball Players
1954-1984

Michael Copeland
Howard Greenblatt

Published by Fox Hall Press

ISBN 978-1-548-35039-0
Library of Congress Control Number: 2017946972

Cover Design by Carson Kenney
Book Design and Editing by Dean Greenblatt

A portion of the proceeds from the sale of Oh What a Move! *goes to the Sons of Thunder Coalition to support programs for Hartford students.*

Contents

Foreword
Basketball's Sociological Influence

Basketball, more than any other sport, has had a tremendous sociological impact within urban centers. Basketball courts are located on practically every corner within cities. The abundance of facilities allows for whole neighborhoods to participate in games. Perhaps the greatest influence is upon the culture of observant youth. Young people have automatic observatory access to their neighborhood heroes, older males participating as basketball players. This extreme influence has created great basketball success or breeding grounds within specific communities; South Chicago, Illinois; and the Bellevue Square Housing Project of Hartford, Connecticut.

This generational inspiration creates monopolies in city basketball, as well as the sport's popularity. It's no wonder that the high schools that feed or represent the breeding grounds dominate competitive basketball within their respective cities and suburban areas (Boys High of Brooklyn, Dewitt Clinton High of South Bronx, Westinghouse High of Chicago, and Hartford High, as examples). I wouldn't be surprised if young basketball players strategically attempted to falsely relocate within those mecca environments, just to engage in these extraordinary programs. Also, I wouldn't be surprised if school officials altered or modified school district lines to influence some form of possible equal parity throughout competitive high school city basketball. I've heard of parents relocating into these breeding grounds not always legally to place their children into these opportunistic environments, but also to have local entertainment access.

The breeding grounds communities attract the attention of many outsiders of those respective communities. Often their high school basketball games have a substantial number of fans in attendance. The summer basketball leagues draw people from throughout the city as well as from the nation. (Rucker's in New York City, the Baker League in Philadelphia, and the Hartford Parks Department Summer Basketball League are examples.) Lastly, certain basketball players individually have impacted sociological development and establishment. I am certain that Wilt Chamberlain, Kareem Abdul-Jabbar, Bill Russell, and Oscar

Robertson, to name a few, influenced, encouraged, and impacted city business, educational efforts, housing developments and availabilities, media responses and citizens' motivation.

Michael Copeland and I are supreme and utmost friends. Actually, he's like a brother to me. I met Michael Copeland during the early stages of my career. Since then we've developed a growing and strengthening bond that has occurred because of our tremendous similarities in culture and consciousness. Even throughout his youthful years, I realized that Michael was beginning to develop the wherewithal to inspire and influence people's thought processes through analyzing, strategic planning, and conveyance. As a player in my Rawson School Summer Basketball League, he established himself as a profound encourager as a leader of his teams. While serving as a counselor for the Trinity College Summer Camp, his charismatic personality inspired much younger kids to follow his direction. I began identifying that Michael possessed skills of a man leading boys while playing for Weaver High School's basketball team. And he displayed his utmost leadership and inspirational guidance as a founder and chief executive officer of his Sons of Thunder Basketball Program, an organization designed not only to provide youngsters structured recreation, but also mentorship throughout their academic endeavors. As a result, I am not surprised that he developed such a biographically and socially scientific work as *Oh What a Move!* Throughout *Oh What a Move!* Michael will teach us that basketball players, brought up and cultivated within the city of Hartford's basketball culture from 1954 – 1984, have tremendous sociological influence on the city and, in fact, the nation. Many of these athletes not only impacted Hartford's societal structure, but also those of their relocating communities.

Enjoy your reading!

Sadiq Ali

Educator, Education Consultant, and author of Benjamin E. Mays Institute: Educating Young Black Males

Preface

Mike Copeland and I share a special bond. We both played basketball at Weaver High School and look back fondly on the experience as one of the most memorable and enjoyable segments of our lives. When he contacted me months ago to interview me for a book he was writing about Hartford basketball players, I was honored that he considered my basketball exploits worthy for inclusion in his project. And when he found out during the interview that writing remains one of the main passions of my life, he requested my help in bringing his concept for *Oh What a Move!* to fruition. It was an offer I felt compelled to accept. My days of playing basketball in Hartford in high school and college spanned the mid-1960s and early 1970s, and Mike's playing career gapped the late 1970s and early1980s. Together we covered a considerable swath of the 1954-84 period that is the focus of the book. Mike's knowledge of the history of Hartford basketball surpassed my own, but we shared an enthusiasm for exploring the fascinating stories of legendary players from our hometown.

Any attempt to provide a comprehensive look at all the great basketball players from Hartford through the years is a futile undertaking. There is not enough space in a single book to cover the subject adequately, and as a result, the profiles we have included are merely representative of the numerous individuals that played significant roles in the evolution of basketball in Hartford. Our investigation was limited, in part, to former players that Mike was able to contact for interviews and their willingness to appear in the book. We also narrowed the scope of *Oh What a Move!* to male players that lived in Hartford during their playing days, realizing that to open the book to the players who lived outside the city and the exceptional female athletes who came on the high school basketball scene in the latter stages of the period we cover, was to broaden the inquiry beyond our capacity. We apologize in advance to all the worthy players omitted from our study.

Mike Copeland had been consumed by this project for three years before my involvement. It is his concept, his choice of subjects, and his basis of knowledge that form the crux of the book. I merely assisted in the execution. I have been the playmaking point guard to his MVP effort. It has been a rewarding and captivating collaboration.

Howie Greenblatt

Part I
Championship Fever
1954-1959

Frank and Ernie Perry
Weaver High School 1954, 1960

Championship fever gripped Hartford at the end of the 1953-54 season. Weaver was the first team in the city to win a state championship and events were held throughout Hartford to honor the victorious Weaver basketball team. An assembly was held in the Weaver auditorium attended by many dignitaries from the city, including Mayor Dominick DeLucco, Superintendent of Schools Robert Black, President of the CIAC and principal of Bulkeley High School Alexander Mackimme, Director of Physical Education in the Hartford Schools Joseph Gargan, and Judge Max Savitt. A plaque was presented to Coach Charlie Horvath, team captain Jackie Hartfield was given a commemorative basketball, and the players were awarded shiny new trophies. A testimonial dinner given by Bill and Max Savitt was held at the Bond Hotel, where the Weaver varsity, JV team, and cheerleaders were celebrated. Once again, school board members and city and state officials were on hand to present awards. The event was dubbed "Weaver Night" and it drew a sizable crowd of Hartford luminaries. At the AME Church in Hartford, the church where the Perry family worshiped, a group of approximately 125 parents and guests gathered to pay tribute to the Weaver basketball team. Many of the faith leaders in the community spoke glowingly of the young men that played on the team. For basketball fans, it was an exciting time to live in Hartford.

Weaver had come close to a title in the past. In 1939 the Beavers lost to Bridgeport Central 47-27 in the semifinals of the CIAC state tournament. In 1940 the team was defeated in the semifinals once again, losing to Stratford, 35-20. In 1945 Weaver beat Commercial High School of New Haven (the school that eventually became Wilbur Cross) in the semifinals of the state tournament, only to lose in overtime to another New Haven school, Hillhouse High School, in the title game. But in 1954 Weaver was finally able to break through to win the school and the city's first state championship. Weaver had raised the bar higher for what constituted a successful high school basketball season in the city. Winning the City Series or a conference title was no longer sufficient.

One of the key players on the historic 1954 Weaver team was Frank "Boo" Perry. Frank Perry grew up in Bellevue Square with his parents, seven sisters, and two brothers. His older brother, James "Cap" Perry and the legendary Bobby Knight, introduced him to basketball at the age of nine. He heard from older players the stories of racial bias that still permeated the sport, establishing obstacles for African Americans to get a fair shake in making a team and earning playing time. But Frank Perry did not allow himself to be deterred by the challenges he would face in becoming a basketball success story and taking his place among Hartford's finest players of his era.

Frank Perry had easy access to the gym at Arsenal Elementary School, where his father was a custodian. It was there that he began to put in the hard work of relentless practice, developing every facet of the game a player needed to succeed, dribbling a basketball with either hand until it felt like an extension of his fingertips, perfecting a smooth shooting motion, getting down the timing and the footwork to score around the basket, reading the way the ball came off the rim to know where to pursue a rebound. Frank Perry knew at an early age that basketball would play an important role in his life. He had played other sports but nothing provided the same kind of satisfaction he derived from shooting hoops. He began to haunt the basketball courts in his neighborhood. Like most of Hartford's future basketball stars, his first real taste of organized basketball came in the city's Park Department League. One of his early coaches was Jake Holmes, a superior motivator who won multiple Hartford Park Department League championships. Jake Holmes provided a solid foundation built on good habits and a winning attitude that Frank Perry would carry with him as he pursued his basketball destiny.

At Brackett Northeast Junior High School, Frank Perry continued to develop an affinity for winning basketball games. Under the guidance of Billy Taylor, another coach that stressed strong fundamentals, Frank Perry led his undefeated teams to championships in each of his junior high school years. When he entered Weaver High School as a sophomore, he earned a starting position on the junior varsity team. He continued to work diligently on his game, mindful of the intangibles that had led him to victory in the past, like guarding the opposing team's toughest player and playing unselfishly with his focus on passing the ball to the open man. He would never put up eye-popping scoring numbers, but his teammates appreciated his enormous value to the team.

As a junior playing in his first year on the varsity team, Frank helped Weaver qualify for the state tournament. In the first round of the Connecticut Interscholastic Athletic Conference tournament, Weaver upset defending champion Hillhouse, 53-42. Gene Haynes led the Beavers with 18 points in the game played in front of 5,000 spectators in the New Haven Arena. After eliminating Hillhouse, the Beavers expected to make a deep run in the tournament. But Weaver lost to New London High School, 53-39, in the quarterfinals. Frank Perry was not used to losing big games, and the defeat in the tournament left a bitter taste in his mouth. He went back to work during the summer, improving all aspects of his game. He played in the Hartford Park Department League with several of his Weaver teammates, learning to play together as a cohesive unit. He was determined not to let history repeat itself in his final season at Weaver by failing to win a state championship.

In his senior year all the effort he had put into basketball through the years was rewarded with a near-perfect regular season. Weaver finished the regular season with a single loss that came early in the season to Bristol. In the first round of the 32nd annual CIAC Class A state tournament, Weaver defeated Crosby High School of Waterbury, 87-63. In the quarterfinal match-up against Hall High, the Beavers prevailed 62-41. And in the semifinals the Weaver players beat Bristol 76-55, avenging the lone defeat on their otherwise spotless record. The only obstacle that stood between Weaver and the state championship was a final game against powerful Hillhouse in the New Haven Arena.

Hillhouse High School had won nine previous state championships. The Academics, coached by the legendary Sam Bender, had defeated Bulkeley (57-49), Torrington (47-39), and Roger Ludlowe (62-43) to make it to the tournament finals. The team was 24-0, ranked number one in the state, and eager to avenge a loss to Weaver in the first round of the 1953 state tournament, the last time Hillhouse had been defeated. Captain Harry Bosley, Gene Davins, and Sal DiNicola led the tall and talented Academics. Sam Bender called the group the best shooting team he had ever coached. Since losing to Weaver, he had made some tactical adjustments in the team's approach, switching from the combination zones he had been employing in favor of a strict man-to-man defense in an attempt to counteract Weaver's quickness, balanced scoring, and full-court pressure. So far no team had been able to solve Hillhouse's aggressive defense and relentless, attacking style of play.

Weaver coach Charlie Horvath had tailored his game plan to take advantage of his team's unique strengths. Coach Horvath was a protégé of Hugh Greer at the University of Connecticut, where he had served as the coach of the freshman basketball team before coming to Weaver. He was also a proponent of the innovative coaching philosophy that Red Auerbach would use with unprecedented success with the Boston Celtics in the NBA. Borrowing elements from both Hugh Greer and Red Auerbach, Charlie Horvath had his Weaver team playing a free-flowing, fast-breaking style of basketball that emphasized pace, ball movement, and quick-strike drives to the basket or pull-up jump shots rather than a structured pattern of repetitive set plays. As veterans of the parks and playgrounds in Hartford's North End, the Weaver players were well suited to the style Charlie Horvath opted to play. They had been playing the African American centric brand of basketball their entire lives. Even against a team as formidable as Hillhouse, there was no need to alter the way they played the game. The Weaver players approached the championship game with the utmost confidence, unimpressed with the Hillhouse legacy and reputation. They were from Hartford; and they knew what they were capable of doing.

The 1954 state championship game was played in front of a packed house of nearly 6,000 fans in the New Haven Arena, providing Hillhouse with a distinct home-court advantage. The underdog Beavers, with Ron Harris, Frank Keitt, Ted "Ron" Jefferson, Jackie Hartfield, and Frank Perry in the starting lineup and Henry "Beans" Brown as the sixth man, came out on fire and never let up. Weaver expanded a 14-12 first quarter lead into a 34-24 bulge at the half. After three quarters Weaver led 44-29, and with 1:20 left in the game and Weaver comfortably ahead by 19 points on the way to a 58-42 win, Coach Horvath pulled his starters and gave some of his reserves a chance to take the floor in the historic win. Weaver shot 50 percent from the floor for the game, hitting 22 of 44 shots in an incredible display of poise under pressure. In his recap of the game on the front page of *The Hartford Courant*, sports writer Jimmy Cunavelis called the win "the greatest victory in Hartford basketball history." Hartford had finally emerged from New Haven's shadow, and the rivalry between the two cities would reach an entirely new level of intensity.

Weaver's state title sent ripples of excitement through the city of Hartford, particularly in the North End, where pride in the team's accomplishments energized the community. Frank Perry and his Weaver teammates were the first team in Connecticut to win a state title starting five African American players. The historic victory mimicked the shift that was occurring in society as well as in sports, with African American athletes proving through their inspired play that they commanded respect both on and off the basketball court.

The emergence of Weaver as a force in high school basketball in the state coincided with the acceptance of the way the game was played in the parks and the projects as a viable iteration of the sport. The Bellevue Square, Stowe Village, and Keney Park free-form style had emerged as a legitimate type of basketball that could be adapted successfully to the high school game. Visionary coaches like Charlie Horvath were willing to permit the players the freedom to create and dictate the terms of engagement on the basketball court. Doc Hurley might have been able to accelerate the transition to the playground approach to high school basketball, but unfortunately he was never given the opportunity to coach at Weaver to implement the style he helped pioneer. The coaches that were tasked with the responsibility of carrying on the Weaver tradition, Frank Scelza, John Lambert, and Dwight Tolliver, recognized the value in maintaining the distinct Weaver brand that had originated in the parks and playgrounds and was vindicated by a state championship.

Since the CIAC sent both the winner and the runner-up of the Class A state tournament to the New England High School Basketball Championship tournament in the Boston Garden, the season was not yet over for either Weaver or Hillhouse. When the two teams met in the first round of the New England tournament, Hillhouse avenged the defeat in the state title game only days earlier by beating Weaver 84-76. Hillhouse utilized an extremely aggressive defense that took advantage of the team's depth by getting Weaver in catastrophic foul trouble. All five Weaver starters fouled out. Weaver was led in defeat by Ron Harris with 20 points, Frank Keitt with 15 points, and Frank Perry with 15 points. It was the final game of Frank Perry's high school career.

After graduating from Weaver, Frank Perry attended Shaw University in Raleigh, North Carolina for a year. He returned to Hartford, hoping to find a college that was a better fit for him than Shaw. A recommendation from John Culyer helped Frank Perry get accepted to Florida A&M, where he was a student for three years before enlisting in the military. He played on a service team with NBA standout Dick Barnett, winning yet another championship. After his military stint, he returned once again to Hartford, where he began his work career. He continued to play competitive basketball in leagues around the city. He was a member of the Hartford YMCA basketball team that advanced to the national championship game, where Frank Perry was named the game's Most Valuable Player. He also supervised the Vine Street School Recreation Program, where he mentored some of Hartford's finest emerging basketball players. His older brother James "Cap" Perry introduced Frank to golf, in the same way he had cultivated his interest in basketball. Frank fell in love with the sport and continued to play for many years. He retired from the Travelers Insurance Company after twenty-two years of service, and in retirement he volunteered in the First Tee Golf Program for Youth, which taught life skills and leadership in addition to the fundamentals of golf. Frank Perry was one of the city's original champions, and the pursuit of excellence marked his entire life.

***

Ernie Perry may have been the first Weaver basketball player that tried to emulate his older brother by winning a state championship, but he would not be the last. Both Rick Mahorn and Ken Mink attempted to duplicate their brothers' Owen and Dennis' 1971 title, but came up just a little short of their lofty goal. Ernie Perry would ultimately fail in his bid to capture a state championship, but like Rick Mahorn and Ken Mink who followed after him, he would emerge from his brother's shadow to forge an identity as an exceptional basketball player in his own right.

The path that Ernie Perry pursued on his route to basketball prominence was very similar to the one Frank Perry had followed. Ernie Perry attended Arsenal Elementary School and Brackett Northeast Junior High School, where, like his brother Frank, he played on undefeated championship teams coached by the legendary Billy Taylor. Ernie Perry also played in the Hartford Park Department League, where he was coached by his brother Frank and Henry "Beans" Brown, Frank's teammate at Weaver. Ernie also remembered playing for the great Doc Hurley, and feeling humbled when he returned to a team huddle and Doc asked him, "Son, why would you make a play like that?" Playing for the Arsenal team in the Park Department League helped prepare Ernie Perry for the level of competition he would face in high school.

As a 5'-11" freshman at Weaver, Ernie Perry became a starter on the

JV team and led the team in scoring and assists while playing outstanding defense. He made the varsity in his sophomore year and helped to spark the team coming off the bench. The team finished with a 12-8 record, a significant let down from the undefeated season the previous year that culminated in state and New England titles. In his junior year Ernie Perry was ready to assume a more prominent role on the team. In previewing his team's outlook for the upcoming season for *The Hartford Courant*, Coach Frank Scelza spoke about his promising point guard Ernie Perry, "He's a fine backcourt prospect. He's the best passer I've seen here. Sometimes he's too fast for his teammates. He's speedy and his only drawback seems that he doesn't shoot enough. He'd rather pass." As the season progressed, Ernie Perry was able to show his coach that he could both pass and score extremely well.

In an early season victory over Bristol, Weaver's Andy Morris hit a shot with nine seconds left on the clock and Ernie Perry sealed the 56-53 win with two foul shots with two seconds to go. Co-captain Ricky Turner paced the Beavers with 18 points, followed closely by Ernie Perry with 15 points as Weaver improved to 3-1 on the young season. The pattern of Ricky Turner and Ernie Perry pacing the Weaver offense continued throughout the season. In a 50-44 Weaver win over Hall, Ricky Turner scored 16 points and Ernie Perry 14 as the Beavers improved to 7-1 on the season. In a City Series match-up with Hartford Public at the Trinity Memorial Field House in front of a capacity crowd of 2,700 spectators, Ricky Turner and Ernie Perry scored 14 points each to lead Weaver to a 49-45 victory. Two weeks later, Weaver defeated Hartford Public again in an exciting 68-66 win that clinched the CDC title for the Beavers. Weaver completed the regular season with a 65-59 come-from-behind win over Hall. With less than a minute left in the game, Ernie Perry hit six straight points to provide the winning margin. Weaver finished the regular season with a 16-2 record heading into the state tournament.

In the play-down round of the CIAC Class A tournament in front of a sellout crowd in the New Haven Arena, Weaver beat Bridgeport Central 56-54 behind 24 points from Ricky Turner, who scored the game-winning lay-up with 42 seconds remaining in the game. Ernie Perry scored 12 points for the game, including two foul shots that tied the game at 52-52 and a jump shot that gave Weaver a 54-52 lead. But in the quarterfinals of the tournament, Hillhouse eliminated Weaver. The Beavers finished the season with a 17-3 record, but the loss to Hillhouse prevented Ernie Perry from matching his brother with a state championship.

Ernie Perry had one more chance for a title in his senior year, and with Ricky Turner graduated, he would have to shoulder more of the offensive load if Weaver was going to have another successful season. Even though he had always been a pass-first point guard and defensive stopper, Ernie Perry possessed the quickness and shooting touch to serve as the primary threat in the Weaver offense. He scored 26 points in a 56-44 win over New Britain as Weaver improved to 3-0 on the season. He struck for 23 points in a 69-53 win over CDC foe Fitch, while playing an exceptional floor game and coming up with key steals and assists. But Weaver faced stiff competition within the city. In a City Series game against Bulkeley in front of 2,300 fans in the Trinity Memorial Field House, Barry Leghorn scored 24 points to lead the Bulldogs to a 51-47 win over Weaver, dropping the Beavers to 5-2 on the season. Ernie Perry scored 13 points to pace Weaver before fouling out in the fourth quarter. Weaver bounced back from the loss to Bulkeley by beating New Britain, 66-48, as Ernie Perry scored 19 points, including 11 straight in a decisive fourth quarter. Weaver defeated Hartford Public, 65-54, at Trinity behind 20 points from Ernie Perry, 16 from promising sophomore John Lee, and 14 from co-captain Tom Stewart. Ernie Perry erupted for 31 points in an 83-57 win over Fitch, improving Weaver's record to 10-6 heading into the state tournament.

But once again Ernie Perry and his Weaver teammates' quest for a state title was thwarted in the quarterfinals of the CIAC state tournament by a school from New Haven, this time losing 61-55 to Wilbur Cross. Ernie Perry's outstanding career at Weaver had come to an end. He averaged 17 points per game as a junior, and as a senior he averaged 19 points per game and was an All-State honorable mention selection. He stayed in Hartford after he graduated from Weaver and played in leagues around the city. In 1963 he played on a Royal McBee team in the YMCA Industrial League with Corky Terry and Bobby Knight. In 1970 he signed to play with the East Hartford Explorers of the New England Basketball Association, where he was selected to the All-Star team several times. On the Explorers he played with talented players like Topsy DelGobbo, Tom Verroneau, Billy Evans, and Jim Kissane, yet he was able to stand out for his elite scoring ability and excellent defense, just as he had during his memorable career at Weaver High School. He was the prototypical point guard, capable of leading a team with his offensive production and defensive intensity, and he inspired the generation of Hartford basketball players that followed him.

George Zalucki

Hartford Public High School 1956

The road to success in basketball, as in life, does not always follow a direct and conventional path. Sometimes the route is circuitous and requires overcoming difficult obstacles. Such was the case for George Zalucki. He was born in Troy, New York, one of six children, and his family moved to Hartford when he was three years old. George Zalucki contracted polio as a child. He was put in an isolation hospital and when he was sent home his parents were told he might never walk again. But through the extraordinary determination and self-motivation that would epitomize his life, George Zalucki not only survived polio, he emerged from his childhood as a promising athlete.

He was initially attracted to baseball, but after watching the Harlem Globetrotters perform, his interests shifted to basketball. He even perfected the knack of spinning a basketball on his fingertip! At Our Lady of Sorrows School in Hartford, where he was coached by Father Fallcey, George Zalucki began to refine his basketball skills. In the eighth grade he led his team to the CYO State Championship, giving him a taste for winning basketball. The following year he enrolled in La Salette Seminary in Hartford, pursuing a youthful ambition to become a priest. At the Seminary he was coached by Father Hurley, who introduced George Zalucki to the finer points of playing in the low post. After a year, however, he realized that the priesthood was not for him, and he returned to Our Lady of Sorrows School for the tenth grade. From there he moved on to Hartford Public High School, where he emerged as a two-sport star in football and basketball. A rugged 6'- 6" in height, he played offensive tackle on the football team and was twice named to the All-Conference team. As a basketball player under legendary Coach Joe Kubachka, George Zalucki developed into a tenacious rebounder.

Since he was a strong student as well as a talented athlete at Hartford Public, George Zalucki attracted the attention of several colleges interested in recruiting him. But he and his parents were intimidated by the college application process, and instead of going on to further his education, he decided to enlist in the United States Marine Corps, where he served honorably for two years, before returning to Hartford. Back in Hartford he worked at a variety of jobs while pursuing a career in music. He still enjoyed playing basketball, and he was competing in a Parks and Recreation League game when his old coach, Joe Kubachka, spotted him.

"What are you doing here?" George Zalucki remembers Joe Kubachka asking him. "You should be playing basketball in college somewhere! Do you remember Johnny Egan from Weaver? He's playing at Providence College. Let me make a call for you."

Joe Kubachka coached Hartford Public basketball from 1951-66. His teams compiled a record of 176-86, and included among the victories were multiple Capital District Conference and city championships, a Class L state title, and two New England High School Championships. He went on to become the first coach of the Hartford Capitals in the Continental Basketball Association. During the course of his distinguished career, he had developed extensive connections throughout the basketball world. In going to bat for his former player after their chance encounter, Coach Kubachka not only resurrected George Zulucki's basketball career, he was instrumental in setting him on a path to a highly successful post-graduate life as well.

George Zalucki credited Joe Kubachka for helping him get accepted to Providence College, but it was his own fierce determination, inner drive, and strong sense of purpose that enabled him to convert the opportunity into an inspiring success story. He had played against Johnny Egan in high school, had watched his cross-town rival lead his Weaver team to a New England High School Basketball Championship, and he knew how Egan had teamed with Lenny Wilkens to give Providence College perhaps the best backcourt in all of college basketball. When Zalucki and Egan were united as teammates at Providence College, they helped propel the school into the national spotlight. With the toughness of an ex-Marine and the grit of someone who had overcome childhood polio, George Zalucki provided a powerful counterbalance to Johnny Egan's flash and finesse. Together they helped Providence College advance to the 1961 NIT semi-final game against Holy Cross. In a game reminiscent of Johnny Egan's heroic performance in the finals of the New England High School Basketball Championship, Providence College was tied 75-75 with Holy Cross. With no time left on the clock, Vinnie Ernst, Providence College's 5'- 8" point guard, went to the foul line with a chance to win the game, when, according to legend, Holy Cross fans shook the basket, causing the ball to pop out. Call it divine intervention with an assist from rowdy fans. Vinnie Ernst had been unable to seal the victory and the game went into overtime. Yet Vinnie Ernst redeemed himself for the missed foul shot by scoring or assisting on all 15 points in overtime, advancing the Friars to the title game against St. Louis University. George Zalucki saved his best game for the finals. In front of a packed house on the old Madison Square Garden basketball court in New York City, he scored 17 points and recorded 10 rebounds as Providence College won the NIT Championship.

There were a number of outstanding basketball players responsible for Providence College's historic win in its first tournament championship, including several with Connecticut roots. Ray Flynn, from South Boston, Massachusetts, would play a starring role in both the 1961 and 1963 Providence College NIT Championships. He would go on to serve as Mayor of Boston and ambassador to the Vatican. Tim Moynahan, a forward on the team and Johnny Egan's roommate, went on to become a lawyer in Waterbury, Connecticut. Richard Leonard, a self-described "farm boy from East Hartford," was a walk-on player at Providence who became a senior Vice President at Pratt & Whitney for over thirty years. Richard Holzheimer, a pre-med student at Providence while on a basketball scholarship, was a physician in Euclid, Ohio. With the exception of Johnny Egan, the players on the Providence College basketball team were not considered blue-chip recruits. They were a collection of students pursuing a college education that happened to enjoy playing basketball. But when they were on the court together, their talents meshed to form a cohesive, high-energy unit that was the equal of any college team in the country.

At the beginning of the 1960s, Providence College was an all-male school with about 2,400 students, most of them commuters. The first NIT Championship and the proud basketball tradition that followed would not have been possible without the contribution of the two players from Hartford. They were instrumental in launching Providence College onto the national stage. As George Zalucki said, "Without that '61 team, Providence College never would have had the start to become what it was for so many years. There never would have been a Marvin Barnes or a Jimmy Walker. The genesis of Providence College's success was that team."

George Zalucki became the father of nine children. He pursued a rewarding and highly successful career as a college coach, lecturer, educator, writer, and international personal development trainer. He lives in Tennessee and Florida, a long way from Hartford, where his basketball journey began, and where he developed the fortitude and resilience to overcome the serious challenges he faced in his youth to emerge as a champion in basketball and in life.

Johnny Egan
Weaver High School 1957

John Francis Egan was born on January 31, 1939 in Hartford, Connecticut. He grew up on Branford Street with his two siblings and his parents, Mr. and Mrs. Patrick Egan, both of whom worked at Royal Typewriter. "My mother was a saint," Johnny Eagan said, "And the nicest person you would want to meet." His dad was a fine hurling player (a popular sport in Ireland), and he supported his son's interest in sports with enthusiasm, attending as many games as he could manage. Johnny Egan's athletic ability took root at an early age. He was fast, strong, and well coordinated, and he had unusually large hands for someone of his modest size. By the fifth grade he was already showing indications of his considerable talents by excelling in a CYO league playing with older players. He attended Northwest Jones Junior High School, where he played both baseball and basketball. He was passionate about basketball and worked hard to develop his skills, sometimes shoveling the snow off the basketball court in Keney Park in order to practice. During summers, he regularly spent entire days playing basketball, starting in the morning and staying on the court until it was too dark to see the ball.

Johnny Egan entered Weaver High School in 1953. He showed sufficient potential as a member of the JV team that he was the only freshman Coach Charlie Horvath brought on the trip to Boston for the 1954 New England High School Championship Tournament. Hillhouse eliminated Weaver in the first round, but the team's defeat fueled Johnny Egan's desire for another chance to win the prestigious title before he completed high school. He showed marked improvement as a sophomore, yet it wasn't until his junior year that the full range of his talent became apparent. In Johnny Egan's junior year, Weaver defeated Manchester High School to win the state championship. He was selected as the tournament's Most Valuable Player and he led the voting for the *New Haven Register* All-State team. He was heralded as the best player in the state, a first for a player from Hartford. As the Connecticut state champions, the Weaver basketball team returned to the Boston Garden for the New England championship tournament, but once again the team was eliminated in the first round. Johnny Egan was still a season away from becoming the consensus number one player in all of New England.

The summer before his senior year, Johnny and several of his Weaver teammates approached Walter "Doc" Hurley to ask if he would coach their team in the Hartford Park Department Summer League. The players were young enough to play in the Intermediate division against other high school age teams, but they chose to play in the Open division against older and more experienced players. Walter "Doc" Hurley, a legendary four-sport Weaver athlete in his own right, had returned to Hartford after attending Virginia State University and working in Virginia as a successful football and track coach. It was a natural fit for him to work with members of the Weaver state champion basketball team. With a booming voice and an imposing stature, Doc insisted on consistent effort and team play. He possessed an intuitive sense of the way the game should be played and coached, dating back to his own experience as an outstanding player at Weaver and Virginia State. He was an early proponent of the fast-paced, free-flowing style of play that became the standard in the parks and playgrounds in Hartford's North End. He relied on guards to make good decisions with the ball, to take the shot when it was available, but to always look to pass to an open teammate that had established better position, especially in the post. He wanted everybody to run the court on every play. On defense he expected full court, man-to-man pressure the entire game, trapping and double-teaming the man with the ball when the opportunity presented itself. Generations of Hartford players bore the imprint of Doc Hurley's distinctive basketball philosophy.

Johnny Egan credited Doc Hurley with instilling the dedication and work ethic that would become a hallmark of his basketball career. Doc Hurley's influence on Johnny Eagan extended beyond the basketball court, just as it did for numerous Weaver students over the years. "Doc Hurley not only prepared you on the basketball court," Eagan said, "But he also had a way of talking to you that made you want to make better choices about life. He made us play at another level." The Weaver entry in the summer league finished with a 7-7 record, but the experience the players gained was a key factor in the team's success in the upcoming season.

Another highlight for Johnny Egan during the summer leading up to his senior year was attending Bob Cousy's basketball camp in New Hampshire, where he continued to hone his unique basketball skills. Bob Cousy, a Holy Cross and Boston Celtics legend, was intrigued with Johnny

Egan's potential. He became one of Egan's most influential mentors, helping him smooth out the rough edges of his game and getting him to think seriously about college. He suggested that Johnny Egan consider Providence College, a school trying to establish a strong basketball program under Coach Joe Mullaney, Bob Cousy's former teammate at Holy Cross. But the first order of business for Johnny Egan was to make the most of his senior year, and for him that meant returning to the New England High School Basketball Tournament for the third time in four years.

Johnny Egan and his teammates returned from summer vacation hoping to repeat as state champions, but even the players must have been amazed by the extent of their accomplishments during the magical 1956-57 basketball season. Egan led the Beavers to an undefeated regular season and a second consecutive state title. For the second year in a row, he was named the state tournament's Most Valuable Player. The team was given another shot at the New England championship. It was an opportunity that Johnny Egan and his Weaver teammates had been yearning for all year. The Beavers faced an undefeated Lawrence Central Catholic High School team playing in its home state. It was a game for the ages that made Johnny Egan a basketball legend.

It was a tense, hard-fought game, witnessed by nearly 12,000 fans in a raucous Boston Garden. Johnny Egan scored only four points in the first half. Weaver coach Charlie Horvath made countless superb coaching decisions during the course of the season, but one of the most inspired was to ask Bulkeley coach Lou Bazzano and Hartford Public coach Joe Kubachka to serve as assistant coaches for the New England tournament. At halftime the three Hartford coaches discussed what adjustments to make for the second half against Lawrence, and Lou Bazzano suggested telling the players to get the ball to Johnny Egan more and let him dictate the flow of the game. Coach Bazzano had seen Johnny Egan take over games against his Bulkeley team, and he was confident Egan could do the same against Lawrence. Charlie Horvath was on the same page with the other coaches, and he was willing to put the game in Johnny Egan's capable hands. He had seen Egan come through in the clutch too many times not to trust his star guard in the biggest game of his high school career.

Johnny Egan scored 20 dazzling points in the third and fourth quarters. Weaver trailed by two points when Johnny Egan was fouled with time about to expire on the Boston Garden clock. After a timeout, he calmly stepped to the line and sank two free throws, sending the game into overtime. In the three-minute overtime period Johnny Egan scored 12 of Weaver's 21 points, leading the team to the historic victory. He had scored 36 points in the title game, 32 in the second half and overtime, in what was considered the greatest individual performance in the tournament's history. The win gave Weaver a 24-0 record and Hartford's first New England High School Championship. Once again Johnny Egan received the most votes for the All-State team in Connecticut, he was a consensus high school All-American, and he was the most sought after high school player in New England. He had led Weaver to high school basketball's Promised Land, and he delivered in a manner that elevated the school to a position of regional prominence.

When he graduated from Weaver, Johnny Egan was acclaimed the best high school player in New England. He became one of the first major recruits to attend Providence College, laying the groundwork for the Friars' rise as a national power in college basketball. He teamed with Lenny Wilkens to give Providence one of the best backcourts in the country. Prior to his junior year he suffered a serious knee injury in a freak accident, but he returned late in the season to help his team reach the NIT finals, only to lose to Bradley University. He was named to the NIT All-Tournament team in 1959. As a senior, he worked hard to regain his form and conditioning following his injury. Though he had lost some of the explosiveness that earned him the nickname "Space" for his exceptional hang time in mid-air, he was still an amazing player for the Friars, leading the team back to the finals of the NIT, which it won by defeating St. Louis University. Once again he was named to the NIT All-Tournament team. He scored 39 points against Villanova in a triple overtime victory, a tournament record at the time. As a senior, he also earned second team All-American honors. The kid from Weaver had come through in the clutch once again, establishing his reputation as one of his generation's most dominant high school and college players. But he wasn't done yet. The biggest challenge of his basketball life was still ahead of him. It remained to be seen if the undersized guard from Hartford's North End could compete at the sport's highest level, the National Basketball Association.

Johnny Egan was selected as the twelfth pick in the NBA draft by the Detroit Pistons. During an NBA career that spanned twelve seasons, he played for the Detroit Pistons, New York Knicks, Baltimore Bullets, Los

Angeles Lakers, Cleveland Cavaliers, and San Diego/Houston Rockets. He played with and against some of the greatest players the sport of basketball has ever known, including Jerry West, Wilt Chamberlin, Bill Russell, and Oscar Robertson, and he not only held his own, he distinguished himself for his adept ball handling, pin-point passing, tenacious defense, and clutch shooting. He played 712 games in the NBA, averaging 7.8 points per game and recording 2,102 career assists. He had his best season as a member of the New York Knicks during the 1963-64 season, averaging 13.0 points and 5.4 assists per game. He went on to coach the Houston Rockets from 1973-76.

Johnny Egan settled in the Houston area, where he started his own insurance firm. Now in his seventies, Johnny Egan continues to stay fit through a regimen of push-ups, swimming, bike riding, and yoga. He has remained involved in charitable causes in Houston. In August 2013 he travelled to Seattle, Washington to participate in a Celebrity Weekend golf tournament to benefit the Lenny Wilkens Foundation, a charitable organization that provides education and health care for children in need. Like Egan, Lenny Wilkens had gone on from Providence College to play and coach in the NBA. He became the only three-time inductee to the Naismith Memorial Basketball Hall of Fame, as a player, an NBA coach, and a coach of the United States Olympic gold medal basketball team. When his friend and former teammate asked for his support with the Foundation's golf tournament, Johnny Egan did not hesitate to give his assistance, and he would return year after year to help his friend and former college teammate. Just as they had stood side-by-side on the basketball court, they teamed up once again in support of Seattle youth.

Basketball remained an important part of his life. He organized basketball clinics for kids, and he occasionally went to a local YMCA to shoot around with the guys. He kept a basketball in his bedroom that he liked to toss around from time to time. He was a long way from Hartford, but maybe when he touched that basketball he was reminded of his youth and the city where his remarkable basketball journey began. He married the love of his life, former Weaver High School cheerleader Joan Grimaldi, who died of cancer at the age of fifty-seven. During their wonderful marriage, they had two children, John and Kimberly, and four grandchildren. In many ways Johnny Egan epitomized the very best of Hartford basketball, not only through his extraordinary accomplishments on the court, but also in the humble and caring manner he had chosen to live his life. He will always be remembered as the kid from Weaver High School in Hartford who reached the pinnacle of basketball success, and he set a standard of excellence for all that followed to strive to attain.

Bob Countryman
Weaver High School 1957

When Weaver High won the 1954 CIAC Class A State Championship to cap-off a 19-1 season, the city of Hartford caught a severe case of championship fever. It was the city's first state title, and the fact that it came at the expense of perennial nemesis Hillhouse High School, made the taste of the 58-42 victory that much sweeter. Not even an 84-76 opening round loss to Hillhouse in the New England High School Basketball Tournament at the Boston Garden – a vindictive choice of scheduling motivated, no doubt, by Connecticut's past dominance of the tournament – could dampen Hartford's enthusiasm, especially in the North End. Wherever people congregated, in corner grocery stores, diners, barbershops, downtown department stores, soda fountains, houses of worship, movie theaters, school hallways, and city parks, the Weaver state championship was a constant topic of conversation. Names like Ted Jefferson and Ronnie Harris, Weaver stars that had been named to the state All-Tournament team, were spoken with almost reverential pride. Kids all over the city played the game with renewed intensity, envisioning their own path to celebrity status. Suddenly high school basketball was the most popular pastime in Hartford, and the excitement generated by Weaver's hoop success left the city clamoring for more.

But the 1954-55 Weaver basketball season quickly tamped down expectations of an emerging dynasty. The championship team of the preceding year was hit hard by graduation, losing four of the five starters, and the lone returning featured player, Ted "Ron" Jefferson, had his season curtailed for medical reasons, leaving veterans like Henry "Beans" Brown, Bob Pollack, Dick Reilly and Jerry Roisman to shoulder an impossible load. The team suffered through a disappointing season, failing to qualify for the chance to defend the title that had brought such elation to the community. But the frustration of an unsatisfying season was tempered by the emergence of a group of promising sophomores. Johnny Egan had been the lone freshman that Coach Charlie Horvath chose to accompany the 1954 team to the New England tournament, and in his sophomore year he showed indications of his vast potential. A number of talented players had arrived from Brackett Northeast School, where legendary

Coach Billy Taylor was in the habit of producing junior high school city championships, ringing up a total of twelve titles over his fabled career. One of the most dynamic players from the esteemed Brackett Northeast program was Bob Countryman.

One of twelve children, Bob Countryman grew up on Suffield Street (now Battles Street) in the North End in a three-room flat with very little running water. The family moved to a five-room apartment with a single bathroom in Bellevue Square when he was four years old. His father, Baurel, made a living as a trucker before becoming a barber for forty-two years. His mother supplemented the family income by working in homes in West Hartford. Bob Countryman attended Arsenal Elementary School and Brackett-Northeast Junior High before arriving at Weaver as a sophomore. He began to play in the Hartford Park Department basketball program when he was in grammar school, and he continued playing through high school. Some of the Park Department coaches that influenced his emerging basketball skills were Orice Smith, Freddie Ware, and Doc Hurley. Like most players in Hartford in the fifties and sixties, he admired the great Bobby Knight, deeming him "The Man". He also looked up to the players that preceded him, recalling names like Rudy Knight, Cap and Boo Perry, Ron Jefferson, Gene Haynes, Jack Hartfield, Frank Keitt, and Sonny Thomas. "They all played the game hard and fast," he said. For his mentors, Bob Countryman singled out some of the most distinguished names in the history of Hartford basketball, Bobby Knight, Cap Perry, Joe Young, Willie and Freddie Ware, and Doc Hurley. His own name would eventually attain a similar level of prominence in the hierarchy of legendary city players.

The Weaver team struggled through a losing season in his sophomore year, but the players gained valuable experience that would reap significant dividends as the core group became juniors. One of the highlights of Bob Countryman's sophomore year was a thrilling double overtime game against a strong Bristol team. Weaver had lost 70-57 earlier in the season to Bristol, but in the rematch in the Trinity Memorial Field House, the improving Beavers gave the defending Central Connecticut Conference champions all they could handle. With time running out in the fourth quarter, Bob Countryman hit a shot to tie the game at 43 all and force the first overtime period. At the start of the second overtime, he scored on a pass from Henry "Beans" Brown that gave Weaver a lead the team would continue to hold in the 50-48 win. Jerry Roisman led the Beavers in scoring with 10 points, and Vern Lee and Bob Countryman each scored eight, helping to offset a rare off night by Johnny Egan, who only managed one point. With his late game heroics, Bob Countryman showed his knack for coming up with big plays in big games, a trait that would be repeated throughout his high school and college career.

Before the start of the 1955-56 campaign, the team benefited from an inspirational pre-season event that Coach Charlie Horvath scheduled in the Weaver gym. Coach Horvath brought in "Mr. Basketball", Bob Cousy, the acclaimed star point guard of the Boston Celtics, along with famed Celtics' coach Red Auerbach, to conduct a basketball clinic for area coaches, fans, and players. Weaver players like Floyd Martin, Johnny Egan, and Bob Countryman had the opportunity to work on techniques and maneuvers with Bob Cousy, bolstering their confidence for the upcoming season. "It should be a very interesting season," Charlie Horvath told Jimmy Cunavelis of *The Hartford Courant* as he previewed the Weaver team in his typically modest and understated fashion. "We've got more size than last year and this bunch may be surprising. They've got the ability and could be good."

The reason for Coach Horvath's subdued optimism going into the season was a solid nucleus of six players that included 5'- 11" John Harrell, 5'- 11" Johnny Egan, 6'- 1" John Sullivan, 6'- 2" Ted McBride, 5'- 11" Bob Countryman, and 6'-3" Bob Shannon. Four seniors, 5'-10" Ray Sailor, 5'- 9" Floyd Martin, 6'- 2" George Bell, and 5'- 11" Bob Murray, were all poised to contribute when needed, and over the next two seasons, the core group of Weaver underclassmen and a strong supporting cast would form one of the most effective and cohesive units in the history of Hartford basketball.

The Beavers started the season with a 7-1 record. In a game against Hartford Public in the Trinity Memorial Field House, Weaver rode the hot shooting of Johnny Egan to a 64-55 win. Egan scored 24 points and Bob Countryman added 14, while George Zalucki paced the Owls with 14 points and Pat Camilli scored 12. It was the first City Series victory for Weaver in two years. But on several occasions Weaver reverted to the inconsistent play that plagued the team the previous year. In a City Series game against Bulkeley, the Beavers led by 11 points with two minutes left in the game and ended up losing. Against a weak New Britain team that was 1-8 in the CDC and 2-11 overall, Weaver had to rally in the final two minutes to win 61-50 in a game that was closer than the final margin indicated. As the team headed into the state tournament, the players understood they would need to tighten up their sloppy play if they hoped to capture another title.

Weaver suffered five losses during the regular season to finish with a 12-5 mark and qualify for the 34th annual CIAC Class L State Tournament. The Beavers defeated Stamford 67-64 in the opening round of the tourney, setting up a quarterfinal match-up against unbeaten Hillhouse. The Academics were led by two-time All-State performer Leon Nelson, a holdover from the 1955 State Championship team known as the Wonder Five that had cruised through a 26-0 season, only to lose to Somerville High School of Massachusetts, 67-65, in the semifinals of the New England tourney. The Wonder Five consisted of Leon Nelson, Gene Davins, Sal DiNicola, Johnny Woods, and Don Perrelli, and at the time was considered by many to be legendary coach Sam Bender's best Hillhouse team ever. But Weaver upset Hillhouse in the 1956 state tournament 59-51, overcoming a boisterous crowd of 4,500 fans in the New Haven Arena. After eliminating the vaunted Academics, Weaver had an easier path to the finals, beating Fairfield Prep 75-58 in the semifinals.

The Beavers opponent in the championship game was a dangerous Manchester High School team, making its first appearance in the finals since beating Naugatuck in 1938. The game was played in the New Haven Arena in front of a capacity crowd of 5,500 spectators. Weaver broke away in the third quarter to beat Manchester, 62-52, for the Beavers' second state title in three years. Johnny Egan led Weaver with 18 points, including eight-of-eight from the foul line. Ted McBride and Bob Countryman chipped in with 11 points each, and John Sullivan scored 10. Manchester was led by Al Cole's 25 points. The players barely had time to celebrate the championship before the team embarked on the trip to the Boston Garden to face the champion from Maine, Morse High School, in the New England High School Basketball Tournament.

Morse High was tall, fast, and experienced and featured two prolific scorers in Ed Marchetti and Wes DeCapus. Weaver was out-rebounded and outshot badly from the floor, falling 78-57. Losing to Morse High from Bath, Maine hurt deeply. Bob Countryman and his teammates were determined to return to the tournament the following year and avenge the bitter defeat.

The Hartford Park Department summer basketball program was started in 1949, the inspiration of Mickey Ross, a former UConn student and successful pharmacist. It was co-sponsored from its inception by *The Hartford Courant* and run for many years by Larry Hutnick, a basketball and baseball standout at Hartford Public and Trinity College, under the direction of James Dillon, Hartford's Recreational Director and the person for whom Hartford's Dillon Stadium was named. The summer leagues were played on 19 outdoor courts throughout the city and were broken down into four age groups: Peewees (9-12), Juniors (13-15), Intermediates (16-18), and Seniors (18 and over). Practically every high school basketball prospect in the city participated in the summer leagues at some point. The leagues provided the opportunity for players to gain experience against top-notch competition in games officiated by board certified officials. High school teammates usually split up according to the proximity of their homes to local parks. But the 1954 Weaver state title team with Frank Perry, Ron Harris, Jack Hartfield, Ron Jefferson, and Frank Keitt, played together as a unit, representing Bellevue Square in the Intermediate Division the summer before winning the state championship. The experience they acquired winning a summer league title undoubtedly contributed to their success the following season.

After losing to Morse High in the New England Scholastic Tournament, Bob Countryman and several of his teammates, including Johnny Egan, Ted McBride, and John Sullivan, made arrangements to play on the same team in the summer league. Although they were young enough to participate as Intermediates, they chose to play in the Senior Division for Keney Park. They approached Doc Hurley and asked him if he would be their coach, and he agreed. In Doc Hurley they had found the perfect coach, a knowledgeable, serious-minded Weaver graduate familiar with the fast-breaking, full-court pressing style they were accustomed to playing under Coach Charlie Horvath. Their summer league team finished in fifth place with a 7-7 record and was eliminated from playoff contention after one game, but the experience they gained was invaluable. Coach Horvath credited the team's summer league involvement for Weaver's incredible success during the 1956-57 basketball season.

In Bob Countryman's senior year, the Weaver basketball team had no apparent weaknesses. John Harrell had graduated, but Russ Carter, a reliable reserve the previous season, became a starter, joining Johnny Egan,

Bob Countryman, Ted McBride, and John Sullivan to form a balanced, cohesive unit. The bench was solid as well, with Carl Littman and Bob Shannon the primary reserves. The team charged through an undefeated regular season, finishing with a spotless 17-0 record. The first team Weaver faced in the CIAC Class L state tournament was Hamden High School, and the Beavers came away with a 60-40 win. Wilbur Cross provided stiffer resistance in the quarterfinal match-up, but Weaver prevailed 68-60. The semi-final game against Warren Harding High School of Bridgeport was played in the New Haven Arena in front of 4,500 fans. The game remained tight most of the way, with Weaver pulling ahead to stay in the third quarter when Bob Countryman's drive to the basket ignited a 14-4 run that sealed a 73-64 win. By the time Countryman picked up his fifth foul in the fourth quarter, the game was already decided.

For the fourth time in five years, Weaver's path to the state championship ran through the Academics of Hillhouse High School. The New Haven Arena was filled to capacity. Weaver fans turned out in force for the game in Hillhouse's back yard, buying more than 2,700 tickets in advance. The teams battled evenly the entire game, with neither squad able to sustain much of a lead. But Johnny Egan's blistering offensive output coupled with Weaver's smothering man-to-man, full-court pressure, eventually took a toll on the Academics. Weaver successfully defended its state title, winning 77-72. Johnny Egan scored a tourney record 33 points, Ted McBride added 16, and John Sullivan 15. Bob Countryman, playing his usual all-out, attacking style, scored six points before fouling out. With a second consecutive state championship safely in hand, the players turned their focus on a goal they had yet to achieve, winning the New England High School Basketball Championship.

In the first round of the tourney, Weaver came back from an early deficit to beat LaSalle High School from Rhode Island, 75-59. It was the first time the Beavers had survived the first round of the New England tournament. Johnny Egan injured his knee on the second play of the game, sending shock waves reverberating through the Weaver faithful in the Boston Garden. But he played most of the remainder of the game and did not appear seriously impaired. The win against LaSalle set up a rematch with Hillhouse, and once again the two powerhouses of Connecticut basketball played an intense game. Weaver took a slim lead late in the first half, and held on to beat the Academics 60-53 to improve to 23-0. But

Weaver was not the only unbeaten team in the tournament. Lawrence Central Catholic improved their record to 27-0 by beating Manchester High of New Hampshire, pitting two undefeated teams against each other in the championship showdown.

High School teams from across the six-state region had been competing for the New England High School Championship since 1921, when New Haven Commercial (later to become Wilbur Cross) beat Rogers-Newport of Rhode Island 35-11 for the first title. The 1957 game between Weaver and Central Catholic High School in Lawrence, Massachusetts was almost universally acknowledged as the most exciting contest in the long history of the prestigious tourney. The game could not have been closer. The evenly matched teams were tied 16-16 after one quarter, 27-27 at the half, and 64-64 at the end of regulation when Johnny Egan made two foul shots with four seconds left on the clock. It took a stunning three-minute overtime period, in which Weaver made its first eight attempts and Johnny Egan single-handedly outscored Central Catholic 12-9, for the Beavers to prevail, 85-73. Johnny Egan scored 36 points, 32 in the second half and overtime, for the finest individual performance in tournament history. John Sullivan added 22 points, Ted McBride 14, and Bob Countryman 7. Weaver became the first team from Hartford to win the New England title and in the process cemented friendships and memories that have endured a lifetime.

Not only was Bob Countryman an outstanding basketball player, he was an exceptional student as well. He had multiple offers from colleges from which to choose, and in the end he decided on UConn, where one of his brothers had gone and where Coach Horvath encouraged him to attend. His original intent at UConn was to pursue a major in Civil Engineering, like his brother. But he met a black chemistry instructor in his lab class, Theodore Williams, who was working on a Ph.D. in Chemistry. Theodore Williams was from Washington, D.C., knew Los Angeles Lakers great Elgin Baylor, and loved basketball. He encouraged Bob Countryman to major in Chemistry, the field of study that became his vocation. Bob Countryman reflected on his indebtedness to Theodore Williams, "That gentleman became my mentor and friend for the rest of my life. He went on to become a master teacher at the College of Wooster in Wooster, Ohio. My mentor passed in 2000. R.I.P. Dr. Theodore Williams."

Bob Countryman enjoyed an impressive basketball career at UConn for Coach Hugh Greer. He moved into the starting lineup as a sophomore after he replaced injured guard Johnny Risley in a game against Manhattan in Madison Square Garden and played well in the UConn win. Bob Countryman's initial start came in UConn's first game ever against Georgetown University, and again he played well as the Huskies defeated the Hoyas in the inaugural meeting of the historic rivalry. Coach Hugh Greer spoke to Bill Lee of *The Hartford Courant* about Bob Countryman's progress, "How many sophomores can you remember as valuable as Countryman has been to this team? I'm glad the Manhattan game gave us the opportunity to learn his true value. I remembered somebody had told me Bob did well on big stadium courts and since this game was in Madison Square Garden, I sent him out there. I had been given correct information. Countryman showed me in that game that he deserved a starting role, and nobody has been able to get him out of the lineup ever since."

Bob Countryman's importance in the UConn lineup as either a reserve or a starter was reflected in an early season game against Yale University in his junior year. The Huskies were struggling against their in-state rival, trailing by six points with less than a minute to play, and then by a single point as time was about to expire. With hope of avoiding an embarrassing loss on their home court fading, UConn's Bob Countryman rose up for his left-handed jump shot and floated in the winning basket as time expired. Bob Countryman had been in tough games before. He had played in front of big crowds. And he knew how to respond to pressure with poise and resolute confidence. He was an outstanding basketball player whose statistics tell only a small part of his remarkable story.

After he graduated from the University of Connecticut with a degree in Chemistry, Bob Countryman became an Analytical Chemist with the U.S. Food & Drug Administration in Boston. He transferred to Los Angeles, where he worked for ten years before relocating to San Francisco as a Forensic Chemist with the Drug Enforcement Administration. He later worked in San Diego in a supervisory capacity. Bob Countryman retired in January 2003 after forty-one years of federal service. He returns to Hartford periodically, where he still gets together with former teammates and friends from his Weaver days and to reminisce, perhaps, about one of the greatest teams in the history of Hartford basketball.

John Norman
Weaver High School 1958

John Norman was born in Greenville, South Carolina. His parents worked as share-croppers, but they left that dreary, low-paying work to seek better educational and employment opportunities in Hartford. In the Rice Heights neighborhood where they settled, baseball seemed to be the most popular sport, so John Norman joined the Little League team, becoming the only African American player. One of his teammates was Johnny Egan, establishing the basis for a friendship that would carry over to Weaver, where they would team up once again to put their high school on the map as a basketball powerhouse. When his family moved to the Nelson Court housing project, where basketball was the most popular sport, the athletically-gifted John Norman first became interested in the game he would go on to play with such distinction in both high school and college in the city of Hartford. He attended the Brackett Northeast School, where his academic and athletic skills began to flourish. He practiced playing hoops at various playgrounds in his neighborhood, and when he realized he had a flair for the game, he developed his skills in both church and Hartford Park Department leagues.

At Weaver High John Norman continued to excel academically, becoming a member of the National Honor Society. He also did extremely well on the basketball court. As Johnny Egan's teammate, he played a key role on what was arguably the greatest Weaver basketball team in history, winning back-to-back State Championships in 1956 and 1957 and the 1957 New England High School Championship at Boston Garden. During his senior year, the 6'-3" center/forward anchored Weaver's inside game, crashed the boards, made timely jump shots, and was a deadly foul shooter, sinking 85% of his attempts. He received Weaver High School's Frederick W. Stone Athletic Prize, awarded to the most outstanding student in sports and academics.

When John Norman graduated from Weaver, he attracted interest from a number of colleges with his impressive academic and athletic credentials. He decided to stay in Hartford to attend Trinity College on a full scholarship, where he thrived academically and became a prolific scorer and rebounder on the basketball team. As a junior he averaged 17.5 points per game and scored 38 points against a strong Williams College team in a losing effort, only two points shy of Trinity's single-game scoring record at the time. John Norman was elected captain of the Trinity basketball team for his senior year, becoming the first African American to hold the position. He scored 803 points during a career cut short by a serious knee injury in his senior year. He was elected to the Trinity College Basketball Hall of Fame and became president of his college alumni class. John Norman graduated from Trinity with a major in History and a minor in Spanish. He went on to earn a Master's degree in Political Science and a Ph.D. in Professional Higher Education Administration from the University of Connecticut. Throughout his distinguished career, he was a trail-blazing college educator and administrator, serving in positions in Connecticut, Vermont, Florida, Massachusetts, and Maryland. His dedication to education inspired numerous young people to pursue careers in the field. He received multiple awards for his achievements in education, and he served on the Board of Directors of institutions such as the Urban League of Greater Hartford, the Hartford Foundation for Giving, and the Doc Hurley Scholarship Foundation. From his humble origins as the son of sharecroppers, John Norman went on to become a standout basketball player in the city of Hartford at both the high school and the college level and to inspire a generation of young people by the example of excellence he set in the classroom as well as on the basketball court.

Benny Thomas
Weaver High School 1958

In his junior year, Benny Thomas was a key reserve on the undefeated 1957 Weaver team that went on to win state and New England championships. Like many of the players that could not crack the starting lineup on a supremely talented team in cities such as Hartford and New Haven, he could have been a starter and featured player for most of the high schools in the state. But he had the maturity and team-first attitude to accept his substitute role. Instead of pouting or stirring dissension on the team, he embraced the chance he was given to come off the bench and ignite his teammates with his energy and enthusiasm. What Benny Thomas remembered most fondly about the 1957 team was not only that it went undefeated, but also how great it felt to play against his teammates in practice every day. "We were so even in talent," he said, "It made our practice sessions much more competitive than the real games. Any member on the bench could have started for almost any other high school team." Benny Thomas would have his chance as a starter in his senior year, but he truly appreciated the once in a lifetime opportunity to be a part of one of the greatest teams in his school and his city's history.

Benny Thomas was born and raised in Hartford's North End. His mother was a seamstress and his father was the co-owner of a laundromat. Benny Thomas had two sisters that played an influential role in his life. Joyce, his younger sister, was a Weaver cheerleader. His older sister, Janet, married a player on the iconic Harlem Globetrotters touring basketball team. Benny Thomas traces his interest in basketball back to the fifth grade, when he saw the Harlem Globetrotters play at the State Armory. He developed his game under the guidance of the Ware brothers, Fred and Willie, long-time Hartford Parks and Recreation directors. The Wares coached Benny Thomas and his friends John Norman and Pernell Hicks on the St. Benedict's basketball team. At Brackett Northeast School Benny Thomas played for the incomparable Billy Taylor, establishing a solid foundation for the sound basketball fundamentals he would display in high school. His junior high school basketball team competed against freshman teams from Weaver, Bulkeley, and Hartford High, preparing him for the type of competition he would face at the next level.

When Benny Thomas entered Weaver as a tenth grader, he was ready for the challenge. He earned a starting spot on the JV team, showing the skill and competitive drive that he would carry over to the varsity the following season. As a junior, he played a crucial role in relief of such talented players as Johnny Egan, John Sullivan, Ted McBride, Bob Countryman, and Russ Carter. It was a close-knit team, the kind coaches dreamed about, where everyone accepted the role assigned to him and sacrificed personal goals for the good of the team.

As a senior during the 1957-58 season, Benny Thomas's full range of skills was on display. He was co-captain of the Weaver team with Russell Carter, forming one of the best back-courts in the state. At 5'-11" and 160 pounds, Benny Thomas was comfortable at either guard position. He was an exceptional ball-handler, jump shooter, and penetrator. He averaged 13 points per game as a senior, and led his team back to the Class L state tournament, where Weaver lost in the second round, ending its reign as state and New England champions. But the ability of Weaver to put such a competitive team on the court after having lost so many of its star players from the undefeated championship season to graduation would become indicative of the school's winning tradition. The Beavers would not have to rebuild very often, they would simply have to reload in order to maintain a reputation as a powerhouse high school program. Winning was becoming habit forming at Weaver, and with the excitement generated by the unprecedented success of the Johnny Egan era, the future of the basketball program looked remarkably bright.

After graduating from Weaver, Benny Thomas attended Lincoln University in Pennsylvania for a year before returning home to Hartford, where he worked hard to raise four boys. He worked at Pratt and Whitney for five years and played basketball in the Industrial League. He retired from the Travelers Insurance Company as Director of Information Systems after thirty years of service in the same city where he had helped his Weaver High School team make basketball history by winning its only New England High School Championship, a memory he will cherish for the rest of his life.

Ricky Turner
Weaver High School 1959

When Weaver High won the New England High School Championship in 1957, the school and the city of Hartford earned a reputation throughout the region as a hotbed of basketball talent. All-American Johnny Egan became Coach Joe Mullaney's first notable recruit at Providence College, and as the Providence basketball program developed into one of the nation's best, the doors were opened for other players from Hartford, like George Zalucki and Jim Benedict, to follow Johnny Egan to Providence. Johnny Egan's amazing story created the false impression among aspiring basketball players in the city of Hartford that success on the basketball court automatically translated into opportunities to attend college on scholarship. Unfortunately, the reality of the situation was that all too few of Hartford's finest basketball players succeeded academically and athletically after leaving high school. The players that were fortunate enough to earn scholarship offers often had to travel to the south or the west to junior colleges or traditionally black schools, and many returned home after a semester or two, disillusioned and bitter at the experience. Ricky Turner was a player that proved the exception to this rule, and his life story serves as a stirring example of how a native son of Hartford's African American community was able to defy the odds and leverage his impressive educational credentials to make a big difference in improving the lives of others.

Ricky Turner grew up in Hartford's Bellevue Square and Bowles Park housing projects with his two older sisters and his grandparents. As a kid, Ricky Turner worked odd jobs to help the family. He mowed lawns, shined shoes, and delivered newspapers while attending a variety of different elementary schools scattered through the North End, including Arsenal, Mark Twain, and Rawson. At Northwest Jones Junior High School he began to find his athletic stride, playing on both the baseball and basketball teams. During the summer between seventh and eighth grade, he played on a VFW-sponsored team. He got along well with his teammates, and he noticed that they were equally as concerned about academics as they were about sports. They talked about the kind of courses they would need to take in high school to prepare for college. It made an impression on him that would influence his thinking about the educational process, especially as it related to his community.

In his first year at Weaver High School, Ricky Turner was the only freshman on the varsity baseball team. He also played on the junior varsity basketball team, a significant accomplishment since the Beavers had recently won Connecticut Class L State Championships in three out of the past four years, as well as a New England High School Championship in 1957. Competition in the school for the limited number of spots on the varsity team was fierce. The usual progression through the ranks at Weaver went freshman team as a freshman, JV team as a sophomore, and varsity team as a junior and senior, provided you had demonstrated sufficient talent and potential to remain in the program all four years. "If your name wasn't Johnny Egan or Russell Carter," Ricky Turner recalled, "You simply had to wait your turn to start on the varsity team."

As a sophomore, Ricky Turner gave up playing baseball to focus exclusively on basketball. "It seems like most of my buddies who were African American were playing hoops, and they were winning," he claimed. "I just wanted to be around a winning atmosphere with my friends." Since the championship seasons, there was a definite buzz surrounding Weaver basketball. The Weaver gym was filled to capacity for every game, with excited fans cheering for the Beavers to notch another win. On the road the opponents' gyms were packed as well, as students from other schools around the state were anxious for a glimpse of the defending New England champions. And when Weaver played a City Series game against either Bulkeley or Hartford Public, the rivalries were more intense than ever. A victory against Weaver was enough to make a success of the entire season. Ricky Turner's decision to focus his attention on basketball was driven by the team's sudden popularity. The baseball team could not compete with the celebrity and respect that playing basketball at Weaver provided. While he remained on the JV basketball team his sophomore year, he looked forward to playing on the varsity as a junior, perhaps even as a starter. He wanted to help maintain Weaver's winning tradition and to carve out his niche as one of the city's best players.

After his sophomore year, Ricky Turner played in the Hartford Park Department Summer League to prepare himself for the competition he would face on the Weaver varsity team. Most of the starters from the championship team had graduated, like Johnny Egan, John Sullivan, Ted

Mcbride, and Bob Countryman. A coaching change had also taken place at Weaver, with Frank Scelza replacing Charlie Horvath. Ricky Turner was uncertain how the change would impact his status. He had expected that Coach Horvath would make him a starter, but he did not know what Coach Scelza had in mind for his role with the team. But Frank Scelza recognized Ricky Turner's talent and potential and put him in the starting lineup along with veterans from the Johnny Egan era, Benny Thomas, Russell Carter, and John Norman. Weaver remained one of the most highly regarded teams in the state, and Ricky Turner's future looked bright.

Ricky Turner returned for his senior year as a confident scorer and determined team leader. He was named co-captain of the 1958-59 team with Oszzo Laysayers, his teammate over the summer on the St. Benedict's team in the Hartford Park Department Summer League. Ricky Turner led the Beavers in scoring and helped the team win the CDC Championship. He saved one of the best games of his career for the state tournament, a 56-54 win against Bridgeport Central. Playing in the New Haven Arena in front of a crowd of 3,207 people, Ricky Turner rallied the Beavers from a seven-point deficit in the fourth quarter to tie the game. With 42 seconds left in the game, he drove through the Bridgeport Central defense to score the winning basket. He led all scorers in the game with 24 points, and he and Ernie Perry scored all of Weaver's points in the fourth quarter, sparking the comeback. But Weaver would not get an opportunity to compete for another state or New England Championship. Wilbur Cross was in the midst of winning four consecutive state titles from 1958-61, and Weaver did not make it back to the finals. Ricky Turner had perpetuated the Weaver tradition of basketball excellence, making the All-Conference team and garnering All-State consideration. It was time to turn his attention to the next phase of his life, getting a college education.

Although Ricky Turner had the desire to go to college, the obstacles that stood in his way would be difficult to overcome. He needed a scholarship in order to afford college, but in spite of his fine performance on the basketball court, he was not recruited by any schools. There were two people that came to his aid when he needed help the most, and without their assistance his life could have gone in a very different direction. The first person that was influential in setting Ricky Turner on the path to a college education was Dr. James Peters, a noted psychologist who spent many hours helping Ricky develop the basic reading and math skills he would need to succeed in college. Dr. Peters also helped him with the task of completing the application, making sure he submitted the forms and information required for the admission process.

The second person that was instrumental in helping Ricky Turner get into college was Joe Beidler, the Weaver football coach. Joe Beidler graduated from Trinity College and spent three years coaching at his alma mater. After his coaching stint at Trinity, he accepted a position as the head baseball coach and assistant football coach at Whitman College in Walla Walla, Washington, where he and his wife Ruth moved in 1949. After two years he became the head football coach as well, and remained at Whitman College coaching both sports until he returned to Connecticut in 1955. Once he was back in Hartford, Joe Beidler coached football and baseball at Weaver and Conard High School in West Hartford until he retired in 1983.

While he was at Whitman College, he became friendly with two men that coached at Linfield College in McMinnville, Oregon, Paul Durham, the head football coach, and Roy Helser, the head baseball coach. Although Linfield College and Whitman College were rivals in the Northwest Conference, Joe Beidler bonded with the two coaches and their families and they spent time together socially. "After leaving Whitman, my new assignment of coaching in high school in Hartford enabled me to make recommendations for student-athletes whom I believed would be successful at Linfield," Coach Beidler said in an interview. The first athlete that Coach Beidler recommended to his friends at Linfield College was Curtis Manns, who had played football for him at Weaver for three years before graduating in 1958. Curtis Manns played football at Linfield for three years as well, giving up the sport as a senior to concentrate on academics. He eventually earned a Ph.D. and served on the faculty of Florida A&M for many years.

Curtis Manns was the first recruit to go to Linfield from Hartford, but he would not be the last. In total, ten student athletes from Hartford attended Linfield College based on the recommendation of Joe Beidler, establishing what became known in Linfield sports lore as the "Hartford Connection". Six members of the "Hartford Connection" went on to become college educators after graduating from Linfield College: Curtis Manns, Pete Dengenis, Bob Sullivan, Bob Ruffalo, John Lee, and Ricky Turner. After graduating from Linfield, where he earned All-Conference recognition in basketball, Ricky Turner went on to earn a Ph.D. at Stanford and to become a counselor and administrator in the California State University system. He seized the opportunity for a college education that two mentors, Dr. James Peters and Coach Joe Beidler, presented to him, and he turned it into an inspiring demonstration of his capacity for academic achievement.

When he was growing up in Hartford, Ricky Turner encountered many outstanding basketball players in the community that would never make it to a four-year college or university because of a lack of academic preparation and proper counseling. Those players that had the opportunity to attend a junior college often failed to complete the course of study, and returned to Hartford to seek employment and perhaps to play a little more basketball in leagues around the city. Ricky Turner understood the problem, and when he was in a position to help, he returned to Hartford to offer a potential solution. While working at the University of California in Irvine, he designed an experimental program that would provide student athletes with help getting into college and staying in college once admitted. He called his program "the student-athlete high school academic mentor project", and he arranged to have it tested in two cities in the country, Compton, California and Hartford, Connecticut. In Hartford 45 sophomore athletes – 15 from each of the three public high schools – were selected to take part in the program. The students and their parents were asked to sign a contract in order to participate. The students agreed to maintain a journal detailing how they spent their day and to meet with a mentor – a volunteer teacher, coach, or counselor – once each week to discuss their progress in the program. They were also required to attend tutoring sessions and to take part in programs with their parents that encouraged better study habits, time management skills, and College Board preparation. The program focused exclusively on athletes because, as Ricky Turner explained when he was in Hartford to implement the program, "As long as they are performing well in sports, and those parents can be clapping in the stands, the schoolwork slides. Too often athletes live a life of joy, without academic demands. Then they think they'll make it on their athletic ability alone. They don't."

Ricky Turner considered it a dream come true to come back to Hartford to put the program he had designed into action and "to give something to the city that gave me so much." He wanted the next generation of

Hartford student-athletes to experience the same kind of success he had found on the basketball court, in the classroom, and in life.

Part II
Fierce Rivalries
1960-1969

Jim Benedict
Hartford Public High School 1960

Jim Benedict was born in Hartford and grew up on Broad Street. His mother worked as a bank teller and his father was a toolmaker. He attended Dominic Burns Elementary School from kindergarten through eighth grade, but his introduction to basketball occurred on the basketball courts at Mitchell House, a non-profit organization that assisted the disadvantaged in Hartford. All Jim Benedict needed to do was hop the fence in his back yard to get to the basketball courts, where he practiced for hours. Interns from nearby Trinity College on assignment at Mitchell House helped him to hone his basketball skills. He was steadily becoming an outstanding basketball player with a deadly jump shot. As a kid, he also played baseball; he was a fine pitcher and center fielder on the Frog Hollow Little League team. But when he gave up four homeruns to an opponent in a Little League game, he decided to focus on basketball. At fourteen Jim Benedict met Father Ford of Immaculate Conception Church, who aided his conversion to Catholicism and encouraged him to join the church's CYO basketball team, where his talent for the sport became apparent. Like many of Hartford's finest players, he began competing in the city's Parks and Recreation League, a proving ground for those with aspirations of playing on one of Hartford's competitive high school teams. Representing teams from Pope Park and Goodwin Park, he fared well against the city's elite young basketball players, providing confidence he could play at the high school level.

As a ninth grader, Jim Benedict attended Hartford Public High School, which boasted one of Connecticut's up-and-coming basketball programs. It did not take him long to prove he could compete successfully at the high school level. He started on the JV basketball team as a freshman, and in his sophomore year he became a starter on the varsity team, averaging 16.6 points per game on the strength of a silky smooth outside stroke.

In his senior year at Hartford Public, Jim Benedict served as co-captain of a stellar Owls' team that was a year away from capturing two consecutive New England High School basketball titles. Returning lettermen Jim Benedict, Stan Poole, and Ed Miller, the other co-captain, would join a trio of promising sophomores, Eddie Griffin, Lenny Kostek, and Bruce

Maddox, to form the nucleus of an exciting Owls' team. The team jumped out of the gate quickly, beating Fitch, Norwich, Hillhouse, and New Britain in the first four games of the season. Hartford Public would rattle off four more victories to improve to 8-0 on the season, before losing to Norwich, 78-70. In the first loss of the season to Norwich, Jim Benedict led the Owls in scoring with 25 points, and Stan Poole chipped in with 18 points and 15 rebounds. In a City Series match-up with Weaver, Jim Benedict scored 24 points and grabbed 12 rebounds to pace the Owls to a 56-50 win over the Beavers. As the team headed towards the tournament, the Owls showed they had the firepower and senior leadership to contend for a state title.

In a play-down game against Ansonia to qualify for the tournament, Jim Benedict had one of the best all-around games of his career, scoring 27 points on 12-of-18 shooting from the field and grabbing 18 rebounds in an 80-58 win. Hartford Public faced a familiar foe in the opening round of the 38th annual CIAC Class L basketball tournament, playing Bulkeley in the New Haven Arena in front of a crowd of 4,096 spectators. The Owls used a balanced scoring attack and outstanding shooting to defeat the Bulldogs, 72-58. Stan Poole and Eddie Griffin scored 19 points each, Jim Benedict added 17, and Bruce Maddox chipped in with 13 for the Owls, overcoming 19 points from Barry Leghorn and 13 from John Beilotti. The team reached the quarterfinals of the CIAC Class L state tournament, before dropping a heart-breaking 60-59 decision in overtime to Naugatuck. It was Jim Benedict's final game of his high school career, and he remained undecided about the next step in his basketball journey.

Jim Benedict's father, Wesley, encouraged his son to enroll in a private school, Bridgton Academy in Maine, an institution that had a tradition of preparing student-athletes for success in college athletics. In his two years at Bridgton, Jim Benedict became a scoring sensation, averaging over thirty points per game. He scored 50 points twice and at least 40 points in nine games. He scored a total of 1,500 points and was named All-New England Prep School Player of the year in 1961. He was recruited by Fairfield University, where he was expected to join his friend from Hartford, Pat Burke and his former Owls teammate, Stan Poole. But very late in the process, Coach Joe Mullaney from Providence College reached out to him, soliciting the support of his former player from Hartford, Johnny Egan, to help persuade Jim Benedict to attend Providence instead of Fairfield.

Providence College had lost out on two highly prized All-American recruits. John Austin opted to attend Boston College, where he was considered one of the top guards in the school's history. Dave Bing chose Syracuse over Providence College, laying the foundation for a career that saw him become the number one pick in the NBA draft, enjoy a successful twelve-season NBA career, and earn a spot in the Naismith Memorial Basketball Hall of Fame. John Austin and Dave Bing's decisions to pass on the offers to attend Providence College opened the door for Jim Benedict and another talented guard, Bill Blair, to accept basketball scholarships to fill out a promising Friars' team. Bill Blair's admittance provided Providence College with an unexpected benefit. When he arrived at Providence, Bill Blair told Joe Mullaney, "You should see my cousin Jimmy," which led to the recruitment of Jimmy Walker, one of the greatest Friars' basketball players in the school's history.

For months Joe Mullaney declined to reveal to his talented freshmen, Jim Benedict and Bill Blair, the names of the recruits that had turned down offers to Providence College, freeing up the scholarships they would eventually accept. Whenever they would ask Coach Mullaney to identify the players, he would simply tell them, "Don't worry about it; you guys are better ball players than they are." Since John Austin and Dave Bing went on to become two of the greatest players in their respective colleges' history, when Jim Benedict and Bill Blair did learn the identities of the players they replaced on the Providence College wish-list, there was certainly no need to feel they had been slighted.

When Jim Benedict was a freshman at Providence College, the rule that prohibited freshmen from playing on the varsity basketball team was still in effect. The legendary Dave Gavitt, who was eventually elected into the Naismith Memorial Basketball Hall of Fame, coached the freshman team. Dave Gavitt, who later served as the first commissioner of the Big East Conference, was able to give Jim Benedict excellent preparation for his three-year varsity career. As a sophomore, Jim Benedict played with John Thompson, the future Boston Celtics' player and esteemed Georgetown coach. John Thompson averaged 26.2 points and 14.5 rebounds per game in his senior year to lead the Friars to a 20-6 record.

In Jim Benedict's junior year, Providence College emerged as a dominant force in college basketball with the arrival of future All-American Jimmy Walker. Jim Benedict teamed with Jimmy Walker, future NBA All-Star

Mike Riordan, Dexter Westbrook, and Bill Blair to form one of the most potent teams in the nation. In his junior season Jim Benedict's Providence College team was the third-ranked team in the nation, compiling a 24-2 record, but lost badly to Princeton and its All-American Bill Bradley in the Eastern Regional finals of the NCAA tournament. All five starters from that team returned for Jim Benedict's senior season, but the center, Dexter Westbrook, was declared academically ineligible, and the Friars could not return to the heights they had reached the previous year. They were eliminated in the first round of the NCAA tournament, compiling a record of 22-5.

But Jim Benedict, the 6'- 4" sharpshooter from Hartford, left his mark on Providence College basketball history. He scored over 1,000 points in his career, with a .455 shooting percentage, a remarkable achievement considering he was a long-range shooter in the era before the three-point shot was implemented. He was elected to the Providence College Athletic Hall of Fame. After graduating from Providence College, he received a Master's Degree from Rhode Island College. The kid from Broad Street, who used to dream about making the Hartford Public team while shooting hoops at Mitchell House, became a star in high school, prep school, and college, and in the process secured his reputation as one of the city's finest players of all time.

Barry and Wayne Leghorn
Bulkeley High School 1960, 1966

In the history of Hartford basketball, there have been a number of outstanding brother combinations that have left their mark on the city, including Dwight and Osee Tolliver, Paul and Rufus Wells, Ben and Fred Mathews, Owen and Rick Mahorn, Bill and Doward Tisdale, Joe and Michael Adams, Kenny and Kevin Hightower, and Pete and Bill Egan, to name just a few. One set of brothers that had a significant impact on Hartford basketball history in the South End were the Leghorn brothers, Barry and Wayne.

Barry Leghorn first became enamored with basketball while playing on a neighbor's driveway court. It did not take him long to notice he had a knack for making baskets. The more he practiced, the easier it became to get the basketball to do exactly what he wanted it to do when it left his fingertips, travel in a precise arc, with just the right amount of backspin, and settle into the net. His father, Russell, put up a hoop for him in his own yard, making it easier to work on his shot. Before long he was shooting baskets all day, every day, developing the touch that would make him a star in the city at both the high school and college level. He started going to local parks to test himself against other young players. He represented Goodwin Park in the Hartford Parks and Recreation League. He continued to develop his game while he attended Naylor Elementary School. He made the basketball team at Burr Junior High School, but he was stricken with pneumonia in ninth grade and missed most of the basketball season. But Barry Leghorn was not deterred. He kept striving to improve, hoping to make the Bulkeley High team the following year.

When Barry Leghorn entered Bulkeley as a sophomore in 1957, he played on the JV team for most of the basketball season. Coach Lou Bazzano's varsity team was stacked with outstanding players like Carmen Perrone, Jackie Gilbert, Mike Thompson, Al Rudis, Mike Shea, and John Chmielewski, forming the nucleus of one of Bulkeley's most successful teams in the school's history. But by the end of the season, Barry Leghorn had cracked the varsity starting lineup. The team made it to the Class L finals of the CIAC State Tournament, losing 69-50 to a powerful Wilbur Cross team that included three All-State performers, Dom Ferrara, Bill

Hulteen, and Don Perno. By virtue of finishing as the runner-up in the state, however, the Bulldogs earned the first appearance in school history in the New England High School Basketball Championship tournament, only one year after Weaver had given the city of Hartford its first New England championship. Bulkeley advanced to the semi-final game in Boston Garden before losing once again to Wilbur Cross. The New Haven school would go on to win the championship in a game that marked the beginning of the end for Connecticut's participation in the tournament after a fight broke out near the end of the title game against Somerville. Barry Leghorn scored 13 points in the consolation game against Westerly, Rhode Island, helping Bulkeley capture third-place in the tournament. Barry Leghorn had emerged as a starter and reliable scorer for Bulkeley as a sophomore, and he was ready to assume a much more prominent role on the team in the following years.

Bulkeley lost high scorer and first team All-State selection Carmen Perrone to graduation in 1958. A fresh batch of future stars, Gene Reilly, Jim Belfiore, Joe Hourihan, Ted Kwash and Leo McGrath, were just arriving on the scene and would eventually help Bulkeley return for another run at the state and New England championships. But in the interim, Coach Lou Bazzano needed someone to step up and assume the scoring and leadership role in Carmen Perrone's absence. Barry Leghorn was up to the task. "Barry shot 48 per cent from the field in each of his last two seasons with us," Lou Bazzano recalled with pride in an interview with *The Hartford Courant* sports writer Jimmy Cunavelis. Lou Bazzano went on to tell Jimmy Cunavelis about an incident on December 18, 1959 that revealed a great deal about Barry Leghorn's character:

"We're playing East Hartford and running away from them in the second half. With five minutes to go Leghorn ties Carmen Perrone's individual Bulkeley game scoring record of 41 points. In a time-out I tell Barry he's tied the mark and that he could stay in the game and break the record.

"Barry decided to leave the game. He said this game was one-sided and that Carmen got his 41 points in a close one. 'Let someone else play,' he said.

"I'll never forget that incident, which typifies the kind of person Barry is," Bazanno concluded.

But Barry Leghorn was capable of lighting it up against strong teams as well as weaker ones. In a quarterfinal game against Naugatuck High in the state tournament, he scored 26 points, going 14 for 17 from the foul line as Bulkeley advanced to the semifinals with a 92-78 win. In a game against Weaver in his senior year, in a contest that would determine the winner of the City Series, he scored 34 points, including 14 of 14 free throw attempts, as Bulkeley beat Weaver, 51-47. His proficiency from the foul line against Weaver was not an anomaly for Barry Leghorn. At one point in his senior year he hit 25 consecutive free throws. He finished the season making 83 percent of his foul shots, a Bulkeley record at the time. Bulkeley won the CDC and City Series titles, before losing to Hartford High in the state tournament. He averaged 23.4 points per game. At the end of the season he made the All-Capital District Conference Team and First Team All-State. He was contacted by several colleges, including a couple from the Ivy League, but he decided to stay close to home and attend Trinity College in the South End of Hartford.

By attending Trinity College, Barry Leghorn was following in the footsteps of another great player from Bulkeley, Charlie Wrinn. At Bulkeley, Charlie Wrinn excelled in baseball, basketball, and swimming. He went on to become a star baseball and basketball player at Trinity. He set the college's scoring and rebounding records, and he led the nation's small colleges in rebounding. After a stellar baseball career at Trinity, he pitched for several years in the Milwaukee Braves organization. He went on to become a coach, social studies teacher, and department head at Wethersfield High School. He continued to play both baseball and basketball in the Hartford area, and he was inducted into the Trinity College Hall of Fame, the Twilight League Hall of Fame, and the East Hartford Explorers Hall of Fame.

Charlie Wrinn was not the only multi-sport athlete from Bulkeley to attend Trinity College. His basketball and baseball teammate at Bulkeley, Charley Mazurek, was a year behind him at Trinity. Charley Mazurek played basketball, baseball, and football at Bulkeley. He was selected First Team All-State in basketball two years in a row, becoming the only athlete in the school's history to win All-State honors in consecutive years. He was also named to the All-Conference and All-City teams two years in a row. He scored 237 points as a junior and 250 points as a senior. Charley Mazurek was also an outstanding pitcher at Bulkeley for three years. He continued playing three sports at Trinity, and he set the college's single game basketball scoring record with 40 points in a game against Bates College. He served as the Chief Executive Officer of CM Plastics Company until he retired.

The success that Charlie Wrinn and Charley Mazurek enjoyed at Trinity sent a strong signal to student-athletes at Bulkeley and throughout the city that the small liberal arts college in Hartford was a viable option for basketball players from the city, a place where they could maintain their passion for competing in sports while preparing for a successful career after graduation. Trinity was a challenging academic institution that attracted serious, thoughtful students. But the school also took intercollegiate athletic competition very seriously. The college's athletic programs were among the oldest in the United States. Trinity began playing baseball in 1868. In 1877 Trinity became the twelfth college in the country to play football. Basketball was introduced on campus in 1894 with a game against Hartford Public High School, and three years later Trinity played Wesleyan for the first time, winning by a score of 26-5. Athletes were expected to compete aggressively and with distinction while pursuing the same rigorous course of study as the rest of the student body. The combination of strong athletic teams and demanding academics made Trinity College an appealing destination for many student-athletes, not only from the Hartford area, but across the nation and many foreign countries as well.

When Barry Leghorn arrived at Trinity, he probably did not have his mind set on breaking Charlie Wrinn's scoring record, but he showed early on that he had the ability to become a special player. His coach on the Trinity freshman team, Robie Shults, knew from the beginning that Barry Leghorn was very talented. "He was the biggest gun on the best club I had up to that time here," Coach Shults told Jimmy Cunavelis of *The Hartford Courant*. "He was my best rebounder and scorer. And when the boys needed someone to throw the ball to in a pinch, they looked for Barry."

In an era when students were required to play on the freshman team in their first year of college, Barry Leghorn enjoyed a standout initial college season. At 6'3" he could score on the inside or from long range. He could shoot with either hand, play tough defense, and rebound with authority. As a sophomore, he picked up right where he had left off as a freshman, averaging 18.8 points per game in his first varsity season. He did just as well his junior year, averaging 18.9 points per game, and in his senior year, playing in his fifty-third varsity game, he scored 15 points against the Coast Guard Academy to break the 1,000 point mark, something no other Trinity player had ever accomplished. Charlie Wrinn had held the previous Trinity three-year scoring record with 850 points, averaging 14.9 points per game over his varsity career. Given the close link that had been established between the two South End institutions, it seemed only fitting that the Trinity career scoring record held by one Bulkeley grad would be shattered by another.

But Barry Leghorn's scoring record at Trinity did not endure for long, thanks to the deadly shooting prowess of yet another Bulkeley High School graduate, Jim Belfiore. Along with Gene Reilly, Jim Belfiore and his life-long friend Joe Hourihan had been key members of the 1962 Bulkeley team that challenged Hartford Public for the city, conference, state, and New England championships, only to come up a few points short each time. Both Joe Hourihan and Jim Belfiore chose to attend Trinity after graduating from Bulkeley, maintaining the pipeline that Charlie Wrinn and Charley Mazurek had helped to establish. Like their predecessors from Bulkeley, Joe Hourihan and Jim Belfiore played multiple sports and would leave their mark on the Trinity basketball record book, Hourihan for assists and Belfiore for scoring.

Jim Belfiore was considered the best pure shooter ever to play at Trinity. He averaged 24.5 points per game for his career and he set the single game scoring record of 47 points against the Coast Guard Academy. He finished his career with 1,368 total points. Just as Wrinn and Mazurek had blazed the path from Bulkeley to Trinity that Barry Leghorn would follow, Leghorn paved the way for players like Hourihan and Belfiore, and they in turn inspired a player like Jack Godfrey to attend Trinity. These were all exceptional athletes and outstanding students that had multiple options when it came to selecting a college, including some Division I schools. The fact that they decided to stay in Hartford speaks volumes about their assessment of the value of a Trinity education and the quality of the teams. Barry Leghorn was one of the finest basketball players of his era and a shining example of the contributions a homegrown product could make to the athletic programs at Trinity College.

***

Even in years following the loss of key players to graduation, the city high schools continued to produce outstanding basketball teams through the decade of the 1960s. Not long after Barry Leghorn graduated from Trinity, another Leghorn appeared on the scene to help fortify Bulkeley's basketball fortunes. At 6'- 2", with a fluid shooting stroke and adept ball-handling skills, Wayne Leghorn became one of the most prolific scorers in the school's history. He began playing on the varsity team as a sophomore and he continued to improve every year. As a junior Wayne Leghorn began to assert himself as one of the finest long-range shooters in the state. Playing alongside such talented players as Jim Fenton, Mark Waxenberg, Vin Kwash, Vito Grieco, Ron Mayette, and Jackie Brown, Wayne Leghorn emerged as a premier scorer. In a game against conference rival Norwich Free Academy in his junior year, Wayne Leghorn gave a clear indication of his offensive dominance. He scored 35 points, hitting 13 of 20 field goal attempts and all 9 of his free throw attempts, while sitting out most of the fourth quarter in a lopsided 83-59 win. His torrid shooting would continue throughout the year, making him a marked man by opposing defenses that still could not shut him down. In a rematch against Norwich later in the season, he scored 29 points, making eight field goals and going 13 for 14 from the foul line, even though the defense was stacked to try to contain him after the first mismatch. Bulkeley won the second game as well, 86-42, with Wayne Leghorn scoring 18 of the team's 31 fourth quarter points. The highlight of Wayne Leghorn's junior year was a win against Hartford Public, a team that had beaten Bulkeley thirteen straight times. For the season he averaged 20 points per game and was named to the All-Capital District Conference team.

In his senior year Wayne Leghorn picked up his scoring pace. Opposing coaches knew that if you wanted to beat Bulkeley, you had to neutralize Wayne Leghorn. But containing the Bulkeley sharp-shooter was easier said than done. In a game against Fitch High School of Groton in which Bulkeley would qualify for the state tournament with a win, Wayne Leghorn was unstoppable. With his brother Barry and his father Russell looking on in the Bulkeley gym, Wayne Leghorn scored a school record 44 points in an 89-67 victory. The previous record of 41 points was held jointly by Barry Leghorn, against East Hartford in 1960, and Carmen Perrone, against New London during the 1957-58 season. In his historic game Wayne Leghorn made 16 of 25 field goal attempts and 12 of 13 foul shots. He scored 14 points in the first quarter, 13 points in the second period, 10 in the third quarter, and 4 in the final period when the game was out of reach. For Coach Lou Bazzano the victory meant that Bulkeley would be making its eleventh state tournament appearance in thirteen years. For the Leghorn family it meant the passing of the torch from Barry to Wayne as the school's single game scoring record holder. Records were made to be broken, but usually not by your kid brother!

Wayne Leghorn averaged 24.2 points per game as a senior at Bulkeley. Since he played in the era before the three-point shot rule was implemented, there was no telling how many points he would have scored if most of his long-range jump shots had counted for three points instead of two. But there was no disputing the fact that he had become one of the best shooters in the history of the school, right alongside his brother Barry.

His outstanding performance on the basketball court and his exceptional work in the classroom drew the attention of multiple colleges and universities. Robie Shults, the varsity basketball coach at Trinity College, would have been thrilled if Wayne decided to follow in his brother's footsteps and become a Trinity Bantam. But one of the schools interested in Wayne Leghorn was Harvard, and the opportunity to go to one of the best universities in the world was too appealing for him to pass up. Wayne Leghorn attended Harvard, but unfortunately, a serious motorcycle accident curtailed his athletic and academic career. He returned to Hartford, and he briefly considered enrolling at Trinity before moving on with his life, giving up on playing basketball in college. He would continue to play in leagues around the city, sometimes on the same team as his brother, reviving memories of the way the Leghorn brothers had once dominated the basketball scene in Hartford's South End.

Stanley Poole
Hartford Public High School 1961

Hartford Public High School was founded in 1638 as the Thomas Hooker Latin School, making it the second oldest public high school in the United States after the Boston Latin School. Over the course of the school's distinguished history, it produced numerous illustrious alumni and outstanding athletic teams. Yet in spite of a winning athletic tradition, it took until the 1960-61 season for the school to capture its first major championship. Stan Poole was instrumental in securing the school's original basketball title.

Stan Poole grew up on Wooster Street in the Southwest section of Hartford with his parents and five younger siblings. His father worked as a mason at a cement factory and his mother tended to the varied needs of a growing family of four boys and two girls. His introduction to basketball and baseball came while he attended Mary Hooker Elementary School. In the absence of organized school teams, Stan Poole, like many of his contemporaries, learned to play sports in the city parks and playgrounds. His initial exposure to organized team sports came through Hartford's Little League program, where one of his teammates was a youth a few years older named John Norman. Stan Poole looked up to John Norman for the way he handled himself on the baseball field, and he followed Norman's career with interest as he developed into an outstanding basketball player, first at Weaver and later at Trinity College. Like many of Hartford's finest athletes, Stan Poole was fortunate to identify a positive role model at an early age and to try to emulate his mentor's academic and athletic success.

Stan Poole attended New Park Avenue Junior High School, where basketball began to supplant baseball as his favorite sport. He scanned the sports' sections of the local newspapers looking for articles about prominent basketball players in the city, like Carmine Perrone, Corky Terry, Bill Schmitt, Johnny Egan, and John Norman, wondering if someday his own name might appear in print, with details about his athletic exploits. When Weaver High School won the New England High School Basketball Championship in 1957, Hartford caught hoop fever and the city was eagerly anticipating the next time one of its teams would rise to regional prominence. Unfortunately, when a near riot broke out in the legendary

Boston Garden as Wilbur Cross defeated Somerville, Massachusetts in the 1958 finals, Connecticut officials announced that the state would no longer participate in the tournament after 1962. The clock was ticking for any team from Hartford with aspirations to replicate Weaver's success.

Stan Poole went about developing his basketball skills in the usual manner, working extremely hard on his own to improve every facet of his game, shooting, ball-handling, passing, rebounding, and defending. He played in pick-up games every chance he had. He participated in the Junior High Division of the Protestant Inter-Church League, once scoring 30 points for his Warburton team in a 57-26 win over Emanuel Lutheran. When the new Southwest Boys Club opened in his neighborhood, he became a regular, playing there as often as he could. He met other kids that shared his interest in basketball, aspiring young players like Ron Copes and Gene Jenkins that would become his teammates at Hartford Public. He played in the Hartford Parks and Recreation League. And while he was making steady progress as a basketball player, he was also paying attention in school, developing his reading skills and preparing to pursue a college track course of study when he entered high school. He inspired confidence in his leadership capabilities among his eighth grade classmates at New Park Avenue Junior High School who elected him class president. He was intent on becoming a fine athlete and a good student so he could play sports in high school and beyond.

When he arrived at Hartford Public, Stan Poole made an immediate impact on the basketball program. He started on the JV team as a freshman and had an excellent season. Hoping to play a key role on the varsity team as a sophomore, he continued to work hard during the off-season. Over the summer he played in a league in Bloomfield with several other Hartford High basketball players, including Stan Egnot, Charles Terry, and Ron Copes. Stan Poole had grown to 6'- 4" and 190 pounds, and his inspired play in the Bloomfield summer league showed that he was on the verge of becoming a dominant force on the local high school basketball scene. Coach Joe Kubachka inserted Stan Poole in the starting lineup at the beginning of his sophomore season, and he maintained his status as a key starter over the next three years. He considered his signature game as a sophomore to have been a win against New Britain High School in which he scored 22 points on 8 for 9 shooting from the floor and 6 for 6 from the foul line. At the end of the season he was named to both the

All-Hartford Times and All-Hartford Courant teams, the newspapers he had been reading wondering if his name would ever appear in the sports' sections. Although the Hartford Public Owls enjoyed a strong season, the team was still two years away from adding several key components to the mix that would elevate a good team to the level of greatness.

As a junior, Stan Poole was joined by a dynamic sophomore guard named Eddie Griffin, along with two other outstanding sophomores, Bruce Maddox and Len Kostik, to form the emerging core of what would eventually become one of the most talented teams in the history of Hartford basketball. After another outstanding regular season, the team received a bid to the 38th annual Connecticut Interscholastic Athletic Conference Class L Basketball tournament. Hartford Public faced a familiar opponent in the first round of the tournament, city rival Bulkeley High. Playing in front of a lively crowd of 4,096 fans in the New Haven Arena, Stan Poole scored 19 points to tie Eddie Griffin and Bulkeley's Barry Leghorn for game scoring honors in leading the underdog Owls to a 72-58 victory. Earlier in the season, Bulkeley had won a meeting between the rivals, but Stan Poole had not played in that game. In the rematch in the state tournament Stan Poole played an all-around impressive game, not only scoring and rebounding with authority, but also turning in a fine defensive performance against the dangerous Barry Leghorn. Senior Jim Benedict aided the Owls' cause with 17 points, even though he was hounded by Bulkeley's defensive ace John Pazdar. Bruce Maddox chipped in with 13 points for Hartford High, while John Beilotti scored 13 points, John Kelly eight points, and John Pazdar nine points for Bulkeley.

The victory against Bulkeley secured a quarterfinal match up for Hartford Public against Naugatuck High School, a team that featured Bill Rado, an All-State performer who later earned All-American Honorable Mention honors at the University of Georgia, and Ed Slomcenski, a 7' center who played on two Yankee Conference Championship Teams and in the sweet sixteen of the NCAA tournament against Duke while he was at UConn from 1961-64. Ed Slomcenski averaged 10.5 points and 9.4 rebounds per game during his UConn career. He averaged a double-double as a junior, scoring 13.8 points and 10.8 rebounds per game, earning All-Yankee Conference honors.

The quarter-final game between Hartford Public and Naugatuck was played on a Thursday night in a terrible blizzard. The start of the game was delayed until two state trooper vehicles could escort the Owls' bus to the arena. But in spite of the miserable weather outside and the fact that he was assigned to guard the towering Ed Slomcenski, Stan Poole played one of the best games of his high school career. He scored 20 points, grabbed 19 rebounds, and blocked seven shots, while neutralizing the much taller Slomcenski. In consecutive state tournament victories, Stan Poole had demonstrated his defensive versatility by guarding the 6'- 3" Barry Leghorn and the 7'- 0" Ed Slomcenski, while scoring effectively and dominating the rebounding action. It was clear that Stan Poole had emerged as one of the elite basketball players in the state. He was named to the All-CDC and All-State first teams. Yet he still had not achieved the goal he had dreamed about as a kid – winning a championship. He would have to wait until his senior year to fulfill his title aspirations.

As a senior, Stan Poole was named the captain of a supremely talented Hartford High team that included Eddie Griffin, Pat Burke, Len Kostek, Bruce Maddox, Otis Woods, and Gene Jenkins. If ever there was a year for Hartford Public to compete for a state and New England Championship, this was the year. The Owls had an abundance of talent, but another team in the state was still favored to come out on top. Wilbur Cross had won three consecutive Class L state titles and two of the past three New England High School Championships, and the Governors were poised to make it four state championships in a row and to repeat as the New England champions. The team's optimism about keeping their championship streaks alive was based largely on the continued presence in the lineup of the incomparable senior Dave Hicks. Dave Hicks was a 6'- 5", 205 pound center, widely regarded at the time as the best player in the school's history. He averaged 19.4 points per game as a senior and he scored 1,268 points for his career. Bob Casey, a former sports reporter for the *New Haven Register,* reflected on Dave Hick's career in an article he wrote in 1971, "Dave Hicks made the game of basketball look easy. He had a cherubic face and big flashy grin. But he ate up the best Hartford Public, Weaver, Hillhouse, and Norwich could offer. He moved with the grace of a cat. He was a man among boys. No one was better than Dave Hicks."

Among his litany of impressive accomplishments, Dave Hicks was twice named first team All-State, he led Wilbur Cross to three straight state titles, he was the MVP of the 1960 New England championship tournament, and he was named a Parade Magazine All-American. Yet in spite of his remarkable success on the basketball court, Dave Hicks led a tragic, unfulfilled life off the court. It was reported that he intended to go to the University of Seattle on a basketball scholarship when he graduated from Wilbur Cross, but the owner of the Harlem Globetrotters, Abe Saperstein, had watched films of some of Dave Hick's high school games, and he offered him a contract. Chip Malafronte of the *New Haven Register* quoted comments Dave Hicks had made to Bob Casey during an interview, "My first year [with the Harlem Globetrotters] I got $12,000, which was pretty good money in those days. Maybe it was not the million-dollar contracts that you read about now. But it meant a lot to me and my family. College would have been nice. But you do the best you can with your life." Dave Hicks spent five years with the Harlem Globetrotters, travelling around the world and entertaining scores of basketball fans. He returned to his home town of Ansonia and opened a restaurant, Dave's Place.

But in the 1960-61 season, Dave Hicks was at the pinnacle of the basketball world in Connecticut, and the Wilbur Cross Governors represented the main obstacle impeding Hartford Public's hopes for its first championship. The teams met twice during the regular season, splitting the two games. Before the two teams would face off in a rubber match in the state finals, they had to overcome stiff challenges in the earlier rounds of the CIAC Class L tournament. As usual, Hartford Public's path to a state title ran through one of its city rivals. In a quarter-final double-header played in front of 4,994 fans in the New Haven Arena, Weaver defeated a powerful Hillhouse team 63-59 and Hartford Public beat Hamden 91-72, setting up a semi-final showdown between the two rival schools from Hartford. Hartford Public prevailed in the semifinal battle, earning the chance to meet Wilbur Cross in the finals. But once again Wilbur Cross denied Hartford Public a state title, defeating the Owls 65-59 for the Governors fourth straight state championship. The sole consolation for the Hartford Public Owls was that both the CIAC Class L champion and runner-up earned a trip to the New England High School Tournament, where they might have one last chance to dethrone the mighty Governors.

In the opening round of the 36th annual New England Interscholastic Basketball Tournament, Hartford Public faced undefeated Smith Academy from Hatfield, Massachusetts in front of a capacity crowd of 13,909 fans in the historic Boston Garden. Smith Academy was riding a 22 game winning streak, but it was doubtful that any of the victories had come against a team as deep and talented as Hartford Public. Hartford won by 20, 63-43, using a balanced scoring attack and dominating the backboards. Eddie Griffin led the way with 14 points, but he was ably supported by Bruce Maddox with 12 points, Len Kostek with 11, Otis Woods with 10, and Pat Burke with seven. Captain Stan Poole once again demonstrated his value to the team by scoring nine points, pulling down 19 rebounds, and playing solid defense against Smith Academy's 6'- 6" center, Bob Kovalski. Bob Kovalski was the game's high scorer with 24 points, but most of his points came early in the game against Hartford Public's 3-2 zone before Coach Joe Kubachka switched to a man-to-man defense and assigned Stan Poole to guard the high-scoring center. The Owls' victory set up a semifinals meeting with Chevrus High of Portland, Maine, a team that had beaten its opening round opponent Portsmouth High from New Hampshire, 62-52. When Hartford High beat Chevrus High, they earned a trip to the finals in their first New England Tournament.

Wilbur Cross defeated New Bedford High from Massachusetts 52-49 in its opening round match-up and then beat previously undefeated Hope High School of Providence, Rhode Island in the semifinals, setting up the fourth meeting of the season between the Owls and the Governors in the finals. Wilbur Cross was heavily favored to win a second consecutive New England title and third in four years. The Governors were accustomed to the pressure of a do-or-die game in the Boston Garden in front of a vocal crowd. But the Owls were not intimidated by the magnitude of the game or the championship pedigree of their opponent. After falling behind 3-1 at the start of the game, Hartford Public quickly surged ahead and never trailed again, leading 13-8, 31-23, and 51-37 at the end of the quarters on the way to a 68-62 win. The Owls caught a break when Dave Hicks picked up his fourth foul with three minutes to go in the second quarter, but on this momentous night, Hartford Public was not to be denied. Eddie Griffin scored 21 points and grabbed 16 rebounds, but he had plenty of help from Len Kostek with 13 points, Pat Burke with 14, and Otis Woods with six points. Stan Poole came up big in the biggest game of his career, scoring 12 points, pulling down 18 rebounds, and playing inspired defense in returning the New England title to Hartford for the first time since 1957. He was named the MVP of the tournament for his outstanding all-around performance. The kid from Wooster Street in Hartford, who had once dreamed about winning a championship, had his wish come true.

As a senior, Stan Poole made All-CDC and All-State honors for the second year in a row. He received Hartford High's Clarence Horace Wickham Award, recognizing the best athlete in the graduating class for exemplary sportsmanship and athletic achievement. After stops at the University of Hartford and Fairfield University, he attended Wilberforce University, earning a B.A. degree in 1968. He played briefly for the Hartford Capitols before joining the U.S. Army and serving in Vietnam from 1969-70. He played on the U.S. Army Championship team at Fort Sam Houston in San Antonio, Texas, where he settled with his wife and children. It was only fitting that Stan Poole completed his military service winning another basketball championship, a habit he had cultivated in his youth in Hartford.

Eddie Griffin
(Hartford Public High School 1962)

The rivalries between Hartford Public High School, Bulkeley High School, and Weaver High School were intense. Whenever the schools competed in an athletic contest, more was at stake than a simple win or loss in the record book, especially in basketball, where the players tended to know each other well from facing off on courts around the city, in the parks, playgrounds, and gyms where emotions ran high, trash talking was rampant, and the reputations of future hoop stars were validated or debunked. Regardless of what happened in the parks, however, the true measure of a player's stature was determined by the results of the games played in the high schools. The first claim to bragging rights went to the players that led their teams to wins in the City Series, but there were other plateaus that needed to be reached in order to gain consideration as one of the elite players and teams in the long and proud history of Hartford basketball, a conference title, a state tournament championship, and, in the former golden era of regional competition, a New England High School Basketball Championship.

The New England High School Championships began in 1921, with New Haven Commercial High School (later Wilbur Cross) of Connecticut beating Rogers-Newport from Rhode Island 35-11 for the title, beginning a long period of Connecticut dominance in the tournament. From 1921 through 1962 high schools from Connecticut won 26 of 37 titles, including 24 of the last 29 tournaments and 12 of the last 13. In 1958, when a near riot broke out near the end of the title game in which Wilbur Cross of New Haven defeated Sommerville High School from Massachusetts, CIAC officials determined that 1962 would be the final year that teams from the state would compete in the tournament. There was no disputing the fact that Connecticut was the preeminent basketball power in the New England region.

During its lifespan, the New England High School Championship was a major sporting event, drawing fans throughout the region. Beginning in 1945, the finals were traditionally played in front of capacity crowds in historic Boston Garden, home of the Boston Celtics, a team that won eight consecutive NBA Championships beginning in 1959. High school teams from all the New England states would dream of someday playing on the parquet floor of the Boston Garden in front of a sellout crowd of 13,909 fans for the high school championship. In 1957 that dream came true for Weaver, when the Beavers became the first team from Hartford to win the New England High School Championship by defeating Lawrence Catholic High School of Massachusetts 85-73 in overtime, capping a 24-0 undefeated season. It was acknowledged that Johnny Egan had turned in the greatest individual performance in tournament history by scoring 36 points in the title game, 32 of which came in the second half and overtime. He had made two free throws with four seconds remaining on the clock to send the game into overtime. By winning back-to-back Connecticut Class L State Championships in 1956 and 1957 and following up with the 1957 New England High School Championship, Weaver could lay claim to the best team in the history of Hartford basketball, and Johnny Egan had earned consideration as the city's best high school player ever. With Connecticut's participation in the New England tournament drawing to an end, it did not seem likely that Weaver's lofty status among the Hartford teams could possibly be challenged. But that was before Eddie Griffin stormed onto the Hartford basketball scene.

Eddie Griffin grew up in the Bellevue Square/Arsenal neighborhood of Hartford. He was an only child, but he had a large extended family, including cousins and his grandmother, with whom he was very close. One of his cousins was John Lee, who would go on to become a legendary athlete at Weaver High School and Linfield College. When Eddie Griffin was thirteen, he joined Mt. Olive Baptist Church, where he sang in the youth choir and played basketball in the church league, which at the time was just as competitive as the Hartford Parks and Recreation League. He also played on teams representing Stowe Village, where he became accustomed to winning championships that were celebrated with banquets at Mark Twain School. There was nothing Eddie Griffin enjoyed more than winning. It became part of his DNA. You only had to watch Eddie Griffin play a single game at any stage of his life, from the earliest games in the church league to his days with the Hartford Capitols in the Eastern League, to see how embedded winning was in his basketball psyche. He always made winning his first priority, and the intense desire to come out of a game with a victory would stay with him throughout his life.

At Brackett Northeast School Eddie Griffin was coached by Billy

Taylor, for whom winning basketball championships had become habit-forming. Billy Taylor was a professional boxer and a long time referee, teacher, and coach in the Hartford School System. As a coach, his basketball teams won 12 City Championships in the junior high program. He was a graduate of Hartford Public High School, class of 1927, where he won four letters as a senior in football, basketball, baseball, and track. He attended Springfield College, where he also coached boxing for a time. Billy Taylor was eventually inducted into the Hartford Public High School Athletic Hall of Fame, an honor that his young protégé, Eddie Griffin, would one day share. During Eddie Griffin's three years on the Brackett Northeast team, from seventh through ninth grade, the school won the City Championship every year. In seventh and eighth grade he was disappointed by the lack of playing time Coach Taylor allotted him on a talent-laden team. It wasn't until the ninth grade, when Eddie Griffin became more of the go-to player, that he felt he was making a fitting contribution to the championship winning streak. He would use that early frustration at being overlooked by his legendary coach at the very beginning of his career as motivation to make an immediate impact on the Hartford Public High School basketball team he was about to join.

Eddie Griffin entered Hartford Public as a sophomore, and after the first two games of the basketball season, Coach Joe Kubachka made him a starter. With Eddie Griffin in the starting lineup, the Owls ran off 10 straight wins. By the end of the season he was recognized as one of the best players in the city and the state. But he had his sights set on loftier goals. The summer following his sophomore season he played with many of his teammates in the Hartford Parks and Recreation League, developing the kind of chemistry that would be needed to become an upper echelon team. Competition in the state was fierce, perhaps at an all-time high. Since Weaver had won back-to-back Class L Connecticut State Championships in 1956 and 1957, Wilbur Cross of New Haven, coming off the 1958 New England High School Basketball Championship in a riot-marred game against Sommerville, had reeled off three straight state championships and was a heavy favorite to repeat in 1961 as well. And in Hartford's South End, loomed a dangerous Bulkeley High School team loaded with talent, featuring tenacious players who exhibited a disciplined, controlled style of basketball that compensated for the team's lack of size. Eddie Griffin understood the challenges Hartford Public would face in his junior and senior years to become the top team in the state, and since Connecticut teams were coming off four consecutive New England Championships, achieving dominance in the state was likely to extend throughout the region as well.

As a junior, Eddie Griffin demonstrated his outstanding all-around athletic skills by earning First-Team All-State honors in football. But his brilliance on the football field was merely a prelude to Hartford Public's historic basketball season. Led by Eddie Griffin and senior captain Stan Poole, the Owls enjoyed one of the finest seasons in the school's history, losing only twice during the regular season on the way to capturing city and conference championships. The team advanced to the Class L finals of the State Tournament, facing off against Wilbur Cross, three-time defending state champions. In a hard-fought game, Wilbur Cross defeated Hartford Public 65-59 for its fourth straight state title, but since the CIAC sent both the Class L champion and runner-up to represent the state in the New England High School Championships, the Owls' season was not over. In the New England Tournament, both Wilbur Cross and Hartford Public advanced to the finals, setting up a rematch of the Connecticut Class L championship game. But this time Hartford Public prevailed, upsetting Wilbur Cross 68-62. Eddie Griffin scored 21 points and grabbed 16 rebounds. Stan Poole was selected as the Tournament's Most Valuable Player, and both he and Eddie Griffin were named to the All-New England Team, adding to their All-State, All-Conference, and All-City honors. Stan Poole was graduating, but Eddie Griffin had one more shot at the prize.

When Eddie Griffin returned to the basketball court for his senior year, he was motivated to achieve the one goal had eluded him – a State Championship. Since three key players from the New England Championship team – Stan Poole, Pat Burke, and Otis Woods – had graduated, the task of winning a state championship would not be an easy one for Hartford Public. A major potential stumbling block was city rival Bulkeley High, led by the incomparable Gene Reilly, a superb athlete who would go on to win All-American honors in basketball and baseball at Central Connecticut State College and to lead the nation in foul shooting in 1966. Jim Belfiore and Joe Hourihan, two future Trinity College Hall-of-Famers, along with Ted Kwash and Leo McGrath, rounded out an impressive starting five, giving Bulkeley a solid nucleus of outstanding players capable of beating any team in the state. The rivalry between

Bulkeley and Hartford Public during the 1961-62 basketball season was one for the ages, pitting two of the best teams in the city's history against one another in four epic games that would decide city, conference, state, and New England championships. Hartford Public emerged victorious in all four games, but not without a serious struggle every time. The margin of victory in each of the two regular season games was two points. In the finals for the Class L State Championship played in front of a sold-out crowd at the UConn Fieldhouse, Hartford Public won by 3 points, 67-64, with Eddie Griffin scoring 26 points in a clutch performance that earned him the tournament's MVP award. Then it was on to the New England High School Championship in Boston Garden, where it was only fitting that the top two teams in Connecticut would meet for the final time in the state's farewell to the prestigious regional tournament.

Both Bulkeley and Hartford Public would have to overcome formidable opponents before their showdown in the New England finals. Bulkeley faced a taller and deeper Cambridge Rindge & Latin team, featuring Mike Jarvis, the future St. John's coach, and Bill Hewitt, a 6'- 7" forward who played collegiately at the University of Southern California and would be named to the NBA All-Rookie First Team as a member of the L.A. Lakers. Sharp-shooting Gene Reilly, who made 32 of 35 free throws in the tournament, led Bulkeley to the win to advance to the championship game. In the quarterfinal round, Hartford Public had to overcome Pittsfield High School's first 1,000 point scorer, Mark Belanger, the lanky future eight-time Gold Glove Award winning shortstop for the Baltimore Orioles, to advance. In the championship game that was close throughout, Eddie Griffin scored 24 points, including 11 decisive points in the fourth quarter, to lead Hartford Public to the 47-39 win over Bulkeley and a second consecutive New England title. He was once again selected to the All-New England team. Bulkeley finished the season with a 20-4 record. All four losses were to Hartford Public, by a total of 15 points, with 8 of those points coming in the final game. The two best teams in New England that historic basketball season were both from Hartford.

In spite of one of the most successful high school careers in the history of Hartford basketball, Eddie Griffin was not widely recruited by college basketball programs. After graduating from Hartford Public, he spent a year at Virginia State University, thanks to the help of Weaver's Doc Hurley, an alumnus of the school, before transferring to Linfield College in McMinnville, Oregon, where he starred in basketball and football, following in the footsteps of his cousin from Weaver High, John Lee, a perennial All-Conference performer at Linfield. Eddie Griffin also won First Team All-Conference Honors in basketball at Linfield in 1965-66 and in 1967-68, but he may have been even more impressive as a football player in college, earning a tryout at fullback with the Dallas Cowboys. Following his graduation from Linfield in 1968, he returned to Hartford to begin a career as a physical education teacher and coach. He had ambitions of playing football for the Hartford Knights when he returned, but his interest was not reciprocated by the team. "The Knights weren't very enthusiastic when I asked for a tryout in 1968," he said, "So I gave up football and stuck with basketball." He played six seasons with the Hartford Capitols of the Eastern Basketball Association, averaging 15.7 points and 3.7 assists per game during the 1969-70 season, his most productive. The experience was not particularly rewarding. "I've always wanted to win and have some fun. With the Caps, it got to be a job."

Eddie Griffin went on to have a successful teaching and coaching career. He won two state championships as a coach at Bulkeley High, the team he had stymied repeatedly during his record-setting 1962 season at Hartford Public. As a player and a coach, Eddie Griffin was all about winning, and his determination to succeed made him one of the greatest high school basketball players the city of Hartford had ever known.

John Lee
Weaver High School 1962

While Eddie Griffin was performing his magic at Hartford Public High School, starring in football, track, and basketball and leading the Owls to two consecutive New England High School Basketball Championships, he had a similarly gifted cousin at Weaver High School steadily building an enduring legacy as one of the greatest athletes in Hartford's history. There has probably never been anyone in the city as proficient in three sports – baseball, football, and basketball – as John Lee. But what set John Lee apart was not merely his remarkable athletic ability. He was a natural leader and one of the finest and most genuine people you could ever hope to meet. He cared deeply about other people, and his sincere humanitarian instincts were reflected in the exemplary manner he chose to live his life.

Although born in Bellevue Square in Hartford, John Lee spent the first few years of his life living in a military apartment complex for low income families on Kane Drive in West Hartford with his mother and six siblings. His mother raised the children on her own, while working for the state of Connecticut for many years. She was a woman of faith, and she made sure her children attended Mt. Olive Baptist Church with her on Sunday. John Lee was on the junior usher board and a member of the church choir. His early exposure to religious values was an important influence on John Lee throughout his life.

John Lee remembered three important relationships from his early days in West Hartford – the Huguley brothers, Jay and Willie, and Walker Cannon. The neighborhood friends introduced John Lee to sports, particularly baseball and basketball, sparking an interest that would persist a lifetime. "These individuals put the ball in my hand for the first time," John Lee said. There was nothing fancy about John Lee's introduction to the two sports he would eventually play with such precision. He and his friends played baseball with a cut-off broom for a bat and a tennis ball in lieu of a baseball. They shot baskets at a peach-basket on a tree with any ball they could find. John Lee's first taste of organized sports came in the West Hartford Little League program. He remembered that one of his earliest baseball rivals was a kid from Hartford named Gene Reilly, someone he would compete against in baseball and basketball throughout high school.

When John Lee entered fourth grade, his family returned to Hartford, moving to Cleveland Avenue. He attended Barbour Street School, where one of his teachers, Mr. Wood, instilled in him an appreciation for poetry. He can still remember some of the poems that Mr. Wood had him commit to memory. It was also while attending Barbour Street School that he became interested in basketball. The school's gym teacher, Mr. Roy, became his first basketball coach. He enjoyed playing basketball, and he continued to play during the summer in the Hartford Parks and Recreation League, representing Stowe Village. His coach in the summer league was "Beans" Brown, a Hartford playground legend and a member of the 1954 Weaver basketball team that won the city's first state championship. Beans was a strict, no-nonsense coach who insisted his players learn to play the game the right way. "We learned to respect the game and our opponent," John Lee said. "We were competitors on the court but friends off the court."

The competition became increasingly fierce the further John Lee advanced in school. In the eighth grade his Barbour Street School basketball team defeated the Moylan School team led by Gene Reilly, who would become his nemesis in baseball and basketball at Bulkeley High School. Meanwhile, his cousin Eddie Griffin was beginning to emerge as an exceptional basketball player at Bracket Northeast School. The three gifted young athletes from Hartford – John Lee, Gene Reilly, and Eddie Griffin – were on a collision course to high school where they would compete against each other in multiple sports for dominance in the city, state, and New England.

When John Lee entered Weaver High School in the fall of 1958, he was an immediate success across a three-sport spectrum. It would become apparent to all three of his varsity coaches – Ernie Bottomly in baseball, Joe Beidler in football, and Frank Scelza in basketball – that they had the privilege of coaching a student athlete quite unlike any they had ever encountered, a player with so much natural athletic talent it would be impossible to identify his dominant sport. Not only was he a superior all-around athlete, he was also eminently coachable, a player with an ideal temperament for competitive sports, supportive of his teammates, respectful of his opponents, unflappable under pressure, and always willing to accept instruction and strive for improvement. All three of his coaches benefited from his leadership capabilities, positive attitude, and charismatic personality, regardless of the particular sport.

In his junior year John Lee helped the Weaver baseball team achieve its first winning season since World War II and first city championship in nearly twenty years. Playing first base and pitching, John Lee led the Beavers with a .383 batting average and 10 runs batted in. He batted .500 in the City Series and made only one error in 99 chances in the field. He was named to the All-CDC first team by the coaches in the conference. He excelled as a quarterback and defensive back on the football field for Coach Joe Beidler. But if there was one coach that could truly appreciate and identify with the all-around athletic brilliance of John Lee, it was his basketball coach, Frank Scelza.

Frank Scelza starred in three sports at Bulkeley High School, football, baseball, and basketball. He served as the captain on both the football and basketball teams, and he was named All-State in both sports. After graduating from Bulkeley, he went to Springfield College, where he continued to excel athletically in three sports, playing football, basketball, and golf. When he graduated from college, he began his career at Hartford Public, coaching baseball and teaching physical education in an illustrious department that included Larry Amann, Joe Kubachka, Joe Cirone, and Lindy Remigino. He coached some of Hartford Public's most renowned baseball players, including Pete Sala, a future HPHS Athletic Hall of Fame inductee, and Nick Koback, a catcher who played in the National League for the Pittsburg Pirates.

Frank Scelza became the head basketball coach at Weaver in 1957. He compiled a 166-66 record at Weaver over 12 seasons, a .716 winning percentage in an era in which Weaver regularly faced the toughest teams in the state during the regular season and in the tournament. The schedule included two games each against City Series rivals HPHS and Bulkeley, contests against the New Haven powerhouses Hillhouse and Wilbur Cross, and games in the highly competitive Capital District Conference. His 1966 Weaver team made it to the finals in the State Tournament before losing to Wilbur Cross by 2 points. He went on to serve as Vice Principal at his alma mater, Bulkeley High School, from 1969-89. Among his many awards and honors, he was elected to the Connecticut High School Coaches Hall of Fame, the Connecticut Football Officials Association Hall of Fame, the Bulkeley High School Athletic Hall of Fame as an athlete, and the Hartford Public High School Athletic Hall of Fame as a coach. Frank

Scelza's name is firmly embedded in the historical record of the city's three venerable public high schools, as a standout athlete, winning coach, and distinguished administrator.

John Lee's high school basketball career would have been even more impressive if he had not been pitted against two of the greatest players in the city's history, Gene Reilly and Eddie Griffin. There was certainly no shame in being recognized as the third best high school basketball team in the city during the 1961 and 1962 seasons, since Hartford Public won the New England High School Championship both years and had to get past Bulkeley four times to capture the second title. Weaver finished 15-6 in John Lee's junior year, losing to Hartford Public in the semi-finals of the state tournament. Weaver was once again very competitive in his senior year, but the team had the misfortune of competing against city rivals that would eventually fight it out for the state and New England championships. Still, Weaver put a team on the floor that in any other year would have held its own against any team in the state. John Lee and Bob Ricks were the co-captains, and they were ably supported by fellow starters Ocell Blocker, John Ward, and Gene Nelson, with two future standouts, sophomores Ben Billie and Len VanTassel, providing valuable minutes off the bench. It was a cohesive team that Coach Scelza admired for the hustle and teamwork it displayed game in and game out, exactly what you would expect from any team led by the incomparable John Lee.

As great as John Lee performed in three sports in high school, he found himself in the familiar circumstances that all too many gifted athletes from Hartford confronted. No colleges stepped up to the plate to recruit his services. In the absence of any substantive efforts to recruit him, John Lee considered enlisting in the Marine Corps. But fortunately for John Lee, and for many athletes from Hartford that would follow him, a pipeline to Linfield College in McMinnville, Oregon had previously been established with the admittance of Curtis Manns, a Weaver football player, in 1958. Thanks to the efforts of Weaver football coach Joe Beidler, who had developed personal friendships with the head football and baseball coaches at Linfield while he was working at Whitman College in Walla Walla, Washington, Curtis Manns became the first of ten student athletes from Hartford to get accepted to Linfield between 1958-67 based on Coach Beidler's strong recommendation. What made the "Hartford Connection" to Linfield so successful was that the students Joe Beidler referred to the college were not only outstanding athletes, they were also young men of exceptional character with extraordinary potential. The incredible promise of the student athletes that Coach Beidler recommended to Linfield was born out by the fact that all of them went on to have highly successful careers after graduating from the college, many as educators and coaches, putting them in positions to serve as mentors and sources of inspiration for another generation of student athletes seeking an opportunity to improve their lives.

Even to his most ardent supporters, like his high school coaches, it seemed unlikely that John Lee could replicate in college the remarkable success he had enjoyed in three sports at Weaver. But John Lee had made a habit of surpassing expectations. By the time he graduated from Linfield College in 1967, he was recognized as one of the greatest all-around athletes ever to attend the school. He received national attention by becoming the first athlete in NAIA (National Association of Intercollegiate Athletics) history to compete in all three national playoffs in football, basketball, and baseball. He helped Linfield College make history as well by becoming the first NAIA member school to compete in all three major tournaments in the same year. As a member of the Linfield baseball team, John Lee received honorable mention All-American honors. He led the Linfield Wildcats to a 26-9 record and the NAIA championship in 1966. During the season he hit .327 with 3 home runs and 20 RBIs, garnering All-Northwest Conference, All-District, and All-NAIA honors. As a receiver on the Linfield football team, John Lee averaged 18.9 yards per reception in 1966, the third-highest average in school history. He caught 30 career receptions, six for touchdowns. He was also the team's placekicker, converting 19 of 32 field goal attempts. In basketball the Linfield team won the Northwest Conference title and qualified for the NAIA championship tournament in John Lee's junior and senior years. He averaged 14.1 points per game as a junior, when the team posted a 21-7 record. As a senior, John Lee averaged 11.1 points per game and the team finished with a 23-6 record. Needless to say, John Lee was inducted into the Linfield College Athletic Hall of Fame for his historic three-sport performance.

After he graduated from Linfield College, John Lee returned to Hartford, where he was hired as a physical education teacher and coach at Weaver. His presence on the Weaver staff had a profound impact on the school. To the students at Weaver, John Lee was not just another authority figure intent on keeping them in line. He was one of their own, a living legend who had emerged from the depths of a housing project to achieve athletic glory, not just in high school, but in college as well. His natural leadership skills and dynamic personality made him an ideal role model, especially for student athletes. He exuded optimism and school spirit. His instinctive cheerfulness, hopefulness, and confidence permeated the entire school. The problems at Weaver did not disappear, but with John Lee around, they somehow appeared more manageable, less overwhelming in their scope. A more optimistic attitude was reflected in the school's athletic success when the 1971 basketball team, composed of players John Lee had mentored as the JV coach, won the LL State Championship for the first time since the Johnny Egan era. The 88-86 victory over city rival Hartford Public marked the return of Weaver basketball to a position of preeminence in the state, and John Lee played an influential role in the school's revival as a coach, teacher, and inspirational leader.

Just as the Weaver administration had recognized the value in bringing John Lee back to the school as a staff member, Linfield was eager for its star athlete to return, and the college offered him a position in the athletic department. It was a difficult decision for John Lee to leave the school and the city he loved for his other alma mater on the opposite coast. But he was accustomed to listening to his inner voice, a moral and ethical consciousness built on a solid foundation of faith, tell him where he was needed the most and could do his best work. He became Linfield College's Athletic Director, but he did not forget about Weaver or the city of Hartford. He revived the "Hartford Connection" to Linfield that his Weaver football coach Joe Beidler had started. Thanks to the efforts of John Lee, a steady stream of players from the city of Hartford attended Linfield, players like Ronnie Smith, Merle Lawrence, Stan Mason, Lance Powell, and Carl Hardaway. John Lee made a tremendous impact at both his alma maters, not only as a great athlete, but as an exceptional person as well. He was a genuine Hartford legend who will never be forgotten by the countless people whose lives he touched.

Bill Jones
Hartford Public High School 1963

Every great basketball player needs a strong supporting cast in order for his or her team to reach its full potential. As good a ball player as Eddie Griffin was at Hatford Public, his team could not have won successive New England Championships without other outstanding players making solid contributions, players like Paul Copes, Brian Smith, Stan Poole, Otis Woods, Lenny Kostek, and Pat Burke. In both the New England Championship years, Eddie Griffin was capably supported by a dynamic and versatile young teammate, Bill Jones, who would go to enjoy a brilliant basketball career at Fairfield University.

Bill Jones grew up in the Rice Heights section of Hartford with four siblings. The Union Baptist Church played an important role in the lives of the Jones family. One of the members of the Church was Donald Harris, a teacher and basketball coach at Moylan School, who recognized Bill Jones' potential at an early age and sought to help him realize the promise he exhibited on the basketball court. Bill Jones would spend time at the Harris home, playing basketball in the back yard, which served as a magnet for many of the most talented young basketball players in the neighborhood. The competition in the Harris backyard was intense, and it helped Bill Jones develop the fundamentals of the all-around game that would become his calling card. "It made me a better player," Bill Jones said of his early taste of competitive basketball at the Harris home.

Bill Jones began playing on Moylan School's baseball and basketball teams in the seventh grade. He remembered that a local educator, Eugene Green, was committed to gaining exposure for basketball in Hartford and arranged for a local television station to televise a Moylan game, an event that excited the entire community and inspired Bill Jones to focus exclusively on basketball. Bill Jones also admired Hartford basketball icon Bobby Knight. "When Bobby Knight entered the parks," he recalled, "It was like Willy Mays or Michael Jordan entering. He had his signature towel around his neck and would take time out to talk to everyone, especially the youngsters. Mr. Knight asked about your family, your grades, and then your hoop game." Bill Jones was certainly not alone in holding Bobby Knight in high esteem. Practically every Hartford basketball player of the era was familiar with his story and his impact on the community. Desmond Conner, staff writer for *The Hartford Courant*, in a tribute to Bobby Knight after his death in 2008, wrote, "Knight attended Weaver High School, but because of the lack of college opportunities available to black people at the time, he was picked from the streets of Hartford's North End to play for the Harlem Globetrotters in the late 1940s and early 1950s, the era of Marques Haynes and 'Goose' Tatum. He had a brief stint with the Knicks in 1955. He was often called 'magical' and a 'basketball genius' because of his wizardry with the ball, especially the no-look pass, mastering it long before it was fashionable."

What made Bobby Knight a legend in Hartford was not merely his extraordinary talent on the basketball court but his selfless mentorship of young people in the community as well. He motivated and inspired everyone he encountered, serving as a positive role model for numerous kids whose lives he touched. It was his unwavering commitment to the youth of Hartford that set him apart and made him such a valuable community asset. He was determined to help as many kids as possible avoid the situation in which he had found himself, graduating high school without any viable college opportunities. Sadly, not much had changed in terms of college accessibility for talented basketball players since Bobby Knight graduated from Weaver. Eddie Griffin was generally acknowledged at the time as one of the two best high school basketball players ever from the city of Hartford. When he graduated from Hartford Public, there were no traditional colleges rushing to recruit him. But Bill Jones, only a year behind Eddie Griffin at Hartford Public, was about to overcome an obstacle that had tripped up far too many of his talented predecessors.

By the eighth grade, Bill Jones was showing clear indications of the dominant player he was to become. He began playing at the Southwest Boys Club and at various parks in the city, anywhere he could find a competitive game against experienced players. He met some of the city's iconic Park Directors, men like John Carter, Joel Gordon, Doc Hurley, Beans Brown, and John Barrows, men who not only helped him develop his considerable basketball skills, but offered guidance on how to prepare for success in the classroom as well. Sometimes it required the efforts of a unified community to steer young people in the right direction. Bill Jones was fortunate to find willing mentors to guide his progress along the way.

In his freshman year at Hartford Public, Bill Jones became a starter on an impressive JV team, but it was as a sophomore on a varsity team destined to make history that he exploded onto the Hartford basketball scene. He was a starter on the team with Eddie Griffin and Stan Poole that won the first of two consecutive New England High School Championships, avenging a loss to Wilbur Cross in the finals of the Class L State Tournament to defeat the Governors in the rematch in the Boston Garden. In his junior year Hartford Public ran the table, winning city, conference, state, and New England championships. In a game against Bulkeley High School, the team Hartford Public had to defeat four times to reach the pinnacle of regional basketball success, Bill Jones hit two free throws to seal the win in the state championship game at UConn.

As a senior captain after Eddie Griffin's departure, Bill Jones continued his strong all-around play. He showed his determination to maintain Hartford Public's dominance by scoring 19 points and recording 23 rebounds as the Owls opened defense of its Capital District Conference championship by defeating Norwich Free Academy, 57-43. At 6'- 4" he could play virtually any position on the floor. He was an adept ball handler, skillful passer, and strong rebounder, and he excelled in the clutch, coming up with big plays when it mattered most. He averaged 14 points and 9 rebounds per game in leading the Owls to a 16-7 record and a berth in the Class L semifinals in the state tournament, a game Hartford Public lost to Hillhouse, the eventual state champions. Bill Jones' outstanding high school career had come to an end, but like many acclaimed performers in Hartford, he was not prepared to hang up his sneakers.

Bill Jones' inspired play at Hartford Public had captured the attention of Fairfield University basketball coach George Bisacca. A pipeline from Hartford Public to Fairfield had been established when Coach Bisacca convinced Pat Burke to attend the university. Pat Burke had been Bill Jones' teammate on the 1961 Hartford Public team that won the school's first New England High School Championship. In the championship game against Wilbur Cross, played in front of 8,837 fans in the Boston Garden, Pat Burke contributed 14 points and 8 rebounds, helping to neutralize the New Haven school's imposing front line. His defense against Dave Hicks, who later starred with the Harlem Globetrotters, was considered a key factor in Hartford Public's 68-62 win. Although Pat Burke was recruited to play basketball at Fairfield University, he was not immediately offered a scholarship. But it only took one freshman game for him to secure a scholarship; he scored 40 points in the freshman team's first game. He went on to have an outstanding college career, averaging 18.4 points per game. When Pat Burke was elected co-captain of the 1966 Fairfield University team, arguably the best team the university ever produced, Coach George Bisacca said, "Burke has been our No. 1 clutch player for the past two years. When the opposition is the toughest, Burke has always been at his best." In his junior year Pat Burke scored a career-high 34 points in an upset victory over Georgetown. In a game against Duquesne as a senior, he scored the go-ahead basket with seven seconds left in overtime, before scoring the winning basket after stealing the inbounds pass. Like his high school and college teammate Bill Jones, Pat Burke was a 6'- 4" leaper with the versatility to play inside and outside and a knack for stepping up in the clutch. Pat Burke died tragically before the end of his senior year. Each year Fairfield University bestows the "Patrick Burke Award" to the basketball player that demonstrates the most determination and hustle. He was elected to both the Hartford Public High School and Fairfield University Athletic Hall of Fame.

Before he was able to reunite with Pat Burke on the Fairfield University basketball team, Bill Jones decided to take a year off to improve his college entrance exam scores and to earn money. He went to work at Royal Typewriter to boost his financial situation, and he played in the Industrial Basketball League with former HPHS teammates Cliff Thornton and Eddie Griffin to stay sharp on the basketball court, earning a league championship in the process.

After a year of working he was anxious to enroll at Fairfield University and join the talented basketball team. He displayed the same versatility at the college level that he had shown in high school, playing effectively at multiple positions and scoring and rebounding with authority. George Bisacca described Bill Jones as, "The best player I ever coached," heady praise from someone that coached at Fairfield for eleven years and led the team to the Tri-State League Championship and three NCAA Division II Tournament appearances before elevating the program to Division I. Bill Jones scored 976 points at Fairfield, and in 1968 he won the "Tap Off Club" Major College Player Award and was named to the All-New England Team. In 1982 he was elected to the Fairfield University Athletic Hall of Fame and in 2006 he was inducted into the Hartford Public High School Athletic Hall of Fame, accomplishing something that had eluded many of the city of Hartford's elite players, gaining recognition for his outstanding achievements in basketball at the college level as well as in high school.

Like the mentors that had influenced him in his youth, Bill Jones remained active in the local sports scene in Hartford. He was a founder of the Greater Hartford Summer Basketball League, and he played for the New Haven Elms and the East Hartford Explorers. He worked for the Southern New England Telephone Company for twenty-five years before retiring in 1993. Bill Jones left behind a lasting legacy of basketball success, playing on some of the best teams his high school and college had ever known.

Cliff Thornton
Hartford Public High School 1963

When Eddie Griffin graduated from Hartford Public High School in 1962 after winning a state title and two consecutive New England High School Basketball Championships, many knowledgeable observers of the local basketball scene anticipated the 1962-63 Owls' team would enter a rebuilding phase. Cliff Thornton and Billy Jones were the only key contributors returning to the championship teams. The two solid veterans were joined by John Joiner, an exceptional defender and reliable scorer, and Billy Gilmore, an emerging star who had transferred from Weaver after his freshman year, along with the Thompson twins, Ron and Lionel, Bob Turner, Sam Vaughn, and Peter Odlum providing support. The Owls would need to rely heavily on the continued emergence of Cliff Thornton as one of the top players in the state if there was to be any hope of defending multiple titles.

Cliff Thorton was raised by his grandmother, but it took a community effort to help him navigate the travails of his youth. He recalled receiving an unexpected break from police officers when he was fourteen and had stolen a shirt from a department store. Instead of arresting him, they gave him a stern warning about the life-long consequences of making poor decisions and getting involved in activities that could result in a criminal record and potential incarceration. The tough talk served its purpose, scaring him straight. The police officers followed his progress at Hartford Public, even showing up at his games to offer encouragement.

As early as his grammar school years at Arsenal School, Cliff Thornton displayed a keen sense of intellectual curiosity. He developed an interest in Greek and Roman history and he frequented various libraries, including the Trinity College library, to read about the subjects. He first began playing organized sports at Barnard Brown Junior High School, where his teams won city championships in baseball and basketball. When he entered Hartford Public in the ninth grade, his mother passed away. He lost interest in school and his grades suffered. It was not until his junior year that he began to take basketball seriously again. The Owls had won the City Series, Capital District Conference, and New England High School titles his sophomore year, and the team was attempting to win back-to-back New England championships. All the attention and adulation the first championship run brought to the team inspired him to become a more complete basketball player. He worked hard on all aspects of his game. During the summer he spent time at Keney Park, watching and listening to Bobby Knight, who taught him that talent alone was not enough to make him a great player: he needed to acquire a killer instinct and a fierce will to win. He applied the lessons he learned from Bobby Knight to his play in the Hartford Parks and Recreation Summer League. In a game against Bellevue Square he erupted for 50 points, demonstrating that he was developing the explosive scoring touch he would use to torch opponents over the next two seasons.

As a junior, playing alongside Eddie Griffin and Billy Jones, Cliff Thornton helped Hartford Public make a clean sweep of all the major high school objectives, winning City Series, CDC, State, and New England titles. He had become one of the best jump shooters in the school's history. His favorite spot on the court to launch his patented jump shot was a few feet beyond the top of the key, but he was lethal from anywhere he had the time and space to get his shot off. He felt tremendous satisfaction that he had been able to play a role in Hartford Public's historic success. But he wasn't satisfied. He had one year left to solidify his own legacy, and he was determined to make the most of it.

In Cliff Thorton's senior year Hartford Public won five of the first six games, losing only to Wilbur Cross in a game that Cliff Thornton scored over 30 points. In an early season matchup with CDC rival East Hartford, Cliff Thornton led a balanced Owls attack with 23 points, Billy Gilmore added 14, John Joiner 13, and Billy Jones 12 in a 73-55 win. Against Norwich Free Academy, Cliff Thornton hit for 20 points in a 55-33 Hartford Public victory that raised the team's record to 8-2. By the time the CIAC state tournament began, Hartford had lost six games during the season, but the players felt confident that with a nucleus of Cliff Thornton, Billy Jones, and John Joiner, it could make a deep run in the post-season.

In a quarter-final game against Notre Dame of Bridgeport in the UConn Field House, the Owls jumped out to a quick 4-0 lead on baskets by Cliff Thornton and Sam Vaughn and never trailed on the way to a 67-54 victory. Notre Dame had been ranked number one going into the tournament, while the Owls had been ranked number 12. After scoring just seven points in the first half, Cliff Thornton heated up after the intermission and finished with 22 points. Billy Jones added 16, John Joiner 13, and Bob Turner 11. For Notre Dame, Bill Pritz was the leading scorer with 13 points, Mike Usdanoff scored 11, and Dave Bike had 10.

Dave Bike was only a sophomore at the time, but on his way to becoming a legend in the state as an athlete and a coach. As a rugged 6'-4", 220 pound senior, he would average 24 points a game in basketball and hit .402 for the baseball team, reaching the state finals in both sports. He turned down full basketball scholarship offers from Fordham University and Boston College to sign with the Detroit Tigers' organization. He was a catcher for eight seasons in the Tigers' minor league system before returning to Bridgeport to attend Sacred Heart University. After graduating from Sacred Heart, he served as the men's basketball coach for 35 years, winning over 500 games and capturing the 1986 NCAA Division II national championship. But in the quarter-finals of the CIAC high school tournament in Storrs in 1963, Dave Bike's Notre Dame of Bridgeport team could not dethrone the defending state and two-time New England champion, the Hartford Public High School Owls.

On the same night Hartford Public defeated Notre Dame to advance to the semi-finals, Wilbur Cross beat Maloney High School 81-61, with Doug Wardlaw getting 18 points, Tony Proto 15, Doug Joiner 13, and Sonny Parker 13. Doug Wardlaw, a junior at the time, was named to the New Haven Register All-State team two years in a row. He scored more than 900 points during his three-year varsity career. His legendary coach at Wilbur Cross, Salvatore "Red" Verderame, called Doug Wardlaw the best guard he ever coached. Doug Wardlaw went on to star at Loyola University in Chicago on a basketball scholarship, before returning to New Haven to work for the New Haven Parks and Recreation Department. Hartford Public's loss to Doug Wardlaw's Wilbur Cross team in the semi-finals ended the Owls' hope of winning a second straight state title. Although Wilbur Cross defeated Hartford Public, the Governors would go on to lose in the finals to cross-town rival Hillhouse, 68-65, starting a streak of three consecutive state championships for the Academics. After a brief hiatus, the city of New Haven had resumed its perch atop the state high school basketball hierarchy.

Cliff Thornton was named to the All-State team, the only player not from the New Haven area to be so honored by the New Haven Register. Instead of going on to college, he decided to join his former teammates

Billy Jones and Eddie Griffin by working at Royal Typewriter. Playing in the Hartford Industrial League, Cliff Thornton scored 44 points for the Royal team in a win over Arrow-Hart-Hegeman, showing he had not lost his shooting touch since graduating from Hartford Public. After working for two years, Cliff Thornton enlisted in the United States Army. He played basketball on the Army team, earning All-Army recognition in both the United States and Europe. When he returned from military service, he enrolled at Post University, earning a bachelor's degree in Marketing. He worked for many years as a manager at the Southern New England Telephone Company, retiring in 1997. He lives in Glastonbury with his wife Margaret and he has five daughters and two granddaughters.

Given the daunting obstacles he had to overcome in his youth, if the list of Cliff Thornton's accomplishments included merely his high school basketball exploits, military service, work career, and family life, he would have earned the respect and admiration of everyone that knew him. But Cliff Thornton was driven to do even more with his life. In 1995 Cliff and Margaret Thornton founded Efficacy, an online non-profit organization advocating drug policy reform. In his effort to educate the public about the need to bring drug use under regulated control, Cliff Thornton spoke to hundreds of thousands of people across the United States, Australia, Canada, Europe, and New Zealand. The Amherst College online newspaper described him as "America's foremost anti-Drug War African American activist". In addition to drug policy reform, he also engaged the public in discourse on such topics as health care and education.

Cliff Thornton has also been politically active, serving as one of the seven co-chairs of the Green Party of the United States. In 2006 he was the Connecticut Green Party nominee for Governor, becoming the first African American to appear on the general election ballot for Governor. As a third party candidate, he received 9,583 votes in his unsuccessful bid for the state's highest office. In 2007 the Drug Policy Alliance honored him with the Robert C. Randall Award for Achievement in the Field of Citizen Action. Cliff Thornton has led an amazing life, overcoming unfathomable hardship to inspire numerous people with his activism. The people of Hartford can take pride in his service to the nation, his dedication to the memory of his mother, and the inspirational example he has set for others to follow.

Ben Billie
Weaver High School 1963

For many of Hartford's elite players, the path to fulfillment in basketball and in life was neither easy nor straight-forward. For Ben Billie, excelling at basketball came naturally. He was a gifted athlete with all the physical tools he needed to dominate on the basketball court, quickness, strength, agility, and uncanny leaping ability. But it took time for him to unleash the determination and the strength of character he needed to overcome the obstacles that tripped up some of his less fortunate peers.

Ben Billie and his three sisters were raised by their hard-working mother on Mather Street in Hartford's North End. With his father gone and two of his sisters already married, Ben Billie lacked direction. As a kid he made some unfortunate choices and was influenced by individuals that made a habit of getting in trouble. But from an early age Ben Billie was guided by a strong moral compass and a desire to rise above his circumstances and do something positive with his life. Basketball became the conduit to a more productive life centered on business, political involvement, community, and service to others.

While on a trip to the South when he was ten years old, Ben Billie saw someone working out on a dirt basketball court, performing ball-handling and shooting skills he had never seen before. He was so impressed, he couldn't wait to return to Hartford to try some of the maneuvers he had witnessed on his trip. He started playing at the Vine Street School gym in the evening, under the supervision of Frank "Boo" Perry, the former Weaver standout. He went to Keney Park to play, where he could learn from great players like Eddie Griffin and Bobby Knight. He played on teams representing Stowe Village and DeLucco Park. Through his total immersion in the game of basketball, the hours and hours of practice and intense observation of older players, Ben Billie was able to escape many of the unwholesome distractions of his environment. He was focused on developing the solid, multi-dimensional game that he would bring to Weaver High School.

Ben Billie started on the Weaver JV team as a freshman, before he was brought up at the end of the season to join the varsity squad, a rare accomplishment for a freshman at Weaver. In a state tournament game against the perennial power from New Haven, Hillhouse High School, Ben Billie scored seven clutch fourth quarter points, helping Weaver to a victory and giving notice that he was a player destined for future stardom. In his sophomore year, Ben Billie played both football and basketball for Weaver, but as a junior he was a starter and a key contributor on a strong basketball team and he decided to drop football and concentrate on basketball. Although the Beavers fell short of their goal of a State Championship, Ben Billie established himself as one of the finest all-around players ever to play at Weaver. He led the team in scoring and rebounding, and he was an adept ball-handler and passer as well as a shut-down defender. He could play all five positions, and Coach Frank Scelza did not hesitate to take advantage of Ben Billie's versatility, moving him around the court to capitalize on mismatches and to defend the opponent's top scorer. Although he was only 5"- 11", he played much bigger, using his explosive jumping ability, strength, and timing to rebound and block shots against much taller opponents, while displaying the quickness and tenacity to defend point-guards. Ben Billie was a truly unique high school basketball player, but he faced substantial challenges to achieve his goal of getting a college education and continuing to play basketball at a high level.

When Ben Billie graduated from Weaver, he did not have the academic credentials to get into a four-year college, but he was determined to continue his education. He started taking classes in the morning while he worked the second shift at Pratt & Whitney. Former Weaver star Ricky Turner introduced him to Dr. James Peters, who arranged for Ben Billie and Weaver teammate Maurice Williams to attend Southern University in Baton Rouge, Louisiana on basketball scholarships. But the scholarship offers fell through at the last minute, and the two Weaver teammates returned to Hartford. Ben Billie was disappointed, but he was not defeated. Through his association with an African American social group known as High Noon, he met Frank T. Simpson, a long-time Hartford resident and the initial employee at Connecticut's first Civil Rights agency. Mr. Simpson told Ben Billie about Winstead Community College and encouraged him to attend. Ben Billie followed the advice and earned a two-year associate degree before moving on to Bryant College, which at the time was located in Providence, Rhode Island. Bryant College proved to be the right situation for Ben Billie at that point in his life, providing him with an opportunity to earn a BA degree in Business Administration while playing competitive college basketball. It did not take long for Ben Billie to establish himself as a dominant force in the Naismith Conference in which Bryant College competed. He averaged 15 points and 13 rebounds per game for Bryant, and he set a school record of 25 rebounds in one game. As a senior at Bryant he was elected co-captain of the basketball team with another Weaver High School graduate, David Greenblatt.

Although David Greenblatt had shown exceptional athletic talent while he was growing up in the North End of Hartford, excelling in pick-up games in both football and basketball, he was caught in a dilemma that many high school students faced. His mother and uncle were partners in a small wholesale grocery business, and they depended on David's help after school to keep the business going. Confronted with the decision to play sports after school or to help his family maintain the business, he chose to work. When he attended Bryant College to pursue a degree in Business Administration, he was free to try out for the basketball team as a walk-on. He impressed the coaches with his toughness, rebounding instincts, and all-out hustle. He not only made the team as the only player not to have played on his high school team, he became a starter and eventually a co-captain. His emergence as a standout college basketball player did not come as a surprise to anyone who had known him at Weaver. If he had opted to play sports rather than work after school, he had the potential to make an impact on both the football and basketball teams. But he had placed responsibility to family over personal considerations, and he had to wait until college to take part in athletic competition.

Just as he had at Weaver, Ben Billie did a little bit of everything at Bryant College. He was a reliable scorer, dominant rebounder, dependable ball-handler, and tenacious defender. But perhaps his greatest contribution to the team was his calm demeanor and composure under pressure. Ben Billie never got rattled. He stayed cool regardless of the situation, and his teammates responded to his calm resolve by playing with confidence and maturity. In 1968 Bryant's starting team of guards Don Gray and Joe Goddard, center George Yates, and the Beaver bookend forwards David Greenblatt and Ben Billie, led Bryant to a number 15 ranking in the nation in team defense among College Division teams as the school competed for its fourth Naismith Conference Championship. As at Weaver, Ben Billie made everyone around him a better player, the true measure of an elite basketball player.

After graduating from Bryant College, Ben Billie returned once again to Hartford, where he became interested in local politics as a way to advance the Civil Rights movement. He also became the manager of an R&B group, Lovely, which opened shows for the Commodores, Spinners, and Curtis Mayfield. He worked at United Bank and Trust for fourteen years, serving as a branch manager for ten years. He was a member of Hartford's Democratic Town Committee and in 1984 he became a Jehovah's Witnesses minister. He remained active in the business community as a financial advisor. The versatility he demonstrated on the basketball court carried over to the exemplary manner in which he lived his life, constantly striving for excellence in all his endeavors and inspiring the people he met along the way.

Billy Gilmore
Hartford Public High School 1965

Billy Gilmore grew up as an only child in the Charter Oak Terrace section of Hartford. His parents were hard-working people who tried to instill good habits and strong values in their son. In his early years he was bothered by some older, more aggressive kids, and he had no siblings or relatives to stick up for him. He had to learn to take a stand and defend himself, and he also discovered he could earn respect on the basketball court. He attended the Mary Hooker School, but since the school did not have a basketball team at the time, he learned to play hoops on the outdoor courts in his neighborhood and at the Southwest Boys Club. At Mary Hooker he demonstrated his all-around athletic ability by breaking the school's high jump record.

In the sixth grade, Billy Gilmore's family moved to the North End of Hartford, a section of the city he found very different from Charter Oak Terrace. Once again he found himself in a situation where it was necessary to earn the respect of the kids in his neighborhood, and once again he turned to sports as his way of gaining esteem. He demonstrated early on that he could hold his own on the basketball court or on the baseball field. As an eighth grader at the Barbour School, Billy Gilmore starred on both the basketball and baseball teams. His coach, Mr. O'Neal, thought that Billy had a future in baseball and wanted him to focus on the sport. But Billy saw that the basketball team attracted crowds of students while hardly anyone attended the baseball games. The disparity in attendance convinced him to concentrate on basketball.

As a freshman at Weaver High School, Billy Gilmore made the JV basketball team and he enjoyed a very successful season. He looked forward to moving up to the varsity as a sophomore and joining a promising Weaver team that included such fine players as Ben Billie and Maurice Williams. But that summer his family moved once again, and he learned he would be living in the Hartford Public High School district. He knew he would have to work extremely hard to prepare for the challenges of playing for a new school with all new teammates. He played in the Hartford Parks and Recreation League with some older players, including Hartford Public standout Lenny Kostek. He listened carefully to his older teammates, absorbing all the pointers and advice they shared with him, knowing it would help ease his transition to his new school. In a game against Bellevue Square he scored 30 points, many of them while being guarded by Arnold Mandeville, a tough defender and notorious trash talker. His offensive outburst against a tough Bellevue Square team convinced Billy Gilmore he was ready to compete for playing time at Hartford Public.

As a sophomore at Hartford Public, Billy Gilmore became friends with the Thompson twins, Ron and Lionel, who were also talented basketball players for the Owls. The friendship helped him to adjust to his new school. By the third game of the season, Billy Gilmore was starting on the varsity team. He blended well with his new teammates, and the Hartford Public team made the state tournament. Billy had concentrated more on basketball than his classes, and although his grades were good enough to maintain his eligibility on the team, they fell short of his mother's more exacting academic standards. She forced him to drop off the basketball team until he improved his grades. From that point on he made sure he met his mother's strict criteria for staying on the basketball team.

In his junior year, with his grades in good shape, Billy Gilmore rejoined the team and had a very successful basketball season. He was the Owls leading scorer, averaging over 18 points per game, and he earned recognition as one of the best players in the state. He led Hartford Public to the Class L finals in the State Tournament, only to lose to the powerful Academics from Hillhouse High School, 64-49. It could be noted that once again Billy Gilmore was tripped up by Academics!

But there was certainly no shame in losing to Hillhouse. They were loaded with All-State and All-American caliber players like Walt Esdaile, Tom Chapman, Billy Evans, and Tony Barone. Billy Gilmore was optimistic about his senior year, hoping Hartford Public would get another shot at a Hillhouse team that was returning its core players from the championship team. He had another fine individual season, but his team did not make it back to the finals in the State Tournament in his senior year. Hillhouse prevailed once again, beating a Notre Dame, Bridgeport team led by the amazing Rodock Cox, an uncanny leaper that dazzled the crowd with his gravity-defying forays to the basket. Billy Gilmore had tried his best. He had overcome disrupting moves, changes between rival high schools, his mother's demanding standards, and repeated challenges to earn respect as a standout basketball player. Although a number of colleges expressed interest in his services after high school, he chose to start a family of his own. He worked hard and retired after a career with the City of Hartford and the Connecticut Department of Transportation, but not before leaving an indelible mark on Hartford basketball.

Jerry Bonadies
Weaver High School 1966

Jerry Bonadies grew up in Hartford during the tumultuous sixties, when white families were exiting the North End for the surrounding suburbs. But the Bonadies family had no intention of leaving Hartford. Jerry Bonadies' Italian-American parents taught their three children about the importance of community and the evils of racism. For Jerry Bonadies, the supreme compliment was to be told that he played basketball like a brother. He was in his glory when he could get on the court in Keney Park and put his soulful game on display, the lightning-quick dribble, look-away pass, fearless drives to the hoop, relentless defense. He had spent countless hours in the park observing and learning from the great players that had left their mark on Hartford basketball, ballers like Eddie Griffin, Bobby Knight, and Frank Perry. He watched the way they controlled the game from the point guard position, running a fast-break with calm efficiency, slowing the tempo when a basket was needed to put away an opponent, setting up a cutting teammate for a layup or a dunk. Jerry Bonadies was a student of the game and Keney Park was his classroom, the place where he could develop the moves and the confident attitude he would bring with him across the street to Weaver High School in hope of building a legacy of his own. When he received the MVP trophy in the intermediate division of the Hartford Summer League representing Keney Park, he felt he was ready to pursue his dream of competing for a state championship wearing a green and white Weaver uniform.

Jerry Bonadies might not have had the confidence to play in Keney Park if not for Ben Billie. As a slender, 5'- 8" kid, Jerry Bonadies did not fit the profile of someone that would be picked to play on the team that had called "next" at Keney Park. But as an All-City performer and team captain at Weaver, Ben Billie enjoyed the status to vouch for another player's ability, even one as unlikely as Jerry Bonadies. Ben Billie and Jerry Bonadies had become friends, and it was their friendship that gave Jerry Bonadies the credibility to play in Keney Park. "He was always there for me," Jerry Bonadies recalled. "Ben Billie had a serious thump game," meaning, of course, that Ben was tough and a good fighter and if necessary, he would have Jerry Bonadies' back. But it was his belief in his own abilities, more than anything else, which enabled Jerry Bonadies to make a name for himself, not only at Keney Park, but throughout the city of Hartford as well.

Jerry Bonadies was convinced he could compete against anyone, and his intense level of self-confidence was perhaps his greatest asset on the basketball court. He had no fear and he would never back down. Sometimes, however, his cockiness worked against him. As a sophomore on the JV team, he felt he deserved to play on the Weaver varsity team. When Coach Frank Scelza refused to promote him, Jerry Bonadies transferred to Bulkeley High School for his junior year. He was determined to become a star basketball player, and if he was not going to get the opportunity at Weaver, he would try Bulkeley. But shortly after making the move, he was filled with regret. The Weaver team he had left behind had the potential to be one of the most talented in the school's history. The front court was solid with Jewett Newkirk, Ben Mathews, and Wayne Jones, ascending juniors during the 1965-66 season. Rufus Wells, a deadly jump shooter, was returning as the shooting guard. Only Ron Sears, the dynamic point guard, was graduating, leaving an opening in the starting five that Jerry Bonadies wanted desperately to fill. If he was going to live the dream of proving himself on the basketball court, in his mind it had to be at Weaver.

He asked Coach Scelza for permission to return to the Weaver team, promising to improve his attitude, and the coach agreed. There were only two teams in the state that appeared capable of keeping Weaver from winning the Class LL state championship in 1966 – Hartford Public and Wilbur Cross. The Governors of Wilbur Cross featured two All-State performers in Bill Reaves and Alex Scott, and they had the talent and the experience to beat any team in the state. Hartford Public was formidable as well, with an array of outstanding players like Pooch Tolliver, Greg Harrell, Steve Waterman, Nate Adger, Bob Nash, and Jake Edwards. During the regular season Hartford soundly beat Weaver twice. Since all City-Series games were played at Hartford High at the time, the Owls had enjoyed home-court advantage for both lopsided victories. But when the city rivals met on a neutral court in the state tournament, Weaver won 78-64, with Jerry Bonadies playing the entire game and orchestrating the Beavers' offense to perfection.

The stage was set for a Weaver showdown with Wilbur Cross for the CIAC Class L State Championship. In a dramatic, see-saw game, the two teams stayed close the entire time. Jerry Bonadies was at his best, breaking the Wilbur Cross full-court pressure, penetrating into the teeth of the defense, dishing out assists to his teammates. But in the third quarter Jerry Bonadies was forced out of the game with a serious knee injury. Weaver continued to fight and had a chance to take a lead in the closing seconds of a tie game, when Wayne Jones drove to the basket. His dunk attempt hit the back of the rim and ricocheted to mid-court, where it was retrieved by a Cross player, who went in for an uncontested lay-up, giving Wilbur Cross the 58-56 win. Until his knee betrayed him, Jerry Bonadies had played one of his finest games. Unfortunately, it would also be his last. The knee injury ended his competitive basketball career.

Jerry Bonadies went on to earn a degree in Education at Central Connecticut State College. He enjoyed a long career at the MDC. Now retired and living in Florida, he still has fond memories of his days at Weaver. "The best thing I cherish about the game is not the game itself, but the relationships that I formed," he said. "I remain friends with many of my Weaver classmates and the people I played ball with. It has made me the person I am today: a man of the people." Jerry Bonadies ultimately achieved the goal he had set in his youth, competing for a state championship for Weaver High School and proving to everybody that he had game.

Rufus Wells
Weaver High School 1966

After Hartford High won the Class L state championship in 1962, Hillhouse High School of New Haven reeled off three consecutive state titles from 1963-65. One of the main reasons for the Academics' dominance in the mid-sixties was the outstanding guard play of Billy Evans and Tony Barone. They were widely recognized as comprising the best backcourt in the state, not so much for their individual skills, although they were both extremely talented players, but for the way they meshed their abilities to form a cohesive unit. When they graduated from Hillhouse and moved on to successful collegiate careers, the distinction of preeminent backcourt in the state was up for grabs. The Hartford Public Owls could build a strong case that Dwight Tolliver and Greg Harrell were ready to assume the mantle as the state's best backcourt. They were amazingly quick, fearless, and adept ball-handlers capable of hitting jump shots from outside or penetrating to the basket. On defense they were able to use their quickness to press full court, making it a nightmarish task for opposing teams to advance the ball past mid-court. They had been playing together since they were kids growing up in Bellevue Square. They knew each other's moves and tendencies and played to each other's strengths. They were dynamic, gifted players in their own right; together they formed a devastating force. Yet there was another pair of guards in the city that may not have been as flashy as Dwight Tolliver and Greg Harrell, but were nevertheless highly effective in blending their skill sets to form a winning combination – Rufus Wells and Jerry Bonadies from Weaver High School.

Rufus Wells was born in Georgia and moved to Hartford when he was about a year old. He was one of seven children. His father, Paul Sr., served in the Navy during World War II and worked at Colt Firearms for many years. His mother, Bernice, worked as a nurse's aide. From an early age, Rufus Wells' parents instilled in their children the importance of getting a good education. They monitored the children's grades throughout their schooling and insisted on improvement if they saw any signs of slacking off. Rufus understood that if he wanted to play sports he would have to perform well in school. The emphasis his parents placed on doing well in school helped Rufus Wells become an exceptional student-athlete.

Rufus had an older brother, Paul Jr., who was an excellent athlete, providing him with a ready source of competition whenever they went outside to play. Since they lived in Stowe Village, the Wells brothers learned to play basketball on the project's outdoor courts. Built in 1952, Stowe Village consisted of 591 units, housing nearly 2,500 residents in eight two-story wood-frame duplexes and 23 three-story walk-up brick buildings. Stowe Village was a challenging place to live, but there were also positive influences trying to steer the kids in Stowe Village in the right direction, people like the Hartford Parks and Recreation coordinator and coach, Beans Brown. Beans Brown had played on the 1954 Weaver High team that won the city and state championships and competed for a New England title. He tried to show young players like Rufus and Paul Jr. how to play the game the right way, insisting on teamwork, discipline, and respect for opponents as well as teammates. Beans Brown coached Rufus Wells until the family moved from Stowe Village to Enfield Street, just as Rufus was about to enter Weaver High School. Beans Brown helped to give Rufus a solid foundation in the game he loved to play.

Rufus Wells attended Barbour School, where he played baseball and basketball. He was a pitcher on the school's baseball team that won the city championship when he was in the seventh grade. He played on the basketball team with future Hartford Public star Billy Gilmore, who was already an accomplished scorer in junior high school. Rufus remembered that the coach, Ted Maher, ran one basic play – pass the ball to Billy Gilmore. "Give the ball to Billy," the coach would shout, and the players, including Rufus, listened. The team won the city championship in basketball as well as baseball, giving Rufus two titles in the same year. Fred Ware ran the open gym at the Barbour School, and he and his brother Willie were influential in providing guidance to Rufus and many other kids from Stowe Village about avoiding the pitfalls of living in the project.

Rufus did well in school academically as well as athletically, and he particularly enjoyed the classes of Mr. Roy, the gym teacher, Ms. Scrum, who went on to teach at Weaver, and Mr. Eugene Green, who became the principal at Lewis Fox Middle School. He also demonstrated his keen entrepreneurial instincts by starting a golf caddying business at the Hartford Golf Club, a job he maintained through his junior year in high school. After his success at Barbour School, Rufus Wells was ready to embrace the challenges that awaited him at Weaver High.

When he entered Weaver as a freshman, Rufus Wells intended to play football and basketball, just as his brother, Paul Jr., was doing. He played on the freshman football team in the fall, but when it came time for him to try out for the freshman basketball team, his father would not allow him to play because he was not happy with the effort Rufus was putting into his academic work. Although Paul Sr. had only received a third grade education in his native Georgia, he wanted his children to be educated. When Rufus raised his grade in math from a B to an A, he was given permission to join the freshman basketball team in the second semester. Rufus had learned an important lesson; his participation in sports was contingent on his success in the classroom. It was a stern message he would not forget.

He played well on a freshman team that lost only one game all season, and he provided additional support for the team's high scorer, Steve Harris. Another freshman teammate was a slick ball-handler named Jerry Bonadies. Rufus Wells and Jerry Bonadies meshed well on the basketball court from the very beginning. They possessed complementary skill sets, with Bonadies' adept dribbling and clever passing enabling him to set up Rufus Wells for silky smooth, rainbow jump shots. It was a promising blending of sublime basketball talent that boded well for the future of the program.

Rufus Wells continued to work hard to develop his game. Like so many of his basketball contemporaries from the North End of Hartford, he became a regular at Keney Park, where he was assured of facing the stiffest competition in the area. One of the main benefits he derived from playing in Keney Park took place after the games ended, when the crowd of spectators thinned out and a few of the local legends, like Doc Hurley and Bobby Knight, would hold center court, discussing topics like education, college sports, and employment opportunities. According to Rufus Wells, a group consisting of twenty to thirty young players would listen attentively to these talks, absorbing pointers about the importance of working hard in school, developing good practice and study habits, becoming solid citizens in the community and avoiding distractions and unhealthy influences. For Rufus the discussions reinforced lessons he had learned from his parents; for many of the other players these were critical life lessons they were hearing for the first time. Rufus Wells took the advice to heart and began thinking about his future after he finished playing basketball in high school.

As a sophomore, Rufus Wells led the Weaver junior varsity team in scoring. In his junior year, he played on a strong starting five with Art Blackwell, Gil Cloud, Ben Mathews, and Charlie Parks. The team lacked a true point guard and Rufus Wells was asked to assume the role of playmaker, even though he was a natural two guard and his offense suffered. One of his strengths as a basketball player was his ability to catch and shoot. At 6'- 1" and 175 pounds, he had a size advantage over most opposing guards, and his explosive leaping ability enabled him to elevate over his opponents to get his jump shot off whenever he wanted. Although he was a fine ball-handler, he was much more effective off-the-ball, where his athleticism and feathery-soft jump shot made him one of the best offensive weapons in Weaver's history. In spite of an abundance of outstanding shooters, the team underperformed. Jerry Bonadies had hoped to fill the point guard position, but he clashed with Coach Scelza over a lack of playing time and transferred to Bulkeley High. It began to look as though all the potential Rufus Wells' freshman and JV teams had shown would never be fulfilled.

But in Rufus' senior year all the components for a successful team fell into place. Jerry Bonadies returned to Weaver and patched up his differences with Coach Scelza. With Jerry Bonadies back to run the point with flair and imagination, Rufus Wells could concentrate on getting open for jump shots. Ben Mathews and Jewett Newkirk returned for their junior year, providing size and toughness in the front court. Ben Mathews was one of the greatest players in Weaver's illustrious history. He could dominate at every position on the court. At a solid 6'- 4", he could overpower smaller players in the post, yet he was too quick and too evasive a ball-handler for traditional big men to guard. He made the game look so effortless that many spectators at Weaver games were under the mistaken impression that he was not trying very hard. But his opponents knew that Ben Mathews was a match-up nightmare, and the fluidity of his game masked an intense competitiveness that was ignored at the risk of looking foolish on the court. Ben Mathews could drive by a defender in a heartbeat, and once he elevated to attack the rim, opposing big men were often at his mercy, left with the equally unpalatable options of fouling him or stepping aside.

Jewett Newkirk played basketball like the football player he instinctively was, seeking out contact rather than avoiding it. He was on a constant mission to intimidate and dominate opponents. What he lacked in touch and finesse, he compensated for with a fierce determination that knew no limits. The notion of backing down was never a consideration. At a rugged 6'-3" and 225 pounds, he played the role of enforcer on the Weaver frontline, waiting for someone to drive to the basket and pay the price for what he considered an insolent affront to the team's defensive stand. He was quick enough to draw charges, athletic enough to block shots at the rim, and ornery enough to inflict a hard foul as a last resort, mercilessly staring down an opponent that objected to his over-zealous physicality. Jewett was the kind of player that teammates revered and opponents resented.

But the player that transformed the 1965-66 Weaver team from a very good team into one of the best in the state was Wayne Jones. The lanky 6'-4" Wayne Jones was unlike any other player in Weaver's history. He possessed the wingspan of a much taller player, an attribute that when coupled with his remarkable jumping ability enabled him to block shots with impunity and soar uncontested for rebounds. His teammates knew he would control every jump ball, and Coach Scelza designed plays to score off the jump ball at the start of the game. Wayne Jones was no ordinary high school center, content to play with his back to the basket and use his superior height and jumping ability to score in the post. One of his unique strengths was his ability to stretch the floor. He was an outside jump shooter with unlimited range before the three-point shot became a part of the game, when few big men ventured beyond the limits of the key. It was impossible for smaller players to challenge his jump shot; he would simply elevate over opposing guards for a clean look at the basket. Taller players were reluctant to get too close to him on the perimeter for fear that he would blow past them for an embarrassing dunk. Most teams did not have the luxury of allowing their center to roam around outside on offense. But with Ben Mathews, Jewett Newkirk, and Rufus Wells available to control the backboards, Wayne Jones was given the freedom to shoot from anywhere on the court, a liberty he willingly exploited as he emerged as a prominent scoring option on a team loaded with firepower.

Although Weaver possessed a formidable lineup capable of competing against any team in the state, the team's hopes for a state championship would not go unchallenged. The Beavers got off to a quick start in the 1965-66 season. In a game against Notre Dame of West Haven the Beavers won their ninth straight game 90-66 to remain undefeated.

Rufus Wells scored 12 points in the first quarter as Weaver jumped out to a 24-10 lead. He finished the game with 22 points, while Ben Mathews scored 23, Jerry Bonadies 16, and Jewett Newkirk 13 in a typically balanced Weaver attack. In his write-up in *The Hartford Courant* the next morning, sports writer Pat Bolduc emphasized the superb floor game Jerry Bonadies had played, referring to the senior point guard as a "brilliant playmaker, setting up play after play and passing for several spectacular baskets." With Jerry Bonadies handling the point with poise and precision, Rufus Wells was free to focus on what he did best, scoring the basketball with his lethal jump shot. When Jerry Bonadies and Rufus Wells were on their game, Weaver looked practically unstoppable.

The biggest threat to Weaver's quest for a state title, came from two powerful teams, cross-town rival Hartford Public and Wilbur Cross of New Haven. On the same night that Weaver was punishing Notre Dame of West Haven in Hartford, the undefeated Owls and Governors faced off in New Haven in front of an overflow crowd of 1,700 fans in the Wilbur Cross gym in what many observers felt was a preview of the likely matchup in the finals of the state tournament. The game did not disappoint. With 43 seconds remaining in the fourth quarter Dwight Tolliver stole the ball and scored a basket to give the Owls a tenuous 67-65 lead. Hartford Public's Larry Ross was fouled with eight seconds left and the Owls clinging to a one point lead. He converted the first free throw, but missed the second. After a Wilbur Cross time-out, Alex Scott threw in a desperation shot from 30 feet to force overtime. Then with time running out in the overtime period and the score tied 74-74, Alex Scott struck again, hitting a jump shot at the buzzer to win the game 76-74. Only a sophomore, Scott was the game's leading scorer with 22 points, while Larry Harper had 19 points and 13 rebounds. Dwight Tolliver led Hartford Public with 21 points. Art Blackwell, who had transferred from Weaver, scored 18 and Larry Ross had 17.

The intensity and excitement of the game did nothing to dispel the notion that Hartford Public and Wilbur Cross were the two best teams in the state and that they were destined to meet in the championship. The impression of the inevitability of a Hartford Public and Wilbur Cross matchup in the finals of the state tournament was reinforced when Weaver and Hartford met twice in the regular season and the Owls won convincingly both times. But in the third meeting between the city rivals in the quarterfinals of the state tournament at Wethersfield High School, Weaver defeated Hartford Public in a major upset, 78-66. Coach Scelza played only five men in the win, starters Rufus Wells, Jerry Bonadies, Wayne Jones, Ben Mathews, and Jewett Newkirk. The strong showing by Weaver demonstrated that the Beavers were capable of beating any team in the state. With their confidence restored, the players looked forward to facing Wilbur Cross in the finals, convinced this was the year they could capture the title.

But Weaver was unable to defeat Wilbur Cross in the championship game, losing 58-56 on a late score by Wilbur Cross. Jerry Bonadies went out with a knee injury in the first half, and without his floor leadership, Weaver struggled. But Rufus Wells played an inspired game, not only making clutch jump shots, but battling Wilbur Cross on the boards as well. Jerry Bonadies said it was the best game Rufus ever played. While Wilbur Cross did a creditable job neutralizing Weaver's big front line, they had no answer for the way Rufus Wells crashed the boards from the guard position. His rebounding and scoring singlehandedly kept Weaver in the game. But in the end it was not enough. Rufus Wells' standout high school career had come to a disappointing end.

At the end of his senior season, Rufus received multiple athletic and academic awards. He was named to the All-City, All-CDC, and All-Tournament teams. He was recognized for his high score on the Physics Achievement Test. As a result of his superb performance on the basketball court and in the classroom, he received multiple athletic and academic scholarship offers. In the end he chose to attend the University of Bridgeport on a full basketball scholarship. Rufus enjoyed a productive basketball career at the University of Bridgeport. He was named captain of the team in his senior year and he made the All-Tourney team in the Annual Pocono Classic Basketball Tournament. He was among the nation's leaders in free throw percentage, and at one point he held the school's record for most points in a half. He also continued to impress in the classroom as he had at Weaver, earning a B.A. in accounting and going back to school later to receive a master's degree.

After he graduated from the University of Bridgeport Rufus Wells served in Vietnam. He went on to start a successful business as a housing consultant. But Rufus never forgot where he came from. Along with his wife Janice and his old teammate Steve Harris, who became a lieutenant in the Hartford Fire Department, Rufus Wells provided funds to send children ten to fourteen years of age from Stowe Village and nearby North End streets to a sleepover summer camp in eastern Connecticut. He wanted the children to experience the natural beauty of the great outdoors, something that kids in Stowe Village might never see. Rufus Wells was one of the lucky ones to go on to a successful career, and he chose to share his good fortune with Hartford youngsters struggling for a better life. Rufus Wells was a class act both on and off the basketball court.

Dwight Tolliver
Hartford Public High School 1967

Every so often in the history of Hartford basketball a player came along with a skill set so unique that he changed the way the game was played in the city. Johnny Egan, with his ability to hang in mid-air and palm the ball with his exceptionally large hands, expanded the role of a 5'-11" guard with his creative drives to the basket and floating tear-drop shots. Eddie Griffin was so strong with the basketball and had such great court awareness that he could dominate a game as a scorer or playmaker. When Dwight "Pooch" Tolliver appeared on the Hartford basketball scene, he weaponized the element of quickness, showing how he could dictate the pace of the game by blowing past opponents at will. For years to follow young players on basketball courts throughout the city imitated his style of play, employing a stutter-step dribble to freeze defenders, making no-look passes to cutting teammates for open layups, and fearlessly attacking the basket against taller opponents. But before he could bring his distinctive game to a wider audience, he had to prove himself on the basketball court.

The 308-unit Bellevue Square public housing project was built in 1941 by the Hartford Housing Authority. It was originally intended as temporary housing for defense workers. At first, access to public housing for African Americans was intentionally limited through a policy of "controlled integration", although over time, due to shifting economic conditions and the exodus of white residents to surrounding suburban communities, there was a gradual shift in occupancy from white to African American renters. Bellevue Square covered 12.57 acres on Wooster, Canton, Pavillion, and Bellevue Streets. It provided housing for approximately 1,300 residents, mostly in three-story brick walk-up buildings with four families per floor. It was called the "brickyard", and it was one of the harshest environments in the city.

There were two major gathering sites for residents of the Square, an outdoor basketball court and a community building. The basketball court became a breeding ground for some of the most talented players in the city. The style of play was intense and physical. No accommodations were made for those that lacked toughness or a desire to compete. Playing against mostly older and more experienced players, the Bellevue Square basketball court was where Dwight Tolliver developed the flashy, up-tempo style of play that became his trademark. He was considered a basketball prodigy, a young player so gifted with natural ability that his potential appeared unlimited. But there had been other talented players from Bellevue Square that had succumbed to the pressures and challenges, and it remained to be seen if Pooch could overcome the pitfalls that had derailed the promising futures of so many of his basketball predecessors.

Dwight Tolliver was raised by his single parent mother in a household of three boys and five girls. His mother worked to feed and clothe the family, serving as a housekeeper in affluent suburbs like West Hartford and Simsbury. Pooch recalled that his mother shopped for clothing at the local Salvation Army store, provoking the disdain of some insensitive neighbors. As the oldest boy in the family, he accepted his responsibility to stay out of trouble and to help care for his siblings. He looked to basketball as his ticket to a better way of life. He began playing at the age of 10, shooting baskets with his friend Howard Jefferson. He attended Arsenal Elementary School before moving on to Brackett Northeast Junior High, where he was coached by the legendary Billy Taylor. During the summer he played in the Hartford Parks and Recreation League, representing Bellevue Square, where he was coached by Eugene Green. His team won the championship in his age group, giving him added confidence as he prepared to enter high school.

When he arrived at Hartford Public as a freshman, he made the JV team, and after three games Coach Joe Kubachka promoted him to the varsity squad, a team dominated by veterans like John Joiner, Bob Turner, Billy Gilmore, and the Thompson twins, Ron and Lionel. Coach Kubachka immediately recognized Dwight Tolliver's potential to impact a game from the point guard position, controlling tempo, seeking out open teammates for pin-point passes, pressuring opposing ball-handlers. As his playing time increased, his confidence soared and his value to the team grew. In a 65-49 City Series win against Bulkeley, he scored 9 second half points while shutting down Bulldogs' guard Mark Waxenberg, pulling the Owls into a three-way tie for the Capital District Conference lead with defending champion Weaver and Norwich Free Academy. As the season progressed, Dwight Tolliver became an increasingly integral part of the team's success. The Owls made it to the finals of the Class L state tournament before losing to Hillhouse 64-49, denying Pooch a championship in his freshman year. He would have three more years to try to capture a title.

The summer following his freshman year Dwight Tolliver was determined to improve his game, particularly his ability to shoot the basketball. Against ordinary competition, he was quick enough to drive to the basket for layups or to pull up for short jump shots. But playing against elite teams like Weaver, Wilbur Cross, and Hillhouse that had big men to protect the rim and savvy, resourceful guards to neutralize his quickness, he recognized the need to expand the range on his outside jump shot. At 5'-10" and 160 pounds he instinctively understood that by making himself a threat to shoot from distance he would open up lanes to penetrate to the basket. He went to work to implement his plans to expand his game, participating in summer leagues, attending basketball camps, and practicing diligently on his own. He was able to earn spending money by working in playgrounds like Bellevue Square and St. Benedict's. He became a regular at Keney Park, playing alongside legends like Bobby Knight, Eddie Griffin, and Boo and Ernie Perry, players he had admired from the sidelines when he was younger. The older players not only helped him fine-tune his game, they also offered advice on the importance of staying focused in school and avoiding trouble. He returned to Hartford Public for his sophomore year a more mature and confident player.

In Dwight Tolliver's sophomore year, Coach Joe Kubachka was trying to put together another team to make a deep run in the state tournament. In Tolliver, Steve Waterman, and Greg Harrell, Coach Kubahka had an outstanding nucleus of young talent around which to build a strong team, and slender 6'- 4" junior Nate Adger provided versatility and agility at the forward position. But the team lacked the size and depth to compete against some of the bigger and more physical teams in the state. Hartford Public was eliminated from the state tournament, and Hillhouse went on to win the Class L state title, defeating Notre Dame of Bridgeport, 57-51. It was the third consecutive state championship for the Hillhouse Academics from New Haven. Winning championships was nothing new for Hillhouse under legendary coach Sam Bender. Over his storied coaching career, Sam Bender compiled a 583-143 record that included nine state championships and six New England High School Championships. Although only 5'- 5" tall, he had played football and basketball at Commercial High School (that eventually became Wilbur Cross), and he was a reserve on the basketball team that won the first New England High School Championship in

1921. The Hillhouse team that beat Hartford Public in the 1964 state championship went 22-0 and was considered perhaps the best team in the school's remarkable history. Called the "Fabulous Five", the starters were Walt Esdaile, Billy Evans, Tom Chapman, Billy Gray, and Tony Barone. The Academics won the 1965 championship as well, behind the inspired play of returning All-State performers Walt Esdaile and Billy Evans. Coach Sam Bender retired after the 1965 state championship at the age of 61, bringing his brilliant coaching career to an end. With the graduation of Esdaile and Evans and the retirement of Sam Bender, the large school coaches throughout the state knew that heading into the 1965-66 season the competition for a state championship was suddenly more wide open than it had been in years.

In Dwight Tolliver's junior year, the Hartford Public Owls were eager to claim the title that had eluded them since Eddie Griffin and company had departed. Returning starters Dwight Tolliver, Steve Waterman, Greg Harrell, and Nate Adger gave the Owls a solid core of players poised to compete for the state championship. But an equally determined Weaver team had the height, quickness, and offensive firepower to challenge any team in the state. The Owls handily defeated Weaver twice on their home court during the regular season, but playing on a neutral court in the state tournament, the Beavers beat Hartford Public 78-66, shattering their hopes for a championship in Coach Joe Kubachka's final season. Wilbur Cross won the 1966 state championship by defeating Weaver 58-56, in the first year that the LL classification was added to the tournament format. It was the fourth year in a row that a New Haven high school had won the title and the second time in three years that a Hartford school had lost in the finals. Both Hartford Public and Weaver were bent on reversing the trend the following year.

The 1966-67 Hartford Public team, under the direction of first year head coach John Cuyler, went undefeated during the regular season. The team played as though it was on a mission, knowing that the window of opportunity for securing a championship was closing as Dwight Toliver and Steve Waterman approached graduation. There were several close games, like the 63-61 win over the New London Whalers on Bob Nash's jump shot with 4 seconds left on the clock. But with Bob Nash and Art Andrews controlling the backboards and Tolliver and Waterman providing a devastating one-two punch on offense, the team marched methodically through an undefeated regular season. After beating Weaver twice during the season in close games, the Owls were wary about facing their city rival in the tournament. But Hartford Public defeated the Beavers, avenging their defeat in the previous tournament and putting the Owls on the brink of a state championship. In the final game of the tournament, with an undefeated season and a state title on the line, Wilbur Cross defeated Hartford Public 74-66. Dwight Tolliver called the game the worst defeat of his entire basketball career. The championship he craved had eluded him all four years at Hartford Public. He would have to wait until he coached at Weaver to experience the elation of a state championship.

In spite of the loss, recognition for his outstanding high school career poured in. For the second year in a row he was named to the All-State, All-Capital District Conference, and All-City first teams. He received All-New England and All-American honors, leading to multiple inquiries from colleges and universities throughout the country. Although he had earned decent grades at Hartford Public, he had not pursued an academic course of study that would have made him an attractive candidate for traditional four-year colleges. It was a familiar narrative in the city of Hartford, a student with the athletic accomplishments to earn a scholarship to college, but not the proper accreditation to meet the minimum admittance requirements. There were exceptions to the rule. Students like Steve Waterman and Rufus Wells were prepared academically as well as athletically to gain admittance to traditional institutions.

As he scrambled to find a school where he could continue to play basketball, Dwight Tolliver accepted a scholarship offer from Winston Salem State University, where he had been recruited by Hall of Fame coach Clarence "Big House" Gaines. Winston Salem State University was founded in 1892 as a subsidiary of the University of North Carolina. The historically African American school had risen to national prominence the year Dwight Tolliver was graduating from Hartford Public, mainly on the exploits of a basketball player from John Bartram High School in Philadelphia named Vernon Earl Monroe, better known as Earl the Pearl. As a senior at Winston Salem State, Earl Monroe had averaged an astounding 41.5 points per game. He was named the NCAA College Division player of the year, and the 6'-3" 185 pound guard led his team to the College Division National Championship. The two time All-American was drafted by the Baltimore Bullets as the second pick in the 1967 NBA draft, and he won the NBA Rookie of the Year Award, averaging 24.3 points per game. He went on to enjoy a Hall of Fame career with the Bullets and the New York Knicks.

It must have been flattering for Dwight Tolliver to have his name mentioned in the same context as Earl Monroe and to be considered as a potential replacement for the All-American at Winston Salem State University. But although he had a successful freshman season at Winston Salem State, he returned to Hartford to resolve personal issues and never went back. He was not willing, however, to give up on his dream of playing college basketball. He talked to Ben Mathews, a friend and long-time rival at Weaver, who was attending St. Gregory's Junior College in Shawnee, Oklahoma, and Pooch decided to resume his education there, taking his wife and child with him. He remained at St. Gregory's for a year and a half before transferring to the University of Rhode Island, where he joined his close friend and former high school teammate, Nate "Shotgun" Adger on the basketball team. Pooch enjoyed success at the University of Rhode Island, where he was named captain of the basketball team and made the All-Yankee Conference team. He received a degree in physical education, and after graduation he returned to Hartford to begin his career as a teacher and a coach.

In 1997 Dwight Tolliver was honored by the Greater Hartford African American Alliance and the Hartford Housing Authority for serving as an outstanding role model for young people in the city. He shared the honor with two other Hartford Public High School graduates, Steve Waterman, his former teammate, and Eddie Griffin, one of his most important mentors. It was fitting that three of the very best players in the city's history had all returned to Hartford to serve as teachers, coaches, and mentors at each of the public high schools. Eddie Griffin coached at Bulkeley for 14 years and won two state titles during his tenure. Steve Waterman served as a teacher in Hartford for 25 years. He was an assistant coach at Hartford Public for 16 years before taking over as the head basketball coach from 1994-1999, compiling a 94-41 record. Dwight Tolliver coached Weaver's boys and girls' basketball teams for 18 seasons. As the boys basketball coach he had a 251-99 record, for a .717 winning percentage. In 1991 his Weaver team finished 23-2 and won the Class LL state championship, defeating Danbury 79-76, giving him the title he had fought so hard to achieve during his high school career. His Weaver teams also won seven

CCC West titles since the conference's formation in 1984. Sitting by his side on the Weaver bench was his assistant coach, close personal friend, and high school and college teammate, Nate Adger, who had helped him secure a scholarship to the University of Rhode Island. As seniors at the University of Rhode Island they had both made the All-Yankee Conference first team, along with Julius Erving. Nate Adger taught math and business at Weaver, while serving as Dwight Tolliver's assistant basketball coach. He left coaching after the 1996 season in order to devote more time to watching his son Kevin play basketball at Bloomfield High School. Nate Adger's death on December 27, 2003 at the age of 56 was a terrible blow to Dwight Tolliver as well as to the city of Hartford for the loss of a truly special person.

Prior to the dinner-dance at the West Indian Social Club in recognition of his service to the community, Dwight Tolliver was asked to reflect back on his career. He mentioned people who had served as his personal role models, men like John Wilson, Ernie and Frank Perry, and Bobby Knight. "Bobby always made sure to encourage you," Tolliver said. "I never found anyone who didn't like the guy." He spoke about how he had tried to emulate Bobby Knight during his own career by striving to pass on the wisdom and experience he had gained during his life to his students at Weaver. "Feeling that you got through to a student is probably the most important thing," he said. As a basketball player, teacher, coach, and role model, Dwight Tolliver had an indelible impact on the city of Hartford.

Steve Waterman
Hartford Public High School 1967

Steve Waterman and Dwight Tolliver – the two names are inextricably linked in the annals of Hartford basketball lore. Bob Saulsbury, the legendary basketball coach at Wilbur Cross from 1966-1994, spoke about the pair in almost reverential terms long after they were no longer playing, "When they were on the floor, they were the best. Two great individuals, they realized the importance of a team effort." Steve Waterman and Dwight Tolliver both grew up in the Bellevue Square housing project. They won All-City, All-State, and All-New England honors as teammates on one of the best Hartford Public teams of all time. They both went on to enjoy successful collegiate careers before returning to Hartford to teach and coach at city high schools. And they were both recognized as outstanding role models for a generation of young people. Steve Waterman and Dwight Tolliver were transformative figures in the history of Hartford basketball, not only for their excellence on the basketball court, but for their positive impact in the community as well.

As Steve Waterman was growing up in Bellevue Square with his four brothers and his twin sister, the church was an important factor in his life. His great grandmother lived on Bellevue Street, next door to Eddie Griffin's family. She was a member of Faith Congregational Church, and she insisted that the Waterman family attend church. Steve's mother was a strong advocate for public education, and she saw to it that her children took school seriously. Steve Waterman remembered his early years as a period of doing homework, performing chores, and attending church, leaving far less time for playing sports than he would have liked. But the disciplined approach to education that his mother cultivated in her children remained with Steve throughout his life and made him a good student with a strong work ethic.

Steve Waterman attended Arsenal Elementary School before going to Brackett Northeast Junior High School. At Brackett Northeast he played for the legendary coach Billy Taylor, where he became accustomed to playing winning basketball. His team won two Junior High School city championships, preparing Steve Waterman for the up-tempo, team-oriented style of play that would become the hallmark of his Hartford

Public teams. In his freshman year at Hartford Public he started at center for the junior varsity team, and by the end of the season he was making a solid contribution on the varsity team. As a sophomore, he played on the varsity team with two lightning quick guards, Greg Harrell and Dwight Tolliver, and a talented forward, Nate Adger, providing a glimpse of the core group of players that would become a dominant force in the state over the next two basketball seasons. The team that Coach Joe Kubachka was assembling was a match-up nightmare for opposing coaches. Greg Harrel and Dwight Tolliver possessed outstanding quickness to go along with exceptional ball-handling, passing, and shooting skills that made them nearly impossible to contain. Nate Adger was a solid rebounder with the ability to score on the inside or from the perimeter. Steve Waterman was the glue that held the team together. He was capable of playing any position on the court, moving into the backcourt to provide ball-handling and outside shooting support, filling the lane on the fast-break to attack the basket, and playing inside to help on the boards and defend taller opponents. If the Owls lacked one component needed to compete with the strongest teams in the state like Weaver and Wilbur Cross, it was the size to battle on the backboards. With the emergence of Bob Nash during the 1965-66 season, Steve Waterman's junior year, all the ingredients were in place for consecutive runs at a state title.

The Owls basketball team that took the floor for the 1965-66 season was one of the most dominant in the school's long and proud tradition. It was Coach Kubachka's final season at the helm, and the team was focused on providing him with a state championship as a parting tribute. As the season unfolded, the chances looked promising that the Owls could deliver on their goal. The team won both the City Series and CDC championships and entered the state tournament as favorites to win the title. When the team learned they had to face city rival Weaver in an early round of the tournament, the players remained confident they could advance. They had beaten Weaver twice during the season, both times by lopsided margins. But when the teams faced off in front of a packed crowd on the Wethersfield High School court on March 8, 1966, Weaver upset Hartford Public 78-66, providing yet another example in the storied history of the rivalry that it was impossible to predict with any certainty the outcome of a game between city schools. It was a bitter defeat for the Owls, one that motivated the team to return the following season more determined than ever to win the state championship.

Although Steve Waterman and Dwight Tolliver were the only two starters returning from the team that lost to Weaver the previous season, the 1966-67 Hartford Public team was a powerhouse. Bob Nash and Art Andrews provided size, length, and rebounding, while Jake Edwards replaced the disqualified Greg Harrell to give the Owls a solid defender and developing scorer at the guard position to complement Pooch Tolliver. Brian Robinson and Mike Pagliaro were key substitutes for John Cuyler in his first season as head coach. Weaver and Wilbur Cross stacked up as the main competition to Hartford Public in their quest for a state title. The imposing Weaver front line of Ben Mathews, Jewett Newkirk, and Wayne Jones returned intact. Gil Hampton and the emerging Cleve Royster provided front court depth, and the back court was solid, quick, and deep, with Mike Mitchell, Bill Davis, Sal Harrison, Buster Gore, Howie Greenblatt, and Doug Morgan. Once again Hartford Public beat Weaver twice during the regular season, but the games were close and the teams were on a collision course to meet in the state tournament for the second year in a row. Hartford Public had completed the regular season undefeated for the first time in the school's history, but the Owls were leery of facing Weaver in the tournament, the upset at the hands of the Beavers the previous March still very much on their minds.

The Class LL quarter-final match-up between Hartford Public and Weaver took place at Maloney High in Meriden. Weaver had lost only three games all season, two to Hartford Public and a third to Wilbur Cross, and they posed a serious threat to the Owls' chances of advancing in the tournament. Weaver fell behind early, and although the Beavers mounted a spirited comeback in the second half with their complete lineup restored, the Owls held on for the victory, avenging their ouster from the tournament the prior year.

The only team remaining in the tournament capable of blocking Hartford Public's bid for a state title was the defending state champions Wilbur Cross, led by All-State performers Bill Reaves and Alex Scott. When the teams met during the regular season, Hartford Public had come out on top. But for the second year in a row Hartford Public was denied the title the team coveted, losing to Wilbur Cross in the finals of the state tournament, 74-66. The team finished with a 21-1 record after going 17-2 the previous year. Steve Waterman was named All-New England, All-

State, and All-City. During his stellar high school career, he had attracted the attention of multiple colleges in the region, including the University of Hartford, the University of Bridgeport, Central Connecticut State, and the University of Connecticut, and Springfield College.

The school that appealed to Steve Waterman the most was Springfield College, which was close enough to Hartford to prevent homesickness, yet far enough away to keep him from getting distracted from his student-athlete responsibilities. Ed Bilik, the highly successful head basketball coach at Springfield College, recognized Steve Waterman's outstanding potential and offered him a full scholarship. Coach Bilik had earned BS and MS degrees from Springfield College and an Ed.D. degree from the University of Oregon. He was the head basketball coach at Springfield College from 1966 to 1986, compiling a record of 322-196. He later became the director of athletics at Springfield College. Throughout his basketball career, Steve Waterman came under the influence of exceptional coaches, Billy Taylor at Brackett Northeast Junior High School, Joe Kubachka and John Cuyler at Hartford Public, and Ed Bilik at Springfield College. Given the quality of coaching he received, it was not surprising that he chose to become a coach.

The transition to a college environment from the comfortable confines of Hartford Public was not easy for Steve Waterman. Although he was having success on the freshman basketball team and in the classroom, he found it difficult to adjust to the cultural and social life on campus, and he considered leaving school and going to work. The first time away from home in a collegiate setting had tripped up many outstanding basketball players from Hartford, causing them to cut short their athletic and educational opportunities. Steve Waterman's ability to persevere through a rough start at Springfield College enabled him to find success on the basketball court and to prepare for a successful career after college.

In his sophomore year at Springfield College, Steve Waterman emerged as the complete basketball player he had been in high school. He averaged 12.8 points per game and 8.2 rebounds. He spent most of the season at the guard position, but Coach Bilik switched him to the forward position with four games left in the season to shore up the team's rebounding deficiencies. At 6'- 1" Steve Waterman led the team in rebounds in three of the four remaining games. He was named to the All-Star teams of the NCAA Regional Tournament and the Worcester Holiday Festival. He continued to improve as a junior, playing primarily as a forward on offense while guarding the opponent's top guard on defense. He got off to a fast start as the team surged to a 7-1 record, raising his scoring average to 16.7 points per game and maintaining his rebounding prowess with over 8 boards a game. He scored 28 points in a win over Tufts University. Coach Ed Bilik recognized his importance to the team in an interview with a Springfield sports writer, "Steve made two All-Tourney teams last year, and it wasn't because he's a great scorer. His overall floor game is tremendous. He really makes us go. When we need the key rebound, the big steal or the great pass to spark our team, Steve's the one who usually does it."

In his senior year Steve Waterman was named captain of the Springfield College basketball team. He had developed into one of best all-around players in New England, excelling at both ends of the court. According to Coach Bilik, "Steve is one of the biggest keys to our team. Without his fine play, we'd be an ordinary ball club. He lends quite a bit of poise and overall knowhow to the squad, which I rate even higher than scoring points." In game after game he demonstrated his value to the team. In a late season game against the University of Hartford in which both teams were competing for a spot in the NCAA College Division tournament, Steve Waterman scored 39 points and came up with a key steal and an assist to Fran Stupakevich from Wallingford, Connecticut with 38 seconds remaining to nail down a 91-89 victory.

If there was one game in his college career that exemplified the kind of basketball player Steve Waterman had become, it was the February 16, 1971 contest against the University of Massachusetts. The game was played at the Memorial Field House on the campus of Springfield College in front of 3,000 fans that had packed the arena, many to see Julius Erving perform in his final collegiate season before turning professional. Dr. J was considered the finest basketball player in the country. In his two year varsity career at UMass, Dr. J averaged 26.3 points and 20.2 rebounds per game, one of only six players in NCAA history to exceed the 20-20 mark in scoring and rebounding. On the night the teams played at Springfield College, UMass had a record of 17-2 on the way to completing a 23-4 season, including a 10-0 Yankee Conference record to win the league championship. Springfield College was 13-7 and heavy underdogs to a UMass team that would earn a post-season selection to the NIT.

Only seven players played in the game for Springfield College, Judd

Hunt, Fran Stupakevich, Dana Anderson, Jim Grassi, Rich "Hot Rod" Hundley, Brad Macomber, and team captain Steve Waterman. Coach Bilik decided to play man-to-man rather than a zone defense, and he assigned Brad Macomber to guard Dr. J. UMass led 31-30 at the half, but pulled ahead early in the second half. With eight minutes left in the game, UMass was up 53-44. Springfield College went into a full-court press that enabled them to cut into the UMass lead. With 22 seconds left in the game, Steve Waterman drove in for a layup to pull Springfield within 62-61. As Tom McLaughlin from UMass tried to inbound the ball to Julius Erving, Brad Macomber intercepted the pass and as he was falling out of bounds, he passed the ball to Steve Waterman who dribbled once and hit a 15-foot jump shot with 4 seconds left to win the game 63-62. Steve Waterman scored 30 points in the game, while Dr. J was held to 18, his lowest scoring total of the season, due primarily to Brad Macomber's inspired defensive effort. In an article written 28 years later by Springfield College alumnus Hal Lynch he quoted Dana Anderson, who scored 11 points for Springfield College in spite of a bad cold, "Without a doubt, Steve Waterman played his greatest game. He was tremendous."

Steve Waterman reflected on the end of the historic game, "I was fortunate enough to receive a pass from Brad Macomber with a few seconds left to play. Yes, I made the shot, even though my jump shot came off the wrong foot! I will never forget Coach Bilik. He made me feel important." Hal Lynch titled his article about the game *Springfield College's Greatest Basketball Victory*. Springfield College finished the season with a 17-7 record, but there can be little doubt that the win over UMass was the most satisfying victory of the year and Steve Waterman's most memorable game in his remarkable career. He scored 1,166 career points at Springfield College and he was later inducted into the Hartford Public High School Athletic Hall of Fame and the New England Basketball Hall of Fame.

After he graduated from Springfield College, Steve Waterman returned to Hartford and continued his education at Central Connecticut State. He became a middle school physical education teacher and held the position of assistant basketball coach at HPHS for 16 years. He was named the head coach at Hartford Public in 1994, replacing the retiring Stan Piorkowski. He compiled a 94-41 record as the head basketball coach at his alma mater. One of the highest compliments that can be paid to a basketball player is to say that he played the game the right way. If you ask any of the coaches for whom he played, any of the teammates that played beside him, any of the opponents he battled against, they will all tell you the same thing – Steve Waterman played the game the right way.

Howie Greenblatt

Weaver High School 1967
In His Own Words

I grew up on Garden Street in the North End of Hartford in a racially and ethnically diverse neighborhood where there were plenty of opportunities to play sports. My first taste of organized sports came in the Hartford Midget Football League. I tried to emulate my older brother David, who was one of the elite players in the league. But I lacked the tools that made him an exceptional football player, like size, toughness, and the willingness to absorb and dole out physical punishment. Some of the teammates I remember from midget football include Bill Mullady, Jewett Newkirk, Vito Grieco, and Kaj Munik, all people I would meet again in other athletic endeavors.

I attended Brackett Northeast for elementary school and Northwest Jones Junior High School. I played shortstop on a Northwest Jones baseball team that won two city junior high school championships. Our team featured two outstanding pitchers, Nolan Lewis and Joe Green, both of whom would have productive multi-sport careers at Weaver. Another teammate I remember was Earl Womack, a gifted natural athlete who had his life cut tragically short when he was stabbed to death in a fight while he was a freshman at Weaver. The shock of losing a friend at such a young age still resonates in my consciousness.

While I enjoyed the experience of playing football and baseball, I did not envision a bright future for me in either sport. I didn't like to get hit in football, and I couldn't hit a baseball very well. Basketball was a different story. My family moved to the Blue Hills Avenue of Hartford when I was in the eighth grade, and I played all the time on the narrow driveway of our house on Thomaston Street, with friends like Ron Berkowitz, Bob Sheketoff, Steve Kass, David Marks, and of course my brother David. I was a regular at the Rawson School gym, where we played spirited pickup games. I frequented the parks and playgrounds in the neighborhood, like Bowles Park, Keney Park, and Elizabeth Park, looking for games against strong competition. It was my hope that my love of basketball would somehow translate into a chance to play at Weaver, but that goal seemed like a stretch, even on my good days when I felt I was progressing as a player.

In my first year at Weaver, I made the freshman basketball team, but I was disillusioned by my lack of playing time and the coach's seeming inability to remember my name. If he finally decided to put me into a game, he simply pointed to me at the end of the bench and nodded towards the scorer's table. I stopped showing up for practices or games, but I doubt the coach even noticed. At the beginning of my sophomore year at Weaver, I was playing in a pickup basketball game during gym class, when I was approached by head basketball coach Frank Scelza. He asked my name and encouraged me to try out for the team. Without his prompt, I'm still not sure I would have attended the tryouts.

I started on a strong JV team, boosting my confidence that I might actually be on track to realize my dream of playing varsity basketball at Weaver. I had been attending Weaver basketball games for a few years, watching players like Ben Billie, Wade Timmons, Len VanTassel, John Bologna, Gil Cloud, and Paul Wells. I was impressed by the excitement generated in the band-box Weaver gym, where students filled the stands, cheerleaders scrunched against the wall, feet stomped on the bleachers in unison to create a deafening din that reverberated in spectators' ears long after the game was over. Weaver seldom lost a home game, and I basked in the party-like atmosphere that swept through the crowded gym as the fans celebrated another victory.

I earned a spot on the 1965-66 Weaver varsity team as a junior, but I played a limited role on a veteran team with a legitimate shot at a Class LL state championship. The starting lineup of 6'-1" Rufus Wells, 5'-9" Jerry Bonadies, 6'-3" Jewett Newkirk, 6'-4" Ben Matthews, and 6'-4" Wayne Jones was one of Weaver's most impressive units of all time. After a strong regular season, we upset Hartford Public in the quarterfinals of the CIAC Class LL state tournament, but we lost to Wilbur Cross in the finals by two points. The disappointment of that defeat still lingers.

I was given the opportunity to play meaningful minutes for Weaver in my senior year, an experience I still consider one of the highlights of my life. Jerry and Rufus had graduated, Ben, Jewett, and Wayne were back for another year, and I shared the guard positions with a talented group of teammates that included Bill Davis, Mike Mitchell, Sal Harrison, and Buster Gore. Unfortunately, we were blocked from getting back to the finals by a great Hartford Public team. The Owls went undefeated during the regular season, beating Weaver three times, before falling to Wilbur Cross in the championship game in the state tournament.

My high school career was over, but not my passion for basketball. I was a good student academically, and I intended to go to college. One of my main considerations was picking a college where I would stand a chance of contributing to the basketball program. During my senior year at Weaver, I went to watch Trinity College play in the Memorial Field House, and I recall leaving the gym convinced that I had found a college that met my academic and athletic criteria. I had already submitted an early decision application to Trinity, and I was accepted. In essence I recruited myself, applying to only one school. But with the pressure of the college selection process completed early in my senior year, I could relax and focus on making the most of my remaining months of high school, which I did. I enjoyed my four years at Weaver tremendously, and I was grateful to all my classmates, teachers, and coaches who had made the experience so memorable. I was amazed the time had flown by so quickly.

I played point guard on a talented Trinity freshman team that included my roommate, 6'-8" center Ron Nussbaum, from North High School in Des Moines, Iowa, 6'-4" forward Jim Wolcott from West Cranston High School in Rhode Island, 6'-3" forward Tom Sasali from Windsor Locks High School, 6'-2" guard Ron Cretaro from Pekin Community High School in Pekin, Illinois, and 6'-2" forward John Durland from Darien High School. We finished the season with a 13-2 record, placing our freshman team among the best in Trinity's history. One of my personal highlights of the season was a 38 point break-out game in an overtime win over Yale University.

If the freshman team had remained intact, Trinity might have been far more successful over the next three years, but the team lost several key players for academic, physical, or personal reasons, and we never lived up to the potential we showed in our first year on campus. In my sophomore year Joe Pantelone, a 6'-7" transfer from UConn, was added to the lineup and over the next two years he would provide our team with a dominant scorer and rebounder. He was the first player in Trinity history to score over 1,000 points in two seasons. As a senior he was named to the College Division All-America Basketball Team. Joe Pantalone died tragically in an automobile accident on December 15, 1974 in Kenitra, Morocco, while serving in the United States Marines. His death came only two days after his promotion from lieutenant to the rank of captain.

The team struggled in my senior year in the absence of Joe Pantalone, but even a subpar season could not detract from the enjoyment of playing with a great group of teammates and for a true gentleman of a coach, Robie Shults. Although scattered across the country now, some of us still get together on occasion, and we appreciate each other's company, just as we did when we were young and competing on the basketball court.

I was selected as the Trinity captain in my senior year. I finished my three-year varsity career with a total of 1,214 points (I looked up the exact figure to make sure my memory wasn't inflating the actual number). I was a distant second in the college's scoring history at the time to Jim Belfiore's 1,369 points. My point total was deceiving, especially to me. I never led a team in scoring at any level except in my senior year at Trinity, when I averaged 21.8 points per game. I always considered ball-handling and passing as my main basketball strengths, with pressing man-to-man defense a close third. I wasn't a great pure shooter like Jim Belfiore or a natural scorer like Joe Pantalone. If anything, I was persistent. One of the accomplishments at Trinity for which I was most proud was receiving an NCAA grant for postgraduate studies, one of five college division players in the country to be so recognized. I used the scholarship to pursue a Ph.D. in English and American Literature at Brandeis University, while I continued to play competitive basketball in leagues in the Boston area. I am honored to be in the Trinity College Basketball Hall of Fame and the New England Basketball Hall of Fame.

I moved back to Hartford in 1976, living on Preston Street with my wife Cindy for the first few years of our marriage before we moved to Wethersfield, where we have been ever since. We have two grown children, Dean and Marcia, a son-in-law Chris Lesser, and two wonderful grandchildren, Zachary and Alexandra Lesser.

I recently visited my former Weaver basketball coach, Frank Scelza, now in his nineties, at his home in East Hartford. I told him I was working with Mike Copeland on a book on Hartford basketball, and we spent the afternoon reminiscing about the glory days of Weaver basketball. I was surprised at the clarity of our recollections as we evoked individual players and particular games from the distant past. The time raced by, as it always does. We could have talked much longer about a subject dear to both our hearts.

Jackie Brown
Bulkeley High School 1968)

Jackie Brown grew up in the Southwest section of Hartford. His mother was an excellent basketball player in her own right, and she brought Jackie Brown to the neighborhood park and encouraged him to shoot baskets. Once he started to see the ball go through the hoop on a regular basis, he was hooked. Jackie Brown was a natural athlete, and he excelled at every sport he played in his youth. He was a dominating pitcher and powerful hitter on Coach Don Harris's Little League team, and he was a superior quarterback in the Midget Football League. Although he enjoyed playing all sports, he felt a special attraction to basketball, and it would not take long for him to show that he had the talent to do special things on the court.

Jackie Brown attended Wilson Elementary School, where in the sixth grade he earned a spot on the Moylan Junior High School basketball team, coached by Don Harris, his Little League coach. The Moylan basketball team had a championship pedigree; it had won multiple championships and was riding a historic winning streak. Jackie Brown played for Moylan from grades six through eight, and his team won sixty-three games in a row and captured three city championships. While never attempting to run up the score, some of the victories during the winning streak were embarrassingly one-sided. There were occasions when Jackie Brown scored twenty to thirty points by half time, more points than the opposing team would score for the whole game. Jackie Brown was a major factor in one of the more remarkable basketball winning streaks at any level in the city of Hartford.

When it was time for Jackie Brown to enter high school, he decided to take the prep school route, hoping the experience would put him on a more reliable track to college. He enrolled at Avon Old Farms School on a scholarship, but he stayed only a few months before returning to Hartford. His father encouraged him to attend Bulkeley High School, a recommendation based largely on the reputation of the legendary basketball coach, Lou Bazzano. Like many of the great basketball players of his era, Jackie Brown was fortunate to come in contact with an exceptional coach that recognized his talent, motivated him to reach his full potential, and helped him to flourish as a basketball player and a man. Jackie Brown only had Lou Bazzano as his coach for two years, but it was enough time to enable him to develop the fundamentally sound game that would make him one of the city's most complete players.

Lou Bazzano was born in New Britain and played basketball and baseball at New Britain High. During World War II he served in the Army and participated in the European Theatre in Germany and France. After he was discharged from the army, he attended Springfield College, where he earned a B.S. in Physical Education and later he earned a Master of Education Degree. He began his coaching career in Plymouth, New Hampshire in spectacular fashion, coaching the football team to a state championship, the basketball team to an undefeated season, and the baseball team to a league championship, all in his first year! From 1953-66 Coach Bazzano led Bulkeley High School to a 202-86 record and three Capital District Conference championships. His teams made two trips to the New England High School Basketball Championship in 1958 and 1962. His traditionally undersized teams played a disciplined, intense style of basketball that gave opponents very little margin of error. Any team that had Bulkeley on the schedule knew it was in for a very tough game.

As a freshman Jackie Brown started on the Bulkeley JV team and dressed for the varsity games, receiving significant minutes in both contests. During a varsity game against cross-town rival Weaver, Jackie Brown scored twelve crucial points in the fourth quarter to seal the victory. In his sophomore year, he played baseball as well as basketball. He led the CDC with a .440 batting average, attracting the attention of some major league scouts. In his junior year he continued to excel in both sports, leading the CDC in scoring while emerging as a top rebounder and continuing his torrid hitting on the baseball field. Several basketball rating services, such as Street & Smith, listed him as one of the country's top one hundred high school players. Yet in spite of his contribution, the team was struggling. Bulkeley needed to win seven of the final eight games to qualify for the state tournament. Jackie Brown was up to the challenge. In the last four games he went on an incredible scoring spree, averaging 37 points a game, helping his team earn a bid to the tournament.

In his senior year Jackie Brown continued his ascent as one of the top basketball players in the state and the nation. He was a first team All-City selection, and he received All-American consideration from several national publications. Multiple colleges and universities were interested in him, but he opted to attend a junior college, enrolling in the College of Southern Idaho, a community college with a tradition of strong basketball teams. It did not turn out to be a good match for Jackie Brown, and he returned to Hartford. But he had made a strong impression on too many people to go unnoticed. Hartford has always been a tight-knit community, where people are quick to lend a hand when they see a native son in need. A friend of Jackie Brown's family from church was an alumnus of Ohio Wesleyan University, and he assisted Jackie in obtaining a full athletic scholarship.

Jackie Brown was only able to play two years at Ohio Wesleyan University because he had transferred, but that was enough time to etch his name in the school's record book. He was a two-time all-conference selection in basketball, and he was twice named the team's Most Valuable Player. He averaged 22.1 points per game, which at the time was the second best career average in the school's history and the best ever for a guard. He was the only guard and one of only three players in the history of Ohio Wesleyan to score 500 points in a season when he recorded 521 points in his junior year. He set the single-game record for a guard when he scored 36 points in a game, and he set the school's single-season records for field goals made (232) and attempted (554). Over his two years at Ohio Wesleyan he scored 993 points and recorded 265 rebounds. Both years he was a second-team All-Ohio Athletic Conference selection. He was elected captain of the team in his senior year and he received the George Staten Award as the school's outstanding athlete. He is a member of Ohio Wesleyan University's Athletics Hall of Fame. He earned a Bachelor of Arts degree in Physical Education and Jackie Brown was invited to participate in the Chicago Bulls' free-agent camp. Over the course of his high school and college career, Jackie Brown established a reputation as one of the finest athletes the city has ever produced.

Cleve Royster
Weaver High School 1968

There was no way of knowing for sure who might show up at the basketball court in Keney Park on any given Sunday morning. If you were a player looking to play against the best competition in the area, or merely a casual fan seeking to watch high quality basketball, Keney Park was the place to be. There were regulars, of course, players like Bobby Knight, Eddie Griffin, Billy Jones, Art Blackwell, Cap and Boo Perry, Pooch Tolliver, Ben Billie, and Ben Mathews, to name just a few. And there were always some younger players eager to establish reputations as the rising stars of the future. The quickest way to earn recognition as a baller was to play well at Keney Park against the city's elite talent. Sometimes players from other parts of the state showed up as well, driving from New Haven or Bridgeport to play a few games in Hartford's well-known park. Players from as far away as Boston, New York City, and Providence occasionally made an appearance. A crowd of basketball fans always turned out to watch the games. On a good day the spectators were six or seven deep around the perimeter of the court, and they made plenty of noise when someone busted a nasty move or threw down a thunderous dunk. Trash talking was an accepted part of the Keney Park experience, and sometimes a well-timed remark received as much attention as a devastating drive to the basket. The following Monday, Hartford High and Weaver would be abuzz about who had done what to whom, especially if an outsider with a reputation had ventured onto the court and been humbled by the local ballers. Unless you were actually there and witnessed the competition first hand, it was difficult to separate hype from reality. But one thing was beyond dispute; if you made it onto the court at Keney Park for a prime time run, you had better bring your "A" game.

Cleve Royster was among the up-and-coming high school players who first earned respect by playing in Keney Park. He was born in Florida and moved to Hartford in the fourth grade. He had a challenging youth. His mother passed away soon after moving to Hartford. Keney Park became a refuge for Cleve Royster, a safe place he could go to play basketball and hang out without worrying about getting into trouble.

He remembered one Sunday when a couple of college kids from out of state came to Keney to play a few games. Cleve was being guarded by the taller of the two players, a quick and athletic 6'- 7" leaper with freakishly big hands. Reluctant to go straight up with his jump shot against his taller opponent, Cleve Royster tried throwing up a hook shot that he had learned from Bobby Knight. "With your length and long arms," Bobby Knight had advised Cleve during one of many counseling sessions in the park, "No one can block that shot." But when Cleve rolled out the hook against the stranger, the ball was swatted so far off the court it took a few minutes to retrieve it, while Cleve waited in embarrassment for the game to resume and the fans to stop laughing at him. It turned out the two players were from the University of Massachusetts, Al Skinner and Julius "Dr. J" Erving. When Cleve learned that it was Dr. J who had rejected his shot, his sense of shame vanished. Dr. J. had averaged 32.5 points per game and 20.2 rebounds in his two years playing for UMass, before leaving early to join the Virginia Squires of the ABA as an undrafted free agent. During his illustrious Hall of Fame career, Dr. J was an NBA All-Star 11 times and he scored more than 30,000 points. Cleve always considered it a badge of honor that the great Dr. J. had blocked his shot with such cold-blooded nonchalance.

While Cleve Royster knew how to act on the basketball court at Keney Park, his behavior in school was another matter. As a seventh grader, he was cut from the Northwest Jones Junior High School basketball team by his coach, Doc Hurley, because of bad behavior. He rejoined the team in the eighth grade with an improved attitude, grateful that Coach Hurley was giving him a second chance. Doc Hurley's strict and demanding approach was just what Cleve Royster needed. Doc Hurley recognized Cleve's outstanding potential as a basketball player and as a young man. Just as he had done for countless other at risk kids, Doc Hurly devoted his time and his effort to make sure that Cleve Royster was on the right track.

Originally from Albany, Georgia, Doc Hurley's family moved to Hartford when his father, William, died. William had given his son Walter the nickname Doc because he wanted him to become a doctor, and while Doc Hurley never attended medical school, he served a lifetime as an inspirational and healing force in the lives of young people in the Hartford community. After an outstanding four-sport career at Weaver, Doc Hurley attended Virginia State University. His college education was interrupted by World War II, when he served in the Marines and fought in the Pacific.

He returned from the war to graduate from Virginia State and become a teacher and coach in Portsmouth, Virginia. He played professional football for the Brooklyn Dodgers of the All-American Football Conference. He returned to Hartford in 1959, where he spent the remainder of his life helping to improve young lives in Hartford by providing guidance, support, and numerous college scholarships.

In a tribute to Doc Hurley written after his death on February 2, 2014, Tom Yantz of *The Hartford Courant* quoted Windsor football coach Rob Fleeting, who had graduated from Weaver in 1988 and had served as the Weaver football coach, "Doc Hurley represented hope. If someone in the community needed guidance, a parent seeking advice on how to get a son or daughter into a college, you'd call Doc. He helped a lot of students go to college with scholarships or by calling college administrators he knew to open up a door." From the time Cleve Royster was in the eighth grade until he helped him to receive a basketball scholarship to Niagara University, Doc Hurley played a critical role in Cleve's life, inspiring him to use his athletic gifts to earn a college education.

In his freshman year at Weaver High School, Cleve Royster met with immediate athletic success. As a member of the track team, he was part of the 880 relay team that won a State Championship. As a member of the Weaver football team, he caught a 40 yard pass against Hartford High in Dillon Stadium on Thanksgiving Day. His outstanding play on the JV basketball team earned him playing time on the Weaver varsity. Cleve Royster's role on the varsity as a freshman was to back up Weaver's powerful front line of Ben Mathews, Jewett Newkirk, and Wayne Jones. As he sat on the bench, he watched the three big men closely, studying the way they comported themselves on the court. Cleve Royster may have struggled at times in the classroom, but he had no problem absorbing the lessons he learned on the basketball court, and he could not have had better mentors than Weaver's vaunted front line. He modeled the way he played the game on what he observed from watching the veterans in action. He tried to rebound and play defense with Jewett Newkirk's fierce intensity. He aspired to shoot the ball with the silky touch and limitless range of Wayne Jones. He looked to emulate Ben Mathew's slick ball-handling, versatility, and calmness under pressure. By taking aspects of the unique styles of Weaver's Big Three and melding his observations into his own game, Cleve Royster became one of the best big men in Weaver's history.

Wayne Jones in particular was a major influence on Cleve Royster. Wayne was a different kind of big man, unlike the prototypical post players that had preceded him in Hartford. He did not play with his back to the basket, but instead he took his game outside, to an area of the court where only the guards usually roamed. He was equally comfortable shooting from deep in the corner or from beyond the top of the key. If he had played in the era of the three-point shot, he would have accumulated many more points than he totaled during his high school career. With his great leaping ability, he could get his shot off at will against shorter opponents that tried to challenge him on the perimeter. If a big man tried to match up with him on the outside, he was capable of blowing past a slower opponent and taking the ball to the basket for a dunk.

But it was not just his teammates that Cleve watched closely; he also paid attention to the opponents he would one day have to face. He was on the bench when Hartford Public eliminated Weaver from the state tournament in 1967, along with Fred Mathews and Nolan Lewis, and he saw up close the way Bob Nash swatted away shot attempts, crashed the boards, and fought for every rebound. When Cleve Royster returned for his sophomore year as Weaver's starting center, he was prepared for the challenge of trying to contain Bob Nash. He was not intimidated going up against the Hartford High star. His experiences at Keney Park had prepared him to face stiff competition, and he possessed the physical tools, confidence, and determination to match up with anyone in the state. In three epic games played during the 1967-68 season, Cleve Royster and Bob Nash provided Hartford basketball fans with an exhibition of big man talent and finesse as exhilarating as anything previously witnessed in the city.

Weaver won the first meeting 62-61 on Cleve Royster's last second put-back of a Doug Morgan miss, avenging Weaver's defeat in the quarterfinals of the state tournament the previous season. Cleve Royster outscored Bob Nash 22 to 17 and battled him evenly on the boards. The game was played in front of a full house in the Hartford High gym. But Hartford Public won the next game 65-60 in overtime behind Bob Nash's 23 points and 15 rebounds. Although he once again held his own on the boards, Cleve Royster was limited to 12 points on a brilliant defensive effort by Owls senior Marshall Cade. Coach Cuyler had success the previous week by using Marshall Cade as a defensive stopper against Bulkeley's star Jackie

Brown, and he applied the same strategy against Weaver in trying to slow down Cleve Royster, while protecting Bob Nash from foul trouble. After the game Coach Cuyler credited Marshall Cade's defense against Cleve Royster as a key to the victory. "This win is unbelievable," the coach exalted, his clothes still dripping wet after getting dunked in the shower by his exuberant players.

The third and final game between the two dominant centers took place in the sold out Central Connecticut State College gym in the quarterfinals of the Class LL state tournament. For the second time in a row, an overtime period was required to decide the outcome. Once again Coach Cuyler had Marshall Cade shadow Cleve Royster the entire game, and the strategy paid dividends. Cleve Royster scored 13 points and grabbed 15 rebounds, but the intense defensive pressure applied by Marshall Cade prevented him from breaking through with one of his typical dominating performances. Although Dee Dee Mathews scored 21 points, Nolan Lewis 18, and Gil Hampton 10, it was not enough to defeat the Owls. Marshall Cade also came up big on the offensive end for Hartford Public, scoring 21 points, and Harold Abrams chipped in with 14 points. But in spite of Weaver's sagging zone defense intended to limit his number of touches, it was the play of Bob Nash that proved the difference. Nash scored 22 points and pulled down 24 rebounds, hitting 10 of his 12 field goal attempts to hold off the Beavers. As the fans filed out of the gym they were aware they had just witnessed another classic Weaver/Hartford High confrontation, one that would be talked about for years to come.

At the end of the 1967-68 season, Bob Nash graduated from Hartford Public and began his inspiring journey to the NBA. Cleve Royster's basketball future was uncertain. Doc Hurley was assigned the unenviable task of informing Cleve Royster he was ineligible to continue playing basketball at Weaver because of his age and grades. But Doc Hurley and Dr. Richard Cobb, the Weaver team doctor, did not abandon Cleve Royster. Dr. Richard Cobb took a proactive interest in the well-being of the student athletes he served. It was not unusual for Dr. Cobb to invite members of the basketball team to his house for a quality home-cooked meal prepared by his wife. For the Weaver players, the generosity, hospitality, and graciousness of the Cobb family were gestures of kindness they would always remember.

Doc Hurley and Dr. Cobb made arrangements for Cleve Royster to attend St. Thomas More School, a college preparatory school with a rich tradition of basketball success. At St. Thomas More, Cleve Royster teamed up with the future Providence College stars Ernie DiGregorio and Nehru King to lead the school to the New England Prep School Championship. In his second year at St. Thomas More the team repeated as New England champions, with Cleve Royster averaging 22 points and 16 rebounds per game. His outstanding performance at St. Thomas More attracted the attention of multiple colleges. He decided to attend Niagara University, following in the path of Wayne Jones, the former Weaver standout who had impressed Cleve with his versatility and long-range shooting ability when he watched him play in high school.

Wayne Jones was a teammate at Niagara University of the great Calvin Murphy from Norwalk, Connecticut. They played together on the 1969-70 Niagara team that advanced to the NCAA East Regional semifinals in Columbia, South Carolina before losing to Villanova University 98-73. Calvin Murphy was a three-time All-American at Niagara. He scored 2,548 points in his three-year varsity career, averaging 33.1 points per game. He played in the NBA from 1970 to 1983 as a member of the San Diego/Houston Rockets, and for four years of his career, from 1972 to 1976, he was coached by former Weaver High great Johnny Egan. Calvin Murphy was inducted into the Naismith Basketball Hall of Fame in 1993.

In the 1970 NCAA tournament elimination game against Villanova, Wayne Jones scored 17 points and led the team with eight rebounds. He followed up that performance with 20 points and a team-leading 12 rebounds against North Carolina State in an East Regional consolation game defeat. Wayne Jones' success at Niagara from 1969-71 under former NBA head coach and general manager Frank Layden, helped pave the way for the admittance of Cleve Royster. Dr. Richard Cobb, Cleve Royster's long-time supporter and benefactor from Hartford, helped to pay the portion of Cleve's college expenses not covered by his basketball scholarship.

Cleve Royster earned a degree in business from Niagara and worked in a variety of positions. His most rewarding endeavor was working with at risk youth. "Those are my guys," Cleve said. "I identify with those kids." He now lives in Virginia, where he continues to make a difference in the lives of young people in his community. His emergence from Hartford to play Division I basketball at Niagara University is a tribute to his determination and strength of character, as well as an acknowledgment to mentors like Bobby Knight, Doc Hurley, and Dr. Richard Cobb, who guided him along the way.

Bob Nash
Hartford Public High School 1968

What does a young basketball player think about during long hours of practice as he moves around on a basketball court, working on his dribbling and shooting, imitating a move seen on TV or in the park, elevating in the air to release a jump shot, or exploding to the rim to try to dunk? Some dream about playing on their high school team and making the state tournament. Others fantasize about playing in college for a team with a shot at March Madness. And some might even dare to imagine a professional career, making it to all the way to The League, the NBA, knowing that the odds against such a far-fetched outcome were enormous. Still, one can always dream, and who knows, sometimes even the most outlandish dreams come true.

Many basketball players growing up in a city like Hartford entertained fantastical thoughts of playing in the NBA. To play it well, the game of basketball required countless hours of practice, both alone and as part of a team. Players worked for years developing sound ball-handling and shooting fundamentals, often spending hours every day on park playgrounds or inside gyms striving to develop the skills they would need to make their high school teams. In the formative years there was ample time during countless practice sessions to imagine playing on the professional level in front of massive crowds in packed arenas in major cities around the country. For the vast majority of players the dream quickly faded away. Only a lucky few ever had the opportunity to excel in high school and to bask in the glowing praise of teammates, coaches, the local press, and the community. Even fewer went on to enjoy success in college, especially at the Division I level, where every player had been a standout in high school. The challenge of facing elite competition in practice and in game situations eroded the confidence of all but the most talented and determined athletes. But even after a significant college career, the chances of getting drafted by an NBA team and making the opening game roster were minuscule. Only a small percentage of exceptionally gifted basketball players made it in the NBA. According to an NCAA study, seventy-five percent of Division I basketball players felt they had a reasonable chance at a professional basketball career, while in actuality only 1.2 percent were even given an opportunity to make an NBA team. Far too many players were seduced by the allure of the NBA, only to neglect preparing for a more realistic and achievable career path. Hartford High's Bob Nash was one of the few for whom the dream of playing in the NBA became a reality.

Bob Nash was born in Athens, Georgia and moved to Hartford as a high school sophomore. He had played basketball in Athens, but nothing in his past experiences had prepared him for the way basketball was played at Hartford Public High School. He started on the junior varsity team as a sophomore and received playing time on the varsity. He worked extremely hard in practice, and he listened carefully to the suggestions of his more experienced teammates. They recognized that Bob Nash had the potential to make the Hartford Public team one of the best in the school's history. But if there was one person responsible for the evolution of Bob Nash from a player exuding raw potential into a future NBA player, it was his coach, John Cuyler.

John Cuyler was a 1951 graduate of Weaver High School, where he was captain of the basketball team. After graduating from Weaver he received an athletic scholarship to attend Florida A&M, a public, historically black university in Tallahassee, where he received a B.S. degree in Physical Education. At Florida A&M he was the captain of a basketball team that won the SIAC championship. He served in the U.S. Army after he graduated from college, completing his active duty with the rank of First Lieutenant. He returned to Hartford after his discharge and went to work as a recreation supervisor, and in 1962 he began a thirty-two year career as a physical education teacher, basketball and golf coach, and athletic director at HPHS. He became an assistant men's basketball coach at the University of Hartford, where he had earned a Master's Degree in Urban Education. During his coaching tenure at Hartford High he led the basketball team to 11 City Championships and seven CDC titles, and he coached seven All-State players. He was named to the Florida A&M Athletic Hall of Fame and the Hartford Public High School Athletic Hall of Fame. After he retired from teaching, he continued to work to improve the lives of young people in Hartford and Bloomfield.

As the first African American head basketball coach in Hartford, John Cuyler had a profound impact on the community. Other qualified African American candidates for a head coaching position in the city, such as Doc Hurley, had been overlooked. Like Doc Hurley, John Cuyler was a Hartford success story, someone who had leveraged his academic and athletic accomplishments at Weaver to attend college, receive a degree, and prepare for a profession of service to others. When he talked to his players about the critically important role of academics in their lives, he spoke with the voice of experience. And his players listened to him. He delivered the message in his usual modest and uplifting manner, treating his players with respect and integrity and appealing to their best selves. It was no accident that a number of his players went on to become coaches and mentors, people like Dwight Tolliver, Steve Waterman, Nate Adger, and Bob Nash who had observed first-hand the influence a positive role model could have in molding the lives of student athletes. John Cuyler was a gifted communicator, capable of expressing his vision and values in a way that motivated his players and encouraged them to strive to reach their full potential in basketball and in life.

Bob Nash could not have found a better coach and mentor than John Cuyler to ease his transition from Athens to Hartford. Coach Cuyler's plan was to give his young transfer student as much experience as possible by having him play extensive minutes in both the junior varsity and varsity games. He knew that Bob Nash was joining a program with outstanding veteran leadership and a history of success. John Cuyler did not put any pressure on Bob Nash to become an offensive force on the team, a role he was not prepared to accept when he arrived from Georgia. The coach had the luxury of allowing his potential star to concentrate on elements of the game where he could make an immediate impact, like rebounding, shot blocking and defending. The strategy of giving Bob Nash the time to develop at his own pace undoubtedly helped him to realize his enormous potential.

The Hartford Public team that Bob Nash joined as a sophomore had tremendous offensive fire power, with Dwight Tolliver, Steve Waterman, Nate Adger, Jake Edwards, and Greg Harrell carrying the bulk of the scoring. There were only a couple teams in the state with the talent to challenge the Owls in their quest for a state championship. Wilbur Cross was anchored by the All-State duo of Bill Reaves and Alex Scott and coached by the legendary Bob Saulsbury. They would pose a serious threat to Hartford Public's title aspirations. And across the city a formidable Weaver team was waiting in the wings, with an imposing front court of Ben Mathews, Wayne Jones, and Jewitt Newkirk, a dangerous backcourt manned by Rufus Wells and Jerry Bonadies, and an exceptional coach in Frank Scelza.

Hartford Public started the 1965-66 season on a roll. When they faced a rugged Norwich team led by Bill Wendt, both teams were undefeated. The game was played at Hartford High in front of 1,500 fans and was officiated by two of the best officials in the state from Board 6, Doc Hurley and Frosty Francis, reflecting the significance of the contest. Hartford rode the hot shooting of Dwight Tolliver and Steve Waterman and the rebounding of Bob Nash to a 79-58 victory in a game that was more competitive than the final score indicated. With the win, Hartford Public improved to 7-0 overall and 5-0 in the CDC. Bob Nash grabbed 13 rebounds in the first half alone and scored 10 of his 16 points in the first quarter, showing how important he was becoming to the Owls. Coach Cuyler lauded his budding star's performance in an interview after the game, "He played a tremendous game." It was clear that by adding Bob Nash's outstanding rebounding and improving offensive skills to the veteran mix of star players, Hartford Public had become one of the dominant teams in the state.

In his article on the game in *The Hartford Courant* the next day, sports writer Steve Nidetz commented that he had talked to Weaver Coach Frank Scelza, who was scouting the game. Nidetz wrote, "Weaver's Frank Scelza, more than just an interested spectator, said as he left the game, 'We'll need all the luck we can get.' His first date with Hartford is Feb. 4. And he spells 'luck' Newkirk, Mathews, and Jones."

Coach Scelza did not have much luck when he returned to the Hartford Public gym with his undefeated Beavers for the highly anticipated February 4, 1966 encounter, losing by more than 20 points in front of a sold-out crowd. Nor did his luck improve when Weaver faced off against Hartford Public in their second regular season meeting, the Beavers again going down to defeat by more than a twenty point margin. The Weaver team would have to wait until the Class LL state tournament to defeat the talented Owls. Playing on a neutral court at Wethersfield High School, the Beavers played an inspired game and upset Hartford Public. The Weaver victory over Hartford Public in the state tournament reinforced a dynamic that came into play whenever the city high schools met. You could disregard the records and the rankings; the players knew each other too well, the coaches were too familiar with their opponents' strengths and weaknesses, the teams were too battle-tested against stiff competition to back down from any challenge. Over the course of the long history of city rivalries, upsets were not uncommon. There was a lot at stake in the outcome of the games, bragging rights within the city borders and often conference or state championships. Weaver's upset victory over Hartford Public added fuel to an already overheated rivalry.

The Hartford Public team that John Cuyler put on the floor for the 1966-67 season was one of the strongest in the history of the school. The team possessed play making and back-court leadership from Dwight Tolliver and Jake Edwards; rebounding, scoring, and court savvy at the forward position with Steve Waterman and Bob Nash; length, rebounding, and rim protection at the center position with Art Andrews. Drew Saltys provided depth at the guard position in the absence of Greg Harrol, who had been declared ineligible. In an early season conference game against New London High School, Bob Nash demonstrated how important he had become to the team's success, hitting a jump shot with four seconds left on the clock to provide Hartford Public with a 63-61 win. It was one of the few close games for the Owls the entire 1966-67 season. The team remained undefeated throughout the regular season, twice defeating a Weaver team that posed the biggest challenge to Hartford Public's hopes for a state championship. But when the two city teams met in the tournament, Hartford Public prevailed for a third time, handing Weaver a tough loss. The Owls advanced to the finals, but Wilbur Cross successfully defended its state title by defeating Hartford Public 74-66.

Bob Nash averaged 10.8 points and 18 rebounds per game as a junior. He was listed in a national magazine as one of the top 500 returning players in the country, along with another Hartford product, Jackie Brown from Bulkeley. It had been an impressive season for Bob Nash, but not one that offered a clear indication he was destined for an NBA career. In his senior year, however, he emerged from the shadow of such stars as Dwight Tolliver, Steve Waterman, and Jake Edwards, to display his remarkable potential. The agile big man started alongside 6'-1" Marshall Cade, 6'-2" junior Ron Mirek, 6'-0" junior transfer from Weaver Willie Martin, and 5'-11" Gene Clancy, with the dynamic 5'-7" Jimmy LaJoy coming off the bench. Bob Nash was a marked man his senior year. Opposing defenses were stacked against him, knowing that if they could slow him down, the chances of defeating the Owls improved dramatically. But in spite of the sagging defenses, double-teaming, and constant pressure, stopping Bob

Nash was practically an impossible task. He continued to dominate the backboards as he had the previous year, collecting 20-plus rebounds in a number of games, but as a senior he became a more effective and versatile scorer, consistently hitting for more than 20 points and going over the 30 point mark several times.

In the opening game of the 1967-68 season, Hartford Public faced Wilbur Cross, the team that had beaten the Owls in the finals of the state tournament the previous season. The game against the defending state champion was not that close, with the Governors from Wilbur Cross, playing on their home court in New Haven, defeating the Owls 95-78. Co-captain Alex Scott, who was on his way to a second consecutive All-State season, led all scorers in the game with 33 points, and he was ably supported by another All-State performer, Clint Davis, with 19 points. Emerging sophomore "Super John" Williamson was also on the Wilbur Cross team. John Williamson was considered one of the best player ever in the Greater New Haven area. He would go on to become a star at New Mexico State before averaging 20.1 points per game in five NBA seasons and 14.1 points in three seasons in the ABA. The Wilbur Cross/Hartford Public game was played in front of a capacity crowd and was especially memorable for the 73-foot shot Alex Scott swished at the buzzer as the third quarter ended.

Although Hartford Public lost the game, Bob Nash served notice that he would be a force to be reckoned with all season long. He scored 26 points and grabbed 24 rebounds in a game that typified the kind of effort opponents could expect from Nash. In the rematch against Wilbur Cross, played on Hartford Public's home court, Nash scored 28 points and pulled down 25 rebounds to hand the Governors their first defeat of the season, 82-76. He helped seal the victory with three consecutive offensive tip-ins with less than two minutes left in the game. Willie Martin scored 16 points and Cornell Thornton 15 as the Owls avenged the team's only loss of the season.

But with the loss of firepower that accompanied the graduation of four starting seniors the year before, it would not be smooth sailing through the season for the Owls. In the first city series match-up against Weaver, the Beavers came out on top 63-62, on a last second shot by Cleve Royster. Weaver's 6'- 5" center Cleve Royster was one of the few players in the state that could match up one-on-one against Bob Nash. They were both outstanding leapers with exceptional rebounding and shot-blocking technique, and they were both fierce competitors that did not like losing to anyone, especially each other. Their intense personal rivalry confirmed that despite all the star players on both sides that had graduated the prior season, the competition within the city remained as intense as ever.

The one-point Weaver win in the first meeting of the season between the schools and their dominant centers was the first of three epic battles. In the regular season rematch, Hartford Public won in overtime, 65-60, in front of a packed house on the Owls' home court. Bob Nash scored 23 points and pulled down 15 rebounds, setting up a third and final meeting in the quarterfinals of the state tournament, in the same kind of win-or-go-home showdown that had been needed to settle the score between the two city rivals three years in a row. The game was played on the campus of Central Connecticut State in front of a sold-out crowd of 4,500 basketball fans. Once again the game could not be decided in regulation time. Weaver's Nolan Lewis hit a jump shot with 12 seconds left in the fourth quarter to send the game into overtime, the second consecutive time an extra period was needed to decide a game between the two Hartford schools. Eventually, Hartford Public prevailed, outlasting Weaver 80-74, on the strength of Bob Nash's 22 points and 24 rebounds and 21 points by Marshall Cade. Cleve Royster scored 13 points and grabbed 15 rebounds as he battled Nash on the boards the entire game. As the fans filed out of the Central gym, they could rest assured that the intense rivalry between Hartford Public and Weaver was alive and well.

Hartford Public's win over Weaver set up a third game of the season against Wilbur Cross in the semi-finals of the state tournament. In a hard-fought game, Wilbur Cross edged Hartford Public 67-65. The Owls had trailed by 55-38 with five minutes left in the third quarter, but fought back to take a two-point lead with 3:34 left in the fourth quarter, only to come up short at the end of the game. Bob Nash's senior year had begun and ended with a loss to Wilbur Cross. He scored 22 points in his final high school game and was solid on the boards once again. His season may have been over, but his basketball career was just taking off.

In his senior year at Hartford Public, Bon Nash received numerous honors for his basketball accomplishments. He was named to All-City, All-Conference, All-State, and All-American teams. He played in several All-Star games, including the two-day Capital District Schoolboy Basketball

Classic at the LaSalette Junior College Seminary in Altamount, New York, where he teamed up with Clint Davis, Alex Scott, and John Williamson of Wilbur Cross to defeat a New York State team that included Julius Erving. Bob Nash was the top rebounder in the tournament and he was named to the All-Tournament team.

In spite of all the recognition and accolades he received, he did not have many options when it came to selecting a college. Like so many of the athletes in Hartford that had come before him, he did not have the academic credentials to attend a traditional four-year institution. Bob Nash obviously had the talent to play Division I basketball; unfortunately, he did not receive scholarship offers.

He attended San Jacinto Junior Collge in Texas, a community college known for quality athletic teams. A number of other former NBA players began their ascent to a professional career at San Jacinto, including Sam Cassell, Steve Francis, Ray Williams, Walter Berry, and Thomas Henderson. At San Jacinto Junior College Bob Nash averaged 21 points a game over two years and he was named a second team junior college All-American. The Division I offers that had been non-existent when he graduated from Hartford Public were suddenly appearing regularly. He elected to attend the University of Hawaii, where he led the basketball team to a 47-8 record during his two seasons, including the school's first NCAA tournament appearance.

In his senior year at the University of Hawaii, the team made a trip to Hartford to play the University of Connecticut. He returned to Hartford as a hero, a rising basketball star leading the 19th ranked University of Hawaii in both scoring (19.3) and rebounding (15.7). His name was being mentioned frequently as a potential top pick in the NBA draft. When he was interviewed by Tom Hines of *The Hartford Courant*, Nash admitted that he had his sights set on a professional career. Willie Martin, the Weaver transfer who had played with Bob Nash at Hartford Public and followed him to the University of Hawaii after two years at Johnson and Wales in Providence, was enthusiastic about his teammate's chances of making it to the NBA. "In the finals when we won the Rainbow Classic, you should have seen Nash play," Martin told Tom Hines. "I've never seen anyone control a game like he did. He looked like Howard Porter [former Villanova star that led his team to an NCAA championship]. He couldn't be stopped. He had 30 rebounds, 27 points, and they weren't in close like in high school. He's shooting from 30-feet now."

Bob Nash was selected in the first round of the 1972 NBA draft by the Detroit Pistons. He was the seventh overall pick in the draft. The 6'- 8", 205-pound forward became the first player from Hartford since Johnny Egan to play in the NBA. He played two seasons with the Pistons, two with the Kansas City Kings, and one with San Diego in the ABA. He played in 236 professional games, scoring over 1,000 points. He scored an NBA career high 33 points for the Kansas City Kings in a 126-120 win over the Denver Nuggets. After completing his pro career, he returned to the University of Hawaii as an assistant basketball coach for 23 seasons, before becoming the head coach from 2007-2009. In 2010 he became the head coach of the Saitana Broncos in the Japanese professional league, where his son Bobby played, and in 2012 he became the head coach for the Toyama Grouses. The basketball journey that began in Athens, Georgia and continued in Hartford, Connecticut took Bob Nash around the globe. He will be remembered as one of the very best to ever play basketball in Hartford.

Nolan Lewis
Weaver High School 1969

Nolan Lewis's athletic career began with baseball and ended with baseball, but in between he managed to play a dynamic stretch of basketball at Weaver High School, where he emerged as one of the city's finest long-range shooters. Basketball was an afterthought for Nolan Lewis. From an early age he had hopes of a professional baseball career, a dream he came close to making a reality. He clawed his way up from a difficult early childhood in Hartford to receive a unique opportunity in baseball with the Kansas City Royals organization, only to see his promising career stymied by injury. A closer look at his legacy provides insights into the uphill challenges that many Hartford athletes faced in realizing their youthful dreams.

Nolan Lewis' athletic journey began in the Bellevue Square housing project in the North End, where he and his younger sister Valerie were born. Nolan Lewis's mother meant the world to him, and he credited her for keeping him on a righteous path that emphasized the importance of high moral standards and respect for others. His mother was employed as a human resource officer, and her parents were pastors of Victory Temple on Florence Street in Hartford, a church his mother eventually pastored and renamed Ramsey Memorial Church of God. "It seemed we were in church every day," Nolan Lewis recalled of his early years.

Nolan Lewis was introduced to baseball by a neighborhood friend, Ronnie McFarlane. When they began throwing a baseball around outside, it was obvious that Nolan Lewis was gifted with an unusually strong and accurate arm. At Arsenal Elementary School he enjoyed taking gym classes with Mr. Roy, an easy going and supportive physical education teacher who taught him the basics of baseball and basketball. The Lewis family moved from Bellevue Square to Enfield Street, and Nolan attended Northwest Jones Junior High School, where he played organized baseball and basketball for the first time. He was coached in both sports by Charlie Gibson, a gym teacher who recognized Nolan's athletic talents. When he was in seventh and eighth grade, his Northwest Jones baseball team won the city championship for junior high schools both years. Nolan Lewis teamed up with an ambidextrous hurler named Joe Green to give

Northwest Jones an unbeatable pitching rotation. Nolan Lewis was not only a star pitcher on the Northwest Jones team, he was one of the best hitters. He could drive the ball with power and he hit for a high batting average. In the championship game in the eighth grade Nolan Lewis hit a towering home run in Dillon Stadium to clinch the title, a fitting ending to a remarkable two year run that gave a clear indication of his potential to dominate a baseball game from the pitcher's mound as well as at the plate.

Nolan Lewis played basketball as well as baseball at Northwest Jones, and he showed impressive potential in both sports. Baseball came more naturally to him; he had to work hard to develop his basketball skills. He had cousins on Colebrook Street, the Hurston family, who encouraged him to play basketball with them. He began to practice more often, shooting hoops for hours at Rawson School. During the summer he played in the Hartford Parks and Recreation League, representing Rawson School. He discovered he had a talent for shooting a basketball, and through hard work he developed a lethal long-range jump shot. He looked forward to competing in both basketball and baseball at Weaver High School.

Once he arrived at Weaver, the transition to high school baseball came easy for him. By the start of his sophomore year, he was the ace of the Weaver pitching staff and one of the team's most reliable hitters, and he began to make his mark on the basketball court as well. But his rise as a Weaver basketball player followed an uneven path. In his sophomore year he was a starter on the junior varsity team for the first four games of the season, when he was replaced in the starting lineup by another player. At that point in his development Nolan Lewis was not a confident basketball player and he could not accept the demotion to second string status. He quit the team, deciding he would concentrate on baseball, where he knew he would play a key role on Coach Ernie Bottomley's team. He had no intention of playing basketball as a junior, when Coach Frank Scelza approached him to go out for the JV team again. Coach Scelza had been impressed with the limited sample of games Nolan Lewis had played the previous year, and he believed that all Nolan needed to become a very good basketball player was more experience.

Nolan Lewis took Frank Scelza's advice, and he played exceptionally well on the JV team, averaging over twenty points a game, including a 45 point explosion against Norwich Free Academy. Frank Scelza rewarded Nolan for his outstanding performance by bringing him up to the varsity at the end of the JV season, even starting him in the quarterfinal game of the Class LL state tournament against Hartford Public. The Owls beat Weaver and went on to play the defending Class LL State Champion Wilbur Cross in the finals, a game Wilbur Cross won 74-66 for its second consecutive title game win against a team from Hartford.

In his senior year, Nolan Lewis played on another strong Weaver team that included Cleve Royster, Gil Hampton, Fred Mathews, Doug Morgan, Mike Polite and John Pinckney. As a senior, Nolan Lewis came into his own as a consistent scorer and long-range jump shooting threat. He scored 32 points in a 78-73 win over Norwich, hitting with uncanny accuracy from long distance. After the game Coach Scelza told Courant Sports writer Steve Nidetz, "We finally found a way to get Nolan open." Nolan Lewis helped to put the game away when he hit four straight jump shots late in the fourth quarter. It was a typical Nolan Lewis performance, keeping Weaver in a game by finding his shooting groove and going on a scoring spurt.

Weaver started the season 9-2, and the team was still doing well with a 12-4 record, when a crushing defeat to Hartford Public turned the promising season around. Weaver led by seven points over the Owls with 36 seconds remaining in the fourth quarter, but Hartford Public managed to tie the game and force a three-minute overtime. Hartford won the game 65-60, and the deflating loss sent Weaver into a tailspin. The team lost the next three games, finishing the regular season with a record of 12-7.

But the team rallied in the state tournament, upsetting third-ranked Rippowam 74-55 in a first round game at Southern Connecticut State College. Nolan Lewis led Weaver with 22 points, most of them coming in the second half on patented long-range jump shots. "Nolan Lewis was simply hot in the second half," Coach Scelza commented to *The Hartford Courant* sports writer Tom Hine after the game. "Cleve Royster was tough on the boards, Mathews took up the slack in scoring in the first half and Gil Hampton and [Doug] Morgan both seemed to get the ball when we needed it." But Weaver was eliminated from the tournament in the next round, ending Nolan Lewis' basketball career for the Beavers.

Nolan Lewis averaged over twenty points a game as a senior and was named first team All-City along with teammates Cleve Royster and Dee Dee Mathews. After one full season of varsity basketball, Nolan Lewis had exhausted his eligibility just when he was beginning to fulfill his potential.

If he could have found a college program willing to cultivate his exceptional talents, there was no telling how far he could have gone as a basketball player. Sadly, there was no second act for Nolan Lewis in basketball. Like so many other outstanding players from the city, academics tripped him up and cut short a promising career.

When he graduated from Weaver, he enrolled in a junior college in Boley, Oklahoma. The results were predictable. Lonely, home sick, and ill-prepared for the academic challenge, he soon quit school and returned to Hartford. He enlisted in the U.S. Army and was assigned to a Special Forces unit, but he suffered a shoulder injury while on active duty training. He received an honorable discharge from the army for medical reasons, and he returned to Hartford for surgery on his shoulder.

Through all his hardships, Nolan Lewis had never given up on his dream of a professional baseball career. When he was back in Hartford playing in a local baseball league, a teammate told him the Kansas City Royals were conducting an open tryout at Quigley Stadium in West Haven. Although hundreds of baseball players from throughout the region showed up for the tryouts, Nolan Lewis impressed the coaches with his pitching ability. He was selected by the Royals to participate in an experimental program devised by the team's new owner, Ewing Kauffman. Fifty baseball prospects from across the country were chosen on the basis of meeting certain physical metrics, such as running 60 yards in under seven seconds, having above average eye sight and reaction time, and having exceptional lateral movement to either side. Nolan Lewis met all the qualifications, and he was the only player from New England selected to enroll in the Kansas City Royals' Baseball Academy.

As part of the program he was allowed to attend Manateo Junior College in Bradenton, Florida free of charge. He attended classes in the morning, and in the afternoon he played baseball under the supervision of Royals' coaches and instructors. Once the program was completed, he would be assigned to a minor league baseball affiliate. The innovative program provided Nolan Lewis with a tremendous opportunity to leverage his athletic ability to receive additional education while preparing for a career in baseball and beyond. Unfortunately, Nolan Lewis never recovered full strength in his shoulder following the surgery, and he was unable to complete the program. He continued to try to rehabilitate the shoulder, and he was given tryouts with the New York Mets and California Angels organizations. Once his baseball career was over, he returned to Hartford once again, where he will long be remembered for his outstanding career at Weaver as a talented pitcher and sharp-shooting basketball player.

Fred "Dee-Dee" Mathews
Weaver High School 1969

Beginning with the 1963-64 season, all city series basketball games were played in the spacious Hartford Public High School gym that had a seating capacity of 2,250 spectators. Previously, the city series contests were played in the venerable Trinity College Memorial Fieldhouse, a dusty, cavernous structure with a portable parquet floor marred by occasional dead spots that betrayed the ball-handler's expectations for a true bounce. Although the Trinity Fieldhouse could sit 1,800 fans, it lacked the intimate feel of a packed gymnasium where the thunderous roar of an excited crowd shook the rafters and sent adrenalin coursing through the players' veins. But while the new gym at Hartford Public provided a vastly superior atmosphere to the Trinity Fieldhouse, it presented a distinct disadvantage to the other city high schools. Since every city series game was played on the Owls' home court, it gave the Hartford Public team an unmistakable home court edge over Weaver and Bulkeley. Just as Hartford Public was in the process of putting together some of the most competitive teams in the long history of the school's basketball program, the task of upending the Owls became even more difficult for its inner-city rivals.

The same year the City Series was transitioning from Trinity to Hartford Public, a freshman by the name of Ben Mathews arrived at Weaver High, and over the course of the next four years, he would play a prominent role in elevating the intensity of the bitter rivalry between the city schools. Ben Mathews was one of the finest basketball players in Weaver High School's history. He played four years of varsity basketball, becoming one of the few players at Weaver to gain varsity experience as a freshman. At a chiseled 6'-4", he was a multi-dimensional force of nature on the basketball court, a rugged rebounder, deadly mid-range jump shooter, deceptive ball-handler, solid defender, and adept passer. He could play any position on the court and defend quick guards as adroitly as he could shut down opposing centers. As a sophomore he made an immediate impact on a Weaver team that had gone 14-4 the previous season and had captured City Series and CDC championships. The team was returning a solid core of veterans, including co-captains Ben Billie and Maurice Williams, Gil Cloud, Len VanTassel, Charles Barlow, and John Bologna. But Coach Frank Scelza did not waste any time inserting Ben Mathews into the mix. In the preseason Coach Scelza told Hartford Courant reporter Pat Bolduc, "Our fourth and fifth starters [alongside Ben Billie, Maurice Williams, and Gil Cloud] will depend upon the type of opposition and what we need most at the time – rebounding strength, defense, or speed. This means that we may use VanTassel and Greg Thornton, or we could go with Barlow and Ben Mathews."

Coach Scelza would not regret the confidence he showed in Ben Mathews in the early stages of his development as a Weaver basketball player. Ben Mathews improved every season, and by the time he was a senior he was generally recognized as one of the best players in the city and the state. Ben Mathews teamed with Jewett Newkirk, a tenacious rebounder and fierce defender who was a mainstay on Weaver's undefeated football team, and Wayne Jones, a tremendous leaper and deadly long-range jump shooter who would play at Niagara University with the great Calvin Murphy, to give Weaver one of the most imposing front courts ever assembled at Weaver. As juniors, the outstanding trio of Weaver big men, in combination with the superb backcourt of Jerry Bonadies and Rufus Wells, had come within seconds of winning the Class LL State Championship, losing to Wilbur Cross 58-56. With Ben Mathews anchoring a veteran lineup, Weaver was poised to make another deep run in the state tournament. As seniors, Ben Mathews averaged 19.4 points per game, Wayne Jones 18.8, and Jewitt Newkirk 9.8. Weaver had another excellent season, finishing with a 17-3 record. The only teams to beat Weaver were Wilbur Cross and Hartford High. With a loss in the state tournament to Hartford High, Ben Mathews' standout career at Weaver came to an end.

***

It must have been difficult for Fred "Dee Dee" Mathews to grow up in the shadow of his talented big brother. Fred idolized Ben, and in order to stay close to his brother and have a front row seat at all the Weaver basketball games, he signed up to be the team's manager. Although Fred Mathews had not played organized basketball as a kid, he enjoyed playing recreational basketball at Vine Street School and at various playgrounds. He accompanied Ben to Keney Park, and at his brother's urging he would sometimes take part in pickup games. Although his game lacked the power of Ben's, Fred showed that he could hold his own in the games at Keney Park. All he needed was more self-confidence and experience to blossom into an exceptional basketball player. He had watched enough basketball to grasp the finer points of the game, and his brother provided an incomparable example of how to compete with poise and desire, qualities Fred would incorporate in his own style of play once he acquired the will to create a legacy of his own.

When Fred entered Weaver in 1965, he had no intention of playing on the basketball team. He tried out for the freshman football team, but after one season he decided football was not in his future. While Fred was serving as manager of the basketball team, Coach Scelza watched him shooting baskets in the gym before practice, and he was amazed to see that Fred was a very good shooter in his own right. Coach Scelza was constantly on the lookout for fresh basketball talent. He would approach a student in a gym class, in the hallway between classes, or in the cafeteria, anywhere he spotted someone he thought might be interested in playing basketball and invite him to come out for the team. The first day of basketball tryouts during Frank Scelza's tenure as head basketball coach was always a lively event, with about half the male population of the school showing up for the opportunity to scrimmage against the best basketball players at Weaver, with many responding to a personal invitation from the coach. Frank Scelza considered the Weaver building his recruiting grounds, and on more than one occasion he uncovered a diamond in the rough who was loaded with potential but lacking in experience. And so it was with Fred Mathews. It didn't hurt Fred's chances of making the team that his older brother was one of the best players Frank Scelza had ever coached, but Fred showed more than enough promise during the tryouts to warrant making the JV team. Fred Mathews became the starting point guard on a very good JV squad, teaming up with Nolan Lewis to form Weaver's backcourt of the future. At the end of the junior varsity season Coach Scelza asked both Fred Mathews and Nolan Lewis to dress for the varsity games, along with promising big man Cleve Royster. When Fred Mathews was playing in a late season varsity game, he passed the ball to his brother Ben for an assist, one of the highlights of his sophomore year.

After Ben Mathews graduated, Fred was ready to emerge from his brother's shadow and step into the spotlight. He had spent the summer before his junior year working diligently to improve, going to Keney Park on the weekends to play against the best competition he could find. At 6'-2", he had above average height for a point guard, yet he had the quickness to beat opposing guards off the dribble. He was an excellent penetrator who took what the defense gave him, waiting until the defender committed to him before dropping a pass to an open teammate, or pulling up for a short jump shot if the defense collapsed. Playing alongside such talented players as Nolan Lewis, Cleve Royster, Doug Morgan, Gil Hampton, Mike Polite, and John Pinckney, Fred Mathews was the consummate playmaker, setting up his teammates for hoops and running the fast break effectively. But in addition to his deft playmaking, Fred Mathews was also emerging as a dangerous scorer, very much in the mold of his brother Ben. He scored a game high 26 points in a 93-59 victory over New London. He hit for 20 points in a 70-50 win over South Catholic. In a 74-55 upset of Rippowam in the first round of the state tournament, Fred Mathews scored 17 points, many of them in the first half as Weaver struggled to wrest momentum from a stubborn opponent.

Yet the most satisfying win of Fred Mathews' junior year came against arch rival Hartford Public. The previous year Dee Dee had watched from the Weaver bench as Hartford Public knocked Weaver out of the state tournament, thwarting the Beavers' hope for a return to the finals and a potential rematch with Wilbur Cross. The game also marked the end of his brother's brilliant high school career. The memory of the sadness that pervaded the Weaver locker room after that crushing defeat was still fresh in Dee Dee's memory as he took the floor against the Owls in the packed HPHS gym.

Fred Mathews was not alone in his quest for revenge against the powerful Owls team that featured the incomparable Bob Nash, Willie Martin, and Marshall Cade. Two of Dee Dee's teammates, Nolan Lewis and Cleve Royster, had also been called up to the Weaver varsity team at the completion of the JV season, and they were equally frustrated by the season-ending defeat at the hands of cross-town rival Hartford Public. Senior Gil Hampton had been a valuable front-court reserve on that Weaver team. On a memorable Saturday night these four Weaver veterans, feeding off the frustration and disappointment of the preceding year, refused to go down to defeat. The game was close throughout, but with 3:38 remaining, Weaver trailed 58-49. Then Cleve Royster took over, scoring 10 of Weaver's final 12 points, including a tap with one second left on the clock that sealed the 63-62 comeback victory. Royster finished with 22 points, Nolan Lewis with 14, Gil Hampton with seven, and Dee Dee Mathews with 12, in a balanced team performance that would have made Ben Mathews proud.

The satisfaction with the victory over Hartford Public was short-lived. In the quarter finals of the Class LL State Tournament, Weaver and Hartford Public faced off once again, the fourth year in a row the city rivals met to determine which city school would advance in the tournament. The game was played before a capacity crowd of 4,500 fans at Central Connecticut State as part of a double-header, with Wilbur Cross advancing to the semi-finals by defeating Hillhouse 80-65 in the first game. The game between the Hartford schools was much closer, with neither team able to sustain a lead. In the closing seconds, with Hartford Public clinging to a 68-66 advantage, Fred Mathews hit a jump shot to send the game into overtime. But Marshall Cade dominated the overtime period to lead Hartford Public to the win, the second overtime victory against Weaver in the last three meetings. Marshall Cade finished with 21 points, with seven points coming in overtime and Harold Abrams scored 14. But it was Bob Nash's outstanding performance that doomed the Beavers. The Owls' dynamic center hit 10 of 12 shots from the field to finish with 23 points, and he dominated the boards, collecting 24 rebounds, seven in overtime. For Weaver, Dee Dee Mathews scored 21 points and Nolan Lewis 18, while Cleve Royster, battling Nash on the boards the entire game, added 13 points and 15 rebounds. In spite of the victory over Weaver, Hartford Public lost in the semi-finals. Wilbur Cross won the State Championship for the third year in a row, beating Bridgeport Central in a record setting scoring performance, 123-82. It was the first time in three years Wilbur Cross did not face a school from Hartford in the finals. Fred Mathews finished the season averaging 17 points per game and winning first team All-City honors.

Fred Mathews returned for his senior year as captain of the Weaver basketball team. He had a mostly new supporting cast that included John Holliday, John Brown, Clarence Love, Greg Stinson, and Lee Otis Wilson. He enjoyed an outstanding season, averaging 20 points, seven rebounds, and seven assists per game, numbers that closely paralleled his brother Ben's senior year performance. He was a first team All-City selection for the second year in a row and a second team All-State performer. But in spite of his exceptional all-around performance on the basketball court, his stellar basketball credentials did not lead to scholarship offers from traditional four-year colleges. He attended St. Gregory's Junior College in Shawnee, Oklahoma. It was not an ideal fit, but Fred Mathews was able to overcome the culture shock of rural Oklahoma and homesickness to remain at the college and become the first member of his family to graduate from an institution of higher education. His basketball and academic accomplishments at St. Gregory's drew interest from several four-year schools, including UCLA, North Texas State, and Georgia State. He chose to attend Wichita State University in Kansas, a basketball powerhouse with outstanding facilities. Fred Mathews returned to Hartford and decided to join the workforce. His basketball career was essentially over, but he had far exceeded any of his youthful expectations about becoming a significant player, building a legacy in Hartford that rivaled his brother's and withstood the test of time.

Willie Martin
Hartford Public High School 1969

Willie Martin was a teammate of Bob Nash at Hartford Public High School and the University of Hawaii. Like Nash, he was originally from Georgia; his home town was Cuthbert in Randolph County. His family moved to Oakland Terrace in Hartford when he was eleven. His uncle, C.W. Martin, helped raise him and was a life-long role model. He attended Barnard Brown Elementary School and he shot hoops at Keney Park, where he met Bobby Knight, a Hartford basketball legend. Bobby Knight recognized Willie Martin's raw potential, and as he did for so many young players, he encouraged Willie Martin to develop his natural talent. As a seventh grader at Northwest Jones Junior High School, Willie Martin was the starting center on a basketball team that won the junior high city championship. It was apparent at an early age that he had the athleticism and the competitive instincts to become an outstanding basketball player.

When he entered Weaver High School as a freshman, he made an immediate impact on the football field, playing on the undefeated state championship team. After the football season he started playing basketball, splitting time on the freshman and JV teams while dressing for varsity games. It looked as though he had a promising future at Weaver in both sports, but when he returned as a sophomore he did not play football or basketball. He had broken his jaw during football practice as a freshman, and it was still bothering him enough as a sophomore to keep him from playing either sport. Rather than try to resume his athletic career at Weaver as a junior, he made the unusual decision to transfer to Hartford Public and get a completely fresh start at a new school.

He still was not ready to play football, but he was anxious to get back on the basketball court. The Hartford Public team he was joining had lost four starters from the team that had finished as the runner-up to Wilbur Cross in the Class LL state tournament. The lone returning starter was Bob Nash, and his presence alone was enough to make the Owls a very dangerous team. Willie Martin started in the backcourt with Gene Clancy, while the forwards were Marshall Cade and Ron Mirek. If Willie Martin was uncomfortable about switching schools in mid-stream, he did not show any nervousness facing his former teammates for the first time. He scored

21 points to lead the Owls in scoring, although Weaver won the game 63-62 on a last second shot by Cleve Royster. Hartford Public would go on to win the next two meetings of the season against Weaver, both in overtime, including a thrilling 80-74 victory at Central Connecticut State in the quarter-finals of the LL State Tournament. The margin of victory in all three games was so narrow that the players on the Weaver team, including Cleve Royster, Nolan Lewis, Fred Mathews, Doug Morgan, Gil Hampton, and John Pinckney, as well as Coach Frank Scelza, must have wondered if the outcome might have been reversed had Willie Martin stayed at Weaver instead of transferring to their arch rival across the city.

The Owls lost to Wilbur Cross 67-65 in the semifinals of the state tournament in Willie Martin's junior year, a game in which he scored only 2 points. He had played very well against Wilbur Cross the previous time the teams met, scoring 16 points in an 82-76 win. Willie Martin had hit clutch shots in the third quarter as Hartford Public closed a big gap and set up a fourth quarter surge led by Bob Nash to seal the victory. His disappointing performance against the Governors in the tournament motivated him to work hard to prepare for his senior year. His determination to make the most of his final year in high school was reflected in his decision to play football again. He became a key member of the Owls' football team and earned first-team All-City honors. But his sights were set on having an outstanding basketball season. Most of the starters from the previous year's team had graduated, including the irreplaceable Bob Nash. Yet in typical Hartford Public fashion, a talented group of players were prepared to take center stage. In the absence of Bob Nash, Gene Clancy, Marshall Cade, and Ron Mirek, the Owls would rely heavily on Willie Martin Ted Rush, Clive May, Larry Reynolds, and Jimmy LaJoy to carry the scoring load and maintain the school's winning tradition.

Unfortunately, Willie Martin injured an ankle, and his senior season did not live up to his expectations for a break-out year on the basketball court. His senior year statistics fell short of the 13.8 points and 9 rebounds per game he had recorded as a junior, when he earned All-City and All-CDC consideration. At 6'-3" and 175 pounds, he possessed all the physical tools needed to excel. He was an outstanding rebounder, capable shooter, and strong defender. But the jury was still out on whether he would ever become the kind of elite player Hartford Public was known for producing.

Any questions about his ability to elevate his game to another level were answered when Willie Martin attended Johnson and Wales. The fact that he even had the opportunity to attend the junior college in Providence, Rhode Island was largely the result of the work of Dr. John A. Yena. Dr. Yena began his career as a teacher at Johnson & Wales, and he also served as an assistant basketball coach. In an effort to build a strong basketball program that would enhance the school's name recognition, he extended his recruiting efforts beyond the local area to places in New England that he knew had a rich basketball tradition. His search for basketball talent led him to Connecticut, where he recruited two starters from Hartford Public's powerful 1966-67 team, Jake Edwards and Nate "Shotgun" Adger. The immediate success that Jake Edwards and Nate Adger enjoyed at Johnson and Wales opened the doors for more players from Hartford, like Mike Polite from Weaver and Willie Martin.

Nate Adger became the most celebrated player in Johnson & Wales' history. During his two years at the school, he led the basketball team in scoring and rebounding both years. Along with Jake Edwards, Mike Polite, Fred Tyson, and Jim Gary, another Connecticut product, Nate Adger helped the 1969-70 Johnson & Wales team reach the NJCAA Championship before losing by a single point to the number-one team in the country in the junior college division. The scoring and rebounding records that Nate Adger set at Johnson & Wales were not broken until the junior college became a four-year institution. Nate Adger went on to reunite with his Hartford Public teammate Dwight Tolliver as a starter at the University of Rhode Island.

Dr. Yana recognized that Nate Adger and Jake Edwards were not only outstanding basketball players, they were exceptional people as well. Their success at Johnson & Wales led him to recruit additional players from Hartford. Mike Polite was the kind of unselfish, team-oriented player that every coach wants on his team. After Weaver High School scratched out a tough 78-73 victory over Norwich Free Academy, Coach Frank Scelza singled out Mike Polite for his strong performance, even though Nolan Lewis had scored 32 points and Cleve Royster and Fred Mathews both had fine games. Coach Scelza told Hartford Courant sports writer Steve Nidetz that Mike Polite was a key difference in the game. "He didn't hurt us when he had to go in for Cleve," Scelza said. "Nolan can score 30 points any night, but what makes the team go is when there is balance. We have four other shooters out there." Mike Polite was a glue player, a solid all-around performer who did not need the ball in his hands to impact a game.

Dr. Yana's ability to evaluate basketball talent led to his recruitment of the players from Hartford and fulfilled his intention of raising the profile of the basketball program. But his contribution to the college went beyond his efforts to build a winning basketball tradition. Dr. Yena went on to serve as the Chief Executive Officer and President of Johnson & Wales, and under his leadership and vision, Johnson & Wales transitioned from a junior college into a university.

When he arrived at Johnson & Wales, Willie Martin was determined to show he could compete effectively at the college level. His confidence had been shaken in his senior year at Hartford Public when his ankle injury kept him from realizing his potential. In his first year at Johnson & Wales he recovered his self-confidence, averaging 21 points per game, and in his second year he averaged more than 30. He earned an Associate's Degree in Business Administration, and he received scholarship offers from several four-year colleges. He decided to attend the University of Hawaii, where he would be reunited with Bob Nash. Although he showed flashes of becoming a valuable member of the University of Hawaii team, he was frustrated by injuries and a lack of playing time and left school. Eventually he returned to his hometown of Cuthbert, Georgia, where he served two terms as mayor. He is the father of four children and remains active in his community. His life journey had come full circle, from Cuthbert to Hartford, with stops in Providence, Rhode Island and Manoa, Hawaii, before ending up back in Cuthbert. Along the way he built an enduring basketball legacy.

Jimmy LaJoy

Hartford Public High School 1969

For athletes in Hartford, playing a team sport in high school was a labor of love, requiring considerable expenditures of time and energy. Basketball, in particular, demanded a lengthy commitment, with the basketball season extending from November into March, if the team was fortunate enough to make the state tournament. But serious basketball players did not limit themselves to in-season activity. Players worked on their games all year long, practicing on basketball courts in parks, playgrounds, gyms, driveways, public housing projects, and schoolyards. Many played in Hartford Parks and Recreation leagues and attended basketball camps and clinics. Aspiring players were willing to put in the time and effort in hope of making a high school team, even if that meant sitting on the bench during most of the game and getting on the court only when the outcome was no longer in doubt. In a city like Hartford, with an abundance of basketball talent, just earning a spot on one of the public high school teams was an impressive achievement, the kind an undersized 5'-7" 115-pound player would be proud to accomplish. But Jimmy LaJoy was not an ordinary player. He would not allow himself to be defined as a basketball player by his lack of height or to accept a subordinate role on a team. He was a gifted athlete who proved that it was impossible to judge a player's heart by his physical stature.

Jimmy LaJoy was the youngest in a family of three boys. Ronnie was in the middle, and David was the oldest. David was an all-around fine athlete who played basketball at Weaver in the aftermath of the Johnny Egan era, when basketball was undergoing a renaissance in Hartford, thanks to the Beavers' success in the New England tournament. Jimmy LaJoy admired his oldest brother and wanted to play sports just like him. Although David was ten years older than Jimmy, he would bring his younger brother with him when he went to play basketball at one of the local parks. Jimmy LaJoy showed at an early age that he was capable of playing with older and bigger players. He could handle the basketball, he could pass, and he could shoot. If the first impression he made when he walked onto a basketball court was that he was too short and slight to be much of a player, by the time he walked off the court everyone was aware that Jimmy LaJoy could

158

play the game exceptionally well.

Jimmy's father worked multiple jobs, supplementing his employment driving a milk truck with bartending. His stay-at-home mother taught Jimmy LaJoy the importance of treating people with kindness and consideration. According to Jimmy, one of his mother's favorite sayings was, "It doesn't cost anything to be nice to people." The lessons he learned from his parents at an early age, working hard and treating people respectfully, stayed with him throughout his life.

As a fifth grader at the Wilson Street Elementary school, Jimmy LaJoy was selected to play on the Moylan Junior High School basketball team. It was a noteworthy accomplishment, establishing him as one of the most promising players in his age group. The basketball program at Moylan was one of the best in the city. The team was coached by Donald Harris, Sr., a teacher in the Hartford system for over 37 years at Moylan and then at Bulkeley High School, where he later served as Vice Principal for ten years. Don Harris, Sr. was a first lieutenant in the United States Army during World War II. He was the first African American elected to the Board of Education in Bloomfield, serving from 1967-75. As a coach, teacher, and administrator in the Hartford school system, Don Harris, Sr. influenced the lives of numerous young people in the city. His tough, no-nonsense coaching style helped Jimmy LaJoy develop winning habits and a disciplined approach to basketball that carried over to high school.

After he completed seventh grade, Jimmy LaJoy's family moved from Rice Heights to New Park Avenue. He enrolled in New Park Avenue Junior High School, where he played basketball under Coach James White, the brother of St. Louis Cardinals great and New York Yankees' broadcaster Bill White. Jimmy LaJoy continued to develop into a fine basketball player in junior high school. He began to play regularly at the Southwest Boys Club, where he became friends with Daniel Cicero, a future teammate at Hartford Public. He watched great players like Jackie Brown, Eddie Griffin, and Stan Poole at the Southwest Boys Club and he became familiar with the pace and intensity of games played at the next level. He received encouragement from Charlie Horvath, the legendary Weaver coach who was the director of the Southwest Boys Club and the father of talented sons who played at the club. Jimmy LaJoy also remembered that Joe Lapenta was a fixture at the Southwest Boys Club, not surprising since Joe Lapenta, a former Boys Club member, dedicated more than 60 years of his life to the Boys & Girls Clubs of Hartford, many as the Executive Director, and he received numerous awards for his service to the youth of Hartford. Like many of the city's finest basketball players, Jimmy LaJoy's path to success in high school was paved by a combination of his own determination and effort and the support of role models and mentors within the community.

Although he had demonstrated his ability to compete at the junior high level and in the recreational setting of the Southwest Boys Club, when Jimmy LaJoy entered Hartford Public High School as a freshman in 1965, he was skeptical that he could play basketball for the Owls. The varsity team's roster was loaded with talent, including players like Dwight Tolliver, Greg Harrell, Steve Waterman, Nate Adger, Bob Nash, Jake Edwards, Drew Soltys, and Art Andrews. It was difficult for Jimmy LaJoy to envision playing alongside players of their stature. But Joe Kubachka, the longtime Hartford Public varsity coach who had guided the 1961 and 1962 teams to New England High School championships, encouraged Jimmy LaJoy to at least attend the freshman team tryouts. He not only made the team, he was named captain and led the team in scoring. In his sophomore year he served as captain of the JV team and led the team in scoring once again, averaging nearly 30 points per game. His performance on the JV team was so impressive that he received playing time on Coach John Cuyler's varsity team that went undefeated the entire season before losing to Wilbur Cross in the finals of the CIAC Class LL State Tournament. Whatever doubts Jimmy LaJoy harbored about playing basketball at Hartford Public were completely dispelled.

He was promoted full-time to the varsity team for his junior year. In his preview of the 1967-68 high school basketball season, *Hartford Courant* sports writer Tom Hines wrote about the contribution Jimmy LaJoy was expected to make to the Hartford Public team: "One of the first off the bench for the Owls will be little Jim LaJoy, a 5-7 junior guard who led the Junior Varsity in scoring last season. A fine shooter and a scrappy defender, LaJoy is one [player] certain to be heard of in the future." On almost any other team in the state, Jimmy LaJoy would have been a starter in his junior year. But the Hartford Public varsity squad he was joining was deep and talented, featuring starters 6'-7" center Bob Nash, 6'-1" Marshall Cade and 6'2" Ron Mirek as the forwards, and 6' Willie Martin and 5'-11" Gene Clancy in the backcourt. Some of the other players competing for playing time off the Owls' bench included Cornell Thornton, Don Chafin, Harold

Abrams, Cliff Mitchell, and Dennis Alexander. For Jimmy LaJoy to play a vital role in the team's success as a junior was an extremely impressive accomplishment. As the season progressed, he transitioned from valuable sixth man to occasional starter. The team advanced to the semifinals of the state tournament, facing nemesis Wilbur Cross on the campus of Central Connecticut State College in front of 4,500 fans. Sparked by All-State performers Alex Scott and Clint Davis, Wilbur Cross opened a big lead that included an amazing 73-foot heave by Scott that went through the nets as the third-quarter buzzer sounded, before Hartford Public mounted a stirring comeback. But Wilbur Cross prevailed in the end 67-65, ending Bob Nash's illustrious high school career and moving on to beat Bridgeport Central in the finals in a record-setting scoring performance, 123-82, for the Governors third consecutive state title.

In his senior year Jimmy LaJoy started for the Owls, playing alongside Ted Rush, Willie Martin, Cleve May, and Larry Reynolds. He had become a reliable scorer, hitting double figures in multiple games. In a critical game against Weaver, Hartford Public avenged an earlier season loss by beating the Beavers 76-56 to create a first place tie for the City Series. Ted Rush scored 18 points, Cleve May had 17, Willie Martin 15, Jimmy LaJoy 13, and Larry Reynolds 11 for the winners, while Fred Mathews scored 19 points, Clarence Love 13, and John Holliday 11 for Weaver. In his write-up of the game, Tom Hines of *The Hartford Courant* credited LaJoy for his game-changing performance: "Little Jim LaJoy was a big factor all afternoon. The Owls needed his ball handling and needed it badly. When he was sidelined with three personal fouls just before the half, Weaver made its comeback. When he was back in play again in the second half, Hartford was in business."

Jimmy LaJoy was the rare player that could impact a game without scoring a point. In a key Capital District Conference game against Norwich Free Academy, LaJoy was scoreless in a 58-48 Owl victory, handing Norwich its first conference defeat. But LaJoy's contribution to the big win did not go unnoticed by Coach John Cuyler. Recapping the game for the *Courant's* Tom Hines, Cuyler commented, "Ted Rush, Cleve May, and Larry Reynolds were great on the boards. And Willie Martin helped a lot from the outside, but I can't believe that Jimmy LaJoy didn't score a point. He sure handled the ballclub." Time and again Jimmy LaJoy propelled Hartford Public to victory with his heady floor game, superb ball-handling, and clever passing. While he had been a dominant scorer on both the freshman and JV teams, he embraced his role on the varsity as a floor general, a pass first point guard intent on setting up his teammates at the expense of his individual offensive statistics. He earned the trust and respect of his coaches and teammates, who knew that Jimmy LaJoy cared only about winning.

At the end of his senior season, Jimmy LaJoy was uncertain about his future. He had not thought seriously about applying to college, anticipating he would merely follow his hard-working father's example and go right to work after high school. But when the opportunity arose to attend Johnson & Wales College and play on the basketball team, he reconsidered his options. A pipeline between Hartford Public and Johnson & Wales already existed. Nate Adger, Jake Edwards, and Willie Martin all went on to play basketball at Johnson & Wales. But Jimmy LaJoy's college plans were derailed. He joined the National Guard and took a job with the United States Post Office, where he worked for over forty years. He has been married for forty-two years and has two sons. He will long be remembered as one of Hartford's outstanding players.

Part III
Teammates and Brothers
1970-1979

Fran Laffin
South Catholic High School 1970

Choosing the right college can be a daunting decision for a high school basketball player, especially if there are multiple options on the table. Some of the factors that need to be considered include the college's location, division, size, strength of schedule, coaching philosophy, and the amount of financial aid available. There is a great deal at stake in making a sound choice. It can mean the difference between dropping out, transferring, or returning home after a few short weeks, or staying on to enjoy a tremendously rewarding and memorable four-year experience, playing competitive basketball, bonding with coaches and teammates that will become lifelong friends, and preparing academically for life after college. No matter how much thought is invested in the process, there is no way to know if you are on the right track. Sometimes it is best to rely on someone else to help make the decision for you – a mentor, a coach, a teammate or, in the case of Fran Laffin, a mother willing to advocate for you to a college she feels is a perfect fit.

Fran Laffin grew up in the South End of Hartford with six siblings. His parents were devout Catholics of Hungarian and Swedish descent, and they instilled the values of their faith in all their children. Fran Laffin enjoyed attending church and became an altar boy at St. Lawrence O'Toole Roman Catholic Church. His faith remained a central part of his life.

At St. Augustine School Fran Laffin felt he had very good teachers who reinforced the core values he learned at home and church. As a young boy, his athletic ambitions were focused on baseball; he had dreams of someday playing in the major leagues. When he entered South Catholic in 1966, he was looking forward to playing on the school's baseball team. He still considered baseball his favorite sport, and he was anxious to compete at the high school level. But fate intervened. Prior to the official opening of the basketball season his friends were forming an intramural basketball team and needed additional bodies to fill out the roster. He agreed to play on the team, and the rest is history. He scored 35 points in a game, and suddenly he was hooked on basketball. He tried out for the freshman basketball team, and although he made the team, he received very little playing time. He knew he needed to develop his skills to become a better all-around basketball player, and he was determined to put in the work to improve his game. Like many of the great players to emerge from the city of Hartford, he looked forward to the summer and the opportunity to play in the parks.

Kids from Hartford interested in playing on their high school basketball teams gravitated to the parks, because that was where they were bound to find the best competition and the most expeditious path to improvement. It was critical to develop the self-confidence that you could not only compete against the players from your own neighborhood and section of the city, but against the players that would be going to the other city high schools as well. Playing basketball in Hartford was like a brotherhood. Even if you didn't know the other players on the high school teams personally, you knew of them. Word spread about the rising talents in the city. The players whose names would appear in the box scores in the local newspapers during the basketball season were the same players that were lighting it up in the parks. The parks were a breeding ground for basketball talent in Hartford. Another potential benefit that aspiring basketball players might derive from playing on the courts in the parks was the possibility of encountering mentors that could assist their development. For Fran Laffin, meeting Coach Gene Reilly and having him take an interest in his improvement served as an important link to his future success.

Gene Reilly was considered one of Hartford's greatest athletes. He was a standout in two sports in both high school and college. As a basketball player at Bulkeley High School, he was the leading scorer on the 1962 basketball team that finished the season 20-4, with all four losses coming to Hartford Public, including the State and New England Championship games. In the State Class L final at the UConn Fieldhouse, he matched Eddie Griffin for game high scoring honors with 26 points. He set the CIAC tournament record by making 30 consecutive free throws, a record that still stands. In the New England High School Championship tournament, he made 32 of 35 free throws. He was selected first team All-State, capping a career that will be remembered as one of the finest ever at Bulkeley High School.

But his exploits in high school merely set the stage for his incredible accomplishments as a two-sport athlete at Central Connecticut State in New Britain, where he was an All-American basketball and baseball player.

He scored 1,597 career points at Central, and he led the nation in free throw shooting percentage as a senior for the nationally-ranked Blue Devils. He still holds the school records for career free throws made with 581 and most in a single game with 21, earning him the nickname Gene "The Machine" for his uncanny foul shooting accuracy. His basketball coach at Central, the legendary Bill Detrick, said that when he required players to make a certain number of free throws in practice, Gene Reilly wouldn't count the ones that hit the rim. "He wanted net only," Coach Detrick was quoted as saying of his star guard. "He was an exceptional defender, too."

Gene Reilly was a great baseball player at Central. Under coach Hank Majlinger, he earned All-American honors and was signed as a pitcher by the San Francisco Giants. He spent two years playing in the Giants' minor league system before he was drafted into the U.S. Army, serving a tour of duty in Vietnam with the 199th Light Infantry Brigade. When he returned home after his military service, the door was still open for him to play Class A minor league baseball, but he decided to take his career in a different direction. "I was 26. That's not an age where you want to start all over again," he was quoted as saying. Instead of playing professional baseball, he chose to try his hand at coaching. He coached baseball at South Catholic and served as a basketball assistant to his older brother, Joe, for two years, before accepting baseball and basketball coaching positions at Portland High School. He coached at Portland High for thirty-five years, winning state championships in both baseball and basketball, as well as numerous honors and awards, such as Middlesex County Coach of the Year, Connecticut High School Coaches Association Basketball Coach of the Year, and the Connecticut Sports Writers Alliance Gold Key Award. He was inducted into the Bulkeley Hall of Fame, the Central Connecticut Athletic Hall of Fame, the Twilight League Hall of Fame, and the New England Basketball Hall of Fame.

Fran Laffin could not have had a more inspirational mentor than Gene Reilly. As his game evolved in his early years at South Catholic, his improved play reflected Gene Reilly's influence, in the attention to the nuances of basketball, the foul shooting accuracy, jump shooting prowess, passing and ball handling skill, calmness under pressure, and defensive determination. But by the time he was a senior, Fran Laffin possessed an asset that Gene Reilly had lacked, a 6'- 5" frame that made him a scoring threat anywhere on the court. In spite of his physical and athletic gifts, it took time and experience for Fran Laffin to realize his potential. His legendary coach, Joe Reilly, referring to Fran Laffin's basketball talent, once remarked to sportswriter Woody Anderson in an interview for *The Hartford Courant*, "He didn't come by it naturally. As a freshman he was about the ninth man. But he was a good learner. He hit the weights very hard. He built himself up."

In his sophomore year he showed indications of the scoring ability that became his trademark, averaging 15 points per game on the JV team. As a junior, he continued to play on the JV team, but his steady progress earned him playing time with the varsity. In a big game against South Catholic's arch rival, East Catholic High School, Fran Laffin was assigned to cover Tim Kearns, a strong and talented 6'- 5" low-post presence who was averaging 28 points per game. The game was played at Central Connecticut State to accommodate the crowd of more than 5,000 fans that wanted to see the two power-house teams compete. Fran Laffin turned in an exceptional defensive effort, holding East Catholic's high-scoring center and future All-State player to 10 points, in a prelude to the 1970 Class L State Championship finals. In a state tournament game against Naugatuck High School, Fran Laffin showed how far he had come as a complete player. He led a spirited South Catholic comeback against a much taller Naugatuck team, closing a gap that had reached 23 points at one point to a single point in the game's closing seconds. Fran Laffin was fouled with no time remaining on the clock and South Catholic trailing by one. He stepped to the foul line under enormous pressure, with the outcome of the game resting squarely on his shoulders, and channeling the foul shooting expertise of his former mentor, Gene "The Machine" Reilly, he calmly sank the two free throws, giving South Catholic the win. Fran Laffin had clearly arrived as a big time clutch performer.

In his senior year at South Catholic, Fran Laffin took center stage as one of the premier basketball players in the state. As usual in Connecticut, the competition for All-State recognition for the 1969-70 basketball season was fierce. Class LL featured such illustrious names as John Williamson and Dan Hardy from Wilbur Cross, Bill Farley from Hillhouse, Rich Semo from Bridgeport Central, and Nate Vinson from New Britain. The Class L category in which South Catholic competed was equally impressive, with players like Tim Kearns from East Catholic, Dick Fairbrother from

Northwest Catholic, Steve Selinger from Wilton, and John Budris from Cheshire vying for All-State honors. By the end of the season, Fran Laffin's name was right at the top of the list. South Catholic enjoyed one of the finest seasons in the school's history, finishing the season with a 20-5 record and a berth in the Class L State Championship. The final game once again pitted South Catholic against East Catholic before a packed crowd at Central Connecticut State. Fran Laffin scored 25 points and grabbed 15 rebounds, leading South Catholic to a 71-67 victory for the school's first state championship. He earned the tournament MVP award and became only the second All-American in the school's history.

Fran Laffin had averaged 21 points and 15 rebounds in his senior year, and he was ranked as the eighth best player in New England. Multiple colleges and universities expressed an interest in him, including the Naval Academy, American International College, Fairfield University, and the University of Bridgeport. Although flattered by the attention his senior year performance on the basketball court had generated, he was frustrated by the difficulty in deciding which school to attend. His mother knew little about basketball and the college recruiting process, but she was sympathetic to her son's indecision and decided to take matters into her own hands. She contacted St. Michael's College in Vermont and told the assistant coach that her son was a great player and that the school should offer him a full scholarship. The coach was skeptical, but he was impressed with Mrs. Laffin's sincerity and impassioned advocacy for her son's ability. He called UConn assistant coach Fred Baracat to inquire about Fran Laffin. Coach Baracat gave Fran Laffin a rave review, telling the St. Michaels assistant that Fran Laffin had all the tools to become an outstanding college player. Fran Laffin received word from St. Michael's that he would receive the full scholarship his mother had so boldly requested.

St. Michael's would look back on the decision to admit Fran Laffin on a full scholarship as one of the best the college ever made. As a four-year starter, he became the only player in the school's history to score more than 2,000 career points, setting the school's all-time scoring record of 2,005 points in the final game of his college career, a loss to Bentley College in an NCAA Division II tournament game. St. Michael's compiled a 60-38 record during Fran Laffin's four-year college career. He was named All-State in Vermont four times, All-New England two times, and All-East two times. He was selected twice to the First Team NCAA All-Regional

Tournament Team. He was named Vermont's Athlete of the Month in December, 1973 and New England Division II Player of the Year for 1974. He was a Second Team NABC All-American selection in 1974 as well as a First Team District I All-Star pick. He was elected to the St. Michael's Athletic Hall of Fame in 1988. Judging from all the accolades he received and records he set at St. Michaels, Fran Laffin, and his mother, made the right choice of colleges.

After he graduated from St. Michael's, Fran Laffin played professionally in Holland for the Basketball Club of Markt of Utrecht for two years, averaging 31 points per game. In one game he scored a career high 55 points. He returned home to Hartford after two years, where he coached the South Catholic junior varsity team, served as a substitute teacher, and attended St. Joseph College to earn his teaching certification. He also played for the East Hartford Explorers in the New England Basketball Association, where he was leading the league with a 30.1 points per game average before being slowed by an ankle injury. Ray McKenna, founder and coach of the Explorers, was quoted as saying of Fran Laffin, "He's a perfect forward. He goes to the hoop all the time. He can rebound (10 per game), shoot from outside and handle the ball. He's the complete player." Not bad for a kid from the South End of Hartford who didn't start his first varsity game until midway through his junior year of high school before going on to win a state title and become the most prolific scorer in his college's history.

Peter Egan
Northwest Catholic High School 1971

As Peter Egan was growing up on Ridgefield Street in Hartford in close proximity to Weaver High School, he was often asked if he was related to Johnny Egan, the legendary basketball player who had led his Weaver team to state and New England titles before moving on to continued success at Providence College and in the NBA. "When I learned how good Johnny Egan was," Peter Egan said jokingly, "Even though we weren't related, I did less and less to discourage the association of our names." Unlike his namesake, Peter Egan attended parochial rather than public schools, but after Hall of Fame careers at Northwest Catholic and the University of Hartford, he was able to build an enduring basketball legacy in his own right, enhancing the fame of the Egan name in Hartford.

Peter Egan attended St. Justin's School, where he was introduced to basketball in gym class. At first he showed little interest in basketball; baseball was his sport of choice, and he played in various youth baseball leagues in Hartford. His seventh grade basketball coach at St. Justin's, Jack Flynn, recognized Peter Egan's potential and encouraged him to play. Jack Flynn became a loyal supporter, attending Peter's games in high school and college. As a freshman at Northwest Catholic High School, baseball remained his primary sport, while basketball was an afterthought. His friends convinced him to try out for the freshman basketball team, but he quit the team because he was frustrated with his lack of progress. He had a change of heart as a sophomore and played on the JV team, where he caught the attention of Charlie Larson, the varsity basketball coach. Coach Larson was a disciplinarian who stressed sound fundamentals and team play, and he insisted that Peter Egan learn to play basketball the right way. "He was constantly on me," Peter said, but Coach Larson was instrumental in helping Peter Egan develop the skill set that would make him an effective player, the ability to assert himself on the backboards, the footwork to maneuver in the post, the touch to score around the basket with either hand, and the range to move outside the key and hit jump shots. By his junior year Peter Egan emerged as a solid rebounder and dependable scorer on the varsity team, averaging 12 points and 12 rebounds per game. Northwest Catholic advanced to the semi-finals of the CIAC Class L state tournament, facing rival South Catholic in front of a capacity crowd at Central Connecticut State. A basket by captain Dick Fairbrother brought Northwest Catholic within one point with a little over six minutes remaining in the fourth quarter. But South Catholic pulled ahead at the end behind the hot shooting of Ed DelMastro and Fran Laffin and won 62-53. Jack Phelan led Northwest Catholic in scoring with 13 points, while Dick Fairbrother had 12, Chuck Harding 10, and Jim Akin 7. Peter Egan scored 9 points and grabbed 8 rebounds, but it was not enough to offset Ed DelMastro's 19 points and 16 rebounds and Fran Laffin's 23 points and 11 rebounds. South Catholic, after losing twice to defending champion East Catholic during the regular season, went on to beat East Catholic in the finals, 71-67.

Among the highlights of Peter Egan's basketball season in his senior year at Northwest Catholic were two victories over arch rival South Catholic and their star center, 6'-5" Ed DelMastro. The wins against South Catholic avenged the loss in the Class L state tournament semi-finals the previous year. In the first win against South during the 1970-71 season, Peter Egan led Northwest to an 80-53 victory by scoring 34 points and grabbing a school record 23 rebounds, while holding Ed DelMastro to 11 points. In the second game he tallied 20 points and 21 rebounds. Northwest Catholic once again made it to the semi-finals of the Class L state tournament, where the team faced off against an undefeated South Windsor High School team.

South Windsor, led by 6'-9" All-State and All-American center Tom Roy, had won the 1970 Class M state title and had moved up to Class L for the 1971 state tournament. Tom Roy averaged 36 points per game as a senior and amassed 2,501 career points, but he was not the only obstacle opponents faced in trying to defeat South Windsor. The team also featured starters 6'-7" forward Phil Levesque, 6'-5" forward Greg Burger, 6' point guard Terry Stoddard, and 6'-2" guard John E. Mason, Jr., with reserves Al Jankowski and Dave Lacy providing capable support off the bench. The team was coached by Charlie Sharos, who accumulated a record of 365-266 over a 30 year career that included 12 league titles and two state championships. Coach Sharos had scheduled regular season games against powerhouse teams like South Catholic, Northwest Catholic, Kolbe of Bridgeport and Wilbur Cross to prepare the team for another run at a state title. South Windsor had defeated Hand High of Madison to win the Class M title in 1970, led by Tom Roy, who was coming off a 60 point performance against Middletown High School in the semi-finals, a game in which he made 26 of 28 field goal attempts and 8 of 10 foul shots. In the semi-final game in the 1971 Class L tournament against Northwest Catholic that ended Peter Egan's high school career, Tom Roy scored 46 points to lead South Windsor to victory. South Windsor went on to defeat East Catholic in the finals 54-34, overcoming East's attempt at a slowdown. Reflecting back on his legendary coaching career after his retirement, Charlie Sharos placed three members of the 1971 Northwest Catholic team on his list of all-time best opponents – Peter Egan, Chuck Harding, and Jack Phelan.

Peter Egan was contacted by numerous colleges after his standout performance at Northwest Catholic in basketball and baseball. He decided to stay close to home and attend the University of Hartford. One of the reasons he chose the University of Hartford was his desire to continue to play on the same team with his Northwest Catholic friend and teammate Chuck Harding. Another reason for his decision was his trust that Coach Gordie McCullough could help him expand his game. Gordie McCullough took over the University of Hartford basketball program for the 1962-63 season. He led the team to an 11-11 record in his first season, but with a sharp shooting freshman named Gary Palladino ready to begin his varsity career, things were looking up for the Hawks. The 1964-65 team recorded the school's first winning season with a 12-10 record. Gary Palladino averaged 19.2 points per game as a sophomore. He reached the 1,000 point mark in two seasons and he accumulated 1,620 points in his three varsity seasons, with a career scoring average of 25.3 points per game. He was a two-time All-New England and All-East performer. Under the guidance of Coach McCullough and the brilliant scoring ability of Gary Palladino, the University of Hartford earned credibility as a formidable Division II program.

One of the keys to Gordie McCullough's coaching success was his intention to recruit top notch talent from the local area, particularly in Hartford. Gary Palladino was followed by players like Robert Foley, Stan Piorkowski, Ken Gwozdz, Tom Meade, Augie Gwozdz, Larry Franciose, and Wayne Augustine. Several of the recruits played baseball as well as basketball and were attracted to the university by the prospect of playing two sports in college. Both Peter Egan and Chuck Harding fit the University of Hartford prototype of playing both excellent basketball and baseball. And they were both from Hartford, which meant they were accustomed to playing highly competitive basketball. Over the next few years, Gordie McCullough recruited several outstanding players from Hartford. In addition to Peter Egan and Chuck Harding, Bill Brown from Hartford Public and Clarence Love from Weaver committed to the resurgent University of Hartford basketball program. The school had become a viable option for talented basketball players from Hartford.

In his freshman year at the University of Hartford, Peter Egan averaged 20.2 points per game and 12.2 rebounds per game and was named the Eastern College Athletic Conference Division II Rookie-of-the-Year. He scored 41 points in a game at Brooklyn College. The team qualified for the first of four consecutive trips to the NCAA Division II regional tournament. As a sophomore Peter Egan averaged 18.5 points and 11.3 rebounds per game. The 6'-5" center was named the team's Most Valuable Player and he was an All-New England first team selection. The team finished with a 17-7 record and once again qualified for the NCAA tournament, losing to St. Michael's in the opening round in spite of Peter Egan's 30 points and 21 rebounds before fouling out in the fourth quarter. As a junior co-captain, he scored 30 points and grabbed 16 rebounds in a 78-57 win against Norwich University to go over the 1,000 point threshold in his career. In his senior year be became the all-time Hawks leader in points and rebounds, finishing his career with 1,854 points and 1,054 rebounds. In a game against City College of New York, he matched his career high with 41 points in a 102-90 victory. He was 17-25 from the floor for the game, hit all seven of his free throws, and pulled down a team-leading eight rebounds. In the opening round of the New England NCAA College Division basketball tournament, the University of Hartford lost to St. Michael's 108-97. Peter Egan played a tremendous game, scoring 30 points and grabbing 21 rebounds before fouling out with 2:28 left to play in the game. Clarence Love from Weaver and Bill Brown from Hartford Public chipped in with 18 and 17 points respectively, while Chuck Harding handed out 11 assists. But it was not enough to overcome the hot shooting of St. Michael's guard Bob Toner, who scored 33 points on 14 of 18 shooting from the floor and five-for-five from the foul line. Fran Laffin, the former South Catholic star, scored 26 points for St. Michael's in the victory that ousted the Hawks from the tournament.

Peter Egan had led the team in scoring and rebounding in each of his final three seasons. A two-time co-captain, he was named All-America twice and All-New England three times. He was also named the University of Hartford Athlete of the Year in 1972, 1974, and 1975. After he graduated he played professionally with Caracas in the Venezuelan National Basketball League, where he averaged 30 points a game, with a high of 43 against the Caracus Beverly Hills team. He has been inducted into the Northwest Catholic Alumni Athletic Hall of Fame, the University of Hartford Athletics Hall of Fame, the East Hartford Explorers Hall of Fame, and the New England Basketball Hall of Fame. Peter Egan married his college sweetheart, Trish, and the couple lives in Rocky Hill. Their 6'-8" son Patrick starred in baseball and basketball at Rocky Hill High School and Qunnipiac University. He played professional baseball as a pitcher for several years at the minor league level. Something about the Egan name just commands attention in the Hartford area.

Charles "Chuck" Harding
Northwest Catholic High School 1971

As Chuck Harding's illustrious career at the University of Hartford drew to a close, one of the many honors he received was the Unsung Hero Award at the annual New England College Basketball Awards Dinner at the Sheraton-Lincoln Inn in Worcester, Massachusetts. The event was sponsored by the New England Sports Information Directors Association for the purpose of honoring the top basketball players in New England. Coach Gordon McCullough praised his star point guard for his contributions to the program. "Chuck is the kind of player most coaches wait a lifetime for," he said. "He is a born leader and, without reservation, I think he is the most inspirational leader our school basketball program has ever had." Coach McCullough was a perceptive evaluator of basketball talent, as he demonstrated throughout his successful tenure as the University of Hartford's head coach and Director of Athletics. But he also understood the intangibles that contribute to a winning program, like an all-purpose point guard who can neutralize defensive pressure with his ball-handling skills, find the open man on the break, score from the outside when necessary, and provide the poise and leadership to carry his team through the rough stretches of a close game. In Chuck Harding, Coach McCullough knew that over four winning campaigns he had found the ideal playmaker to serve as his team's catalyst and proxy coach on the floor.

Chuck Harding grew up in Hartford with his parents and five siblings. His father owned a rug store and his mother was a nurse at St. Francis Hospital. He attended Batchelder Elementary School, where he began playing basketball under the direction of Nick Matto, who ran the Parks and Recreation program at the school. His family moved after he completed fourth grade and he went to Noah Webster School for about a year before attending St. Joseph Cathedral School. His coaches at Cathedral were Bill Rice and Andy Manzi, Hartford police officers. Chuck Harding recalled his coaches occasionally falling asleep on the bench from fatigue after working twelve hour shifts prior to a practice or a game. But it was their dedication that gave the boys at Cathedral the opportunity to play competitive basketball. Chuck Harding emerged as a leader on the team, displaying his instinctive capabilities as a floor general while averaging 15 points per game. Sometimes after practice the team would pile into Officer Rice's big Cadillac to go for a ride. "Those rides were hilarious," Chuck remembered. "They were almost as much fun as the games."

When Chuck Harding arrived at Northwest Catholic High School, he made an immediate impact on the basketball program. He led the freshman team in scoring and assists and helped the team win the City Championship for freshman teams. He started for the JV team as a sophomore and led the team in scoring, averaging 15 points per game. He received playing time on the varsity team, bolstering his confidence that he was ready to move up to the next level. As a junior he was the starting point guard on the varsity team, playing alongside Peter Egan, Jack Phelan, and Dick Fairbrother, three prolific scorers that would go on to become standout college players. Chuck Harding's willingness to sacrifice his individual scoring statistics to focus on distributing the ball to his teammates was instrumental in the team's success. He meshed particularly well with Peter Egan, the 6'-5" center who would become his close friend and college teammate. Peter Egan was the beneficiary of numerous Chuck Harding assists, a practice that would carry over from high school to college. Together the two Hartford natives formed a dynamic inside-outside combination that would torment opposing teams for years to come.

Northwest Catholic reached the semi-finals in the CIAC Class L state tournament in both Chuck Harding's junior and senior year. In his junior year, Northwest Catholic was riding a nine game winning streak into the semi-final game against rival South Catholic on the campus of Central Connecticut State. Although South Catholic played the game without 6'-5" senior Paul Lukas, the scoring and rebounding of 6'-5" sophomore Ed DelMastro and 6'-4" senior Fran Laffin carried the Rebels to a 62-53 victory over Northwest Catholic. The two South Catholic big men combined for 42 points and 27 rebounds and held Peter Egan to 9 points and 8 rebounds to seal the win. Chuck Harding scored 10 points in the bitter loss. But the defeat motivated Chuck Harding and his teammates to return with renewed determination the following season. After a strong 15-5 regular season that included two wins against South Catholic, avenging the season-ending defeat the previous year, the Indians were optimistic about their chances in the Class L state tournament. Northwest Catholic beat New London, Glastonbury, and East Haven before facing South Windsor, a team many considered the best suburban team in the state's history. South

Windsor had four starters and nine seniors returning from the 1970 Class M state championship team. The team was tall, talented, and deep, but it was the presence of 6'- 9" Tom Roy in the middle that made South Windsor unbeatable in his senior year. He averaged 36 points per game and 27 rebounds on his way to earning All-State and All-America honors. He scored 2,501 career points, breaking the state and New England scoring records, and he disappointed countless Connecticut fans when he announced his decision to play for Coach Charles "Lefty" Driesell at the University of Maryland rather than attend UConn. Northwest Catholic's loss to South Windsor in the semi-finals of the 1971 Class L tournament marked the end of Chuck Harding's stellar high school career. But he still had a lot of basketball left to play as he and Peter Egan took their scintillating act a few miles down the road to the University of Hartford.

In his freshman year of college, the 5'-10" Harding picked up where he had left off in high school, playing inspired basketball at the point guard position and directing his team to multiple post-season tournaments. He joined a stellar freshman class that included Peter Egan, Gary LaRocque, and Steve Sheerer. All four freshmen were from the local area and played two sports at the University of Hartford. As a group they made four consecutive appearances in the NCAA Division II basketball tournament. Gary LaRocque, a 6' shooting guard and defensive stopper from West Hartford, was an outstanding shortstop on the baseball team, compiling a .305 career batting average, while scoring 962 career points on the basketball team. Steve Sheerer, a 6'- 2" swingman from Windsor Locks, was a star soccer player as well as a defensive ace on the basketball team, managing to score 635 points during his career and grabbing 352 rebounds, while winning the Outstanding Defensive Player Award three times. Peter Egan, a catcher on the baseball team, finished his basketball career with 1,855 points and 1,054 rebounds. Chuck Harding's aggressive style of play – constantly diving on the floor for loose balls, setting up his teammates for open shots, battling taller opponents for rebounds, and hitting clutch shots from long range or on fearless drives to the basket – was essential to the winning formula that propelled the team to four post-season appearances.

One incident his freshman year exemplified the intensity and desire that marked Chuck Harding's record-setting career at the University of Hartford. The Hawks were scheduled to play a game at Bates College in Lewiston, Maine on a date that conflicted with his brother's ordination into the Franciscan Order at St. Joseph's Church in Winsted, Connecticut. Chuck was determined to honor both commitments. He witnessed the ordination, then flew out on a private plane to Lewiston for the game, before driving back to Connecticut in order to participate in his brother's first mass. He travelled 600 miles in a 24 hour period that included playing a basketball game, a genuine expression of his devotion to family and the U of H basketball program.

In his sophomore season at the University of Hartford, Chuck Harding averaged 11.5 points per game and 4.8 assists. At the team's annual awards luncheon at the end of the season, Chuck Harding and Peter Egan were selected by their teammates as co-captains for the 1973-74 season. Chuck Harding was also honored with the Most Desire Award, given to the player that had displayed the most effort and energy throughout the season. In his junior season, although hampered by a knee injury, Chuck Harding led the Hawks to a 20-4 record. He was named second team All-New England College Division, and he was awarded the U of H Outstanding Player Award. Prior to the NCAA College Division New England Regional Tournament, Coach Gordon McCullough spoke to *The Hartford Courant* sportswriter Bill Lee about Chuck Harding's unique desire on the basketball court. "Harding typifies our hustling style," McCullough said. "He must have hit the floor 500 times since he came here, mostly of his own volition diving for loose balls. He took a rebound from a 6-8 St. Anselm's player this year and hit the floor so hard he was stunned. I knew he would get back up. Chuck always does. He did get up and helped us win in overtime."

As a senior, Chuck Harding served as the team's co-captain for the third year in a row. He guided the Hawks to a fourth straight NCAA Division II Tournament appearance. The team lost to St. Michael's in the opening round 108-97, but the Hawks beat Sacred Heart of Bridgeport 102-91 in the consolation game, as the four local seniors that had been the core of the team for four years all finished in double figures, with Peter Egan scoring 28 points, Chuck Harding with 17, Gary LaRocque with 10, and Steve Scheerer with 10. It was a fitting way to end their careers on a winning note. Chuck Harding, who had seven assists in the game, brought his career assist total to 586, a school record. He had scored 801 points in his career. He was a two-time All-New England selection. The recognition given to the University of Hartford's assist leader each season is now called the Chuck Harding Award. His hustling, team-oriented style of play helped pave the way for the program's ascendancy to Division I status. As a team leader and consummate point guard, he made every one around him a better player.

Chuck Harding was inducted into the Northwest Catholic Alumni Athletic Hall of Fame and the University of Hartford Athletics Hall of Fame. He stayed connected to the game for many years by serving as a highly-regarded basketball official for IAABO Central Connecticut Board 6. He lives in Wethersfield with his wife Peg and remains close friends with some of the teammates he led with such precision and determination on the basketball court.

Dennis and Ken Mink
Weaver High School 1971, 1978

When Weaver High played Hillhouse for the 1978 CIAC Class LL state championship, there was a familiar name in the Beavers' starting lineup that evoked memories of the 1971 finals against Hartford Public, the last time Weaver won the coveted title. In 1971 Dennis Mink had been a key member of the championship team, a fluid 6'- 6" center who could score, rebound, and defend. His younger brother Ken was the leading scorer on the 1978 team, an explosive outside shooter, capable of breaking open a game with one of his patented hot streaks. The Weaver faithful had experienced a similar situation in 1976, when a younger brother tried to duplicate the 1971 championship run of his older brother, only to come up three points short in the title game. Could the Mink brothers, Dennis and Ken, succeed where the Mahorn brothers, Owen and Rick, had come ever so close?

Dennis and Ken Mink grew up in Stowe Village with their younger brother Marvin and two sisters, in the loving care of their mother, Julia M. Mink. All three of the Mink brothers played basketball at Weaver, but Dennis' path to high school athletics was complicated by the diagnosis of a heart ailment when he was seven years old. He was told to curtail his physical activity, and so he became an avid reader and focused on his schoolwork, resisting the temptation to join his friends on the Stowe Village basketball courts. Eventually, the attraction of playing basketball became too compelling for him to ignore, and he competed for Stowe Village in the Pee Wee division of the Parks and Recreation summer basketball program, along with future Weaver teammates Dave Tyson and John Holliday. He discovered he had a knack for the game, but he was concerned that he was jeopardizing his health by continuing to play.

When he arrived at Weaver, he did not intend to try out for the freshman basketball team, but Coach Frank Scelza had other ideas. Frank Scelza had made a habit of approaching students anywhere in the school and recruiting them for the basketball program. It was unlikely that a student with Dennis Mink's exceptional height could escape Frank Scelza's notice. When the coach approached the tall freshman in the cafeteria, Dennis told Frank Scelza about his health concerns, and the coach arranged for a medical examination that gave Dennis clearance to play basketball. Dennis Mink became a starter and the high scorer on a talented freshman team.

Although his basketball career at Weaver was off to a promising start, Dennis Mink was disappointed with his progress in the classroom. He expressed his concerns to his guidance counselor, George Thomas, a legendary former history teacher at Weaver with a charismatic approach to relating to young people. George Thomas recognized Dennis Mink's academic potential and helped to connect him with programs that would improve his chances for success. Dennis Mink credited George Thomas for making him a more focused and motivated student, qualities that would enable him to excel in the classroom as well as on the basketball court.

As a sophomore, Dennis Mink led the Weaver JV team in scoring and rebounding, providing encouragement that he would become a valuable member of the varsity the following season. But he continued to seek out opportunities that would help him succeed as a student as well. The summer after his sophomore year he participated in an enrichment program for Hartford youth at Trinity College, an experience that would have a profound impact on his life. He met Dr. John Norman, the director of the program. John Norman had been a member of the undefeated 1957 Weaver basketball team that won the state and New England championships. After Weaver, he attended Trinity College, where he excelled in basketball and academics. He became interested in Dennis Mink, monitored his progress at Weaver, and helped him with the college selection process. Dennis Mink was fortunate to have two outstanding mentors in his corner, George Thomas and Dr. John Norman, and he tried to follow the sound advice they provided him.

In his junior year, Dennis Mink emerged as a reliable scorer and rebounder on the Weaver varsity team in John Lambert's first year as head coach. The Beavers started the season by winning seven of the team's first nine games. In a Capital District Conference game against previously undefeated Norwich Free Academy, Dennis Mink scored 23 points in an 89-84 Weaver victory. Weaver played a powerful East Catholic High team in Manchester in front of 1,000 fans, and Dennis Mink led all scorers with 21 points in a 76-68 Weaver win. But in a key City Series matchup against Hartford Public, the hot-shooting Owls beat Weaver 92-71 to drop Weaver to 8-3 on the season. Prior to the Weaver game, Hartford Public had lost three games in a row, but when it came to the city rivalry, both teams knew that the won-loss records could be disregarded. Bragging rights in the city were at stake, and regardless of the teams' records or standings in the conference, the games were sure to be intense and hard-fought.

By the time Weaver faced Hartford Public two weeks later in the rematch, the Beavers had suffered a devastating blow. Four Weaver players, including two key starters, Lee Otis Wilson and Owen Mahorn, had been dismissed from the team for disciplinary reasons. Yet Weaver still managed to give Hartford Public a tough game that went down to the wire. Ted Rush scored on a drive to the basket with less than three seconds left in the game to lift the Owls to a 64-62 win. Dennis Mink, Myron Goggins, Lee Hunt, Herbie Johnson, and captain Alfie Williams kept the game close, but hampered by a depleted roster, they were unable to prevent Hartford Public from completing its first City Series sweep since the 1966-67 season. Weaver still qualified for the CIAC Class LL state tournament, but the team was eliminated in the first round by Hillhouse, 80-65. Dennis Mink led Weaver in scoring against Hillhouse with 17 points. For the year he had averaged 16.9 points and 14.1 rebounds per game. Although the season ended in disappointment with the first round loss to Hillhouse, the dismissal of four of his teammates, and the sweep by Hartford Public, Dennis Mink had shown he was one of the best big men in the state. And he was only getting started.

Dennis Mink and Myron Goggins were named captains of the 1970-71 Weaver basketball team. The lineup that would take the floor for the Beavers at the start of the season was not only one of the strongest in the school's history, it ranked among the best teams the city and the state had ever produced. Lee Otis Wilson, a 6'-3" forward with a lethal jump shot that would light up UConn opponents the following year, had led the team in scoring as a junior, averaging 23 points a game. Myron Goggins, an intimidating presence on the court at 6'-5" and a clutch shooter capable of hitting big shots, had averaged 14.4 points and 11.8 rebounds per game as a junior. Owen Mahorn, a powerfully built 6'-4" guard with a sweet left-handed shot, had averaged 10 points per game as a sophomore, and he was poised to become one of the most dominant players ever to wear a Weaver uniform. Keith Smart, a 6' guard, had played against Hillhouse in the state tournament as a freshman and had shown he was ready for the pressure of big games. Over the next three seasons, he would become one of the most dangerous point guards in the state. Dennis Mink, at 6'- 7", could dominate in the post with his length, but he was also comfortable facing the basket and taking his smooth jump shot. The reserves were solid, with juniors Dave Tyson (6'- 4"), Vincent Hylton (5'- 9"), and Keith Price (6'- 0") as well as senior guard Robert Lomax all capable of stepping in and making valuable contributions off the bench. But many teams looked unstoppable on paper, only to underperform on the basketball court and failed to live up to the preseason hype and over-zealous expectations. The formidable 1970-71 Weaver team would be tested immediately by the perennially strong Governors of Wilbur Cross High School.

Many promising teams had been humbled facing Wilbur Cross in New Haven, where home court losses were as rare as leap years. Although Weaver trailed most of the game and was down 61-50 at the end of the third quarter, the team played with poise and determination, staying within range as Wilbur Cross began to show the effects of the Beavers' pressing defense. Weaver trailed 87-86 with 17 seconds remaining in the fourth quarter and a Cross player on the foul line. Myron Goggins rebounded the missed free throw, and Dennis Mink hit a layup with eight seconds on the clock, giving the Beavers a stunning 88-87 victory. The one-point win over Wilbur Cross in New Haven was the perfect start to a magical season, giving the Beavers confidence the team could beat any school on their schedule. In a game against Enfield a week later, Weaver put on a dazzling offensive display in a 118-67 win. Dennis Mink scored 27 points and grabbed 28 rebounds for one of the more impressive lines ever recorded in a Weaver scorebook. But it was not just Dennis Mink elevating his performance; the entire team was clicking at a staggering level. The Beavers remained unbeaten at 6-0 after a 90-83 win over conference rival New Britain. The scoring and rebounding totals reflected the team's remarkable balance. Dennis Mink sat out the first quarter, yet still managed 18 points and 27 rebounds. Myron Goggins also scored 18 points and grabbed 13 rebounds. Keith Morgan scored 17 points. Lee Otis Wilson and Owen Mahorn each added 14 points, with Owen, Weaver's "Big O", collecting 19 rebounds to aid the cause.

Norwich Free Academy, which had its own ten-game season-opening winning streak snuffed out by Weaver the previous year, proved that the 1970-71 Beavers were not invincible, upending Weaver 73-68 in Norwich. Dennis Mink was held to 11 points and 8 rebounds, far below his usual output for the season. Weaver avenged the loss when Norwich played the Beavers in Hartford, winning 92-67 by returning to the balanced, high-powered offense that carried the team all season. Weaver shot 55 percent from the field in another dynamic display of offensive wizardry. Keith Morgan led the way with 24 points. Dennis Mink scored 22 points and pulled down 18 rebounds. Myron Goggins had 14 points, 15 rebounds, and a strong defensive effort against Norwich's tough frontcourt, and Owen Mahorn chipped in with 13 points and 14 rebounds. It was exactly the kind of all-around team effort the Beavers needed heading into the teeth of the schedule, highlighted by an upcoming game against a team that remained undefeated late in the season, Bridgeport Central High School.

The game between Weaver and Bridgeport Central in Bridgeport was a matchup of two of the state's best teams, and at the end of the game the Hilltoppers of Bridgeport Central emerged as the superior team. Bridgeport Central was averaging over 103 points a game while giving up only 62 points a game. In 6'- 6" All-State senior center Rich Semo, who had recently become the fourth player in Bridgeport Central's history to score 1,000 points, the Hilltoppers had the size to contend on the inside with Dennis Mink and Myron Goggins.

The game stayed close until the fourth quarter, when Bridgeport Central began to pull away. But Dennis Mink scored eight points in quick succession to pull Weaver within five points at 89-84 with two and a half minutes to play. Bridgeport Central held off Weaver at the end, hitting key foul shots to win 97-88. Dennis Mink, who had led the stirring Weaver comeback, scored 22 points to pace the Beavers. But the game had a major impact on his future that extended far beyond his point total. He had managed to impress the opposing team's head coach, and the impression he made would help determine where he would go to college.

Tom Penders excelled in basketball and baseball at UConn and was one of the few athletes, along with Hartford native Randy LaVigne, to appear in both the NCAA basketball tournament and the College World Series. In his two years as the basketball coach at Bridgeport Central, he guided the team to 23-2 and 20-1 records. After the two exceptional seasons, he moved on from Bridgeport Central into the college coaching ranks. His first stop was Tufts University, and from there he went to Columbia, Fordham, Rhode Island, Texas, George Washington, and Houston. He worked for more Division I programs than any coach in history, compiling a career record of 649-437. Only three college coaches coached more games than Tom Penders, Jim Calhoun, Mike Kryzewski, and Jim Boeheim. His success at every one of his stops earned him the nickname Tom Turnaround. When Tom Penders watched Dennis Mink play against his Bridgeport Central team, he obviously liked what he saw. Dennis Mink became Tom Penders' first blue-chip recruit when he started his college coaching career at Tufts University. Together they would be instrumental in transforming the Tufts' basketball program from a run-of-the-mill NESCAC team into a regional force. Tom Penders teams were 54-18 during his coaching tenure at Tufts and Dennis Mink was the main catalyst for his success.

After losing to Bridgeport Central, the team remained focused on leading Weaver to a state championship and, as usual, Hartford Public stood in the way of the Beavers' title aspirations. Weaver finished the regular season strong heading into the Class LL state tournament. The Beavers defeated Stamford 93-83 in the opening round, with Dennis Mink leading the way with 29 points and 16 rebounds. In the quarterfinal round, Weaver beat Lee High School, the team that had knocked undefeated Bridgeport Central out of the tournament. Weaver played Wilbur Cross in the semifinal round, and for the second time in the season, the Beavers eked out a one-point victory, wining 94-93. The game clinching bucket came on a Robert Lomax layup off a feed from Myron Goggins with six seconds remaining in the game.

The Weaver victory over Cross set up an all-Hartford final at the University of Connecticut. Hartford had defeated Danbury, Norwich, and Roger Ludlowe to join Weaver in the championship game. In front of a sellout crowd of 2,331, the two rivals battled evenly the entire game. The score had been tied 16 times, including at 86-86, when Weaver took possession with 19 seconds to play. Myron Goggins hit a jump shot from the corner to give Weaver an 88-86 win and the school's first state championship since 1957. Dennis Mink had ended his high school career on the highest note possible, capturing an elusive state title.

In deciding to attend Tufts University, Dennis Mink had selected a strong academic institution with an ascending basketball program. He enjoyed outstanding success over his three year career at Tufts, setting the university's all-time scoring mark with 1,447 points. He averaged 20.4 points per game over his career. In his senior year, he averaged 23.4 points per game, establishing a single-season school record at the time. He was named Player-of-the-Week in the Eastern Collegiate Athletic Conference Division III balloting when he had 40 points and 15 rebounds against WPI, 39 points and 14 rebounds against MIT, and 27 points and 20 rebounds against Wesleyan. He led the team in rebounding, averaging 11.8 boards per game over his career. After his senior year, he was named to the UPI All-New England Division III basketball team.

Dennis Mink was not only successful on the basketball court at Tufts, but in the classroom as well. He graduated with a degree in political science and a minor in secondary education. He returned to Hartford after his graduation from Tufts to teach social studies at Weaver. He became the director of the Upward Bound Program at Trinity College for 18 years, and he retired from Capital Workforce Partners after ten years of service.

***

Weaver High School played in three Class LL state championship games in the 1970s, and Ken Mink was involved in all of them. In 1971 he watched intently from the University of Connecticut stands as his brother Dennis and his teammates defeated Hartford Public 88-86 to win the title. He was a sophomore reserve averaging five points a game for Weaver in 1976, when the Beavers lost to Lee High School of New Haven 80-77. His best chance for a championship of his own came in 1978, when Weaver survived a string of close games in the tournament to reach the finals against Hillhouse. In the years leading up to the final game of his high school career against Hillhouse, Ken Mink developed into one of the finest offensive threats in Weaver's history.

As a kid growing up in Stowe Village, Ken idolized his brother Dennis. In his eyes Dennis could do no wrong. But unlike Dennis, whose development as a basketball player was delayed by the diagnosis of a heart defect, Ken began playing at a young age. He played in the Parks and Recreation summer basketball league as well as for Wish School, where his team was undefeated. When he was in the fifth grade, his family moved to Martin Street and he attended Clark Elementary School, where he admired the principal, Vernal Davis, a graduate of Weaver who had a long and distinguished career in education in the Hartford school system. Ken Mink was coached in the Parks and Recreation league by the legendary Willie Ware, the first African American captain of the Weaver basketball team during the 1935-36 season. At Lewis Fox Middle School, Ken Mink played for Coach Wilbur Jones on an outstanding team that included Alan Broughton, Kevin Shannon, and Nigel Edwards, all future teammates at Weaver. The team lost only one game in two years, sending a strong signal that the Weaver basketball program was about to be replenished with a group of highly talented young players.

Ken Mink arrived at Weaver with the self-confidence that would become his trademark. Even as a freshman, he felt he deserved playing time on the varsity team, a conviction he was not bashful about sharing with his coach and his teammates. As a sophomore he played on a veteran team that could compete with any high school in the state. The team possessed speed and size. On one end of the spectrum there was George "Shorty" Davis, who Woody Anderson of *The Hartford Courant* called "the best 5-9 player in the state". George Davis led the team in scoring and assists and was considered the team's most consistent player. On the other end of the height range was 6'- 7", and still growing, Rick "Too Tall" Mahorn. Rick Mahorn averaged 12 points and 12 rebounds a game as a junior, but his statistics told only a small part of the story. His value to the team as an intimidating presence around the basket was on display in a 77-71 win over Hartford Public at the Civic Center when he blocked five shots in the first quarter. To complement the long and the short of it on the Weaver team was a capable supporting cast that included 6'- 4" Carlton Butler, 6'- 3" Tim Syms, 6'- 2" Daryl Turner, 5'- 9" Ron Smith, 5'- 10" Gerry Hamilton, and 6'- 3" Ken Mink. Coach John Lambert thought that his current team was even quicker than his 1971 group that had won the state championship. But there was one thing the two Weaver teams had in common – they both had a Mink and a Mahorn.

Like the 1971 team, the 1976 Beavers made it to the Class LL finals. In the 1976 championship game the Weaver team faced a Lee High team from New Haven that was led by Sly Williams, a 6'- 7" All-State and All-American candidate who later played for the University of Rhode Island before moving on to play in the NBA for the New York Knicks, Atlanta Hawks, and, very briefly, for the Boston Celtics. Sly Williams averaged 32 points and 24 rebounds per game for Lee in his senior year. In the championship game he scored 31 points to lead Lee past Weaver 80-77 in overtime. Weaver finished the season with an 18-4 record. But the senior dominated team was moving on, and it would be left to players like Ken

Mink and Kevin Shannon to set the stage for another Weaver run at the state championship.

In his junior year at Weaver, Ken Mink became one of the team's major offensive weapons. He displayed the ability to shoot his smooth left-handed jump shot from long range and to make strong drives to the basket. Two of his favorite shots were a fade away jump shot and a sweeping hook shot. He averaged 17.6 points per game as a junior, and he received plenty of support from his reliable running mate, Kevin Shannon, who averaged 14.3 points per game and pulled down nine rebounds a game. The team won 14 games during the season, before losing to Brian McMahon of Norwalk in the semifinals of the state tournament, leaving his senior year as Ken Mink's last chance to win a state title.

Weaver opened the 1977-78 season by playing Cheverus High School in Portland, Maine. Ken Mink scored 20 points and Kevin Shannon scored 15 in a 68-62 Weaver victory. Weaver's first loss of the season came at the hands of Wilbur Cross in the New Haven Coliseum. Ken Mink scored 24 points in the 76-71 Weaver loss. The Beavers regained their footing in consecutive games against teams from Springfield, Massachusetts. Kevin Shannon scored 25 points and Ken Mink hit for 20 in a 74-66 win over Springfield Technical, and then in a game against Springfield Classical High School, Ken Mink erupted for a career high 36 points and Kevin Shannon added 25 in a 96-66 Weaver victory.

Both Weaver and Ken Mink remained hot over the next several weeks of the season, racking up victories over teams like Bulkeley, New Britain, Hartford Public, Springfield Classical (again), and Hillhouse. But the team ran into trouble heading into the tournament, losing consecutive games to rivals Hartford Public and Wilbur Cross. Hartford Public, desperate for a win to keep alive the team's hope of qualifying for the tournament, beat Weaver 79-64 behind Ken Smith's 33 points and nine rebounds. Nigel Edwards led Weaver with 18 points and Ken Mink contributed 16. In Weaver's next game against Wilbur Cross, Bernard Draughn banked in a shot with 21 seconds left in the game to seal a 102-101 win. Ken Mink scored 26 points, Nigel Edwards scored 17 points and handed out 13 assists, and Kevin Shannon scored 14 in the high-scoring loss. The Beavers suffered a third crushing defeat in a row in New Britain when the Golden Hurricanes' Mel Kline threw in a 35-foot prayer at the buzzer to defeat Weaver 62-60 and win the CDC championship. The Beavers finished the regular season with an 11-6 record as the tournament was about to get underway.

Weaver appeared to right the ship in the CIAC Class LL Region I tourney, but by the narrowest of margins, winning by a single point in each of the first two rounds. In the quarterfinals of the state tournament at Hall High School, Weaver defeated New Britain 77-75 behind 27 points by Ken Mink. Weaver played Hartford Public in the semifinals, winning 79-76 as Ken Mink's two foul shots provided the winning cushion. He scored 27 points as Weaver won its fourth straight game to improve to 15-6. Only Hillhouse stood in the way of a Weaver state title.

The Class LL championship game between Weaver and Hillhouse was played at Crosby High School in Waterbury in front of a crowd of 2,200 noisy spectators. The game was close throughout, with neither team able to establish much of a lead. With a little over a minute left in the fourth quarter, Weaver's Devon Henry made a baseline jump shot to pull the Beaver's within one point. Weaver worked for a final shot and tried to get the ball to Ken Mink with eight seconds remaining in the game, but the pass was intercepted, and Hillhouse won 56-55, capturing its sixteenth title in twenty-three tries.

Ken Mink had averaged 25 points a game in the tournament and 24.3 points per game for the season. He led Weaver in rebounding with 8.2 boards per game. He finished his career with 948 total points. His outstanding senior season was recognized with All-City and All-State honors. He may have fallen just short of his goal of winning the state championship, but he had secured his legacy as one of the best players in the state.

After he graduated from Weaver, Ken Mink attended the University of Hartford for parts of two chaotic years. As a freshman, he seemed to make a smooth adjustment from high school to college, serving as a valuable secondary scorer behind senior Mark Noon, the Hawks all-time leading scorer with 2,113 career points. At the end of his freshman year he was named to the second team Little All-American team. In the season-opening game his sophomore year, Ken Mink scored 35 points in a 68-65 loss to Southern Connecticut. As the losses continued to pile up for the Hawks, he transferred to Virginia State, where he competed for playing time on a very solid, veteran Division II team. He eventually left the program and returned to Hartford, where he continued to play in leagues around the city. Through the efforts of John Wilson, the executive director of the South Arsenal Neighborhood Development Corp, and Pat Santinello, a local donut shop owner, Ken Mink received a tryout with the Bay State Bombardiers in Worcester, Massachusetts. He became active in politics, and he ran for mayor of Hartford against Mike Peters. He eventually relocated to Indiana with his daughter. "She is the most important thing in the world to me," Ken Mink said, "Not basketball." There are still many people in Hartford that still recall watching Ken Mink play his exhilarating brand of basketball and thrilling at his exceptional talent.

Ted Rush
Hartford Public High School 1971

Most of the elite basketball players in Hartford demonstrated their jumping ability on the court, leaping for rebounds, soaring for dunks, or blocking shot attempts. In a city graced with outstanding athletes, it was difficult for a high school basketball player to earn a reputation as an exceptional jumper. But Ted Rush earned his credentials as one of the premier jumpers in the city's history through his performance on the Hartford Public High School outdoor track team. In the 1970 city track meet Ted Rush took first place in the long jump, high jump, and triple jump. He took first in the triple jump in the CIAC Class A meet and the State Open meet. In 1971 he won both the triple jump and long jump in the Eastern Connecticut Track Coaches Relays at Farmington High School. A week later he won two first place medals in the annual Rippowam Invitational Track and Field Meet in Stamford. He was ranked eighth in the country in the triple jump in his senior year. Ted Rush could really jump, as his success on the outdoor track team proved beyond a doubt. But his performance on the Hartford Public basketball team as an all-around remarkable talent was equally impressive.

Ted Rush was born in the Bronx, New York and moved to the Charter Oak Terrace neighborhood in Hartford, where his mother worked for the Community Renewal Team. He was the oldest of four boys and took responsibility for his younger brothers. He attended the Mary Hooker Elementary School, where one of his teachers, Mr. Leonard Berliner, offered encouragement and helped him become a better student. At New Park Avenue Junior High School, basketball began to play an important role in his life. His junior high coach was Jimmy White, who recognized Ted Rush's potential and helped him develop the skills he would need in high school. Ted also spent many hours at Colt Park and the Southwest Boys & Girls Club working on his game. He played in the Courant-Hartford Parks and Recreation League, where he competed for a championship in the Pee Wee division. He was tall and slender and wore glasses, and through hard work and determination he developed into a fine basketball player even before he arrived at Hartford Public.

As a freshman at Hartford Public, he immediately distinguished himself in both basketball and track. He was a starter on the JV basketball team when he was spotted in a gym class by legendary track and field coach Lindy Remigino and asked to come out for indoor track. Lindy Remigino graduated from Hartford Public in 1949, and three years later he was a Gold Medalist in the Helinski Olympics in the 100 meters and 4x100 medley relay. During his running career, he established multiple state, New England, and national records. As the track and field coach at Hartford Public for 42 years, his teams won 31 CIAC State Championships, 19 Greater Hartford Championships, and 25 City Championships. His overall dual meet record at HPHS was 282-49-1. He produced 12 track and field All-Americans, including two-time honoree Ted Rush. Under Lindy Remigino's tutelage, Ted Rush became one of the outstanding track and field athletes in the nation. Before he left Hartford Public, Ted Rush would also earn recognition as one of the best basketball players in the school's history.

In his sophomore year Ted Rush became one of the highest scoring sophomores ever at HPHS, averaging 17 points per game. In an early season game against New London, he led a third quarter spurt that helped seal an 85-69 win, finishing with 14 points. He continued to improve throughout the season, becoming one of the mainstays of the offense with Willie Martin, Clarence Knight, Larry Reynolds, Cleve May, and Jimmy LaJoy. As the season progressed, he began to assert himself as one of city and conference's most dominant players. He scored 20 points in a 74-60 loss to Weaver, and he followed up with another 20 point performance in a 70-50 win over Bulkeley. At the end of the season he was an All-Capital District Conference selection, and he still had two more years to build on his growing legacy.

Ted Rush was named captain of the Owls' basketball team as a junior. Playing alongside a solid group of veterans that included Cleve May, Berone Richardson, Clarence Knight, Ralph Storey, and promising sophomore Bill Brown, Ted Rush hoped to improve on the team's 11-6 record the previous season. A close and tense 86-82 loss to defending Class LL state champion Hillhouse in New Haven, gave evidence that the Owls were ready to challenge the elite teams in the state. In a City Series game against Bulkeley, Hartford Public improved to 6-3 on the season with an 80-45 win. Ted Rush led the Owls' attack with 21 points, followed closely by Clarence Knight's 20. But three straight losses followed the Bulkeley win, including an 83-80 defeat to New Britain, despite Ted Rush's 28-point, 14-rebound effort. The Owls appeared in jeopardy of falling out of tournament contention, when Ted Rush stepped up his game by recording 33 points and 13 rebounds in a 92-71 win over a depleted Weaver team that was missing four key players. He scored 22 points in a 64-61 victory over New London and followed up with 28 points in a 64-44 win over Bulkeley, in spite of playing with a sore knee. Ted Rush scored 20 points, including the winning basket on a twisting layup with three seconds left in the game, to beat Weaver 64-62. The win gave Hartford Public the City Series title with a perfect 4-0 record and ignited a seven game winning streak that propelled the Owls into the state tournament. Hartford Public was eliminated in the first round of the tournament by 20-1 Bridgeport Central. Ted Rush once again was named to the All-CDC first team. After his strong season as a junior, he was determined to make a serious run at a state championship in his senior year.

He had his best chance for a title in his senior year when he played on a talented HPHS team that included Kemp Mitchell, Bill Brown, Osee Tolliver, Chuck Cummings, and Bill and Doward Tisdol. The Owls beat South Catholic in the season opener and defeated New Britain 76-67 in the first conference game. Ted Rush led Hartford Public in scoring in the New Britain win with 23 points, and he received support from Doward Tisdol with 19 points, Kemp Mitchell with 16, and Bill Tisdol with 12. Hartford Public easily defeated Enfield 93-58 behind Ted Rush's 18 points, 16 from Doward Tisdol, and 12 from Osee Tolliver. Ted Rush scored 24 points and pulled down 14 rebounds as the Owls improved to 4-0 with an 85-62 win over New London. But even as Hartford Public raced out to a fast start of the season, a dominant Weaver team was having no problem keeping pace, beating teams by sizable margins and scoring at a blistering pace. It was one of the best Weaver teams in the school's history, featuring a talented lineup that included Dennis Mink, Myron Goggins, Lee Otis Wilson, Keith Morgan, Owen Mahorn, Dave Tyson, Bob Lomax, Vincent Hylton, and Keith Price. The two powerful teams from Hartford were on a collision course to see who could prevail in the city, conference, and state.

In the first meeting of the season between Hartford Public and Weaver, the Owls maintained their perfect 10-0 record in the conference by beating the Beavers 60-57. Hartford Public continued to pile up the wins with an 86-61 thrashing of Bulkeley, a game in which Ted Rush scored 16 points and grabbed 16 rebounds. Although only about 6'- 2", Ted Rush was able to use his excellent timing and exceptional leaping ability to out-rebound taller opponents throughout his career. Given his outstanding shooting touch, it came as no surprise when he surpassed the 1,000 point plateau, but his uncanny ability to secure rebounds remained one of the team's most valuable assets.

When Hartford Public faced Weaver in the second meeting of the season, the Beavers played an inspired game to hand the Owls their first City Series and CDC loss, 103-81. Ted Rush had a strong game with 24 points and 23 rebounds, but it was not enough to overcome Weaver's balanced scoring attack and substantial rebounding advantage. Sophomore Keith Morgan paced the Beavers with 31 points. Lee Otis Wilson added 20, Dennis Mink contributed 18, and Darwin Jones chipped in with 15. Weaver out-rebounded the Owls 72-54, with Keith Morgan, Lee Otis Wilson, and Dennis Mink each grabbing 13, while Owen Mahorn pulled down 10. Weaver improved to 15-4 with the convincing win that cast a shadow of doubt over Hartford Public's hopes of a championship.

Hartford Public clinched the CDC championship on the final game of the regular season, beating Fitch of Groton 96-67. Doward Tisdol led the Hartford Public offense with 25 points and Ted Rush added 23. The Owls finished the regular season with a 17-2 record, one of the best in school history. After the game Coach John Cuyler spoke to Tom Hine of *The Hartford Courant* about his team's success, "It's been a good year. We were inexperienced to start with, but I'm satisfied with the way the kids came on … more than satisfied. We've had some high points. Teddy Rush broke the 1,000 point mark; Bill Brown, who missed our last few games after an operation, won about six games for us all by himself; Chuckie Cummings has come on real well, the Tisdol brothers, Osee Tollliver, Kemp Mitchell. All of them have. I'm very satisfied." But senior captain Ted Rush was not ready for his season to end. He had his sights set on a championship as the Owls headed to the state tournament.

In the first round of the CIAC Class LL tournament, Hartford Public defeated Danbury 87-66. Doward Tisdol scored 26 points and grabbed 20 rebounds. Ted Rush also had a strong game, scoring 18 points and hauling in 23 rebounds. Hartford Public won the next two games in the tournament, defeating Norwich in the quarterfinals and Roger Ludlowe in the semifinals, to advance to the championship game against arch rival

Weaver. It was only the second time in history that two schools from Hartford met in the finals, with Hartford Public beating Bulkeley in the first encounter in 1962. The game was played at the University of Connecticut in Storrs in front of a capacity crowd. The two teams were evenly matched, with Weaver holding a height advantage and Hartford Public possessing an edge in quickness. The game came down to the final shot to decide the winner. With seconds remaining on the clock, Myron Goggins hit a 17-foot jump shot to give Weaver a thrilling 88-86 victory. Keith Morgan led Weaver in scoring with 30 points, Lee Otis Wilson scored 21, Bob Lomax had 12, and Myron Goggins scored 12, including the game winning basket. Ted Rush scored 29 points and grabbed 16 rebounds to pace the Owls in the final game of his remarkable high school career.

Ted Rush was named the Class LL state tournament Most Valuable Player and he was selected to the All-State team. He was a three-time All-City and All-CDC selection. After he graduated from Hartford Public, he attended Florida A&M, the alma mater of his basketball coach, John Cuyler. But after a successful freshman year, he was sidelined by a knee injury that ended his college career in basketball and track and field. He left Florida A&M and returned to Hartford. He resumed playing basketball in various leagues, including a stint with the Bay State Bombardiers of the Continental Basketball Association. Eventually he relocated to St. Petersburg, Florida with his wife, Evelyn, and their four children. In 2016 Ted Rush was inducted into the Hartford Public High School Athletic Hall of Fame for his accomplishments in track and field and basketball. He was the rare athlete that soared to great heights in two sports.

Owen Mahorn
Weaver High School 1972

In the early 1970s one of the best summer leagues in New England was held at Crompton Park in Worcester, Massachusetts. The rosters of the ten teams in the league were filled with the names of current and former collegians from schools throughout the New England region, players like Billy Evans, Jim O'Brien, and Terry Driscoll from Boston College, Mike Boylan and John Grochowalski from nearby Division II power Assumption College, Marvin Safford, a local high school All-American who played at the University of Southern California, and Ed Siudet and King Gaskins from Holy Cross. Players from UConn, Providence College, and UMass regularly drove to Worcester for the chance to play against elite competition. Crompton Park was like Keney Park on steroids, not so much for the level of talent – Keney Park regulars could hold their own against any teams in New England – but just for the sheer number of quality players that were attracted to the league, including many that went on to play professionally or semi-professionally once their college careers ended.

One team in the Worcester Parks Summer League, Charlie's Surplus, consisted mainly of players that were either from Hartford or had played college ball in Hartford. Charlie Epstein, a Worcester entrepreneur and basketball fan, had heard about a team from Hartford that was dominating the highly competitive Enfield Summer League, and he contacted the team's coach, Andy Gwodz, to ask if the team would like to come to Worcester to represent Charlie's Surplus in the city's summer league. The players agreed, and soon they were making weekly trips to Worcester. The original team included Ken and Augie Gwozdz, Wayne Augustine, Larry Franchoise, and Coach Gordie McCullough, all from the University of Hartford, John Lee from Weaver and Linfield College, and Howie Greenblatt from Weaver and Trinity College, although players like Wayne Jones and Cleve Royster, both from Weaver High and Niagara University, and Fran Laffin from South Catholic and St. Michael's would later be added to the mix. John Lee, a coach and teacher at Weaver at the time, brought Owen Mahorn along with him to Worcester in his sleek Dodge Charger. John Lee had become a mentor to Owen and helped him develop into the exceptional player who led his Weaver team to the state championship in 1971 as a junior.

At 6'- 4" and 235 pounds, Owen Mahorn was a match-up nightmare for opposing teams at Crompton Park. He was too big and strong for guards to contain, yet too quick and agile for big men to guard on the perimeter. The tall front-court of the Charlie's Surplus team allowed Owen Mahorn to play the guard position, where he was comfortable handling the ball and utilizing his unique abilities to maximum advantage.

Amidst all the great players competing at Crompton Park, Owen Mahorn stood out for his athleticism, raw talent, and instinctive feel for the game. Spectators in the stands, in awe of his dazzling display of basketball virtuosity, clamored to know who he was and where he was from. Most of the local fans assumed he was a big time college player from another region of the country who had thus far eluded their attention. Opposing players were amazed to learn he was still in high school and talked to him after the games, trying to entice him to consider giving their own colleges a look. His teammates, all college graduates, encouraged him to stay laser-focused on basketball and academics, predicting he had a legitimate shot at a future NBA career. His legend grew with every game, as word spread of his prodigious talent, and more fans from the Worcester area flocked to Crompton Park for a first-hand view of a basketball prodigy. Mark Epstein and his brother Bob grew up around Crompton Park watching their father Charlie's teams compete. Mark Epstein called Owen Mahorn the most dominant player he had ever seen in the Worcester Summer League – high school, college, or pro. Basketball fans in Worcester were learning what people in Hartford already knew; Owen Mahorn was a remarkable basketball talent seemingly destined for greatness.

Owen Mahorn grew up in Bellevue Square with his sisters Pamela and Audrey, his younger brother Ricky, and his mother Alice. By the time he was in the seventh grade, Owen began to show outstanding promise as a basketball player. His Northwest Jones team beat perennial power Brackett Northeast for the Junior High School City Championship. He credited Doc Hurley, a towering presence at Northwest Jones and throughout the city, for setting him on a solid course for the future by teaching him that success in basketball required hard work, a team-oriented approach, and a dedication to doing well in the classroom. During the summer he played in the Hartford Parks and Recreation League with some of his future teammates at Weaver like Dennis Mink and Myron Goggins. He also became friends with Bill Brown, a future rival at Hartford Public. Although

Brackett Northeast reclaimed the championship when Owen was in eighth grade, he had indicated he was on his way to becoming a major force on the Hartford basketball scene.

Even before he arrived at Weaver, Owen Mahorn was familiar with the mystique that surrounded the high school's basketball program. He had attended Weaver games, enthralled by the lively atmosphere in the noisy gym, the rhythmic, synchronized dance routines of the cheerleaders, the loud student section rooting for the Weaver team and berating the opposition, the deafening roar that followed a blocked shot or soaring slam. He knew about the bitter rivalries with the other city public high schools, Hartford Public, and Bulkeley, and he was aware of the long drought since the Beavers had last won a state championship. He wanted to be a part of the proud Weaver tradition, and he already possessed the confidence that would make him a difference maker.

As a freshman at Weaver, Owen Mahorn played baseball and football as well as basketball. When he made the football team as a running back on offense and linebacker on defense, the coaches did not have a helmet big enough to fit him and had to borrow one from Trinity College. Owen was easy to spot on the football field, not only for his considerable size, but also for wearing the only gold helmet for the Green-and-White Beavers. But Owen decided early on to focus his athletic prowess solely on his favorite sport, basketball. He led the freshman team to a 10-1 record while also playing for the successful JV team and getting minutes on the varsity squad. John Lee, the legendary three-sport athlete at Weaver and Linfield College who had returned to his high school alma mater as a teacher and coach, took an interest in Owen and helped him establish the work ethic he would need to gain admittance to college when the time came.

The summer following his productive freshman year, he attended a two-week summer program at the Hotchkiss School that enabled inner-city student-athletes to experience an educational and athletic environment similar to the one on a college campus. He also played in the Parks and Recreation League, continuing to develop his multi-faceted game, and he worked for the Community Renewal Team in Keney Park. Owen was fortunate in the early stages of his life to have individuals like John Lee and Doc Hurley and institutions like The Hotchkiss School, the Parks and Recreation Department, and CRT assisting him to gain access to a college education.

In his sophomore year Owen Mahorn emerged as a valuable starter for first-year varsity coach John Lambert. Coach Lambert inherited a strong Weaver team from Frank Scelza, who had accepted an administration position at Bulkeley High. In his three years as the JV coach, John Labert had lost only two games each season, and the players he had nurtured on the junior varsity level formed the nucleus of his first varsity team. In addition to sophomore Owen Mahorn, the Beavers were led by Lee Otis Wilson, Dennis Mink, Myron Goggins, Alfie Williams, Herbie Johnson, Lee Hunt, and Bob Lomax, with freshman sensation Keith Morgan beginning to assert himself as a key component by the end of the season. But the Beavers were still a year away from making a serious run at a state championship.

Weaver finished the 1969-70 season with an underwhelming 11-7 record, reflecting the team's inconsistent play. Weaver trounced Bulkeley 90-45 in the first meeting of the season between the city rivals, yet in the second game the Bulldogs pulled within eight points of the Beavers with 6:50 left in the game, before fading at the end in a 69-55 loss that was closer than the final score would indicate. Weaver was led in scoring by Lee Otis Wilson with 27 points, Dennis Mink with 19, Myron Goggins with 11, and Owen Mahorn with 8. A few nights later Weaver defeated East Catholic 76-68 in a non-conference game to raise its season record to 8-3. Dennis Mink led Weaver with 21 points, while Owen Mahorn scored 15 points, Bob Lomax 14, and Myron Goggins 12. East Catholic, playing without the team's captain, Tim Kearns, was led by Tom Juknis' 16 points as the team's record fell to 11-3.

As the season progressed, Weaver's sporadic play continued. Against Hartford Public, in a crucial conference showdown, the Owls defeated Weaver soundly, 92-71, behind 33 points from Ted Rush, 20 from Clarence Knight, and 14 from Kemp Mitchell. For Weaver, Myron Goggins scored 17 points and recorded 13 rebounds, while Lee Hunt and Dennis Mink each scored 12 points, Lee Otis Wilson 11, and Owen Mahorn 10. As a sophomore, Owen showed that he did not need to have a big scoring night to impact a game. Playing at the guard position with Weaver's big front line, his steady ball-handling, accurate passing, and calm leadership were indispensable to the team. Although he was capable of an offensive eruption in any game, he always let the game come to him. If his team was doing well without his scoring output, he was content to distribute the ball to his teammates and contribute in other areas. But he seldom failed to produce big rebounding numbers, even if he was having a quiet night scoring the basketball. His dominance on the boards was a key factor in Weaver's success, often providing the difference between victory and defeat. As the 1969-70 season drew to a disappointing end for the Beavers, the team's balanced scoring and Owen Mahorn's continued development as a solid scorer and dominant rebounder boded well for Weaver's future.

At the start of the 1970-71 basketball season, Weaver unveiled a devastating lineup that few teams in the state could hope to match. The team started 6'-4" junior Owen Mahorn and 6'-0" sophomore Keith Morgan at the guard positions, 6'-5" senior Myron Goggins and 6'-3" senior Lee Otis Wilson at the forward positions, and 6'-6" senior Dennis Mink at center. Among the key reserves were 6'-3" junior Dave Tyson and 6'-3" senior Darwin Jones in the frontcourt and 5'-9" junior Vincent Hylton, 6'-0" senior Bob Lomax, and 6'-0" junior Keith Price in the backcourt. It was one of the strongest, deepest, and most versatile teams in the school's history. The Beavers jumped out to a fast start, winning 11 of the first 12 games, the only loss coming against a tough Norwich Free Academy team. But, as usual, the fate of Weaver's basketball season rested on how well the team would fare against arch-rival Hartford Public. Weaver went into the first meeting at the end of January at a distinct disadvantage, forced to play the game without senior guard Bob Lomax and swingman Lee Otis Wilson, the team's leading scorer. It would have been a tough assignment to beat the 12-1 Owls under any circumstances; yet in the absence of Lomax and Wilson, the task was made even more daunting. Coach Lambert attempted to depart from the team's usual fast-paced, free-wheeling style in favor of a slower, more deliberate approach. The strategy failed to pay dividends as Hartford Public jumped out to an early lead and held off a late Weaver rally to win 60-57. It was the fourth consecutive win for Hartford Public against Weaver. The Owls were led by Bill Brown, making only his second start of the season, with 15 points. Ted Rush, who left the game for a while after a collision with Myron Goggins, contributed 14 points. Osee Tolliver, playing a dazzling floor game while setting up his teammates with pinpoint passes, added 10 points, the same number as Doward Tisdol. For Weaver, Owen Mahorn scored 10 points and grabbed 15 rebounds, helping the Beavers out-rebound the Owls 45-31 for the game. Keith Morgan scored 17 points and Myron Goggins added 14 points and 10 rebounds. With the loss to Hartford Public a shadow of uncertainty was cast over a season that had begun with so much promise.

Weaver bounced back from the defeat to Hartford Public with a 92-67 victory over Norwich, avenging a 73-68 loss earlier in the season. In the continued absence of Lee Otis Wilson, the other four regular starters all came up big, with Keith Morgan scoring 24 points, Dennis Mink adding 22 points and 13 rebounds, Myron Goggins with 14 points and 15 rebounds, and Owen Mahorn with 12 points and 14 rebounds. Although Weaver improved to a 13-3 record, the team's momentum was short-lived. Facing the undefeated Hilltoppers of Bridgeport Central, a team coached by former UConn star Tom Penders and led by 6'- 6" senior center Rich Semo, Weaver went down to defeat, 97-88. With only a few weeks left before the start of the state tournament, it remained unclear if Weaver could right the ship in time to make a run at a championship that had eluded the team since the Johnny Egan era.

In the rematch between Weaver and Hartford Public, the Beavers served notice that they had not given up on their quest for a state title. With Lee Otis Wilson reinstated, the Beavers had their full arsenal of lethal weapons back on the court again. Keith Morgan scored 31 points in leading Weaver to a 103-81 win. Ted Rush scored 24 points and pulled down 23 rebounds in a losing effort. Weaver won the rebounding battle 72-54, once again showing the team's dominance on the boards. Over the course of the season, Weaver and Hartford Public had shown they were two of the best teams in the state. As the regular season was winding down, a third meeting between the two teams in the state tournament loomed as a distinct possibility.

In the opening round of the 1971 CIAC Class LL State Tournament, Weaver defeated Stamford 93-83. Owen Mahorn scored 18 points and pulled down 16 rebounds, Dennis Mink had 29 points and 16 rebounds in one of the most dominating performances of his productive career, Myron Goggins had 14 points and 10 rebounds, Lee Otis Wilson scored 14 points, and Keith Morgan scored 12 points. The Weaver victory set up a quarter-final matchup against Lee High of New Haven, a team that had pulled off the biggest upset of the tournament by defeating top-ranked Bridgeport Central, 81-75. In the game against Lee High, Lee Otis Wilson must have thought the contest was set up in his honor because of the shared first name. He came off the bench with Weaver trailing 15-5 with a little over three minutes remaining in the first quarter and proceeded to go on a scoring rampage, hitting 14 of 25 field goal attempts and 9 of 10 foul shots for a total of 37 points in an 81-69 win. With Lee Otis Wilson controlling the scoring, aided by Keith Morgan's 18 points and 13 from Dennis Mink, Owen Mahorn was able to concentrate on the boards. Battling Lee High's 6'- 7" center Calvin Carrington, Owen, who only scored four points in the game, grabbed 22 rebounds, while Myron Goggins and Lee Otis Wilson had 12 boards each as Weaver's dominance of the backboards in the tournament continued.

The victory over Lee High set up a meeting with always-dangerous Wilbur Cross in the semi-finals. In a game for the ages that many fans fortunate enough to get inside the packed Quinnipac gym called the best in the 49 year history of the tournament, the two rivals battled to the bitter end. With six seconds remaining in the game and Wilbur Cross leading by one point, Keith Morgan found Bob Lomax underneath the basket with a stunningly precise pass to give Weaver a 94-93 victory. It was Weaver's second one point win of the season over Wilbur Cross. Lee Otis Wilson once again led the Weaver scoring with 26 points, but Keith Morgan chipped in with 22, Dennis Mink 15, Owen Mahorn 11, and Myron Goggins 10 in a typically balanced attack. The Beavers hit on 50 percent of their shots. Wilbur Cross was led by the team's two All-State performers, Roland Jones and Mickey Heard with 31 and 30 points respectively. Owen Mahorn pulled down 21 rebounds, giving him a staggering 43 boards in the past two games, both against rugged New Haven teams. Wilbur Cross' season ended with a 17-5 record. Weaver, 16-4, advanced to face 17-2 Hartford Public in the finals.

In the long history of the rivalry between Weaver and Hartford Public, the schools had never met in the finals of the state tournament. The two teams were extremely evenly matched. Both possessed outstanding, quick guards, fine shooters, and fierce rebounders. If Hartford Public had an advantage in the first meeting when neither Bob Lomax nor Lee Otis Wilson played, Weaver enjoyed an edge in the finals, since Bill Brown was out for the season with an injury and Bill Tisdol was not at full strength. Weaver had a height advantage, but Hartford Public had an edge in quickness. The 2,231 fans that packed into the UConn Field House expected a close, intense, hard-fought game, and they were not disappointed. The teams were tied 16 times, and they were never separated by more than seven points. In the end Weaver edged Hartford Public 88-86 on a jump shot by Myron Goggins in the closing seconds of the game. Owen Mahorn had come up with the biggest rebound of the game, grabbing a Doward Tisdol miss with 19 seconds to play to give Weaver a final possession that resulted in the winning basket by Myron Goggins. The jubilant Beavers cut down the nets, celebrating one of the finest moments in the school's history.

Weaver opened defense of its CIAC Class LL State Championship the following season with a convincing 97-74 win over Norwalk High School. Keith Morgan scored 28 points, Owen Mahorn 25 points, and Mike Harris, making his first varsity start, scored 21. But a week later, Weaver fell 89-80 to a high-powered Wilbur Cross team determined to bring the state title back to New Haven at the end of the season. Sophomore Jiggy Williamson led Wilbur Cross with 25 points, while Mickey Heard scored 20 points, Roland Jones 21, and George Powell 21. Co-captain Owen Mahorn led the Beavers with 23 points and 18 rebounds. Wilbur Cross coach Bob Saulsbury singled out Leroy Williams, who did not score in the game, for a fine defensive job against Owen Mahorn. The tactic of playing a box-and-one to slow down Owen Mahorn became a regular feature of the 1971-72 season. Bulkeley Coach Joe DiChara tried a similar strategy in his team's second game against Weaver, after losing the first game 64-44. He used guard Pete Palermino to shadow Owen Mahorn the entire game and nearly pulled off the upset before bowing 52-50. Owen was held to seven points, while fighting strep throat in addition to the mongrel defense, while Keith Morgan picked up the slack with 17 points, including the game winning shot. Bulkeley was let by Steve Snyder's 15 points, Ron LaVigne's 14, and Pete Palermino's 13. In the next game against East Catholic, Owen was sidelined by strep throat, and the Beavers lost by two points, 51-49.

Although Weaver defeated Bulkeley twice, the team lost twice during the regular season to a Hartford Public team intent on avenging the two-point loss in the state championship game the previous March. In the first meeting, with Owen Mahorn still sidelined with strep throat and a fever, the Owls romped to a 97-68 victory. In the second game of the season between Weaver and HPHS, Doward Tisdol erupted for 38 points, Nick Oliver scored 22, Osee Tolliver 15, and Bill Brown had 10 points and 14 rebounds to defeat the Beavers 89-79. Keith Morgan scored 28 points for Weaver, while Rufus Oten came off the bench to score 21 points.

Owen Mahorn scored 16 points and pulled down 11 rebounds, but it was not enough to overcome Weaver's foul trouble and Hartford Public's inspired defensive effort. The Owls clinched the City Series and raised the team's record to 16-1, while Weaver fell to 14-4. The two teams met for a third time in the quarter-finals of the Class LL state tournament in a game played at the University of Hartford. The Beavers fought back from a 10 point deficit before falling to the Owls 69-67. Owen Mahorn scored 18 points and grabbed 27 rebounds and Keith Morgan scored 32 points and pulled down 12 rebounds, but Hartford Public's balanced scoring attack, led by Doward Tisdol's 18 points, Nick Oliver's 17, Bill Brown's 14, and Osee Tolliver's 11 proved to be the difference in the game.

With the defeat to Hartford Public in the tournament, Owen Mahorn's dazzling high school career came to an end. As a senior he had averaged 22 points and 18 rebounds a game and was a first-team All-State selection. He received All-American recognition and was named one of the top 100 high school players in the nation. He received an athletic scholarship to attend Fairfield University, where he played basketball for two years. As a freshman he averaged 10.4 points and 14 rebounds per game, coming off the bench. He scored a season high 24 points in an 82-75 win over St. Bonaventure, hitting 90 per cent of his shots from the field and six of seven attempts from the foul line. Owen became a starter as a sophomore, averaging 15.5 points per game and leading the team in rebounding with 8.2 per game, playing alongside 6'- 9" Steve Balkun from Northwest Catholic and 6'- 9" Mark Plefka from East Hartford High School, Fairfield's leading scorer. After he left Fairfield he returned to Hartford, where he continued to amaze local basketball fans for years with his play in leagues around the state. Hartford's "Big O" passed away after a long illness on March 11, 2015 at the age of 61. His funeral service at Fuqua Funeral Home in Bloomfield was attended by numerous friends, former teammates and coaches, and adoring family members, paying tribute to one of Hartford's most admired and beloved athletes.

Sadiq Ali

(formerly Bill Brown)

Hartford Public High School 1972

Bill Brown began his freshman year at Hartford Public High School in 1968, only months after Dr. Martin Luther King, Jr. had been killed in Memphis, Tennessee. Dr. King's assassination sparked unrest in cities across the United States, including Hartford. Two days after the assassination, Walter "Doc" Hurley was teaching a Physical Education class at Northwest Jones Junior High, when he was interrupted by school officials and asked to go immediately to Weaver High School to try to deal with a crowd of about 500 students that had gathered outside the school. When he arrived at Weaver, Doc Hurley told the students that they were not going to destroy the school, because without the school they would have no place to receive an education. The critical importance of education, especially for African American student-athletes seeking to improve their lives, was one of Doc Hurley's guiding principles and a cause to which he devoted most of his life. He perpetually advised the students he encountered in the parks and in the schools to come up with a plan for their lives, a plan that included a college education. Educational opportunities in the African American community would become a dominant concern for Bill Brown as well, and the central focus of his life's work.

He became aware of the importance of education at an early age. The concept of prioritizing academics was driven home to him by his parents and grandfather. They constantly reminded him how difficult it was for them to make a living. Neither his grandfather nor his father had completed high school, yet they were hard working, principled, and devoted family men. Bill Brown wanted them to be proud of him, and he understood that the key to earning their respect was to be successful academically as well as athletically. His family provided early motivation for him to work hard in the classroom and on the basketball court.

Bill Brown began playing basketball in the seventh grade, thanks to the influence of his friend and future high school rival, Owen Mahorn. Since he had started relatively late, he had his work cut out for him to catch up to Owen and some of the other boys he knew who represented Stowe Village in the Parks and Recreation League, future Weaver High basketball standouts like Michael Lomax, Myron Goggins, and Dennis Mink. According to Bill Brown, Dennis Mink in particular was a special basketball player, capable of dominating the kids in his age group. Two of the mentors in his youth that helped Bill Brown learn to compete against his more experienced peers were his coaches Dexter Williams-Bey and Freddy Blocker. Bill Brown claimed that Freddy Blocker was a great motivator. "He saw something in me that I didn't see in myself," Brown said. Freddy Blocker taught Bill Brown to go all out pursuing rebounds. "Before my other skills took root," Bill Brown said, "I was a good rebounder first. The offensive boards were my specialty." Tenacious, aggressive rebounding would become a Bill Brown trademark at both Hartford Public High School and the University of Hartford.

In his first year at Hartford Public, Bill Brown led the freshman team in scoring and rebounding. As a sophomore, he was so dominant at the JV level that he was quickly promoted to the varsity team and became a starter. In only his second start of the season, the Owls faced Weaver in a key City Series match up in front on 2,200 fans in the Hartford Public gym on Forest Street. Hartford Public was undefeated in the Capital District Conference with a 9-0 record, while Weaver was right behind the Owls in the conference standings at 9-1.

It was a typically hard-fought, rugged, and intense game between the two city rivals, but unlike most of the previous games between the schools that turned into high-scoring, fast-paced affairs, Weaver, playing without two key starters, seniors Bob Lomax and Lee Otis Wilson, attempted to slow the game down. But the Owls did not let the slower tempo of the game disturb their offensive rhythm, defeating the Beavers 60-57 for their fourth straight victory over Weaver. Bill Brown played the entire game and finished with 15 points and 10 rebounds, both team highs. Ted Rush, who sat out a portion of the second quarter after a hard collision had knocked him out of the game, scored 15 points, Doward Tisdol 10, Osee Tolliver 10, and Bill Tisdol seven points. For Weaver Keith Morgan scored 17 points, Myron Goggins 14, and Own Mahorn had 10 points and 15 rebounds. It was Hartford Public's biggest win of the season, and Bill Brown played a key role in lifting the team to victory.

After a successful sophomore season, Bill Brown expected that his junior year would be even better. The reason for his optimism was an outstanding group of teammates that included Kemp Mitchell, Chuck Cummings, Ted

Rush, and Bill and Doward Tisdol. But his hopes of competing for a state championship were dashed when he strained ligaments in his ankle and was limited to half a season. Even without Bill Brown to anchor the center position, the team was strong enough to make a deep run in the state tournament, before falling to arch rival Weaver in the finals, 88-86. Bill Brown was left to ponder what might have happened if he had been healthy enough to play in the finals. He had success against Weaver in the past, thriving on the opportunity to play against friends like Owen Mahorn, Dennis Mink, and Myron Goggins. The Owls narrow loss to Weaver in the 1971 finals served as motivation for Bill Brown to come back stronger for his senior year and compete for another state championship.

The 1971-72 Hartford Public team was quick, talented, and intent on avenging the defeat to Weaver the previous March in the state championship game. In his senior year the 6'- 3" Bill Brown had emerged as one of the most feared rebounders in the state, capable of dominating the backboards, even against considerably taller opponents. In a mid-season City Series game against Bulkeley, Bill Brown scored 21 points and led all rebounders with 18, as he and Doward Tisdol (21 points and 14 rebounds) contributed to the Owls decisive 53-27 advantage on the boards. Hartford Public won the game 75-63, improving to 9-0 on the season. Bulkeley stayed close most of the game, but the Owls punishing effort on the backboards wore the Bulldogs down and created foul problems for their big men. The Bulkeley guards, Steve Snyder and Pete Palermino, led the Bulldogs in scoring with 16 and 15 points respectively. Forward Ron LaVigne scored 12 points and center Jerry Devine scored 10 points, before both fouled out in the fourth quarter. The Bulldogs learned the same lesson that every Hartford Public opponent was forced to absorb – as long as Bill Brown was crashing the boards, the Owls would be a very tough team to beat.

As satisfying as a victory over Bulkeley in the City Series was for the Owls, Weaver was the team they had in their sights the entire season. Hartford Public beat Weaver twice during the regular season, setting up a quarter-final showdown in the state tournament. The Owls had been down this same path in the past, dominating Weaver on their home court in the regular season, only to fall short in the state tournament, losing an elimination game on a neutral court. It was the scenario that unfolded in 1966 and again in 1971. But this time Hartford Public would not be denied. Behind a balanced scoring attack, the Owls eked out a 69-67 win.

Doward Tisdol led the team in scoring with 18 points, while Bill Brown scored 14 points and pulled down 14 rebounds. Nick Oliver contributed 17 points, Osee Tolliver 11, and Daryl Brown nine points. "We've been doing that all year – balanced scoring," Hartford Public coach John Cuyler told *Courant* sports writer Woody Anderson after the game. "And all the close games we've won. The kids just won't give up." The team's record improved to 20-1, and with Weaver out of the way, the chances of returning to the championship game for the second straight year looked promising. Weaver finished with a 17-5 record, with three of the losses coming at the hands of the Owls. The Beavers had fought valiantly in their final game, fighting back from a 10 point deficit with 3:20 left in the fourth quarter, only to come up two points short, largely on a botched inbounds pass that struck the rafters in the University of Hartford gym. Keith Morgan scored 32 points and recorded 12 rebounds for the Beavers, while Owen Mahorn had 18 points and pulled down an amazing 27 rebounds. Weaver out-rebounded Hartford Public 62-47 in another classic match-up in the intense rivalry.

Hartford Public's hopes for a state championship ended with an 83-77 loss to Wilbur Cross in the finals. The Owls finished 21-2, with both losses to Wilbur Cross. Bill Brown, Doward Tisdol, Nick Oliver, Osee Tolliver, Keith Knight, and Daryl Brown formed the core of one of the best teams in the school's history. In the state finals, however, the Owls were up against one of the best Wibur Cross teams ever. The victory by Wilbur Cross would mark the first of three consecutive state titles, culminating in the 2004 state championship by a team that was considered the number one high school team in the country.

From 2001–2003 Hartford Public made it to the Class LL state finals each year, only to lose the championship game. As a senior in 2002, consecutive defeats in the state finals were a bitter pill for Bill Brown to swallow. Yet thanks to his strong work ethic and his consistent effort in the classroom, Bill Brown's basketball career was far from over. He was recruited by such schools as Davidson College, Central Connecticut State College, the University of Hartford, and UConn. During the recruiting process, he had been impressed by a charismatic assistant coach at the University of Connecticut by the name of Jim Valvano, who would go on to win a national championship as the head coach at North Carolina State University in 1983. But in the end Bill Brown decided to attend the

University of Hartford, where he would become one of the finest players in the history of the school.

Over his four year career at the University of Hartford, Bill Brown scored 1,023 points and recorded 651 rebounds. He played in three Division II NCAA Tournaments. During his first three years at the University of Hartford, Bill Brown teamed with Pete Egan to provide the team with a devastating rebounding tandem. In a 79-74 win over Southern Connecticut State University, Pete Egan scored 28 points and grabbed 14 rebounds while Bill Brown hit for 20 points and pulled down 18 rebounds. It was the kind of overpowering performance on the backboards that made the Hawks such a difficult team to contain. As a senior co-captain, Bill Brown led the Hawks in rebounding with 10.4 boards per game and was the second leading scorer with 13.9 points per game. In a game against city rival Trinity College, Bill Brown scored 17 points and added 11 rebounds in an 85-81 win, recording yet another double-double. In his final home appearance of his college career, Bill Brown scored 19 points as the Hawks edged Williams College 80-79 to become the fifth player in University of Hartford history to reach 1,000 points, joining the select group of Gary Palladino, Pete Egan, Ken Gwozdz, and Wayne Augustine. The victory gave Coach Gordon McCullough the 200th win of his career.

Gordie McCullough would retire at the end of the season after 14 seasons as the head basketball coach with a career record of 201-117, giving him the most wins in the school's history. He led the Hawks to nine straight winning seasons. He stayed on as the Director of Athletics and golf coach after his standout basketball coaching career. After the Williams College game Bill Brown told sports writer Terry Price of *The Hartford Courant* that he had felt a lot of pressure at the start of the game, not because he was in reach of scoring 1,000 points, but rather that he wanted to make sure that Coach McCullough secured his 200th victory. In typical Bill Brown fashion, he was able to set aside the distractions of the dual milestones and focus on what he did best – play intense, winning basketball.

After graduating from the University of Hartford, Bill Brown became a teacher in the Hartford school system and a recreation coordinator at the Rawson School summer program. He continued to play competitive basketball well into his 40s, and he was a founding member of the Greater Hartford Over-Thirty League. His commitment to bettering the lives of students in Hartford never wavered. He founded the Benjamin E. Mays

Institute in 1995, an all-male African American academy at Fox Middle School in Hartford for seventh and eighth grade students. In 2015 he published *Benjamin E. Mays Institute: Educating Young Black Males* under the name he adopted when he became a Muslim, Sadiq Ali. The book describes the creation of the school in Hartford and the lessons he learned from the experience of implementing his educational philosophy. In 2016 he organized the Black Male Education Summit that was held at Virginia State University, where Doc Hurley was educated. He resides in Richmond, Virginia with his wife and daughter. As an athlete, educator, author, consultant, and mentor, Sadiq Ali made an indelible impression on the city of Hartford.

Jack Phelan
Northwest Catholic High School 1972

As a kid growing up in Hartford, Jack Phelan enjoyed tagging along with his older brother Kenny on excursions to neighborhood parks where they could always find other boys eager to play basketball. They played games of two-on-two, three-on-three, or if there were enough guys around, they would pick sides, divide up into skins and shirts, and run full court. For Jack it was a pleasure to hang around with his brother, and playing pick-up basketball on asphalt courts was a perfect way to spend long afternoons that often extended into evenings, until it grew too dark to see the ball and everyone would head home. The Phelan brothers were athletic and competitive and they could hold their own against any kids their own age and many that were older. They took the games seriously and always played to win, with a fierce determination that made them difficult to beat. The Phelan brothers only knew one way to compete, and that was all-out, with maximum effort on every play. The only way to stay on the court, especially with older players, was to keep winning. The intense mindset gave them a competitive edge that would enable them to be successful as they moved on to high school and college. Throughout his life Jack Phelan was able to sustain the youthful passion he assimilated playing basketball with his brother Kenny. He was permanently hooked on hoops.

Jack Phelan's father worked at Pratt & Whitney and his mother was a nurse who worked for many years at St. Joseph Cathedral, where the family worshipped. Jack attended St. Joseph Cathedral School on Asylum Avenue. He has fond memories of his teachers at the school, primarily Sisters of Mercy who instilled in him the values of faith, family, and a strong work ethic. His first experience in organized basketball came from playing on the school's CYO team. The team went 24-0 and won the CYO New England Championship. He showed sufficient promise to make his grammar-school team as a fourth grader. He also played on the Elizabeth Park team in the Hartford Parks and Recreation League that won the city championship in the Pee Wee division, beating the team from Love Lane Park. He thrived on the experience of winning championships and set his sights on continuing the practice when he reached high school.

As a freshman at Northwest Catholic High School, Jack Phelan played for Coach Lee Callahan on a team that finished third behind Hartford Public and Weaver in the City Series League for freshman teams. He was a starting forward on Coach Charlie Larson's varsity team as a sophomore, playing alongside juniors Peter Egan and Chuck Harding and seniors Dick Fairbrother and Jim Akin, all future college standouts at area schools, Egan and Harding at the University of Hartford and Fairbrother and Akin at Wesleyan University. The team was riding a nine game winning streak going into the semi-finals of the CIAC Class L State Tournament against a powerful South Catholic team that had beaten Northwest Catholic twice during the regular season. The game was played in front of a packed house at Central Connecticut State as part of a double header, with East Catholic defeating Windham in the opening game 67-61 behind Ed Fitzgerald's 19 points and 17 by Tim Kearns. The night's second game between rivals Northwest Catholic and South Catholic was close throughout, with neither team able to gain separation. But with Ed DelMastro and Fran Laffin helping South win the battle of the boards 51-41, Northwest Catholic could get no closer than one point in the fourth quarter before losing 62-53. Jack Phelan led Northwest Catholic in scoring with 13 points, giving notice, as he had all season long, that he was ready to assume a prominent role in the program's future in the years to come.

Northwest Catholic returned to the semi-final game of the Class L state tournament in Jack Phelan's junior year, facing an undefeated South Windsor team led by the superb big man, Tom Roy. Behind 46 points by their consensus All-State and All-American center, South Windsor defeated Northwest Catholic, ending the Indians' quest for a state title in the semi-final round for the second consecutive year. As a junior Jack Phelan had averaged 15 points and 10 rebounds per game, emerging as one of the best all-around players in the state. At 6'-3" he had the size, quickness, athleticism, leaping ability, and defensive tenacity to excel at multiple positions on the floor. He had some of his best games against the Indians' toughest opponents, like a 16 point, 17 rebound performance in an 80-53 win over South Catholic and a 22 point effort in a narrow 59-55 loss to unbeaten East Catholic. But he was disappointed that his team had once again failed in the attempt to win a state championship, a situation he hoped to rectify in his senior year.

As a senior, Jack Phelan was the captain and leader of a balanced Northwest Catholic team that included Mike Kilmas, Bob Gardner, John

Zalucki, Lenny McIntee, and Brian Hickey. Phelan was literally a Jack-of-all-trades for the Indians, jumping center, handling the ball against pressure defense, anchoring the middle of the 1-3-1 zone or guarding the opponents' top scorer, regardless of position. He was capable of playing every position on the floor, and in the course of the game he frequently shifted from guard, to forward, to center as the situation and circumstances of the game dictated. But he was not only versatile; he was also extremely effective in the clutch. Facing arch rival South Catholic in a key conference match-up at the University of Hartford in front of 1,500 fans, the Indians trailed by nine points at the half. Northwest Catholic fought back to tie the game at the end of regulation and send the contest into overtime. Jack was fouled by South's Steve Farrell with one second left on the clock in overtime. He stepped to the line and sank both foul shots to win the game 62-60. In a close game against Hartford Country Conference rival East Catholic, Jack Phelan took charge late in the game to score seven of the Indians' final 11 points. He finished with a team-leading 15 points and a game-high 17 rebounds, for one of his frequent double-doubles in a 49-42 win. In a game against a solid St. Paul team that had a 14-3 record going into the game, Jack Phelan recorded a triple-double, scoring 21 points, pulling down 19 rebounds, and handing out 12 assists.

But the Indians did not play with the kind of consistency that would indicate they were prepared to make a deep run in the tournament. After beating South Catholic in overtime in their first match-up of the season, Northwest Catholic lost the rematch 58-54, in spite of Jack Phelan's 17 points and 9 rebounds. The same scenario unfolded in the series with East Catholic, with Northwest Catholic winning the first game 49-42 before losing the second game a week later 48-44, when Jack Phelan was held to 10 points after getting into early foul trouble guarding East's 6'-4" center Kevin Tierney, who scored 20 points. But Coach Charlie Larson had intentionally scheduled non-conference games against some of the best teams in the state, like defending Class LL champion Weaver High School and perennial powerhouse Wilbur Cross, in order to prepare his team for the pressure of the state tournament. In a home game against Weaver, Jack battled the Beavers' rugged star Owen Mahorn evenly before fouling out with four and a half minutes left in the game. Without Phelan's ball-handling, passing, scoring, and rebounding, Northwest Catholic could not stay close and lost the game 75-55.

Northwest Catholic played Wilbur Cross twice during the 1971-72 season, losing badly both times. But losing to Wilbur Cross was hardly a disgrace. The Governors from New Haven had one of the best teams in the school's illustrious basketball history. Wilbur Cross featured two sets of two-time All-State players in seniors Mickey Heard and Roland Jones and sophomores Bruce "Soup" Campbell and Jim "Jiggy" Williamson. The team went undefeated and was on the way to capturing three consecutive Class LL State Championships in 1972, 1973, and 1974. The 1974 team, with Campbell and Williamson as seniors, was named by the Washington Post as the best high school team in the country and by the New York Post as "the best high school team in the world." In the first meeting between Northwest Catholic and Wilbur Cross, Roland Jones scored 38 points and pulled down 15 rebounds, while Mickey Heard scored 17 points and grabbed 22 rebounds to pace the Governors' 119-63 win. Jack Phelan left the game in the first quarter with an ankle injury and did not return, ending all hope of a close game. The second game against Wilbur Cross was the regular season finale for both teams. Jiggy Williamson scored 32 points and Soup Campbell had 21 in the Governors' 102-64 win, completing a perfect 20-0 regular season. But Northwest Catholic trailed by only 10 points at the half and had four players in double figures, led by Phelan's 15 points and John Zalucki's 14 to finish the regular season with a deceiving 13-7 record. The Indians had faced the stiffest competition in the state and perhaps in the entire country. There was no team on the horizon that could impress or intimidate them. It was a masterful stroke of scheduling by Coach Larson. Northwest Catholic would not lose another game.

After playing in Class L in past tournaments, the Indians had dropped down to Class M, improving the team's chances of winning a state title. Still, there was no easy path to a state championship in talent-rich Connecticut. Northwest Catholic faced Norwich Tech in the opening round of the tournament, winning comfortably 88-59 behind a balanced scoring attack. Five players scored in double figures for the Indians, with Jack Phelan getting 17 points, Bob Gardner 10, Mike Kilmas 18, John Zalucki 12, and Lenny McIntee 16, while playmaker Brian Hickey scored seven points. The Indians won by combining balanced scoring, hard-nosed defense, and determined rebounding against a bigger opponent, a winning formula that would carry the Indians through the tournament. In the second round Northwest Catholic defeated East Lyme 49-38, overcoming a half-time deficit. In the quarter-finals, Northwest Catholic had to come back once again after trailing at the half to defeat Guilford High School 75-55, with six players scoring in double figures. Concerned about the team's slow start in the early rounds of the tournament, Coach Larson made defensive modifications for the final two games, switching from the zone that had been the team's primary defense to more man-to-man principles. The adjustments paid immediate dividends. The 20th ranked Indians defeated St. Thomas Aquinas in the semi-finals, setting up a Class M finals match-up at the University of Connecticut against the defending champions from Kolbe-Cathedral of Bridgeport and the team's amazing scorer, 6'- 4" guard Walt Luckett.

Walt Luckett averaged 41 points per game as a senior on his way to shattering Tom Roy's New England career scoring mark with 2,691 points. He scored 995 points in his senior year. In the finals against Northwest Catholic, he scored 36 points on 17 of 30 shooting. During one stretch in the second half he scored 18 of his team's 20 points. He also pulled down 14 rebounds. But his stunning individual effort was not enough to overcome the Indians' balanced scoring attack. Jack Phelan, playing one of the finest all-around games of his career on the biggest stage, scored 22 points and grabbed 15 rebounds. He was ably supported by 6'- 3" John Zalucki with 17 points, Bob Gardner with 14, and Mike Kilmas with 10. Northwest Catholic only trailed 37-31 in the rebounding totals against the taller Friars. When Kolbe came within 69-65 with less than a minute to play, Jack Phalen hit four of six foul shots to seal the 72-67 victory. Walt Luckett was named the tournament MVP, but Jack Phelan was able to cut down a piece of the nets for winning the state championship he had coveted.

After he graduated from Northwest Catholic, Jack Phelan attended St. Thomas More of Colchester for a year. The Chancellors won the New England Prep School Championship, Jack's second title in two years. When it came time for him to consider his options for attending college, he hoped to stay in-state, preferably at a school like Fairfield, where his brother Kenny had played, or at UConn, the program he had followed intensely while growing up in Hartford. But although both Fairfield coach Fred Baracat and UConn coach Dee Rowe showed interest in Jack Phalen, neither coach pursued him with sufficient enthusiasm to convince Jack he was a valued recruit. There may have been lingering questions about his weight or his lack of height to play the forward position in college. But the coaches failed to consider the unequaled competitive desire he brought to the game, the inner drive that compelled him to work harder than anyone else in relentless pursuit of excellence. Both Fred Baracat and Dee Rowe would later admit that they had had missed the boat on Jack Phalen and should have recruited him more aggressively.

Jack Phelan ended up attending St. Francis College (now St. Francis University) in Loretto, Pennsylvania, where he had an outstanding career. Dave Magarity, who was an assistant coach at St. Francis College in 1973 and helped recruit Jack, told Jim Shea of *The Hartford Courant* about his first impressions of Jack as a college player: "Jack was bigger then, he looked like a linebacker. We used him at the point, but he could play all five positions. He was a great athlete, but more than anything else, he was a consummate competitor, a killer on the floor." One of the highlights of Jack Phelan's college career was a 42 point outburst against Duquesne University of Pittsburg in his senior year in an 89-85 St. Francis win. Jack hit on 20 of 25 attempts from the floor, a performance that broke Maurice Stokes' single game field goal record and raised his shooting percentage for the season to an uncanny 60.6 per cent. Duquesne featured point-guard Norm Nixon, who averaged 17.2 points, 4 rebounds, and 5.5 assists during his four year college career before going on to a twelve year NBA career that included two championships with the "Showtime" Los Angeles Lakers.

As a senior captain, Jack Phelan led St. Francis to a 15-11 record that included an upset win against a strong UNC-Charlotte team. He averaged 16 points a game as a senior. But his time at St. Francis was also marked by a terrible personal tragedy when his brother Kenny died in an automobile accident on I-84 in Farmington. Jack gave Jim Shea of *The Hartford Courant* an indication of how much his brother meant to him, "He was the person I was closest to. He was my idol. He meant everything in the world to me. To be without him even now is still very tough. I owe everything to him." Kenny's loss was a devastating blow to Jack Phelan and one of his main motivations for eventually moving back to the Hartford area to try to console his mother and sister.

After graduating from St. Francis, Jack Phelan had the rare opportunity to try out for professional teams in two different sports. He was selected in the sixth round of the NBA draft by the Golden State Warriors, but after a promising training camp, he did not stick with the team. He was also invited to attend a tryout for the Pittsburg Steelers in Three Rivers Stadium. Jack had not played football since his sophomore year at Northwest Catholic, where he once scored three touchdowns in a game against Manchester High School, catching six passes for 100 yards, including scoring strikes of 30 and 25 yards, and rushing five yards for another score. But the strength and athleticism he had shown at St. Francis drew the attention of the Steelers' organization, and he was signed to a one-year contract, contingent on making the team as a defensive back. He did not survive the cut, but he was called back again for a second look, a remarkable achievement for someone that had not played a down of football since his sophomore year of high school.

Denied a professional career in either basketball or football, Jack Phelan turned his attention to coaching. He served as an assistant basketball coach at Niagara, St. Francis, and Fairfield before being named the head coach at the University of Hartford in 1981. He described to Jim Shea of *The Hartford Courant* his feelings about returning to Hartford, "It was almost like someone had a hand out steering me back here near my mother (his father died shortly after his brother), my sister ... I was a city of Hartford kid, I'm a native, a hometown boy, that's what I am. It was a great opportunity for me."

He coached at the University of Hartford until 1992, overseeing the school's transition from Division II to Division I. He currently serves as the highly respected Athletic Director at Farmington High School. He has a wide group of friends in the area, including former teammates and opponents while at Northwest Catholic, former players, assistant coaches, and associates from the coaching days at the University of Hartford, and the numerous Farmington High students he had influenced through the years in his capacity as Athletic Director. He remains one of Hartford's most important athletes of his generation.

Keith Morgan
Weaver High School 1973

When Weaver High won the school and the city's first state championship in 1954 and followed up that momentous achievement with back-to-back state titles in 1956 and 1957, the future of the basketball program appeared bright. The triumphant Weaver basketball teams captured the excitement, enthusiasm, and imagination of the entire community. Youngsters throughout the North End played basketball with renewed purpose and determination, hoping someday to duplicate the feats of the mighty Beavers. The basketball teams at Weaver feeder schools like Northwest Jones, Brackett Northeast, Mark Twain, and Rawson, came under increased scrutiny as die-hard fans anxiously awaited the next wave of great players to replenish the pipeline. Household names like Egan, Countryman, McBride, Hurrell, Shannon, Carter, and Sullivan were spoken with reverential pride for the glory they had bestowed on Weaver High School.

But the decade of the sixties brought turmoil rather than exhilaration to the Weaver community. It was an era of strife and violence as the nation was racked by war, civil disobedience, and a wave of assassinations. Medgar Evers, John F. Kennedy, Malcolm X, Martin Luther King, Jr., and Robert Kennedy were all murdered, setting off repeated waves of despair through a shocked society. Unrelenting social, cultural, and political upheaval racked the country. Within Weaver High, the assassination of Dr. Martin Luther King, Jr. on April 4, 1968 raised the anger and frustration in the building to the boiling point as students threatened to tear the school apart. Doc Hurley, who had helped to mold the championship basketball teams as a summer league coach and mentor, was called to Weaver from his Physical Education class at Northwest Jones to try to quell a disturbance by a large group of angry students in front of the school. He was able to convince the students that destroying the school was tantamount to extinguishing their dreams for the future. Weaver survived, but the innocence, optimism, and school pride that had flourished in the fifties, seemed diminished, along with the glowing reputation of the basketball program.

As the sixties unfolded, the Weaver basketball team continued to earn praise as one of the state's elite programs. But when Hartford Public High

School won back-to-back New England High School titles and its first ever state championship in 1962 by beating cross-town rival Bulkeley 67-64, the spotlight clearly shifted away from Weaver to the other city high schools. The Weaver championships receded into the background, overshadowed by Hartford Public's emergence as the new dominant basketball power in the city. The names of the basketball heroes from Weaver that had dominated the fifties were replaced by a new crop of emerging Hartford legends, like Eddie Griffin, Billy Jones, Pat Burke, Stan Poole, and Otis Woods. Weaver made a few gallant attempts during the decade to resurrect the glory days of state basketball dominance. In 1966 the Beavers came within two points of defeating Wilbur Cross for the state championship, and in 1968 Weaver mounted another spirited run at the title, only to lose to a Bob Nash-led Hartford Public team in overtime in the quarter-finals of the state tournament. The 1967-68 Weaver team featured a dynamic starting line-up of Freddie Mathews and Nolan Lewis at guards, Gil Hampton and Doug Morgan at forwards, and Cleve Royster at the center position. Doug Morgan was a reliable scorer and effective rebounder for the Beavers. Like all of his teammates, he was sorely disappointed that Weaver had come up short in its bid for a state title. Doug had a younger brother, Keith, who had followed the Weaver team with interest throughout the season, and Keith shared his brother's frustration with the defeat to Hartford Public in the tournament. It would not be long before Keith Morgan played a major role in reversing Weaver's championship fortunes.

Keith Morgan grew up in Stowe Village with Doug, his two sisters, and his mother, a registered nurse. He began playing basketball with Doug at an early age. When he attended Fred D. Wish Elementary School, he starred on the school's basketball team, along with Stan Manson, a future Weaver teammate. When he arrived at Weaver in 1969, he played wide receiver on the football team, on one occasion scoring four touchdowns in a game. But basketball was his sport of choice. He had witnessed firsthand the large, raucous crowds attending Weaver games, particularly City Series showdowns in the spacious HPHS gym on Forest Street, and he yearned to play in such an energy-charged atmosphere. Even as a freshman he displayed the explosive shooting ability, deft ball-handling skills, and play-making instincts that indicated he was destined to become a great high school basketball player. He started on the JV team, but it was not long before he was seeing action on the varsity. At the end of the regular season, he received playing time in state tournament games. But it was in his sophomore year that Keith Morgan emerged as a key player on one of the best teams in the history of Weaver High School.

A cloud of uncertainty hung over the Weaver basketball program as the 1970-71 season began. A year earlier long-time head coach Frank Scelza had accepted an administration position at his alma mater, Buckeley High School, and John Lambert took over as the varsity coach after a successful stint as the JV coach. John Lambert had captained the baseball team at Presque Isle High School in Maine. He served three years in the United States Army before entering St. Bonaventure University, where he lettered in baseball. He was a teacher and baseball coach at Vinal Technical Regional High School in Middletown for five years. He began coaching at Weaver in 1966, leading the JV basketball team to records of 18-2, 14-4, and 18-2 in successive years before taking the reins of the Weaver varsity. In his first year as varsity coach the team finished a lackluster 11-7, but with all the key players returning, the 1970-71 Weaver team was optimistic about its prospects. Senior co-captains Myron Goggins and Dennis Mink gave Weaver a versatile big-man tandem that could match-up with any front court in the state. Myron Goggins, 6'-5", had averaged 12.9 points and 14.8 rebounds per game as a junior. Dennis Mink, 6'-6", had averaged 14.6 points and 13.1 rebounds per game. Working together, they gave the Beavers an imposing dual-threat combination that few teams in the state could handle.

Lee Otis Wilson, a 6'-3" senior forward who Frank Scelza had called the best shooter he ever coached, had led the team in scoring at 23 points per game. A lethal long-range jump shooter, Lee Otis Wilson was also known for his tremendous leaping ability, giving the Beavers yet another weapon that could finish above the rim. At one of the guard positions was Weaver's "Big O", Owen Mahorn, one of the most physically imposing Beavers of all time. At 6'-4" and 230 pounds, Owen Mahorn was comfortable anywhere on the court, fighting for rebounds on the backboards, handling the ball on Weaver's blistering fast break, setting up the offense, or punishing defenders one-on-one. He was the rare player that combined devastating strength and power with agility and finesse, making him a match-up nightmare for opponents. He could operate with equal effectiveness from the guard, forward, or center position, providing Coach Lambert the versatility to attack the opposition in a number of different ways. The veteran core of the Weaver team offered very few, if any, weaknesses for an opponent to exploit.

The main concern heading into the season was whether the Beavers had the quickness and foot speed to contend with some of the faster run-and-gun teams on the schedule, like Wilbur Cross, Bridgeport Central, and Hartford Public. Keith Morgan quickly showed he possessed the talent to erase any doubts about the team's prospects. As a brash sophomore, he played with energy and exuberance, pushing the ball up the court at top speed. If he crossed mid-court before the opposing defense had a chance to set up, he did not hesitate to pull up and launch a long jump shot, or if he saw an open lane to the basket, he attacked with impunity. He never lacked confidence, and like all great shooters, if he missed a few shots, he was not afraid to keep shooting, fully expecting that his next shot would be on target. Yet he understood his responsibility as a point guard to distribute the basketball to his teammates, and he threw passes with pace, creativity, and accuracy. Although he was surrounded by outstanding veteran players, the 5'-11" sophomore was the catalyst for the Weaver team as it began the quest for an elusive state championship.

Coach John Lambert would not have to wait long once the season began to gauge the team's potential. The first two games on the schedule were away games against perennial powerhouses Wilbur Cross and Bridgeport Central. Weaver won both games. By the time Weaver raced past Bulkeley 80-59 in the twelfth game of the season, the Beavers had lost only once, an early season 73-68 defeat at Norwich Free Academy, the two-time defending Capital District Conference champions. But when Weaver faced Norwich at home in early February, the Beavers won easily, 92-67. Keith Morgan paced the Weaver offense with 24 points, while Dennis Mink added 22 points and 13 rebounds, Myron Goggins contributed 14 points and 15 rebounds, and Owen Mahorn chipped in with 12 points and 14 rebounds. With the win Weaver improved to 13-3 on the season, including 11-2 in the rugged CDC. But as the season unfolded, Weaver had some hiccups along the way. Lee Otis Wilson was suspended mid-way through the season for several games for disciplinary reasons. The Beavers lost a total of four games during the season, giving ample evidence that they could be beaten. Hartford Public rolled through the regular season with a 17-2 record, capturing the CDC title for the third time in the past five years with a 15-1 conference record. Although Weaver finished in a tie with Hartford Public in the City Series race, the Beavers came in second in the conference, finishing with a 14-2 record.

After the regular season finale against Fitch High of Groton, a 96-67 Hartford Public win, Owls' coach John Cuyler expressed his satisfaction with the team in an interview with Tom Hine, *The Hartford Courant* sports writer. "It's been a good year. We were inexperienced to start with, but I'm satisfied with the way the kids came on … more than satisfied. We've had some high points. Teddy Rush broke the 1,000 point mark; Bill Brown, who missed our last few games after an operation, won about six games for us all by himself; Chuckie Cummings has come on real swell, the Tisdol brothers, Osee Tolliver, Kemp Mitchell. All of them have. I'm very satisfied." Weaver also won its final game of the regular season, beating New London 79-55. But losing out to Hartford Public for the conference championship was a disappointment to the Beavers heading into the tournament. A rematch loomed in the Class LL finals.

On the path to the championship game Weaver first defeated Stamford and Lee High, before meeting nemesis Wilbur Cross in the semi-finals. The game between Weaver and Wilbur Cross was played in the new gym on the Quinnipiac campus. The gym's capacity was listed as 1,800, but estimates put the over-flow crowd at 2,500, as fans stood along all four sides of the court. Reportedly, two bus-loads of Weaver students that had purchased tickets for the game, a group that included the Weaver cheerleaders, were not admitted until the second half. Those fortunate enough to witness the entire game, recalled the event as one of the most exciting, hard-fought, and intense battles in the 49-year history of the CIAC state tournament. With 2:48 left in the game, Weaver clung to a 90-86 lead, but Wilbur Cross fought back to take a 93-90 lead with less than a minute to play. A fight broke out in the stands that later carried over outside the gym, and it took 15 minutes to restore sufficient order for the game to resume. Owen Mahorn scored on a layup to bring Weaver within a point, 93-92, and when Wilbur Cross turned the ball over for failing to inbound within five seconds, Weaver held the ball, hoping to win on the final shot of the game. Tom Hine described the final frantic seconds in his excellent recap of the game in *The Hartford Courant*, "The Beavers froze the ball for 35 seconds and Keith Morgan then hit [Bob] Lomax all alone underneath the hoop with a perfect pass. Lomax, underhanded, whipped the ball straight up, banked it off the board, and it dropped through for the clincher."

Weaver's thrilling 94-93 win over Wilbur Cross set up an all-Hartford final for the Class LL championship. Hartford Public had eliminated Danbury, Norwich, and Roger Ludlow in the tournament to set up a meeting with Weaver in the finals. The two Hartford teams had split their two City Series games, with Hartford Public winning the first game 60-57 and Weaver taking the second game in a rare blowout, 103-81, ending a 15 game Owls' winning streak. In the second game in Hartford Public's gym, the Beavers scored 33 points in the first quarter to take a 12 point lead. Keith Morgan set the pace for Weaver, striking for 15 points in the first quarter on his way to a personal best 31 points. He shot 15 for 30 from the field and grabbed 13 rebounds, while leading a devastating Weaver fast break. Ted Rush offered the stiffest resistance to the Weaver onslaught, scoring 24 points and hauling in 23 rebounds, but the Owls were beaten badly on the boards, 72-55. Keith Morgan, Lee Otis Wilson, Dennis Mink, and Darwin Jones had 13 rebounds each, and Owen Mahorn pulled down 10. Keith Morgan had set a blistering pace for the game, putting unrelenting pressure on the Owls' defense. After the game he confessed his exhaustion to Woody Anderson of *The Hartford Courant*, while he made a bold prediction about the eventual outcome of the state tournament, "I went all out. I'm tired. I think we'll go all the way now."

As John Cuyler's Owls prepared to face Weaver for the state championship, the lopsided defeat to the Beavers only three weeks earlier weighed heavily on their minds. The Owls were not at full strength for the critical final game. The team had lost Bill Brown to a season ending operation and Bill Tisdol was still on the mend from a recent injury. Meanwhile, Weaver's high-powered offense was firing on all cylinders in the tournament, averaging 89.3 points over the previous three games. Five Weaver players were averaging in double figures for the tournament, led by Lee Otis Wilson with 26 points a game (coming off the bench to spark the Beavers, just as he would the UConn Huskies in the years to follow), Dennis Mink with 19 points per game, Keith Morgan with 17.3, Myron Goggins with 11, and Owen Mahorn with 10. Weaver had won the rebounding battle by substantial margins in each of the tournament games, led by Mink, Goggins, and Mahorn. For the Owls, sophomore Doward Tisdol was averaging 25 points per game for the tournament, followed by 13.3 for Kemp Mitchell, 13 for Ted Rush, 11.6 for Osee Tolliver, and 11.3 for Chuck Cummings. But when it came to a clash between Weaver and

Hartford, particularly in a game with a potential state championship in the balance, the records and the statistics could be ignored. The players had known each other since they were kids, competing in the elementary schools, junior highs, and Parks and Recreation leagues. They all knew what was at stake – bragging rights in the community, the city, and the state. Although the game would end after thirty-two minutes of playing time, unless overtime was necessary, the memory of the outcome would last a lifetime.

The championship game was played in front of 2,331 fans in the Field House on the University of Connecticut campus in Storrs. In a game that was close throughout, with neither team able to pull ahead by more than seven points, there were 16 ties. With a minute left to play in the fourth quarter the game was knotted at 86. The fans were on their feet; the students from both schools cheering in a frenzy of excitement. The Owls grabbed a rebound and held for a final shot. Osee Tolliver drove to the hoop with 20 seconds on the clock and his layup attempt rimmed out. Doward Tisdol's follow-up rebound also missed. What happened next remains in dispute. Some of the players and coaches claimed they heard a whistle, although officials Don Paris and Pat Mazzarella said it had not come from them. Owen Mahorn alertly grabbed the rebound off the Tisdol miss, and the Beavers held the ball for one final shot. The ball came to Myron Goggins and he threw up a jump shot from the corner that settled through the net for the win. Keith Morgan finished with 30 points on 13 of 22 from the floor and 4 for 5 from the line. He had come up huge once again, scoring at least 30 points in both the semi-finals and finals. Lee Otis Wilson finished with 21, Bob Lomax and Myron Goggins with 12 each, and Owen Mahorn with seven points and eight rebounds. Ted Rush scored 29 points and grabbed 16 rebounds to pace the Owls, and he was named the tourney MVP. Doward Tisdol scored 17 points and pulled down 15 rebounds, while Kemp Mitchell, Osee Tolliver, and Bill Tisdol each had 12 points. After eight consecutive championships by either Hillhouse or Wilbur Cross, the title was back in Hartford, and for Weaver High School, the 14 year championship drought was over.

The following season Weaver returned three starters from the championship team in co-captains Owen Mahorn, David Tyson, and Keith Morgan, but the Beavers could not make it back to the finals to defend their title. Keith Morgan averaged 19 points and 9 assists per game in his junior year, and he scored a career high 38 points against New Britain High. As a senior, playing alongside Stan Manson, Larry Young, Mike Harris, Moses Dillard, and Jerry Curry, Keith Morgan had a disappointing season. He played forward instead of guard to help shore up the team's rebounding, and although he averaged 25 points a game, Weaver missed his dynamic floor leadership. He scored 33 points in a 78-76 loss to Hartford Public, going over 1,000 points for his career. But his frustration continued to mount as the losses piled up. Weaver ended the regular season with a 9-9 record, having to win five of its last seven games to qualify for the tournament. In a play-down game against New Britain High played at Bristol Central, Weaver lost 64-56 to finish at 9-10. Keith Morgan did not start, but he ended as the game's high scorer with 23 points. It was not enough to give Weaver a win that would have allowed them to advance to the next round and face Wilbur Cross, the eventual tournament champion. His Weaver career had come to a disappointing end, yet Keith Morgan took part in something that only a very few players from Hartford ever experienced – the thrill of a state championship.

Peter Harris
Northwest Catholic High School/Weaver High School 1974

It was not an easy task to make a high school basketball team in the city of Hartford. Many students that had their hearts set on playing in high school were seriously disappointed when they found out they had not made the coaches' final cuts. Some aspiring players accepted the bad news reluctantly and moved on to pursue other interests. Others continued to work hard on their games in hope of taking another stab at earning one of the coveted spots on the roster. Yet there were a few players that were stubbornly convinced of their ability to become successful high school players and refused to take no for an answer. Through sheer determination and perseverance, they stuck with basketball until they finally received the break they needed to show what they could do. Peter Harris was one of the rare players that overcame seemingly insurmountable odds to take his rightful place among the elite basketball players of his era.

Peter Harris grew up in the North End of Hartford with advantages that many of his peers lacked. His father, Jim Harris, Jr., was born in Cuthbert, Georgia and served in the U.S. Air Force during the Korean War. Jim Harris graduated from Hartford Public High School and the University of Hartford. He worked in the State Welfare Department and served as an assistant director of the state Office of Economic Opportunity before he joined the staff of Governor John Dempsey, serving as a special assistant to the governor and the administration's Civil Rights Coordinator. He was a past president of the Greater Hartford NAACP and the Executive Director of the Community Renewal Team. During his distinguished career in public service, he served on numerous boards and commissions and became one of Hartford's leading Civil Rights advocates. He was able to provide his family with a comfortable lifestyle while serving as an outstanding example of service to his community.

Peter Harris began playing basketball in his driveway, constantly shooting hoops with his neighborhood friends until it was too dark to see the ball and his grandmother insisted the games come to an end so she could enjoy a little peace and quiet. Peter and his friends moved on to play in the Hartford Parks and Recreation League, representing Keney-Barbour. He played other sports with his friends as well, but basketball was his passion, and he already was imagining playing for Weaver High School someday.

But when it came time for Peter Harris to enter high school, at the urging of his parents he attended Northwest Catholic High School. He was a starter on the freshman team and received playing time on the JV squad. In spite of his early success on the basketball court at Northwest Catholic, he missed his friends that were going to Weaver. His grades suffered, and he tried to convince his parents that he would be happier and do better at Weaver. He managed to persuade them, and he enrolled at Weaver for his sophomore year. But to his disappointment, he was cut from the Weaver JV team. He questioned if he had inadvertently jeopardized his chances for playing high school basketball. Yet his dream had been to play at Weaver with his friends, and he was not ready to give up on his goal.

He played baseball at Weaver as a sophomore and joined the track and field team. He was still intent on playing basketball. He tried out for the team as a junior, but he was cut once again. He was disheartened, but he continued to play recreational basketball whenever he had the chance. He was playing in a Police Athletic League game one evening when Weaver head coach John Lambert happened to spot him. In typical Peter Harris fashion, he was a blur of activity, outracing all the other players as he dashed up and down the court, tossing in long range jump shots in bunches, stealing the ball, coming out of nowhere to grab rebounds, whipping pin-point passes to his teammates. Coach Lambert was impressed, and he asked Peter Harris to come back out for the team. It was the opportunity he had been dreaming about for years, and he was not going to let it pass without giving his best.

Peter Harris was thrilled to make the Weaver team, but he did not expect to play very much. Circumstances intervened in his favor to alter his outlook for exensive playing time. George "Shorty" Davis, a promising sophomore and the younger brother of Co-captain Nick Davis, was expected to start, but he severely sprained an ankle and missed the first seven games of the season. In the first game of the 1973-74 season, Weaver led Norwalk High School 36-33 at the half, but as the game was winding down, Norwalk opened a comfortable lead. Coach Lambert inserted 5'- 6", 113-pound Peter Harris, hoping for a spark off the bench. Peter Harris scored six quick points and disrupted the Norwalk offense, harassing the guards and making steals. Norwalk's James Kovacs scored the winning basket with 12 seconds left on the clock to defeat Weaver, 72-69. Jasper McBride led Weaver in scoring with 26 points, but Peter Harris had shown that his speed and tenacity could impact a game. John Lambert made him a starter and for the rest of his senior year Peter Harris became a bright spot in a dismal Weaver basketball season.

The second game of the season was against Northwest Catholic, the school Peter Harris had left after his freshman year to play at Weaver. Northwest Catholic was the defending Class M state champions, defeating Nonnewaug of Woodbury, 65-49, in the title game the previous March. Northwest remained a formidable team, relying heavily on two exceptional big men, 6'- 4" sophomore Bill Egan, who would go on to play at the University of Hartford, and 6'- 9" Steve Balkum, who would play at Fairfield University. Weaver took a 38-31 lead into halftime, but Northwest Catholic's superior size wore Weaver down in the fourth quarter, coming out on top 58-51. Bill Egan led Northwest Catholic with 22 points, and Steve Balkum added 14 points and 20 rebounds. Weaver was led in scoring by Nick Davis with 22 points, and Peter Harris added 14 points, showing he could be a valuable contributor to the Beavers' offense.

Even as Peter Harris began to assert himself on offense, the team continued to struggle. After staying close in Weaver's first two games, the team stumbled badly in the third game, losing 90-70 to a South Catholic team that would go on to win the Class L state championship. Sophomore Ron Smith led Weaver in scoring with 19 points, and Peter Harris scored 15 for the 0-3 Beavers. South Catholic demonstrated superb scoring and rebounding balance, with Bill Eller hitting for 18 points and 17 rebounds, Ted Mauro registering 15 points and 15 rebounds, and Randy LaVigne adding 16 points and 10 rebounds. Weaver's woes continued against East Catholic, losing 66-50 at the University of Hartford. East Catholic coach Stan Ogrodnik registered the 100th victory of his distinguished career. Stan Ogrodnik would compile a record of 162-49 in nine seasons at East Catholic that included two Class L state championships and three state runner-up finishes. He would go on to become a legendary college coach at Trinity College, where he had a 469-190 record over 27 seasons, including seven NCAA tournament bids, four ECAC Division III New England titles, two NCAA Elite Eight appearances and one Final Four appearance, making him one of the most successful basketball coaches in Hartford of all time.

When Weaver faced East Catholic during the 1973-74 season, the teams were heading in opposite directions. East Catholic's record was 5-0 after the victory; Weaver was 0-5. The once mighty Weaver basketball program had fallen on hard times. But like Peter Harris, Weaver was resilient and would bounce back from adversity. Weaver had won the Class LL championship in 1971 and would make it back to the finals in 1976, only to lose to Lee High, 80-77 in a classic game. Peter Harris served as a bridge between two of the school's all-time great point guards, Keith Morgan and George "Shorty" Davis. Although he played on a team with a losing record, Peter Harris consistently played with pride, hustle, and a fierce competitive spirit, in the tradition of the Weaver players that had come before him and as an inspiration to those that would follow. He was playing out his dream of wearing the Weaver uniform, and he acquitted himself with distinction.

Throughout the difficult season, Peter Harris and his teammates continued to battle. In a City Series game against Bulkeley, Weaver ended a seven-game losing streak with a 65-50 win. Peter Harris and Alex Groves led the team in scoring with 14 points each. Nick Davis added 10 points and 8 rebounds, and Shorty Davis, back from his ankle injury, chipped in with 10 points. With Peter Harris and Shorty Davis playing together, Weaver could boast of one of the quickest and most dynamic backcourts in the area. In a CDC matchup against Norwich, Peter Harris led Weaver to a 64-48 win, scoring 19 of his game-high 29 points in the second half to overcome a halftime deficit. In a loss to powerful Bridgeport Central, he scored 33 points. Peter Harris had emerged as a big-time high school scorer.

Weaver finished the season with a dismal 3-18 record, hitting a low point in the school's history. In his senior year Peter Harris averaged 14 points, eight assists, and four steals per game. He was selected to the All-City and All-CDC first teams, but he was not recruited by any colleges. After graduating from Weaver, he attended Greater Hartford Community College, where he scored 1,100 points in two seasons, averaging 26.2 points per game. He served as captain of the 1975-76 team. One of his teammates at GHCC was Jasper McBride, who was a teammate at Weaver as well. After two years at GHCC, Peter Harris attended Western New England College, where he had two highly successful years on the basketball team. At Western New England he teamed up with 6'-5" Greg Burton, who had played alongside him at GHCC. In 2003 Peter Harris was inducted into the Western New England Downes Athletic Hall of Fame.

Even after he completed his outstanding college basketball career, his passion for the game remained strong. He went on to become a successful community college coach at Naugatuck Valley Community College, Middlesex Community College, and Manchester Community College. In the 1984-85 season, Peter Harris coached his Middlesex Community College team to a 22-3 record and an upset of previously unbeaten Mattatuck Community College to win the New England Community College championship. His team had four Hartford area players on the roster: Frank Henry and Kevin Ward from Hartford Public, Wendell Williams from Bloomfield, and Steve Blocker from Weaver.

Peter Harris has been happily married to his college sweet heart for 33 years and they have two children. He currently serves as the Director of Enrollment Management at Manchester Community College, the only African American to hold that position in the Connecticut State College and University system. Peter Harris never gave up on himself as a basketball player and his habit of persistence helped him lead a highly successful life.

Ted Mauro
South Catholic High School 1974

Many of Hartford's most impressive basketball players displayed their enormous potential at an early age, dominating recreational and scholastic leagues throughout the city, providing clear indications of future success. But others struggled to gain traction in the sport they loved to play, enduring repeated failures to stick with teams they wanted desperately to make, or siting on the bench longing for meaningful playing time. Eddie Griffin had to wait his turn at Brackett Northeast School to show what he could do. Rick Mahorn was famously cut from the Weaver junior varsity team. Some young players were defeated by the sting of similar setbacks and sought other outlets for their youthful energy. Certain players channeled their frustration into motivation to work even harder to develop the skill and intensity they would need to achieve their goals. Ted Mauro was a basketball star in the making that refused to allow early obstacles to stand in the way of an illustrious career.

Ted Mauro grew up on Douglas Street in Hartford's South End with an older brother and a younger sister. His father came from Italy when he was twenty-four years old and married Ted's mother, a Bulkeley High School graduate. Ted attended St. Augustine School, where he tried out for the basketball team in the sixth and seventh grades and was cut both times. He finally made the team in eighth grade, but he mainly sat on the bench and rarely played in the games. Rather than getting discouraged over his inability to play at St. Augustine, Ted Mauro was motivated to improve as a basketball player. He spent countless hours at Goodwin Park, seeking out games against older and more experienced players. In the evenings he played in open gyms at schools like Burr and Kennelly. By his own admission, he was not a particularly good basketball player as a kid, but he had a passion for the game, and through sheer determination and force of will he kept working to get better. He knew he would be attending South Catholic, a school with a rich basketball tradition and a demanding coach in Joe Reilly, and if he had any hope of making the team, he would have to show marked improvement on the court.

When Ted Mauro arrived at South Catholic in 1970, he barely made the freshman team. He played about five minutes a game and was a nonfactor in the team's accomplishments. "I was horrible," he said, writing off his freshman season as a humbling experience. Meanwhile, the entire school was still excited about the preceding basketball season, one of the most amazing in South Catholic's history. On February 13, 1970, South's Dan Moore shattered the New England single game high school record by scoring 71 points in a home game against Bullard-Havens of Bridgeport. The scoring outburst was as surprising as it was exhilarating. Dan Moore's previous high game of the season had been 17 points against East Catholic. He had missed seven games during the season due to recurring ankle sprains, and the week before the Bullard-Havens game he had been confined to bed with a high temperature. He averaged about 12 points a game, and Coach Reilly relied on him more for his excellent defense than his scoring output. Yet for one surreal game, Dan Moore was unstoppable. His teammates kept feeding him the ball until the previous record of 68 points, set by Steve Pound of Stern High in Millisocket, Maine in 1968 was eclipsed. The state single game scoring record had been 64 points, set by Jim Fitzsimmons of Fairfield Prep during the 1968-69 season. Dan Moore's record setting performance was only a part of the hoopla surrounding the 1970-71 basketball season. South Catholic went on to win the Class L state championship, defeating rival East Catholic 71-67 in the finals, and the school was still abuzz with excitement over the title.

That same season Weaver beat Hartford Public 88-86 in the Class LL title game on a 17-foot jump shot by Myron Goggins with four seconds left in the game. Hartford had captured state championships in the two large school groupings. Enthusiasm for basketball in the city was at a fever pitch. When Ted Mauro began his career at South Catholic, he could not help but get caught up in the basketball mania that gripped the school, and he was determined not to let the disappointment of a subpar freshman season derail his dreams of playing in a championship game for South Catholic. As a sophomore, he had grown considerably, approaching the 6'- 5" and 190 pounds he would reach in high school. He started on the JV team, where he began to develop the shooting touch that would make him a dangerous scorer around the basket and the range to face the basket and hit jump shots. He dressed for the varsity, but he did not get to play in any of the games. Yet he watched and he learned, applying the techniques he observed during the varsity games in his JV games. He continued to work on improving his game during the offseason by playing constantly at

Goodwin Park in anticipation of assuming a more important role in his junior year.

Ted Mauro became the starting center as a junior on a team that included Bill Eller, Randy LaVigne, Steve Happenny, Mark Borofsky, Ron Macaluso, Greg Ciccaglione, Marty Jordan, and Joe Zubretski. South jumped off to a 4-0 record to start the season, but in a game against Wethersfield High School, 5'-10" point guard Steve Happenny suffered a serious knee injury that required season-ending surgery, and without his heady playmaking and reliable ball-handling, the Rebels struggled the rest of the season, losing nine of the team's final fourteen games. The disappointment of a mediocre season served to bring the team closer together. South Catholic had a number of tough losses, including some in overtime, but the players gained valuable experience playing together as a unit. With the entire starting five and the core group of reserves returning intact, the prospects for the following season appeared extremely promising.

The senior-laden Rebels jumped out to a fast start to begin the magical 1973-74 basketball season. In the season opener Ted Mauro led all scorers with 19 points to lead a crushing 100-70 win over St. Bernard of Uncasville. Four other players scored in double figures for South, displaying the kind of balanced scoring that would become representative of the team's effort all season long. Hitting the century mark in points in the first game of the season reflected a conscious shift in offensive strategy implemented by head coach Joe Reilly. He spoke to Woody Anderson of *The Hartford Courant* about the team's new wide-open, fast-break approach, "It was my responsibility to play a type of game so that everyone got involved. I've never had eight seniors before. So we went to the speed-up game. We didn't know if it would work but it looks like the kids have made it work." Over the first five games of the season South Catholic averaged 93 points a game, dominating opponents with balanced scoring, aggressive rebounding, and tenacious man-to-man defense. It was a formula that would guide the team to one of the most successful seasons in the school's history.

In a game played at Wethersfield High School, in the town where he would eventually reside, Ted Mauro exploded for 35 points, helping South Catholic overcome twin 29 point performances by Wethersfield's Larry Ayers and John Sunde in an 86-83 win. Randy LaVigne contributed 15 points and Bill Eller added 10 as South Catholic improved to 6-1. But the season would not be without disappointment. In a key conference showdown against rival Northwest Catholic played at the University of Hartford, the game was tied in the closing seconds when Steve Balkun, Northwest's 6'- 9" center and future Fairfield standout, scored on an offensive rebound to upset South 62-60. Ted Mauro scored 14 points and grabbed 18 rebounds, but Steve Balkun had a game-high 27 points and grabbed 19 rebounds to lead Northwest Catholic to victory. The loss was South's third of the season and exposed the team's vulnerability heading into the state tournament, especially when its usual height and rebounding advantages were offset by a dominant center. South bounced back in the finale to the regular season, defeating Bloomfield 84-61 to finish the regular season 16-3. Ted Mauro scored 15 points and pulled down 15 rebounds, while Randy LaVigne scored 18 points and had 10 rebounds and Bill Eller had 14 points and 10 rebounds. When South's big three of 6'-5" Ted Mauro, 6'-4" Bill Eller, and 6'-3" Randy LaVigne were hitting shots and crashing the boards effectively, the team was extremely difficult to beat, as the Rebels' tournament opponents were about to learn.

After winning the Hartford County Conference championship, South Catholic faced Bassick High School of Bridgeport in a play-down game in the CIAC Class L state tournament. Ted Mauro scored 31 points, including 19 in the first half, to lead South to an 84-69 victory. In a first round matchup, South Catholic played East Hartford High School in a packed Bloomfield High gym. East Hartford High featured the type of dominant big man in 6'- 6" center Mark Plefka that had given South problems in the recent loss to Northwest Catholic. Mark Plefka averaged 21 points and 20 rebounds per game over the season, and he represented a serious threat to South's chances of advancing in the tournament. But the East Hartford team knew that South was a formidable opponent. Before the game East Hartford head coach and former University of Hartford great Ken Gwozdz spoke of the respect he had for the South Catholic team to Woody Anderson of *The Hartford Courant*, "South Catholic has to be the second best team in the state behind Wilbur Cross. South has good height and does everything well. We'll have to use different defenses against them. If we make too many changes we'll be playing right into their hands. We've sacrificed weekends and vacations to get this far. South will know it's been in a game."

South Catholic shook loose from a stubborn East Hartford team with a 12-0 run in the third quarter on the way to a 52-39 victory. The win set up a rematch with South Windsor High School, the Central Valley Conference champion that had beaten South Catholic 103-77 earlier in the season. But South Catholic prevailed, advancing to a semi-final matchup against New London High School. In 6'- 7" center John Delagrange, a future UConn teammate of South's Randy LaVigne, and 6'- 5" Mark Royster, the 21-1 Whalers had the size to compete with the Rebels on the boards. John Delagrange led all scorers with 22 points, but South's balanced scoring attack, with five players in double figures, including 16 each by Ted Mauro and Randy LaVigne, proved decisive in a 64-49 Rebels' win.

The 1974 Class L final was played in front of a spirited crowd of 6,479 fans in the New Haven Coliseum, setting a tournament attendance record at the time. Ted Mauro scored 17 points and grabbed 13 rebounds as South defeated a talented Naugatuck High team 71-57 to win the title. He had averaged 19 points and 12 rebounds per game for his senior year, a significant improvement over his junior year statistics, and he was named first team All-State. He had played a key role in helping South Catholic capture the title that was only a remote dream when he arrived at the school.

The entire school rallied around the championship basketball team. For the remainder of the school year, students wore strands of the net the players had cut down wrapped around their fingers, honoring the team with "net rings". The players were treated like heroes by a grateful student body. For the eight seniors on the team, the euphoria over winning the title was tempered by the need to make decisions about their future. Before his senior year, Ted Mauro had signed a letter of intent to attend Fairfield University on a basketball scholarship. But after he had committed to Fairfield, the school recruited three players bigger than him, and he was concerned he might not get to play significant minutes in his freshman year. He asked Fairfield to release him from his scholarship, and he reopened the recruiting process after South Catholic won the championship. After visiting a number of schools, he decided to attend St. Michael's, a Division II school in Winooski, Vermont, where he felt he could play immediately. A pipeline from South Catholic to St. Michael's had been established when Fran Laffin and then John Balczuk enrolled in the college. Fran Laffin became one of the most successful basketball players in St. Michael's history. He set the St. Michael's career scoring record with 2,005 points and won numerous state, regional, and national awards, including New England Division II Player of the Year for 1974 and NABC Second Team All American the same year. It was the same year that Ted Mauro was graduating from South Catholic after winning the state championship. If Ted was looking for a role model in whose footsteps to follow, he could not have found a better one than Fran Laffin.

Ted Mauro enjoyed a productive college career. He had career averages of 16.1 points and 7.1 rebounds per game. In his junior year he averaged 22 points per game, placing him among the top Division II scorers in the nation. He shot nearly 55 percent from the field and 75 percent from the foul line while scoring 1,548 career points. He was twice named to the All-ECAC team and to both the UPI and NEBCA All-New England teams. Ted Mauro played professionally for a year for Mecap of Vigevano in the Italian Pro League.

While he was at St. Michael's, the team scheduled games in Hartford to play the University of Hartford. For Ted Mauro the games were an opportunity to play in front of fans that had cheered for him when he was at South Catholic and to compete against his former teammate, Bill Eller. In Ted Mauro's junior year the game was played in the Hartford Civic Center and in Ted Mauro's senior year the game was played at the University of Hartford, where Ted Mauro scored 18 points in an 84-81 win. After the game he admitted to Tom Yantz of *The Hartford Courant*, "It was real nice to win here in front of the home folks." Even though he was attending college in Vermont, he remained at heart a Hartford native and he always appreciated the support of the local fans.

Ted Mauro returned to the Hartford area when he finished playing basketball. He married his high school sweetheart, Joyce Haydasz, in 1981. He serves as the president of M&M Group Benefits, Inc. in Newington, Connecticut. Ted and Joyce live in Wethersfield and are the proud parents of three sons, Jesse, Dana, and Luke. Over the years, Ted has been involved in Wethersfield's Youth Basketball League, teaching the finer points of the game he played at an extraordinary level in high school and college.

Randy LaVigne
South Catholic High School 1975

Joe Reilly was one of the most revered and respected coaches in the history of Hartford basketball. He coached at South Catholic High School for twenty-seven years. His teams won five state titles, including the 1991 Class L State Championship the year the school closed. After he finished at South Catholic, he coached at Bloomfield High School for two years and Newington High School for five years before retiring in 1998 with an overall record of 512-288. In 2002 he was inducted into the New England Basketball Hall of Fame as a member of the inaugural class. In 1977 he was named the Connecticut High School Coaches Association Coach of the Year. He was twice named the Region I Coach of the Year for New England and New York. In 1970 he coached the South Catholic baseball and basketball teams to state championships.

During his career, Joe Reilly coached some of the city's finest basketball players, and he helped them to develop the skills that made them outstanding college players. But he was not only interested in his players as athletes; he was also concerned with their personal growth. Each October he took his South Catholic basketball team on a weekend retreat to Vermont to get to know his players as individuals and to develop team chemistry away from the pressures of the basketball court. He was an astute evaluator of basketball talent, capable of helping his players reach their maximum potential. When he passed away in 2004, he left behind a legacy of coaching excellence that many of his former players chose to emulate, including his sons Joe, the head basketball coach at Wesleyan University, and Luke, the coach at East Catholic. When Joe Reilly made the announcement in April 1975 that Randy LaVigne, South Catholic's star baseball and basketball player, had decided to attend the University of Connecticut the following fall, he paid Randy a glowing compliment that was quoted in *The Hartford Courant*. "He has unlimited potential," said Reilly. "He is not just a good athlete, he is a great one and he'll get better. He's the best all-around athlete we've ever had at South Catholic." Randy LaVigne's outstanding performance in two sports and in the classroom over his career at South Catholic and UConn served to justify the confidence Joe Reilly placed in him.

Randy LaVigne grew up in the South End of Hartford, the youngest of four athletically and academically gifted boys. His mother, Vickie, was committed to helping her sons succeed, and she made the effort to attend all the boys' games. His father, George, was a Hartford police officer who was passionate about sports and ran the scoreboard clock for South Catholic basketball games. His three brothers, Rich, Bob, and Ron, were outstanding baseball and basketball players in high school and college. Randy's own athletic prowess became apparent at an early age. When he was eleven, he won a baseball competition at Yankee Stadium prior to a Red Sox-Yankee game that received state and national attention. He was the best player on the Kennelly School basketball team. He played both basketball and baseball in the CYO League, representing his local parish, St. Lawrence O'Toole Roman Catholic Church. The St. Lawrence O'Toole baseball team won the CYO New England championship when Randy was in the seventh and eighth grades. Even before he entered high school, Randy LaVigne had distinguished himself as one of the city's most promising young athletes.

From the time he arrived at South Catholic High School in the fall of 1971, Randy LaVigne excelled in athletics and academics. As a freshman, he played on the JV basketball team and was a starter on the varsity baseball team. As a sophomore at South, he was a starter on the varsity basketball and baseball teams, while continuing to shine in the classroom. The basketball team began the season winning its first four games, but starting point guard Steve Happenny injured his knee in a game against Wethersfield High, and the team struggled the remainder of the season. When Randy LaVigne returned the next year, he was the only junior to start on a South team that featured eight seniors. He emerged as a key player on a veteran team with state title aspirations. In a game against Sacred Heart of Waterbury in front of the South Catholic home fans, Randy LaVigne scored 18 points and pulled down 15 rebounds in a 99-56 win. Ted Mauro, South's 6'-5" center, scored 17 points and had 16 rebounds, while 6'-4" forward Bill Eller scored 16 points and grabbed 18 rebounds. Steve Happenny had 14 points and six assists, Ron Macaluso had 10 points and 12 rebounds, and Greg Ciccaglion scored eight points. South Catholic jumped out to a 22 point first quarter lead and was never seriously challenged in improving to 4-0 on the young season. It was the kind of balanced scoring attack and team rebounding effort that augured well for the remainder of the season. Coach Reilly had strayed from his usual disciplined, more methodical offensive approach to allow the team to run more and take advantage of the veteran players' experience and decision-making capabilities. Throughout his career, Joe Reilly displayed an ability to adapt to his players' skills and temperament, putting them in schemes that optimized their chances for success. As the 1973-74 season progressed, the team coalesced around the blending of inspired coaching with talented players functioning as a cohesive unit.

South Catholic had last won the Class L State Championship in 1971, the year before the current crop of seniors were freshmen. The senior group wanted nothing more than to win a title of their own, and in Randy LaVigne they had a teammate with the versatility and offensive firepower to make the dream a reality. He had the size and rebounding ability to help Ted Mauro and Bill Eller battle on the backboards, yet he could slide smoothly into the back-court to help the guards bring the ball up the court against pressing defenses and set the offense. He was comfortable anywhere on the court. Randy was second on the team in assists, third in rebounds, and he led the team in steals. His knack for stealing the ball, especially in clutch situations when the outcome of the game was hanging in the balance, accounted for a number of key baskets over the course of his career. His unique ability to come up with crucial steals would resurface at UConn and contribute to several important victories.

The first test for South Catholic in the 1974 CIAC Class L basketball tournament was a play-down game against Bassick of Bridgeport at Sheehan High School in Wallingford. Randy Lavigne scored 18 of his 22 points in the second half, Ted Mauro scored 31points, and Bill Eller scored 19 to overpower Bassick 84-69. South Catholic faced East Hartford in the first round of the tournament in a game played before 2,000 fans at Bloomfield High School. Playing smothering man-to-man defense, South Catholic prevailed 52-39. After the game, East Hartford coach Ken Gwozdz, the former University of Hartford basketball and baseball star, spoke to Woody Anderson of *The Hartford Courant* about South's defense, "We didn't get a chance to do a lot of things on offense. South is one of the better defensive teams we faced this year. We knew it would be a tight game and that whoever got momentum would win." Bill Eller paced the South attack with 18 points. Randy LaVigne scored 8 points and pulled down a team-leading 10 rebounds, while Ted Mauro scored 13. Mark Borofsky played stifling defense against East Hartford guard Dave Malick, holding him to 8 points, 10 below his average. East Hartford was led by 6'-6" senior center Mark Plefka, who scored 20 points and had 20 rebounds.

Next up for South in the tournament was New London High School, which had defeated Torrington 65-57 to reach the semi-finals. New London came into the semi-final game at Eastern Connecticut State College with a 21-1 record and riding a 19 game winning streak. New London's featured player was 6'-7" junior center John Delagrange, who would eventually join Randy LaVigne, Jim Abromaitis, and Jeff Carr in UConn's stellar 1975-76 freshman class. John Delagrange led all scorers in the game with 22 points, but it was not enough to offset 16 points each from Randy LaVigne and Ted Mauro, 12 by Bill Eller, and 10 by Mark Borofsky. South Catholic won 64-49 to improve to 21-3, setting up a state championship matchup against Naugatuck High School at the New Haven Coliseum. The title game was played in front of an enthusiastic crowd of 6,479, a CIAC tournament attendance record at the time. It was televised throughout the region to an audience anxious to catch a glimpse of several of the state's elite players. In a see-saw first half, South Catholic led at halftime 32-31. Using full-court, man-to-man pressure the entire game, South managed to build a 48-39 cushion going into the fourth quarter. South turned to a more deliberate, ball-control style in the fourth quarter to quash any chance of a Naugatuck rally. The Rebels came away with a hard-fought 71-57 victory to earn the right to cut down the nets as the 1974 Class L state champions.

In his junior year Randy LaVigne averaged 14 points and 10 rebounds per game, but he often served as the third option on the offense behind seniors Ted Mauro and Bill Eller. As a senior he operated from the center position in addition to his customary guard-forward swingman role from the championship season because of South Catholic's lack of height and experience. Playing with an entirely new cast of teammates that included John Basile, Rich Reardon, Frank Sumpter, Steve Ayers, and Joe Horvath, Randy became the focus of the offense. In previewing his South Catholic team's prospects for the new season, Joe Reilly told Woody Anderson of *The Hartford Courant*, "It's not a question whether Randy makes All-State, but whether he makes All-American."

In South's second game of the season against defending Central Valley Conference champion South Windsor, Randy put his senior leadership skills on full display, scoring 12 of his 23 points in the fourth quarter, making a key steal that led to two foul shots, and assisting on three baskets late in the game that sealed a 58-55 victory. Over the first three games of his senior year, Randy LaVigne averaged 21 points, 18 rebounds, 7 steals, and 6 assists per game. He was putting up eye-popping numbers against everyone South Catholic faced. In a game against city rival Hartford Public High School he scored 28 points and grabbed 13 rebounds in a 61-57 win. He had 20 points and 13 rebounds against Bloomfield. Playing arch rival East Catholic in front of 2,400 fans on the campus of the University of Hartford, he scored 18 points in a 61-46 win, boosting South's record to 6-2. In a 58-45 win against Wethersfield before an overflow crowd in the South Catholic gym, Randy scored 18 points. He hit a long jump shot at the buzzer to end the third quarter that gave South a 36-30 lead and shifted the momentum in the Rebels' favor. Promising sophomore Steve Ayers, who would go on to star at Central Connecticut, chipped in with 10 points against the team from his home town as South improved to 8-2. Randy LaVigne's senior presence in the lineup enabled the team to play with poise and confidence. His unselfish, error-free style was a big part of the team's early success.

But the team's youth and inexperience began to take its toll in the tough Hartford County Conference. A tall and talented Xavier team took over second place in the conference behind St. Paul of Bristol by beating South Catholic 48-45 in Hartford for the Rebel's second consecutive home loss. Steve Ayers led a spirited South comeback in the fourth quarter by scoring seven straight points to cut Xavier's lead to three, but it was not enough to overtake the Falcons. Randy LaVigne was the game's high scorer with 23 points to go along with 15 rebounds. After the game Xavier coach Art Kohs spoke to Woody Anderson of *The Hartford Courant* about Randy LaVigne's performance, "He's the best player I've seen all year. He gives away four inches to Champion [6'-7" Xavier senior center Ken Champion] but LaVigne outjumped him three times."

In a game against Northwest Catholic played at the University of Hartford, South Catholic gave up a 42-32 halftime lead in a 75-71 loss. South's defeat left the teams tied for third place in the conference with identical 5-5 records, as the Rebel's fell to 14-6 on the season. South continued to dominate teams outside the conference, however, and in a game against South End rival Bulkeley, Randy LaVigne scored 30 points and pulled down 21 rebounds in an 81-58 victory. Yet South's inability to pull out close games against the better teams in the conference did not bode well for the upcoming state tournament. In a first round matchup against Rippowan of Stamford at the University of New Haven, South Catholic pulled within one point late in the fourth quarter before falling 54-50. Randy LaVigne led all scorers with 23 points in the last game of his high school career and Steve Ayers added 12. South Catholic finished the season at 14-9. The team had made the state tournament 11 years in a row. Randy LaVigne had averaged 22 points and 15 rebounds a game his senior year. He was recruited by numerous colleges, not only for his basketball exploits, but for his pitching and hitting prowess as well.

His outstanding performance on the baseball team had caught the attention of major league baseball scouts who were eager to sign him to a contract straight out of high school. But Randy was ranked sixth in his class academically and he was a member of the National Honor Society. He intended to go to college, and there were many schools vying for his athletic and academic talents, including top southern baseball schools and Ivy League institutions such as Brown and Princeton. In the end he was swayed by the University of Connecticut's offer of a full scholarship and the opportunity to play both baseball and basketball. The lure of UConn's exceptional baseball program helped guide his selection. He told Terry Price of *The Hartford Courant*, "Everybody was really impressed with UConn's baseball. It is one of the best in the East and was probably the biggest influence in my decision." Randy had already pitched a no-hitter in his senior year at South Catholic, and he wanted to see if he could continue his dominance at the major college level. He was also excited about joining Dee Rowe's successful basketball team and testing himself against elite competition.

Randy LaVigne arrived at UConn as a member of a celebrated in-state recruiting class. He joined Jeff Carr from Bulkeley and Robinson Prep School, Jim Abromaitis from Holy Cross High School in Waterbury, and John Delagrange from New London High School as prominent Connecticut high school players that turned down multiple scholarship offers to play for their state university. The signing of the four Connecticut high school stars caught the attention of young players like Corny Thompson from Middletown High School and Mike McKay from Warren Harding High School who would join them at UConn when the 1975 crop of freshmen were seniors. The trend of signing elite high school players from Connecticut would be vital to UConn's success over the next several years and help build the basketball program from a regional to a national power.

In his freshman year the Huskies' basketball team finished with a 19-10 record and made a run in the NCAA tournament before losing to Rutgers 79-73 in the Sweet Sixteen. As a sophomore, the team finished 17-10 and Randy averaged 7.8 points per game and 4.3 rebounds. But his value to the team was epitomized by his contributions in the first two games of the season. In the season opener at home against Boston University in front of a sellout crowd of 4,460, Randy LaVigne stole the ball with five seconds remaining in overtime and drove the length of the court for a layup that sealed the victory. In the next game against Yale University, the score was tied at 46 when Randy once again stole the ball and went the length of the court for a layup that put UConn ahead to stay. He had 14 points, seven rebounds, and three assists for the game in a 56-50 UConn win. No differently than in high school, he had shown he could impact a game in a variety of different ways, only now he was doing it on a much larger stage. In a stunning upset of Holy Cross, the number two ranked team in New England, Randy LaVigne put UConn ahead for good with a jump shot from the baseline with less than 8:00 minutes left in the game. He followed up the basket with a key steal and feed to Dennis Wolf to shift the momentum in the Huskies' favor. Randy LaVigne scored 15 points, his career high at that point. The UConn starting five of Randy LaVigne, Joe Whelton, Jeff Carr, Jim Abromaitis, and Tony Hanson, had shown the team had the ability to compete with the best teams in the East. After the Holy Cross game Randy LaVigne told Terry Price of *The Hartford Courant*, "We've been building towards this for a long time. We've been really looking forward to it. This is the best team effort of the year. Everybody played a big role."

In a consolation game against Fairfield University in the Hartford Civic Center to determine third place in the Eastern Collegiate Athletic Conference, Randy LaVigne came up big once again. Nursing a slim lead with a few minutes remaining in the game, Fairfield attempted to hold the ball. But Randy LaVigne stole the ball, setting up a three-point play by Tony Hanson that tied the game. The score remained tied until Fairfield missed a shot with 10 seconds left on the clock and Randy was fouled as he pulled down the rebound. He made both ends of a one-and-one to seal the victory. Randy finished with 12 points, while Tony Hanson was the game high scorer with 36 points. For senior Tony Hanson from Holy Cross High School in Waterbury, it was the seventh time during the season he had scored more than 30 points. He had scored over 20 points 21 times, bringing his career total in points to 1,990. After the win against Fairfield, Randy LaVigne told Terry Price of *The Hartford Courant*, "We didn't want the season to end. We want to keep going. I think it has been a great year. There were a lot of big wins and very few disappointments. Everybody has had a great time."

During his sophomore year at UConn, Randy LaVigne was nominated for the Academic All-American basketball team. As an accounting major, he had accumulated a 3.3 grade point average that included a perfect 4.0 for the fall semester. His academic performance was as impressive as his work on the basketball court and the baseball field. After his success on the UConn basketball team as a freshman, he transitioned seamlessly to baseball. In his first start as a pitcher for the Huskies' baseball team, Randy LaVigne pitched a one-hitter in a 9-0 win against Boston College. He faced only 30 batters, three over the minimum, giving up a single, walking three, and striking out six as the Huskies improved to 16-5 on the season. But he saw only spot duty as a pitcher, mainly because the team had returned the entire pitching staff that had led the nation with a 1.71 earned run average.

The summer between his freshman and sophomore years at UConn, Randy LaVigne led the Greater Hartford Twilight League in batting as a shortstop, going four-for-four on two separate occasions, and he was named Rookie-of-the-Year. In his first appearance on the mound for UConn as a sophomore, he pitched a two-hitter, allowing singles in the first and seventh innings on the way to the team's first shutout of the season in a 3-0 win over Brown University as the team improved to 18-3. Over the summer he won the Greater Hartford Twilight League batting title with a .440 average and was named to the All-Star team. In his first two years at UConn, Randy LaVigne distinguished himself in basketball, baseball, and in the classroom as perhaps no other student in the history of the university ever had. Yet he was just beginning to hit his stride.

But before he could experience the elation of dual championships as a senior, he would have to endure the struggles of a challenging junior year on the basketball court. UConn was off to a fast start to the 1977-78 season when Randy LaVigne sprained his ankle during a game against

Boston University. Although leading at the half, the Huskies ended up losing to B.U., and losses to the University of Massachusetts and Niagara University followed, sending the season into a tailspin. UConn finished the season with an 11-15 record and failed to qualify for the post-season for the only time during Randy LaVigne's four years. With the infusion of four quality freshmen in Randy's senior year, Corny Thompson from Middletown, Mike McKay from Bridgeport, Jim Sullivan from East Boston, and Clay Johnson from Waterbury, the Huskies hoped to rebound from the disappointments of the previous season.

The Huskies jumped out to another fast start in Randy LaVigne's senior year. In a game against Rutgers University in the UConn Fieldhouse, Randy hit a twelve-foot jump shot from the baseline with two seconds left on the clock to send the game into overtime. Clay Johnson hit the deciding shot in overtime to give UConn a 69-67 win as the team improved to 9-2. After the game George Smith of *The Hartford Courant* asked Randy if he had ever made a bigger shot than the one that kept UConn alive at the end of regulation time, "I doubt it. It doesn't seem real. I practiced that shot 100 times. It was really an easy shot." Randy, a tri-captain in his senior year, finished with 13 points, but once again his scoring output was secondary to his all-around contributions to the game and the leadership he provided on the floor.

As a senior, Randy LaVigne helped UConn win New England Championships in both basketball and baseball. On March 3, 1979 UConn beat the University of Rhode Island 58-50 at the Providence Civic Center. Randy LaVigne held U.R.I. All-American Sly Williams, who was averaging 25 points per game, to a season low nine points. The victory over U.R.I., UConn's tenth win in its last eleven games, set up a NCAA second round tournament showdown against 25-3 Syracuse University. The game was played before a Providence Civic Center record crowd of 12,336 and a national television audience. Powerful Syracuse, with two 6'-11" players in Roosevelt Bouie and Dan Shayes, jumped out to a 25 point lead in the first half, but had to hold off a frenetic UConn rally in the second half that brought the Huskies within four points before losing 89-81. UConn finished the season with a 21-8 record. Randy LaVigne scored 311 points in his senior year for a 10.7 per game average. He led the Huskies with 112 assists, 56 steals, and an 85.1 foul shooting percentage. But in the immediate aftermath of the crushing loss to Syracuse, he expressed regret to Woody Anderson of *The Hartford Courant* that he had not concentrated more on basketball, "I love basketball. But I never reached my potential. I spent most of my time preparing for a baseball career."

The loss to Syracuse was Randy LaVigne's last basketball game for UConn, but it was not the end of his athletic career. Three days after losing to Syracuse, Randy LaVigne hit a homerun against the University of North Carolina on UConn's spring baseball trip. The Huskies' finished the baseball season with a 31-13 record and won the New England and Eastern regional titles to qualify for the College Baseball World Series in Omaha, Nebraska, where the team was eliminated in two games. Randy LaVigne set single-season records in hits (56), runs scored (42), runs batted in (36), doubles (14), home runs (8), and total bases (104), and he tied the record for triples. He set a UConn career record with 15 home runs, and his 104 total bases was an all-time New England record. He received numerous awards for his achievements at UConn, including an Outstanding Senior Athlete Award from the UConn Club, an ECAC Merit Medal, UConn's most prestigious award for academic and athletic achievement, and the Bill Lee Memorial Athlete of the Year Award as the state's top athlete as chosen by the Connecticut Sports Writers' Alliance.

Randy LaVigne was selected in the seventh round of major league baseball's free agent draft by the Chicago Cubs. He spent five years in the Cubs organization before returning to the Hartford area to pursue career opportunities beyond professional baseball. But he always retained his passion for sports and helping young athletes. During minor league off seasons, he assisted Joe Reilly at South Catholic and served as the JV coach at Northwest Catholic for his former UConn teammate Tony Hanson. After his baseball career he worked as an accountant for Price Waterhouse in Hartford, before accepting a position as assistant Athletic Director for sports development and assistant baseball coach at the University of Hartford. He remained active at the University of Connecticut and served on the selection committee that brought Jim Calhoun to the school as the head basketball coach. In 2007 he received the UConn baseball Distinguished Alumni Award. He also received the UConn Medallion for distinguished service to the university. Randy LaVigne and his wife, Dr. Andrea Dennis-LaVigne, live in Simsbury and they have a son, Justin.

When Scott Burrell, a baseball and basketball star at Hamden High School, announced that he was accepting an athletic scholarship to UConn rather than signing with the Seattle Mariners who had made him their first round draft pick, comparisons were immediately drawn to the last great two-sport Huskies' athlete, Randy LaVigne. In an article in *The Hartford Courant*, George Smith quoted UConn baseball coach Andy Baylock on the likelihood of Scott Burrell succeeding in two sports at UConn, "We've had a few combo kids at UConn since I've been there and I get excited about that. The last one was LaVigne. I remember him flying down to join us on our spring trip and we put him right into the game. He got three hits. You know why? Because he was an athlete." Andy Baylock knew what Joe Reilly and every other coach Randy LaVigne ever played for learned right away; he was a great athlete, one of the best the city of Hartford ever produced.

Jeff Carr
Robinson School 1975

The public housing projects spawned a disproportionate number of Hartford's most renowned basketball players. In the North End, projects like Bellevue Square, Nelson Court, and Stowe Village regularly provided Weaver High School and Hartford Public High School with fresh talent. In the South End, Charter Oak Terrace and Rice Heights sent quality players to Bulkeley. Charter Oak Terrace, a 1,000-unit, barracks-style complex, was built by the Hartford Housing Authority in 1941 on farmland near the south branch of the Park River. It was intended to serve as temporary housing for workers from the burgeoning defense industry, but like the other housing projects scattered throughout the city, it eventually became home to many families in need of affordable housing. The concentration of large numbers of young people made the basketball courts in the projects popular places to meet and compete. But not every youngster was drawn to the basketball courts. If you did not have an aptitude for the game or the desire to face tough competition, you avoided the courts and sought other less demanding pursuits. Although Jeff Carr possessed the size to play basketball when he was growing up in Charter Oak Terrace, he lacked interest in the sport. It would take time for him to grow comfortable with his large body and begin the unlikely basketball journey that transformed him from a reluctant hoopster in Charter Oak Terrace into a legendary basketball player at the University of Connecticut.

As a sixth grader at the Mary Hooker School, Jeff Carr was tall and awkward, and his size 13 sneakers gave every indication he would continue to grow. He was self-conscious about his lack of coordination and avoided organized sports. By the time he attended junior high school, he was already 5'- 11", and he started going to the Southwest Boys Club, where the older boys encouraged him to try playing basketball. But he still was not ready to embrace the sport. When he entered Bulkeley as a freshman he was 6'- 4", and he was constantly asked if he was a basketball player. He repeatedly answered no, but the question kept coming up, gnawing at his patience. He told Woody Anderson of *The Hartford Courant*, "I got tired of saying 'no' so I started to play." But he was so far behind the other freshmen at Bulkeley in terms of skill development and understanding of the game that he knew it would be difficult for him to catch up. When he was contacted by the Robinson School in West Hartford and offered the opportunity to attend, his mother helped convince him it would be beneficial for him to accept. He transferred from Bulkeley and repeated his freshman year at Robinson.

It did not take him long to establish himself at the small private school as a basketball player with enormous potential. As a freshman he started immediately on the Robinson varsity. He grew stronger and more confident as the season progressed, and the team went on to win the New England Class B Championship. By the time he was a sophomore, Jeff Carr was 6'- 8" and 210 pounds. Robinson lost in the semifinals of the New England Class B tournament in his sophomore year, the only time in his four years at the school the team failed to win the championship. Jeff Carr did not yet have the consistency and finesse he would develop as he gained more experience. But he already was a fierce rebounder, intimidating shot blocker, and effective scorer, and he would only get better.

In his junior year Robinson School brought in a new head basketball coach to help with Jeff Carr's development. Tom Lyons had been an assistant coach at Bulkeley, and one of the new duties he embraced at Robinson was to drive Jeff to school every day. Jeff Carr continued to make significant strides as a basketball player, and the team had another solid season, winning the New England Class B Championship. Robinson School won the title in Jeff Carr's senior year as well. During his prep school career, Jeff Carr scored 1,559 points, collected 1,200 rebounds, and blocked more than 200 shots. He averaged 27 points and 20 rebounds for his career. He was twice named the Most Valuable Player in the New England tournament and in his senior year he was named Robinson's Athlete of the Year. The school compiled a 65-17 record over Jeff Carr's four years to go along with three New England titles. He had crammed in an impressive list of accomplishments in only four years of organized basketball.

When Coach Lyons arrived at Robinson, he encouraged Jeff Carr to begin thinking about where he would like to go to college, a process he had yet to give even the slightest consideration. But letters from colleges from around the country started to arrive, and it became apparent that Jeff Carr would have multiple choices from which to choose. He visited the University of Minnesota on a recruiting trip, and although he liked what he saw, he was a little overwhelmed by its size and distance from home. After he was approached by UConn, he attended a game at the Field House and felt very comfortable. He liked the coaches and the school's proximity to Hartford. He told Terry Price of *The Hartford Courant*, "I decided on UConn mainly because of its great fans. The coaches are great and the fact that it's close to home also helped me make up my mind." After narrowing down his choices to a handful of in-state schools and a few out-of-state schools, Jeff Carr announced his intention to attend the University of Connecticut.

Once he was accepted to UConn, Jeff Carr knew he would have to work hard to earn playing time. Head coach Dee Rowe had told Jeff he was the only center he had recruited and that he expected Jeff to back up John Thomas at the position. But Jeff Carr was not going to be satisfied in a limited role as a reserve; he hoped to become a starter in his freshman year. He understood that the competition for playing time would be fierce. In addition to returning veterans like John Thomas, Tony Hanson, Joe Whelton, Al Weston, and Dennis Wolf, Jeff Carr was joining a talented group of incoming freshman in Jim Abromaitis, John Delagrange, and Randy LaVigne. Like Jeff Carr, the three other freshmen recruits were from Connecticut, but they had played for high schools with outstanding basketball programs and had competed against the top talent in the state. Although he had been successful against the competition Robinson School faced, he had only been playing basketball for four years and he did not know how he would stack up against more experienced players from big-name high schools.

In order to prepare for the rigors of his first season at UConn, Jeff Carr played in the Greater Hartford Summer Basketball League. He played for Tuesday's II, a veteran team composed mostly of former Hartford Public High School players like Dwight Tolliver, Steve Waterman, and Jake Edwards. It was precisely the kind of confidence-building experience Jeff Carr needed, to play with savvy, skilled ballplayers that had been tested at every level of basketball competition, in the parks, in high school, in college, and in rugged industrial leagues around Hartford. Jeff Carr demonstrated that he was up to the task. In a summer league game against his future UConn teammate, 6'-7" Jim Abromaitis from Holy Cross High School of Waterbury, Jeff Carr led his undefeated Tuesday's II team to an 87-71 victory over previously unbeaten Bristol. He scored 22 points and pulled down 14 rebounds, while holding Abromaitis to 15 points, showing he was ready to accept the challenge of playing at UConn.

Jeff Carr started all four years at UConn. As a freshman, he averaged 7.8 points and 7.9 rebounds per game. He had two games in which he recorded 19 rebounds. In his best game of the season he scored 17 points and grabbed 15 rebounds in an 80-78 win against Hofstra in the NCAA tournament on the way to a Sweet 16 appearance. His tip-in at the end of regulation sent the game into overtime. His production fell off at the beginning of his sophomore year while he fought an early season illness, but after a breakout game against the University of Massachusetts in which he scored 19 points and grabbed 14 rebounds, his play steadily improved and by the end of the season he finished with 7.5 points and 8.3 rebounds per game. As a junior he averaged 10.1 points and 6.4 rebounds per game, and as a senior he averaged 10.2 points and 7.6 rebounds per game. The kid from Charter Oak Terrace who shied away from basketball until he was in high school finished his UConn career with 987 points.

As a junior at UConn, Jeff Carr worked as an intern for a semester at Long Lane School in Middletown. In an interview with Owen Canfield of *The Hartford Courant*, he reflected on how fortunate he was to escape the kind of difficulties the youth at Long Lane School encountered, "I see kids with real serious problems, in trouble, and I know I could have been that way. But I was lucky. I was pushed. At Bulkeley, I was pushed to go to Robinson Prep, and there I was pushed to go to college. And I'm still being pushed. Through basketball, I learned how to deal with people. I got to know people."

After he graduated from UConn, Jeff Carr worked as a counselor at Mansfield Training Center. He returned to Long Lane School as a youth services officer before accepting a position as a parole officer in Hartford, supervising kids on probation trying to reintegrate into the community. He worked as an assistant basketball coach at Trinity College under Stan Ogrodnik and he coached a youth travel team, where Marcus Camby was one of his players. Jeff Carr lives in Bloomfield with his wife Beverly. He remains a devoted UConn basketball fan, proud of the success of the program that recruited him from a small prep school and gave him a chance to excel as a big-time college player at his state university.

George "Shorty" Davis
Weaver High School 1976

It was a well-known and often repeated narrative that Rick Mahorn was not a big star at Weaver. He emerged as a valuable starter in his senior year, yet even during that special 1975-76 season, when Weaver barely missed out on the state championship his brother Owen had helped to capture in his junior year, Rick only gave hints of the punishing NBA big man he would eventually become. In Rick Mahorn's senior year Weaver finished with an 18-4 record and a CDC title, securing the team a place among the best in the school's history. The senior-laden team had a strong core of exceptional players, including Ron Smith, Daryl Turner, Tim Syms, Carlton Butler, and Gerry Hamilton, but a significant part of the group's dominance was due to the spectacular efforts of a multi-talented guard named George Davis, who was known by the nickname "Shorty", a moniker as unlikely as his rapid rise through the hierarchy of Hartford basketball.

George "Shorty" Davis and his brother Nick were born in Birmingham, Alabama and raised by their mother and stepfather. The family moved to Hartford in 1969 in search of better opportunities than were available in the Deep South. At first they lived on Enfield Street, and Shorty attended Northwest Jones Junior High, where he made his first friends in Hartford, including Benji "Bird" Wilson, a future teammate at Weaver. When the family moved to Stowe Village, Shorty Davis switched to the Fred D. Wish School, where he played on the basketball team for Coach Duchene. To develop sound fundamentals, the coach would devise competitions for his players in practice, and the reward for doing well was to attend Weaver basketball games. Shorty Davis had the opportunity to watch stars like Owen Mahorn and Keith Morgan perform, inspiring his own dreams of someday wearing the green and white Weaver uniform. His team at Wish School won the city championship, and he was given an award as the most improved player on the team, bolstering his confidence that he would someday play in high school. In the summer he enjoyed playing on the Stowe Village team in the Hartford Parks and Recreation League, where he gained valuable experience. Shorty Davis was ready to make his mark as a Weaver High basketball player.

By the time Keith Morgan graduated from Weaver in 1973, the basketball team had slid into mediocrity. The excitement of the 1971 state championship in which Keith Morgan had played such a prominent role as a sophomore was already beginning to fade in memory as a hopeful batch of new players arrived on the scene to replace those that had departed in the ever-shifting rhythm of scholastic sports. In his disappointing senior year Keith Morgan played alongside such players as Jerry Curry, an All-State football player, Merle Lawrence, Mike Harris, Sam Booker, and Stan Manson. Nick Davis, Shorty's older brother, was a promising forward on the team who was a strong rebounder with a reliable jump shot. In a 90-80 loss to Hartford Public in January 1973, Keith Morgan scored 22 points, while Nick Davis chipped in with 10 points.

As his career progressed, Nick Davis continued to improve. He co-captained the 1973-74 Weaver team with Jasper McBride, and although the wins were scarce, Nick Davis had a number of impressive games, including a 22 point performance against Northwest Catholic, a 17 point effort against Lee High, a 14 point game against Hartford Public, and a 13 point game against East Catholic. Unfortunately for Weaver, the games all resulted in defeats. The losses mounted up, and the Beavers failed to qualify for the state tournament, in contrast to so many Weaver teams in the past. If there was any consolation for Nick Davis in his disappointing senior season, it was the opportunity to play with a group of determined, resilient teammates, including his kid brother. With Keith Morgan gone, Weaver lacked a spark to ignite the team, and when Shorty Davis arrived on the scene, it appeared that Weaver might have found the catalyst the team needed to return to relevance.

With the Davis brothers playing well together, the Beavers began to show signs of returning to competitive respectability. In a City Series game against Bulkeley played at Hartford Public High School, Nick Davis scored 10 points and pulled down eight rebounds, while Shorty Davis scored 13 points in a 65-50 victory. Weaver shot 55 per cent from the field, helping the Beavers end a seven-game losing streak. After the game Coach John Lambert told Bodhan Kolinsky of *The Hartford Courant* that he hoped the victory would give the team momentum, "The boys really hustled. This game could turn the team around. They showed a lot of desire. They just have to hang in there, that's all."

Along with the Davis brothers, two senior guards, Peter Harris and

Alex Groves, paced the Beavers' win against Bulkeley with 14 points each. Peter Harris was the real "Shorty", a 5'- 6", 112 pound blur of energy on the court, setting up teammates with pin-point passes, hitting acrobatic shots, even darting past unsuspecting opponents to snare rebounds (he had six for the game). If George Davis needed convincing that a lack of height was not necessarily a deterrent, Peter Harris was the man to provide living proof of what could be accomplished through sheer determination and force of will. For players like Peter Harris and Shorty Davis, height was a state of mind. They played the game with flair and exuberance, using their exceptional quickness, guile, and tenacity to make life miserable for their taller opponents. Their own teammates knew how valuable they were to the cause and were thankful to have them on their side.

Throughout Weaver's long history, dating back at least to the North End school's first state championship in 1954, the Beavers' preferred style of play was frenetic, up-tempo, pressing, full-throttle basketball, an approach that depended on extremely quick, relentless guards that could attack the basket, apply full-court defensive pressure, and shoot well from distance against a retreating defense. The distinguishing strategy of the most successful Weaver teams was to wear down the opposition through constant pressure at both ends of the court. Without strong guard play to minimize turnovers, harass ball-handlers, and provide rapid-fire scoring, the Weaver strategy could veer towards reckless, undisciplined, and counterproductive chaos. But when applied effectively by speedy, intrepid guards, the quick-strike, attacking style often worked with lethal efficiency. Shorty Davis would become the next in a long line of outstanding Weaver point-guards to thrive in a run-and-gun, mayhem-inducing system.

Shorty Davis became a starter on the Weaver JV team as a freshman, averaging 15 points a game, before Coach Lambert promoted him to the varsity team later in the season. He quickly justified the coach's confidence in him by scoring 14 points on seven for seven shooting in one of his first varsity games. In his sophomore year Shorty Davis was hampered by an ankle injury that forced him to miss half the games as the team, co-captained by his brother and Jasper McBride, struggled through a challenging season. Shorty Davis was frustrated by the accumulated losses and was determined to reverse the situation the following year. He went out for the cross-country team to help him get back in shape and to improve his stamina after his lay-off. During the summer, he played for

C.H. Blanks in the Greater Hartford Summer Basketball League, scoring 26 points and dishing out eight assists in a win over New Britain that earned him Player of the Week honors in the High School Division. He was fine-tuning his game in preparation for a break-out junior year.

In the second game of the 1974-75 basketball season, Weaver played Chevrus High of Portland, Maine in Hartford. Shorty Davis served notice that in his junior year he had become a serious scoring threat by netting 21 points in an 81 to 49 Weaver win, the team's second straight victory to start the season. Weaver's fast start continued, with the team winning five of the first six games, the lone loss coming to Norwich Free Academy, 79-69. The defeat at Norwich had ramifications that eventually led to the demise of the Capital District Conference, one of the premier high school leagues in the state. During the game, the Beavers were called for 34 fouls, and the players felt a number of the calls were suspect, intended to discourage them from playing their usual aggressive, pressing defense. When the Norwich team came to Weaver for a rematch on February 7, 1975, a fight broke out among the spectators during half-time, and the officials suspended the game. Norwich, which was losing 34-30 at the half, refused to complete the game, even if it was played on a neutral court without spectators. A controversial vote by the principals of the CDC schools upheld Norwich's decision not to make up the suspended game. Norwich and Fitch pulled out of the conference, and since New London, Enfield, and East Hartford had withdrawn from the league in 1972, there were only four schools remaining, New Britain and the three Hartford public high schools. New Britain left the decimated conference after the 1983-84 academic year, leaving only Weaver, HPHS, and Bulkeley, essentially gutting the once mighty league. The immediate impact of the decision to suspend the game between Norwich and Weaver was to deny the Beavers an opportunity to tie for the conference championship, but in the long run it led to a complete realignment of the competitive landscape in Hartford and the surrounding communities.

In the midst of the distraction over the half-time fight during the Norwich game and the damage suffered to Weaver's reputation as an unsafe venue for athletic events, Shorty Davis remained a consistent performer throughout the year, and Weaver put together an outstanding season, finishing the regular season with a 15-3 record and qualifying for the state tournament after a hiatus of several years. But the Weaver players, unaccustomed to the pressure of the tournament, were eliminated by Enfield in the first round in a major upset. The shocking loss galvanized the spirit of the key group of player's that would be returning the following season. Two of the players that would be counted on were Rick Mahorn and Ken Mink, who both had brothers that played on the 1971 state championship Weaver team. Shorty Davis and his teammates had their sights set on another Weaver title, and they were anxious for the 1975-76 season to arrive.

Shorty Davis continued to use the summer vacation to improve his game. Playing for the Stowe Co-Op All Stars in the Greater Hartford Summer Basketball League, he scored 25 points in an 87-85 victory over Upper Albany to earn Player of the Week honors. By the start of his senior year he had developed into one of the finest players in the state. Together with Ron Smith, the two 5'- 9" guards formed a dynamic backcourt, capable of overwhelming opponents with a devastating offensive barrage. In a key early season matchup, Weaver defeated Wilbur Cross 96-92 in New Haven to improve to 2-0 on the season. Six Weaver players fouled out of the game, including the entire starting team. But Weaver prevailed behind Ron Smith's 33 points and 20 by Shorty Davis. Weaver's fast start to the season continued, with the Beavers winning the first seven games, before facing Hartford Public at the Hartford Civic Center in front of 5,095 spectators. Hartford Public blitzed Weaver 93-70, and the disheartening loss convinced the Beavers they needed to play their best and exert maximum effort to compete against the elite teams in the state. For the rest of the season Weaver played with a fierce sense of urgency that carried them into the state tournament, where they were determined to make it to the championship game.

In the first round of the 1976 CIAC Class LL State Tournament, Weaver faced a far more dangerous opponent in Wilbur Cross than the Enfield team that had knocked the Beavers out of the tournament in the first round the year before. Since Weaver won the state championship in 1971, Wilbur Cross had won three consecutive titles before finishing as the runner-up in 1975, losing to Bridgeport Central by a single point, 70-69. But the Enfield game had taught the Beavers a lesson about playing tentatively in the tournament, and the Weaver players came out firing, setting a blistering pace that had the Governors reeling. By the end of the first half, Weaver led 56-38 after making 25 of 42 attempts from the field. Shorty Davis scored 26 points in the first half, on his way to a game-high 38 points, in a performance that ranked among the best in Weaver's tournament history. Daryl Turner had 21 points, Ron Smith 18, and Carlton Butler 15 as Weaver handled Wilbur Cross 108-80.

Weaver's dominance in the tournament continued until the Beaver's faced Lee High in the finals. Sylvester "Sly" Williams, one of New Haven's all-time great players, scored 31 points and pulled down 14 rebounds to lead Lee over Weaver 80-77 in overtime. Shorty Davis scored 26 points, including a basket that cut the Wilbur Cross lead to 78-76, before a foul shot by Weaver's Gerry Hamilton was offset by two foul shots by Wilbur Cross' Al Galbraith with eight seconds remaining in overtime to complete the scoring. Daryl Turner scored 13 points and Rick Mahorn 12 for Weaver. Shorty Davis had scored 117 points in the four tournament games, averaging 29.25 points per game. For the season he averaged 22 points a game. He was named first team All-State, capping a brilliant high school career. He had led Weaver back to the promised land of the state tournament finals, restoring his high school and his community's battered pride.

After high school Shorty Davis served as a special police officer at Bloomfield High School. He continued to dazzle basketball fans with his spectacular play in leagues around the area. He was a volunteer coach for several years at the Michael Adams Basketball Camp, a free program for North End youth between the ages of 10 to 14 sponsored by SAND, the Hartford Parks and Recreation Program, and the Hartford Foundation for Giving. As an instructor at the camp, Shorty Davis served as a role model and inspiration for young people, some of whom were from the same neighborhoods where he lived when he came to Hartford from Birmingham as a kid. He also instructed the campers in the fundamentals of basketball, an area in which he had displayed his expertise during his legendary days at Weaver High School.

Rick Mahorn
Weaver High School 1976

Predictions by Hartford basketball enthusiasts that Owen Mahorn would one day play in the NBA never came to fruition. Given the extraordinary difficulty in making it to The League, the expectations that Owen would succeed where so many others had failed were overly optimistic, even for someone with his prodigious talent. No player from Weaver had made an NBA roster since Johnny Egan was selected in the second round by the Detroit Pistons as the twelfth overall pick in the 1961 draft. While many from the North End thought that Owen Mahorn had a legitimate chance of reaching the NBA, it was his younger brother Rick that eventually achieved the ultimate basketball goal.

Derrick "Rick" Mahorn grew up in his big brother's considerable shadow. Rick idolized Owen, who was five years older than Rick and was already a Hartford basketball legend when his younger brother entered high school. Their father, Owen Sr., had left the family when Rick was an infant, and Rick did not see him again until he was twenty-three years old and playing in the NBA. Owen filled many roles in Rick's early life – protector, hero, role model, and mentor. Owen's influence helped Rick discover the drive and inner motivation to become a great basketball player. When he arrived at Weaver, Rick was 5'- 11" and weighed 196 pounds, with a physique that did not suggest future basketball stardom. He opted to play football, where he showed promise as a tight end and defensive lineman. But he wanted to follow in his brother's footsteps, and that meant trying to play basketball as well as football at Weaver. He tried out for the junior varsity as a sophomore, but he was cut from the team. Rick Mahorn faced doubters and detractors at every point on his journey to a professional basketball career, but he was not easily deterred. He continued to work diligently to transform himself from a football player into a basketball player.

In the summer before his junior year at Weaver he grew seven inches and returned to school in the fall at 6'- 6" and 205 pounds. He made the Weaver High varsity, but rarely played. "I averaged about two points a game," he told Woody Anderson of *The Hartford Courant* in an interview in 1978. Yet Rick needed time to grow comfortable with his added height.

As a senior, he would begin to give glimpses of the remarkable basketball player he was destined to become.

Rick Mahorn started on an outstanding Weaver basketball team in his senior year. Playing alongside players like George "Shorty" Davis, Daryl Turner, Gerry Hamilton, Ron Smith, Tim Syms, and Charlton "Slo Joe" Butler, Rick Mahorn helped Weaver win the 1975-76 Capital District Conference basketball title with a 5-1 record. In the conference title-clinching game against New Britain, Rick Mahorn contributed 14 points in a 103-78 Weaver victory, while Shorty Davis scored 26 points and Tim Syms came off the bench to spark the Beavers with 12 fourth quarter points. Weaver had beaten New Britain earlier in the season 96-82. In the first meeting Ron Smith led the Beavers in scoring with 28 points and Daryl Turner flirted with a triple-double with 20 points, 8 assists, and 9 rebounds. Rick Mahorn made a solid contribution to the effort with 12 points, 17 rebounds, and 6 blocked shots, in the kind of all-around performance that evoked memories of his brother Owen. Weaver finished the regular season with a 16-3 record, easily qualifying for the state tournament. The Beavers advanced to the finals behind the dazzling play of Shorty Davis, who scored 117 points in four tournament games, setting up a championship matchup against Lee High School and Sylvester "Sly" Williams, the team's spectacular 6'- 7" senior center.

Sly Williams was a two-time All-State selection and high school All-American. He scored more than 1,400 points at Lee, averaging 22 points and 16 rebounds per game for his career. In his senior year he averaged 31 points and 22 rebounds per game, leading Lee High to a District League title and a shot at the team's first state championship, if Lee could defeat Weaver in the finals. Sly Williams was widely recruited out of high school and would go on to play at the University of Rhode Island after verbally committing to Providence College, sparking a bitter dispute between the two schools. He left U.R.I. after his junior year, setting the school's single season scoring record in the process, to sign with the New York Knicks, who had made him the twenty-first overall pick in the NBA draft. Sly Williams played in parts of seven NBA seasons with the Knicks, Atlanta Hawks, and very briefly with the Boston Celtics. He signed to play with the Celtics for the 1985-86 season on one of the greatest Boston teams of all-time, but left the team after appearing in only six games. He returned to New Haven, never to play professionally again. It would have surprised the spectators at the 1976 Class LL State Championship game to learn that of the two future NBA players on the court, Sly Williams and Rick Mahorn, Rick would have the longer and more productive pro career.

The game against Lee High provided Rick Mahorn the opportunity to duplicate the accomplishment of his brother Owen – help Weaver win a state championship. But Sly Williams had other ideas. He was all over the court in the packed New Haven Coliseum, hitting shots from inside and outside, deftly handling the ball to neutralize Weaver's press, snaring offensive and defensive rebounds, and soaring to block shots. He scored 31 points and pulled down 14 rebounds, but no shot in the game was more important than the layup he hit with one second left in the fourth quarter on a three-quarter court assist from Ken Woodsen to send the game into overtime. Both Sly Williams and Rick Mahorn fouled out in the overtime period, but Weaver could get no closer than one point with 41 seconds left in overtime before Lee put the game away with foul shots, winning 80-77. Shorty Davis led Weaver in scoring with 26 points, while Daryl Turner with 13 points and Rick Mahorn with 12 were the other double-figure scorers for the Beavers. In his one year of varsity basketball as a reliable starter, Rick Mahorn had fallen just short of achieving his goal of a state title. But the championship that eluded him in high school would eventually come his way in college and the NBA.

As a standout football player at Weaver, Rick Mahorn could have had a chance to play collegiately, yet he was convinced that he had only skimmed the surface of his potential as a basketball player, and he was determined to continue to develop his capabilities in college. There were a few schools that agreed with him. One of his prime options for a basketball scholarship was Virginia State, Doc Hurley's alma mater. But as he told Woody Anderson of *The Hartford Courant*, he felt more comfortable with his visit to another Virginia college, Hampton Institute, "Everybody told me to go to Virginia State. There was a lot of pressure. But when I visited Hampton there was no pressure. When my mom said she liked it, I liked it."

When Rick arrived at Hampton, he knew very little about the school. He was not even aware that it was Division II. He was lonely and homesick and considered returning home to Hartford. As a freshman he averaged five points and six rebounds per game for a team that finished with a 13-16 record. But as he became more acclimated to the school and the basketball program, he resolved to become a better player. He was disappointed that he was not a starter at the beginning of his sophomore year, yet in his interview with Woody Anderson of *The Hartford Courant* he said, "I wanted to be someone right away. But then I realized I could be a major factor coming off the bench." With his improved attitude, his playing time and productivity began to soar. Yet it took a trip to Hartford to play a homecoming game in the Weaver gym for him to realize just how good he might be. Playing in front of family, friends, former teammates, coaches, and well-wishers from the Hartford community, Rick Mahorn played the game of his young life. He scored 37 points and had 22 rebounds while playing all 40 minutes against Virginia State, the school he had shunned in favor of Hampton. From that point on his career exploded. He averaged 24 points and 12.6 rebounds per game for his sophomore year, and he was named to the NAIA All-American team. Hampton finished with a 24-7 record and won the District 19 championship, an area that included Virginia, Maryland, Delaware, New Jersey, and eastern Pennsylvania. Rick Mahorn had emerged as a big-time college basketball player, but he was not done yet.

As a senior Rick Mahorn's numbers improved to 27.6 points and 15.8 rebounds per game. He led the NAIA in rebounding. His team won three NCAA Division II championships, fulfilling the goal of winning a title that had eluded him at Weaver. He was a three-time first-team NAIA All-American selection. He set 18 school records and was named to 36 All-Star teams. When he arrived at Hampton, Rick Mahorn's ambition was to complete his college education and return to Hartford to teach. His stunning success in basketball forced him to reevaluate his career goals. As he told Michael Vitez, Courant Staff Writer, in a December 2, 1981 interview, "I never had any visions of playing pro ball. The only visions I had were of going to college and getting an education." The unimaginable dream of playing in the NBA was suddenly within his reach.

Rick Mahorn was selected in the second round of the 1980 NBA draft by the Washington Bullets as the 35th overall pick. By his second season with the Bullets, he was averaging 15 points and a team-leading nine rebounds per game. Head coach Gene Shue told Michael Vitez of *The Hartford Courant*, "Mahorn has done very well. Rick is an integral part of this team and he is going to get better and better." Rick Mahorn's professional career spanned two decades. He played five seasons for Washington before being traded to the Detroit Pistons, where he was a key member of the team that won the 1989 NBA championship. But immediately after winning the NBA title, the Pistons left him unprotected in the expansion draft, and he was selected by the new Minnesota Timberwolves. It was a devastating blow to Rick Mahorn, who thought he had found an NBA home in Detroit. He never played for the Timberwolves, signing instead with the Philadelphia 76ers, where he teamed up with Charles Barkley to form the Thump 'N Bump rebounding tandem. After two seasons with Philadelphia he went to play overseas in Italy. He returned to the United States to play four seasons for the New Jersey Nets before finishing out his NBA career with two seasons with the Detroit Pistons and one with the Philadelphia 76ers. After he retired from the NBA he served as a coach in the CBA and as an assistant coach for former Pistons' teammate Bill Laimbeer with the WNBA's Detroit Shock, before becoming head coach of the Shock until the team relocated to Tulsa, Oklahoma. He is currently a radio analyst for the Pistons and is the father of six children.

In spite of the fame he achieved during his lengthy career in the NBA, Rick Mahorn never lost track of where he was from. He returned to Hartford on numerous occasions to give of his time, energy, and financial resources to help the kids from the inner city. During the summers he was a familiar sight in the North End, conducting free instructional basketball camps, visiting with his mother and family, showing up in the parks to encourage youngsters and meet up with old friends. As he told Tom Condon, Courant Staff Writer, in a 1984 interview, "I love working with kids, and I want to be involved in the Hartford community." He bought his mother a home in the West End, helping to make her life more comfortable after the years of impoverishment in the North End. In 1999 Rick Mahorn was honored with the "1999 Celebrity Dad Award" in a ceremony at Hartford Hospital, where he was born. It was a particularly gratifying tribute for Rick, since his own father was never involved in his life. One of the speakers at the event, Doc Hurley, hugged Rick Mahorn and expressed his gratitude for all that he had done in the community, "All during your career you've been a role model for our young people. I love you, man."

Rick Mahorn has continued his efforts to impact the lives of young people through his work in Detroit, where he is considered a Pistons' legend. In February 2017 he served as the host of the twelfth annual

Detroit Pistons Foundation's recognition of Black History Month, an educational and fund raising event intended to provide college scholarships for Detroit high school students. Prior to the event at the Detroit Institute of Arts, Rick Mahorn visited schools in Detroit, educating students on the importance of black history. He was quoted on the Pistons' website extolling the virtues of the Foundation's work, "In the past 12 years, we've not only been able to make an impact on many students' lives, but had the opportunity to shed light on our country's history and embrace all people of all races and religions as equals." In both Hartford and Detroit, Rick Mahorn always stood tall as a role model and advocate for inner-city youth.

For all his accomplishments at Weaver, in college, in the NBA, in coaching, and in broadcasting, one of his goals in life remained unfulfilled. That situation was rectified on Mother's Day in May 2015 when he received his diploma at Hampton University's graduation ceremonies, 35 years after he left school for the NBA. His inspiration for completing his college degree was his mother Alice, who passed away in 1993. Keith Langlois, Web Editor for the Detroit Pistons' website, quoted Rick Mahorn's comments on the example his mother set for him regarding the value of education, "She started it. She was 16 when she had my older brother, but she wanted to graduate high school. She went to night school and she graduated six months before he [Owen Mahorn] did. It was inspiring to me."

When Rick Mahorn's own children were graduating from college, he knew it was time for him to honor his commitment to his mother's memory by completing his degree requirements at the age of 56. Two of his daughters, Moyah and Alexandria, graduated from Oakland University, where his son Derrick II is attending, and a third daughter, Jordan, who Rick proudly refers to as "my chemical engineer", graduated from the University of Michigan. When asked by Keith Langlois why he felt it was necessary to complete his degree after such a successful career, Rick Mahorn stated, "It's the importance of fulfilling a dream that you started – that's the thing to me. You start something, you complete it and then you move forward to other people and pass it along." Rick Mahorn carried the dream that started at Weaver High School to NBA stardom and beyond, and in the process he became one of Hartford's greatest and most revered athletes.

Robert Lee
Hartford Public High School 1976

Robert "Boo Boo" Lee grew up in Bellevue Square in a family of ten children. He was having behavior problems in elementary school, and his parents contacted Project Concern, a state-funded busing plan that provided inner city students the option of attending suburban schools. Through Project Concern, one of the nation's earliest voluntary busing programs, Robert Lee was able to attend Sedgwick Elementary School in West Hartford. While he was at Sedgwick, an affluent couple, David and Norma Nash, took an interest in Robert and wanted to help make his transition to Sedgwick easier. Robert Lee ended up staying in the Nash's home Monday through Friday and returning to Hartford on the weekends. He enjoyed living in West Hartford, but he was not entirely comfortable in his new school and he missed his old neighborhood. Eventually, he decided to return full time to Bellevue Square. Throughout his transition, there was one person that stood by him and offered constant support, his cousin and future teammate at Hartford Public, Charles "Duffy" Jernigan.

Although Robert Lee played football, baseball, and basketball in his youth, he was particularly drawn to basketball. His father was a former Weaver basketball player, and young Robert had his sights set on playing in high school. When he arrived at Hartford Public in 1972, Robert Lee and Duffy Jernigan led the freshman team to an undefeated season. In his sophomore year, his JV team went undefeated as well. He was a starter on the varsity team as a junior, and the Owls jumped out to a fast start, going 10-1 to open the season.

Robert Lee established himself as one of the best players in the state. In a Capital District Conference game against Fitch, Robert Lee scored 16 points, including eight in the second quarter, as Hartford Public opened up a 17 point halftime lead on the way to a 75-60 win. At 6'- 2" and 175 pounds, he was strong and athletic and could score on the inside or from the outside. He averaged over twenty points a game as a junior and was named first team All-City and second team All-State. But without Duffy Jernigan in the lineup, opposing defenses could concentrate on keeping Robert in check, and the offense sputtered at key points in a game. Robert Lee needed his sidekick to return, and in his senior year the cousins would be reunited for the final time.

At the beginning of Robert Lee's senior year, Hartford Public once again started the season on a positive note, winning the first six games before stumbling against a strong South Catholic team, 59-47. One of the highlights of the season was a match up against Weaver in the Hartford Civic Center. Both teams were playing well; Weaver was undefeated and Hartford Public's only loss came to South Catholic the previous week. Weaver was led by Shorty Davis, who was averaging 24 points per game, while Ron Smith was averaging 21 points per game and Daryl Turner 11. Rick Mahorn was controlling the boards for the Beavers, averaging 11 rebounds a game. Hartford Public was paced by Robert Lee's 22 points per game and Duffy Jernigan's 15. The game was part of a doubleheader in front of 5,095 spectators, with New Britain beating Bulkeley in the opening game 63-57. In the second game, Weaver scored the first six points, but Hartford Public pulled steadily ahead and took a 20-12 first quarter lead. The Owls scored 33 points in the second quarter to take a commanding 53-28 lead at the half and were never threatened for the rest of the game. Robert Lee led all scorers with 31 points, while Keith McLachlan, the Owls' 6'- 2" senior center, scored 17 and Duffy Jernigan 14 in the 93-70 rout. The Beavers were led by Shorty Davis' 15 points and 14 by Rick Mahorn. The embarrassing, lopsided loss would help motivate the Beavers to play harder and smarter for the rest of the season. Weaver made it all the way to the championship game in the Class LL state tournament before losing to Lee High School and two-time All-State performer Sly Williams 80-77 in a thrilling overtime final.

Robert Lee had averaged 23 points a game in his senior year that included a 38 point game against Fitch, giving him 1,100 points for his career. He was named to the first team Class LL All-State team and was recognized as one of the elite players in the state, on a par with fellow All-State selections like Sly Williams, Shorty Davis, Mike Gminski, Wes Mathews, Bob Dulin, Bill Egan, Chuck Aleksinas, and Corny Thompson. Yet there were no colleges interested in recruiting him. Uncertain about his future, Robert Lee took the advice of a childhood friend, Reggie Lennon, and looked into attending prep school. He applied to Cheshire Academy and was offered a partial scholarship. He needed to come up with a thousand dollars on his own to pay the tuition. He approached Community Renewal Team executive director James Harris, and was given a job that allowed him to earn the money he needed to attend Cheshire Academy.

At Cheshire Academy the full range of Robert Lee's extraordinary offensive talent was put on display. In the last two games of his second and final year at Cheshire Academy, Robert Lee exploded for performances of 68 and 57 points within a few days of each other. The 68 point effort came in a 105-95 loss to Boston University in a game he told Bohdan Kolinsky of *The Hartford Courant* he probably could have scored more but "I was slowed down by the flu." His coach at Cheshire Academy, Phil Brady, explained to Bohdan Kolinsky just how unstoppable his star swingman was during the game, "In the first half, they (B.U.) played a zone and Robert scored 35. In the second half, they put a transfer from Tulane on him and Robert popped in 33." In the second game of his one-man scoring spree, Robert Lee poured in 57 points in an 83-82 win over Deerfield Academy. For Robert, the 57 point game was more satisfying than the 68 point effort, "[It] was the best because it was the last game here [at Cheshire Academy] and we won." His last two points of the game came on free throws that sealed the victory. Cheshire Academy finished the season with a 13-8 record, with the majority of the games against college sub-varsity teams. Coach Brady was disappointed that the team was overlooked to compete in the New England Class B Prep School championships, which would have given Robert Lee the opportunity to continue on his amazing roll of scoring outbursts.

Robert Lee had averaged 34.6 points per game his first year at Cheshire Academy and 31.2 points per game over the two years combined. He scored a total of 1,279 points in two seasons. And he took the academic side of school seriously. He told *The Hartford Courant*'s Bohdan Kolinsky, "When I first came here, things were pretty shaky. My mother and I decided coming here for two years would be the best. I'm hanging in there. I want to establish myself in the classroom too." Coach Brady explained to Bodhan Kolinsky how Robert Lee's commitment to academics was paying off, "Robert came to us with eight acceptable credits. We told him he would have to stay two years if he came here in November of 1976. He has good grades in three courses but is having a tough time with algebra (he never took a math course at Public)."

With his improved performance in the class room, a number of Division I institutions were showing interest in him, including Providence

College, Niagara University, and, not surprisingly, Boston University, where he had torched the sub-varsity team for 68 points. After meeting with legendary head coach Dave Gavitt and NBA star Ernie DiGregorio, Robert Lee wanted badly to go to Providence College, but the Friars opted for another player, a rejection that haunted Robert for years. He ended up attending Tennessee State University. He returned to Hartford after graduating from college, and worked for the State of Connecticut. He is married to his soulmate, Sandra Lee. He is a member of the Hartford Public High School Athletic Hall of Fame and the Pearl Street (Waterbury) Summer League Hall of Fame. For years Hartford area fans could watch him in the South Arsenal Neighborhood Development Over-30 and Over-40 basketball leagues, along with other great players from the city like Billy Jones, Eddie Griffin, Nate Adger, and Owen Mahorn, and catch a glimpse of the skills that made Robert Lee one of the most dominant ballers of his era.

Charles Jernigan
Hartford Public High School 1977

When Charles "Duffy" Jernigan's All-State cousin, Robert Lee, departed Hartford Public to attend Cheshire Academy, the responsibility for leading the Owls' basketball team fell squarely on Duffy's broad shoulders. It was a challenge that he welcomed, because it gave him the opportunity to redeem himself for losing his eligibility the second semester of his junior year. The team had jumped out to a fast start, compiling a 10-1 record to begin the season, giving notice that the Owls were serious contenders for the Class LL state championship. But the team faltered in the absence of Charles Jernigan's all-around excellence, the deadly long-range jump shot, fierce rebounding, and unflappable court presence that made him one of the state's premier players. He knew he had let down his coaches, his teammates, and the entire student body. Given a chance for redemption in his final year at Hartford Public, Charles Jernigan led the Owls on an improbable pursuit of a championship that would carry the team all the way to the semi-finals of the Class LL state tournament.

Charles Jernigan grew up in Bellevue Square with his parents and three sisters. He was drawn to the basketball court, where he watched local legends like Bobby Knight, Eddie Griffin, and Dwight Tolliver compete. He admired Keith Morgan, the former Weaver star, a big guard like himself that could swing to the forward position when necessary and shoot from distance. Like many of his peers, his first exposure to competitive basketball came in the Hartford Parks and Recreation League, where he had the good fortune to play for knowledgeable, inspirational coaches such as Ames Mandeville, Greg Maddox, and Steve Waterman. In reminiscing about his personal basketball journey, Charles Jernigan spoke glowingly of his early coaches. "They had a way of encouraging you," he said. "They made you want to get to the next level."

He played baseball and football while he was growing up, but no other sport intrigued him like basketball. He felt as though he had found his true calling on the basketball court, and he played as often as he could, hoping for the chance to play in high school. In his first year at Hartford Public he was a standout on an undefeated freshman team. As a sophomore, he played JV basketball, and he helped lead the team to another undefeated season. He dressed for varsity games, embracing his first taste of playing in front of large, enthusiastic crowds. He became a starter as a junior and developed into one of the team leaders. But basketball was the only thing that mattered to him; he completely neglected the academic side of the student-athlete equation. His grades plummeted, and he was declared ineligible for the second semester. A less determined athlete than Charles Jernigan might have given up and dropped out of school, turning to the streets for a different kind of education. But Duffy had other ideas that didn't involve letting his talent and his dreams wither. He returned to the team as a senior, ready to play inspired basketball and help an overachieving team make an unlikely run at a title.

The 1976-77 Hartford Public team stumbled out of the box, losing the first two games. In the season opener against Wilbur Cross in New Haven, the Owls suffered an 84-81 loss in double overtime. Wilbur Cross was led by Billy Jones' 22 points, while Hartford Public was paced by Charles Jernigan and Ken Smith with 27 points each and Don Ager with 19. The Owls bounced back after the season-opening losses, beating defending Class LL champion Lee High School of New Haven 77-68 and defeating Wilbur Cross 69-66 in the rematch of the earlier meeting. But in spite of the strong showing against the two New Haven schools, the Owls struggled through a disappointing early part of the season. The team lost the next five games, falling to 2-7 on the season, before rebounding against New Britain in an 84-66 home court win. Charles Jernigan continued his impressive play, scoring 25 points and grabbing 19 rebounds in the New Britain game, followed by Ken Smith with 22 points and Don Ager with 18. The team's record did not accurately reflect Charles Jernigan's effort and intensity, but he was playing as though he was on a mission of personal redemption, and the strong support provided by Ken Smith and Don Ager indicated that the Owls should not be taken lightly.

With the bitter double-overtime season-opening loss to Wilbur Cross still fresh in his mind, Charles Jernigan found himself in a similar situation in a critical early February game against cross-town rival Bulkeley. The Bulldogs' Terry Paluch scored the last eight points in regulation to send the City Series' game into overtime, tied at 64. Bulkeley quickly scored the first four points of overtime to appear to take control of the game, only to see Charles Jernigan hit two long jump shots, the second a fall-away prayer from over twenty feet out with three seconds on the clock, to send the game into a second three-minute overtime period. Charles Jernigan was in the zone, the rare sweet-spot where a basketball player senses he can do no wrong and the game is in his ultra-hot hands. He hit two more long jump shots to begin the second overtime. But Bulkeley refused to fade, as Joe Tancredi and Kevin Conneely scored to keep the game deadlocked. It was the kind of scenario Charles Jernigan used to dream about as a kid, the crowd on its feet, the game on the line, everybody in the building watching intently to see his next move. With less than a minute remaining in the second overtime, Duffy drilled a shot from the deep corner to put the Owls up by two. There was still time for Bulkeley to answer, but not in this game, not on this night. Mike Williams grabbed a rebound of a missed foul shot and found Charles Jernigan in the lane for the final basket with four seconds on the clock.

Charles Jernigan scored 37 points, including the last four, in a game that Hartford Public had to win to keep alive any hope of making the state tournament. At 5-8 after the win, the Owls needed to win five of the remaining six games to qualify for the tournament, but with Duffy's ability to take over a game and his teammates lending solid support, the unthinkable suddenly seemed possible. When the thrilling game against Bulkeley ended, Owls' coach John Cuyler spoke to Woody Anderson of *The Hartford Courant* about Charles Jernigan's heroic performance, "Show me a better player than Jernigan. I've seen Wes Mathews play. Jernigan is better." Wes Mathews played for Warren Harding of Bridgeport, the defending Class L state champions. He averaged 34 points per game in his senior year, when Warren Harding lost to South Catholic in the 1977 Class L final 78-76. He went on to play point guard for the University of Wisconsin-Madison. He was the fourteenth pick in the 1980 NBA draft by the Washington Bullets, and he played nine seasons in the league, earning two NBA championships with the Los Angeles Lakers. In comparing his star player to Wes Mathews, Coach Cuyler was setting the bar extraordinarily high.

Bulkeley head coach Joe DiChiara also praised Charles Jernigan's performance in post-game comments to Woody Anderson, "He was phenomenal." In addition to his 37 points, Duffy also grabbed 20 rebounds. His all-around brilliant play continued as Hartford Public's desperation late season drive for the tournament turned into the home stretch. He scored a game high 22 points in a 74-56 win over Norwich as the Owls' record improved to 6-8 on the season. Hartford Public faced Weaver in its next game, badly needing a win to stay alive in the hunt to qualify for the tournament. The Owls defeated Weaver 67-61 in the Hartford Civic Center in front of 4,000 fans for the team's fourth straight win. Charles Jernigan and Don Ager led the Owls in scoring with 17 points each, while Ken Mink paced the 10-6 Beavers with 22 points. Hartford Public had beaten Weaver 84-65 in the teams' first meeting only a few days earlier, giving the Owls a regular season sweep over their North End arch-rivals. If Hartford Public could win two out of the final three regular season games against South Windsor, Holy Cross of Waterbury, and Lee, a third meeting with Weaver in the state tournament loomed as a distinct possibility.

Hartford Public beat South Windsor, setting up a crucial game against undefeated Holy Cross. The Crusaders had compiled an 18-0 record, led by All-State candidate 6'-3" Clay Johnson, who would go on to play at UConn. The Owls jumped out to an early 20-10 lead on Charles Jernigan's third dunk of the first half, but Holy Cross stormed back in the second half to win the hard-fought game 66-63. After the game, Holy Cross head coach Tim McDonald spoke to Woody Anderson of *The Hartford Courant* about Charles Jernigan, who scored 18 points in defeat, "We were fortunate to win. That Jernigan is just super. He's the best player we've played against. By far."

The loss to Holy Cross left the Owls with the unenviable task of needing to beat Lee High School, the defending Class LL champion, for a second time to qualify for the tournament. Led by guard Ken Smith's 24 points, 18 by Charles Jernigan, and 12 by Don Ager, Hartford Public edged Lee 78-76 to finish 9-9 on the regular season and slip into the tournament. The Owls faced Penney High School of East Hartford in a play-down game at Bloomfield High. Penny overcame a nine point Owl lead with 2:48 left in the game to close within 61-60 with under a minute to go. Charles Jernigan came up with a steal with four seconds remaining on the clock to seal the victory, and as he was falling out of bounds near the Owls' bench, he threw in a shot from over thirty feet away for the final points in the 63-60 win. Ken Smith led the Hartford Public attack with 24 points and Charles Jernigan added 18 as the Owls played their way into the tournament.

The Owls' victory against Penny set up the third meeting of the season against Wilbur Cross at Plainville High School. After a 33-33 tie at the half, the Owls had to fight back from a hot shooting Wilbur Cross third quarter to eke out a 64-62 win. It was Hartford Public's first victory over Wilbur Cross in the state tournament in over a decade. Charles Jernigan paced the Owls with 16 points, Ken Smith had 14, Beresford Wilson 11, and Daryl Wells 10. It was the third game in a row for the Owls decided in the final seconds by a margin of three points or less.

Hartford Public moved on to face top ranked and undefeated Holy Cross of Waterbury at Bristol Central High School. Holy Cross was the last team to defeat the Owls prior to the tournament, but in the quarter-final rematch Hartford public rode the hot outside shooting of Ken Smith, a game high 26 points, and Charles Jernigan, 23 points and 17 rebounds, to a 74-67 win. Although the final margin was seven points, the game was not that close. The Owls built a 22 points late in the third quarter behind the hot outside shooting of Ken Smith and Charles Jernigan. After the game, John Cuyler commented to Bruce Berlet of *The Hartford Courant* about his team's performance, "It was the best game we've played this year as a team, but we just have to learn to slow it down and show some patience. We're deadly from the outside, but they put pressure on us and we almost cracked. I guess we just can't stand prosperity."

Hartford Public's unexpectedly deep run through the tournament came to an abrupt end in a semi-final game against Stamford in the New Haven Coliseum. After starting the season 2-7 and needing to win the final regular season game against Lee just to qualify for the tournament, the Owls won 10 of the last 12 games to finish with a 12-10 record. Against Stamford, Hartford Public pulled within a point in the third quarter before falling 86-68. Charles Jernigan continued hitting from long range and finished with 23 points, while Ken Smith had 12, Don Ager 11, and Sabinas Couloute 10. Beresford Wilson, the 6'-4" center who joined the Owls in the tenth game of the season and helped turn the team around with his rugged rebounding, added eight points in the loss. Woody Anderson of *The Hartford Courant* called Charles Jernigan "the most exciting player in the tourney". For the season, Duffy averaged 22 points and 13 rebounds per game while shooting over 50 percent from the floor, with many of his shots coming from beyond 20 feet. He scored over 30 points three times, with a season high of 38. He was named to the Class LL All-State team as well as the All-City team, capping a superlative high school career by one of the best shooters in the city's history.

Charles Jernigan attended Eastern Connecticut State College for a year, where he had success on the basketball team. But he wasn't happy at Eastern and returned to Hartford, where he met with former Weaver star athlete John Lee, the Athletic Director at Linfield College in McMinnville, Oregon. John Lee was able to secure a scholarship for Charles Jernigan to attend Linfield. Duffy enjoyed Oregon so much he lived in the state for fifteen years before returning to Hartford, where he was still fondly remembered as one of Hartford's finest basketball players. Reflecting on his basketball career, he said, "I'm amazed on a weekly basis how people come up to me and tell me what my game meant to them." He added that he recognized his responsibility to give good advice to young players. "I didn't listen to good counsel the way I should have when I was a youth," he said. Charles "Duffy" Jernigan was able to overcome some of the early personal challenges he faced to emerge as a stronger and wiser man as well as a Hartford basketball legend.

Kevin Shannon
Weaver High School 1978

There were many reasons why Hartford became a hotbed of boys' basketball talent over the decades – the extensive network of parks and playgrounds in the city; the influence of early ambassadors of the sport like Doc Hurley, Bobby Knight, the Ware brothers, and the Perry brothers; and the insular nature of the neighborhoods and the housing projects that kept kids close to home – to name just a few. But one explanation for the competitiveness of Hartford basketball that stands out was the opportunity for youngsters to play together on feeder school teams and in Parks and Recreation programs long before they teamed up in high school. The familiarity bred during the formative years of learning how to play the game enabled young players to recognize each other's tendencies, to know when to pass the ball and when to shoot, to help out on defense, to look up after a rebound to see if someone was open. There was always going to be a fair amount of one-on-one play, hero ball, and trash talking, but the experience of playing together and learning to trust teammates was invaluable, especially as players progressed from the youth leagues and junior high school teams to the rigorous competition of Hartford's high schools. The players you grew up with and played alongside in high school were more than just teammates; they were like brothers.

Family was very important to Kevin Shannon. One of the fondest memories of his youth was taking very long car rides with his parents, siblings, and extended family to Alabama to visit his grandmother's farm. It was a chance for his family to reconnect with their heritage and to relate how they had to work together to survive in the deep South. The stories resonated with Kevin and became central to his identity as a basketball player and a man. The connectedness of a family was a concept he embraced, and he extended the sense of belonging within a close-knit group to his teammates as well.

Kevin grew up on Cleveland Avenue in Hartford with three siblings. His father worked construction and his mother worked in the cafeteria at Clarence A. Barbour Elementary School. Kevin attended Barbour School, where he and Calvin Clayton became friends and teammates on the school's basketball team. Calvin was the superior player at the time, and when they would go to the Hartford YMCA to play, Calvin had to make sure that Kevin was picked on a team. But it did not take Kevin long to develop into a fine basketball player. By the sixth grade he was considered one of the better players in his age group, along with Al Broughton, Kenny Mink, and Nigel Edwards, future teammates at Weaver High School.

At Fox Middle School Kevin Shannon emerged as an athletic force on the basketball court. By the seventh grade he was able to dunk, providing a preview of the signature explosiveness that would become his calling card at Weaver. He teamed up with Al Broughton to give Fox Middle School one of the most dominant junior high teams in the area. Weaver head coach John Lambert heard about the team's prowess and came to watch the talented group compete. Kevin Shannon also played on a travel team in the off-season that was coached by three well-known members of the community, Wilbert Jones, a gym teacher at Fox Middle, Tom Butterfield, who coached JV basketball and track at Weaver, and Wayne Jones, a Weaver basketball legend who went on to play at Niagara University. The dynamic team of coaches helped prepare Kevin Shannon for the rigors of high school basketball.

One of the members of Kevin's large extended family was his cousin, Keith Morgan. Ever since Kevin Shannon watched Keith Morgan score 30 points for Weaver in the 1971 Class LL state championship victory over Hartford Public High School, he wanted to go to Weaver to play on the basketball team. He had progressed far enough along in his development to play on the varsity team as a freshman, along with Al Broughton and Ken Mink. In his sophomore year, Kevin Shannon was appearing regularly in key games for one of Weaver's most memorable teams. The 1976 Beavers featured George "Shorty" Davis and Rick "Too Tall" Mahorn, but the roster was filled with talented players like Gerry Hamilton, Ron Smith, Daryl Turner, Tim Syms, Carlton "Slo Joe" Butler, Ken Mink, and Al Broughton. Although Weaver lost 80-77 in overtime to Lee High School in the finals of the 1976 Class LL state championship, Kevin Shannon and the other underclassmen on the team received valuable experience that helped them prepare for their own run to a title in 1978. In an interview with Woody Anderson of *The Hartford Courant*, Kevin Shannon credited the 1975-76 team for Weaver's fast start the following year, "I talked to those players a lot. They told me what I should do to be better. But I didn't think I'd have it this good. I put it all together."

In his junior year, Weaver jumped out to a 9-1 start to the season, and Kevin Shannon led the team in scoring at 18.8 points per game and rebounding at 7.7 per game, and he was second on the team in assists to senior Bob Scott. In an early season game against one of the many out of state opponents on the Weaver schedule, Kevin Shannon scored a game-high 34 points and grabbed 13 rebounds as the Beavers beat Springfield Tech 73-69. Al Broughton, the superb 5'- 5" Weaver guard, contributed 13 points, seven assists, and eight rebounds to the victory, while sharp-shooting Bob Scott also added 13 points. Against a previously undefeated Bulkeley team, Al Broughton paced the Weaver attack with 20 points, including a tie-breaking three-point play with 1:19 remaining in the game to help Weaver gain a 58-53 win. A key play came late in the third quarter when Kevin Shannon dunked on a fast break, bringing the Weaver home crowd and his teammates to their feet and giving Weaver some much-needed momentum. "Weaver is the quickest team we've faced," Bulkeley coach Joe DiChiara told Woody Anderson of *The Hartford Courant* after the game, "And we couldn't adjust to their speed But we're okay."

The Bulldogs of Bulkeley High School proved they were, indeed, okay, as Coach DiChiara had predicted, by defeating Weaver 78-66 in the next meeting between the city rivals. It was the first time Bulkeley had beaten the Beavers since 1966. Joe Tancredi, a 5'- 9" guard for Bulkeley, scored 30 points, helping the Bulldogs improve to 11-2 on the season. Although Weaver lost for only the second time in the season, the lack of defensive intensity Weaver had displayed against Bulkeley continued to haunt the Beavers for the rest of the season. An 84-65 loss to Hartford Public followed the Bulkeley defeat, dropping Weaver to 10-4 and ending any chance of contending for City Series or Capital District Conference titles. Three more Weaver losses followed in quick succession, including a 99-75 beat-down by Wilbur Cross, and Weaver looked to the state tournament as a way to salvage a once-promising season that was spiraling out of control.

But as the tournament got underway, Weaver proved it was not ready to give up on the season, even if the students and fans showed their lack of confidence in the team by purchasing only 22 advance tickets to a play-down game against Hillhouse at Platt High School. There were only 205 spectators on hand as Weaver defeated Hillhouse 79-71, eliminating the 15-time state champions from the tournament. Weaver placed six scorers in double figures: Ken Mink with 17, Tim Rush with 13, Kevin Shannon with 12, Bob Scott with 12, Bill Dortche with 11, and Nigel Edwards with 10. It was the kind of balanced scoring attack the team would need to make any kind of run in the tournament.

Weaver faced 18-2 North Haven at Maloney High School in Meriden and won 85-71 as Bob Scott continued his fine outside shooting, and 6'-5" senior center Bill Dortche was tough on the inside in support of the steady play of Ken Mink and Kevin Shannon. The Beavers defeated Trumbull High School in the quarterfinal matchup at Quinnipiac, but Weaver's hopes of returning to the finals were dashed in the semifinals, losing to Brian McMahon of Norwalk. Brian McMahon went on to beat Stamford in the finals of the Class LL tournament for the school's first state title. Weaver finished the season with a 14-8 record, losing six of the team's last eight regular season games after a 9-2 start. Ken Mink had averaged 17.6 points per game and Kevin Shannon had averaged 14.3 points and nine rebounds per game. Both would return for the 1977-78 season, prepared to take another shot at a state championship.

An early season barometer of a Weaver basketball team's success during the year was how the Beavers fared against teams from New Haven. At the beginning of the 1977-78 season, Weaver lost two of the team's first four games to Lee High and Wilbur Cross. But individually, Kevin Shannon was off to a fast start, indicating he was ready to stake out a claim as one of the elite players in the state. He scored 22 points in the 78-62 loss to Lee. He followed up with a 25 point game in a 74-66 win against Springfield Tech, and he hit for 25 again against Springfield Classical High School in a 96-66 Weaver victory. Meanwhile, Ken Mink was finding his stroke as well, scoring 20 points in the Springfield Tech game, 36 against Springfield Classical, and 28 over Bulkeley in a 75-58 Weaver win. With Ken Mink and Kevin Shannon on their game, Weaver possessed one of the most impressive duos in the state, and with talented players like Nigel Edwards, Moses Thompson, Cordell Reese, Joe Williams, and Devon Henry offering valuable support, Weaver emerged as a force in the state, more than capable of winning a championship.

Kevin Shannon and Ken Mink each scored 23 points in an 83-70 win over New Britain, as Weaver improved to 9-2 at the start of the season for the second year in a row. In a key contest against Hartford Public, Ken Mink scored 38 points and Kevin Shannon added 17, and Weaver clinched the City Series title with a 97-88 victory. Cordell Reese and Devon Henry continued their strong play with 11 points each. Ken Smith, the superb Hartford Public guard, scored 32 points in a losing effort. Ken Mink scored 28 and Kevin Shannon added 25 as Weaver ripped Springfield Classical 91-63 to improve to 10-3 on the season. Alan Allison came off the Weaver bench to play and inspired game, finishing with 12 points, 7 rebounds, and 5 assists. In a preview of the Class LL tournament championship game that was still a month away, Weaver defeated Hillhouse in New Haven, 75-70. Kevin Shannon scored 26 points and pulled down 10 rebounds and Ken Mink scored 20 points as Weaver improved to 11-3. But the path to the tournament finals would not be an easy one. Within a week's time, Weaver suffered three consecutive crushing defeats, losing to Hartford Public 79-64, falling to Wilbur Cross 102-101, and dropping a heart-breaking 62-60 loss to New Britain on a 35-foot heave at the buzzer by Mel Kline. Time was running out for Weaver to get back on track for the tournament.

But Kevin Shannon was not ready for his final season at Weaver to come to an end. In the second round of the CIAC Class LL Region I tournament, Kevin scored off a rebound with 27 seconds remaining in the game to give the Beavers a 68-67 win over Windham High School in front of an estimated crowd of 1,500 fans at Glastonbury High School. In the quarter-finals of the Class LL state tournament, Kevin Shannon hit a twisting layup off a pass from Joe Williams to give Weaver a thrilling 77-75 victory over New Britain in a packed Hall High School gym. And in a stirring semifinal showdown with Hartford Public, reminiscent of all the critical tournament games between the arch rivals in years past, the hard fought game came down to the wire before Weaver prevailed 79-76. Kevin Shannon completed a crucial three-point play in the fourth quarter that helped give the Beavers a lead that Hartford Public could not overcome.

The victory against the Owls gave Weaver the right to meet Hillhouse, a 58-52 winner over Westhill of Stamford in the other semifinal game, for the Class LL state championship. A crowd of 2,200 fans filled the Crosby High School gym in Waterbury. It was Weaver's sixth appearance in the championship game; for Hillhouse it was the twenty-third. Weaver had won four times; Hillhouse had captured 15 titles. The game was tied at 12 after the first quarter, and Weaver led by two at the half, 31-29. Neither team could pull ahead in the second half. With Weaver trailing by three points with 1:20 remaining in the fourth quarter, Devon Henry hit a jump shot to pull the Beavers to within one point. Kevin Woodward hit his second straight layup to build the Hillhouse margin back to three, but Devon Henry made two foul shots to close the gap to one point again. Maurice Best of Hillhouse was fouled with 14 seconds left, but when he missed the foul shot, a Weaver player grabbed the rebound and called time out. A play was designed in the huddle to get Ken Mink the ball, but the pass was intercepted. Weaver did not get off another shot, and Hillhouse won 56-55, ending Kevin Shannon's outstanding career.

Kevin Shannon averaged 15 points and 10 rebounds in his senior year. He was selected to the All-CDC first team. Several colleges expressed interest in him, but he felt the need to go right to work to help his family. He will long be remembered for the excitement he brought to Hartford basketball with his high-flying game.

Kevin and Kenny Hightower
Bulkeley High School 1979

From 1954-1984, local college coaches often looked closely at the high schools in Hartford as a source for talented basketball players to replenish their teams. Basketball programs at the University of Hartford, Central Connecticut State, Trinity College, and Wesleyan University looked at players from all over the country, but the coaches understood that the local pool of talent from the Hartford area was as strong as anywhere. The recruiting process was simplified by only having to travel a short distance to watch local players compete. Perceptive coaching staffs could sometimes identity players that had not yet drawn the attention of more remote programs and try to win the recruiting battles before they were really underway. Another important factor that gave local coaches a distinct recruiting advantage was the established pipelines that had been developed over the years between their schools and particular high schools. The local colleges regularly tapped into the talent pool provided by Hartford area high schools to gain a competitive advantage in their conferences.

High school coaches were attuned to the kind of players that might be attractive to local college programs, and tried to steer their kids in a direction that would prove mutually beneficial. In 1979 Bulkeley head coach Joe DiChiara knew he had two blue-chip basketball players that would be a good fit for any college, but especially the fundamentally sound and player-oriented style used by Bill Detrick at Central Connecticut State. The two Bulkeley players had complimentary skill sets. One was 6'- 3", 175 pounds and was comfortable at the guard position, where he could put his reliable pull-up jump shot, strong passing game, tremendous leaping ability, and adept ball-handling skills to good use. The other was 6'- 4", 170 pounds and played the forward position, working smoothly along the baseline in search of open lanes to the basket and superior rebounding position. It was not a forgone conclusion that the two players would attend the same college, but they had played together their whole lives and worked so well in tandem it made sense for them to continue down the same path. After all, Kevin and Kenny Hightower were identical twins, and it was perfectly natural for them both to go from Bulkeley High School to Central Connecticut State, following in the footsteps of other

281

great players that had experienced success at both schools, like John Pazdar, Gene Reilly, and Jimmy Muraski. After outstanding careers at Bulkeley, Kevin and Kenney Hightower would have Hall of Fame careers at Central Connecticut.

Kevin and Kenny Hightower and their six siblings were raised in Charter Oak Terrace by their mother. The twins first became interested in basketball at the Southwest Boys & Girls Club, where they met Clarence "Sonny" Thomas, the club director. Sonny Thomas had been a baseball and basketball star at Hartford Public, where he was elected into the school's Athletic Hall of Fame. He was named first team All-State in basketball in his senior year, when he captained the Owls to city and conference championships. After he graduated from HPHS in 1955, he played professionally with the Harlem Magicians, before returning to Hartford, where he spent over 30 years with the Boys and Girls Club of Hartford. Sonny Thomas introduced Kevin and Kenny Hightower to basketball, talking to them about the right way to play the game and offering guidance on how to behave away from the basketball court as well. From that point on Kevin and Kenny were hooked on basketball and devoted their free time to trying to improve their games.

The twins attended Quirk Middle School, where Kevin and Kenny played together on the basketball team. They entered Bulkeley High as freshman in 1975, the year after the new Bulkeley High School campus was opened in September 1974. Like most freshmen, they spent their first year in high school getting acclimated to the pace of the game and the coach's system. As sophomores they both played on the varsity team, but neither started or played major roles. Yet the Bulldogs enjoyed one of the finest seasons in the team's recent history, finishing with a 15-5 record. The team was eliminated in the first round of the Class LL state tournament by Westhill of Stamford. One of the highlights of the season was a 78-66 win over Weaver at home, Bulkeley's first victory over a city opponent since 1966. The win heralded Bulkeley's return to relevance in the city after a sustained absence, and with the Hightower brothers about to assume more prominent roles in the program, the Bulldogs' future looked promising.

In their junior year at Bulkeley, the Hightower brothers became key players on the basketball team. The Bulldogs jumped out to a 4-1 start to the season, with all five starters averaging in double figures, led by senior center Kevin Conneely's 13.5 points per game. But once Bulkeley began facing some of the tougher teams in the conference, the losses started to pile up. The Bulldogs dropped consecutive games to New Britain (66-56) and Weaver (75-58), and the team's record fell to 4-3. In a game against Prince Tech, Kevin Hightower hit a shot with three seconds left in overtime to give Bulkeley a 70-69 win. He scored 13 points in the game, while Kenney finished with 23 points, including eight in the fourth quarter to help send the game into overtime. Bulkeley's record stood at 6-8, and prospects of a tournament berth were beginning to fade. In the rematch with Prince Tech the Bulldogs prevailed once again, winning 67-54. Kenney Hightower was the game high scorer with 21 points and Kevin Conneely, on his way to All-City honors for a very solid season, added 20 points and 14 rebounds. Bulkeley finished the season with an 8-11 record, but the Hightower brothers had gained valuable experience and considerable playing time, and were poised for break-out seasons the following year.

Bulkeley began the 1978-79 season with a record of 2-4, not the kind of start the team had been hoping for in the Hightower brothers' final year. But as the season progressed, the Bulldogs started to play better, reviving hopes for an appearance in the state tournament. The team was encouraged by City Series wins against Weaver and Hartford Public. In the 70-67 victory over Hartford Public, Kevin Hightower scored 22 points and grabbed eight rebounds, while Kenny finished with 12 points and 14 rebounds. But in the rematch against Hartford Public, the Owls earned a tough victory, defeating the Bulldogs 76-62 behind 25 points and 11 rebounds from Tony Camby, 24 points and 12 assists from Michael Adams, and 8 points, 9 rebounds, and 10 assists from Joe Adams. Kenney Hightower had 26 points and 15 rebounds for Bulkeley and Kevin had 16 points. The Bulldogs finally climbed over the .500 mark at 8-7 by beating Rockville 56-54. Alex Garcia led the Bulkeley attack with 16 points, which included converting a one-and-one opportunity from the free throw line with three seconds remaining in the fourth quarter for the game's final margin. Kevin Hightower added 15 points and 10 rebounds. Bulkeley was peaking at precisely the right time, gaining momentum heading into the tournament.

In the first round of the Class L state basketball tournament, Bulkeley beat South Windsor at the University of Hartford. In the quarterfinal round, however, Bulkeley lost to Bristol Central 59-55 in a game played at Hall High School. Bristol Central was led by All-State performer Bruce Kuczenski, a 6'- 8" center who would go on to play at UConn from 1979-1983. Kevin Hightower paced the Bulldogs with 15 points and Kenny added 11. Going into the tournament, Coach Joe DiChiara praised Kevin Hightower for his exceptional season. He told Bondhan Kolinsky of *The Hartford Courant* that Kevin was "one of the most unselfish players I've ever had. He averages 19.5 points a game but still manages to run our fast break and pass the ball off quite a bit. I think he's one of the top prospects in the area." Apparently Bill Detrick, the head coach of Central Connecticut State College, agreed with Joe DiChiara's assessment. He was able to convince both Kevin and Kenny to continue their educational and basketball careers at Central.

Bill Detrick was the ideal coach to help the Hightower twins develop into outstanding college basketball players. During his legendary career at Central, he was able to earn his players' trust and confidence and to maximize their talents. Bill Detrick had attended Central Connecticut State College when it was known as Teacher's College of Connecticut. He was the only student-athlete in the college's history to earn 12 varsity letters, four each in football, baseball, and basketball. After graduating from Central, he coached at Litchfield High School and in Irvington, New Jersey, before returning to Central as a professor and a coach. He led Central to 468 victories during his 29-year tenure as head coach. He was also a highly successful coach of the golf team at Trinity College for 23 years. When he retired from Central, the gym in Kaiser Hall was named in his honor. Bill Detrick passed away in 2014 at the age of 86.

Coach Detrick recognized the unique skill sets that Kevin and Kenney brought to the team. Kevin was capable of playing multiple positions. He had the ball-handling and passing skills to play point guard, and with his fine shooting touch and explosive ability to drive to the basket and finish above the rim, he could easily slide over to the two guard or small forward positions. Because of his length, quickness, leaping ability, and defensive instincts, he was usually called upon to guard the opponent's top perimeter scorer. In his senior year Kevin was instrumental in helping Central put on a late season surge to qualify for the NCAA Division II New England Regional tournament. Coach Detrick spoke to Tom Yantz of *The Hartford Courant* about an intangible quality that distinguished Kevin Hightower from the majority of his peers, "Certain players have that extra intensity.

It's something that is activated in a close game or when the team needs it. And it can't be taught. Kevin has that."

Kenny Hightower was equally vital to the team's success, although he approached the game from a very different perspective than his brother. Kenny was an exceptional rebounder. At 6'- 4", he could play any of the frontcourt positions. He willingly sacrificed his offense to give Central the dominant rebounder the team needed to counter the taller lineups the Blue Devils usually faced. Kenny was relentless on the boards, displaying toughness and a fierce desire to win that mirrored Coach Detrick's own competitive spirit. The Hightower twins displayed a commitment to success that motivated everyone on the team to play harder. They led the team by their indomitable example of unselfishness and effort.

Kevin Hightower was one of only two players in Central's history to serve as co-captain for three seasons. The team finished 18-9, 18-9, and 21-9 in the three seasons of his captaincy, losing to American International College 65-64 in the NCAA Division II New England Regional basketball tournament in his senior year. He was fourth on the school's all-time career scoring list with 1,477 points. As a senior, he won the prestigious Frederick M. Gladstone Award as the college's top male athlete, the same award his coach Bill Detrick won when he graduated. Kevin was inducted into the Central Athletic Hall of Fame in 2007.

Kenney Hightower was one of only four players in Central history with over 1,000 points and 1,000 rebounds. He finished his career with 1,175 point and 1,129 rebounds. Kenny Hightower had a year of eligibility remaining after Kevin graduated, and along with talented teammates like Tyrone Canino, Johnny Pruitt, and Rich Leonard, he helped Central achieve a school record 26 victories against only six losses. In a game against Assumption College in his senior year, he scored 24 points and recorded 28 rebounds. He was the school's second all-time leading rebounder. Kenny was inducted into the Central Athletic Hall of Fame in 2006. At Bulkeley High School and Central Connecticut State College, the Hightower twins were one of the most exciting and productive brother acts ever to emerge from the city of Hartford.

Part IV
Enduring Legacy
1980-1984

Norman Bailey
Northwest Catholic High School 1980

Norman Bailey was one of the most exciting and celebrated players ever to burst onto the Hartford basketball scene. By the start of his senior year at Northwest Catholic, he had been contacted by hundreds of college basketball programs, and he was being recruited by some of the best known coaches in the country. John Thompson, the legendary Georgetown University basketball coach, attended a Northwest practice, watched Norman Bailey play in a game, and then went to Norman's house to talk to his family. In December 1979, George Smith wrote a piece in *The Hartford Courant* titled *Everyone's Talking About Northwest's Norman Bailey*. The article began with quotes from Hartford County Conference coaches praising the Northwest Catholic standout:

"When he was a freshman they called him 'Stormin' Norman.' He was flashy. Since then he's matured. Now they call him Norman. He will devastate the league this year." St. Paul Coach Fran Serratore.

"I almost pray he dumps the ball off. He's an exciting player to watch. Hopefully I won't have to watch him score too much this year." East Catholic Coach Jim Penders.

"He was good when he started as a freshman. He's big and yet can play the guard spot, which makes him a very, very strong college prospect." South Catholic Coach Joe Reilly.

Northwest Catholic's own coach, Charlie Larson, recognized how fortunate he was to have Norman Bailey on his team. He explained to George Smith of *The Hartford Courant*, "We've had a lot of good basketball players at Northwest and he's got to be one of the best ever. He's got a family that is genuinely interested in what he has besides basketball, too." In referencing the remarkable Copes-Bailey family, Coach Larson touched upon one of the key factors that contributed to Norman's distinctiveness as a player and a person.

Norman Bailey and his twin sister, Nadine, were the youngest of thirteen children. He spent the early part of his life living in Charter Oak Terrace, where his five older brothers, all high school athletes, and his sisters collectively served as his babysitters and athletic mentors. According to Norman Bailey, "My siblings were taught to fill in when our parents were taking care of other responsibilities." His father, Kenneth, known affectionately as KB, worked for Acme Auto for 28 years, and his mother, Mamie, started out by cleaning homes in West Hartford. Mamie Bailey's inspirational life story was featured in an enlightening profile by Tom Condon in the May 13 (appropriately), 1984 edition of *The Hartford Courant* titled *13 Children, 13 Triumphs in Life of Mamie Bailey*. Tom Condon described how Mamie Bailey, née Mamie Pearl Weaver, was born in the North End, where she was raised by an aunt and her grandparents. She married Alex Copes as a teenager. Her education stalled when she was in the sixth grade. She divorced Alex Copes and married Kenneth Bailey in 1949 (a marriage that would last for fifty-six years and produce twenty-six grandchildren and thirty-five great grandchildren). She tried to finish school at night, but when she was forced to abandon her studies to care for her children and to work, she made a promise to herself that all of her children would receive a quality education and advance as far as their abilities would carry them.

To her credit, she kept her promise. Not only did all thirteen children complete high school, ten were awarded Bachelor's Degrees, five received Masters' Degrees, and one became a Ph.D. Glenda Copes Reed graduated from Smith College and served as the director of corporate public involvement for Aetna Insurance Company. Dr. Paul Copes served as the principal at Weaver High School and became Superintendent of Schools in Bloomfield and Executive Director of Education for the Community Renewal Team. Lt. Col. (retired) Ronald Copes attended Lincoln University in Missouri on scholarship and was awarded the Silver Star Medal for combat duty in Viet Nam. He went on to receive a Master's Degree in computer science and to teach in the Army ROTC program at Morgan State. Norman's twin sister, Nadine, graduated from Temple University. And the list goes on, with each individual success story adding to the amazing saga of one of Hartford's most illustrious families.

Mamie Bailey eventually began working at the Albany Avenue Senior Center, where she served as the Executive Director for over thirty-five years, until her retirement in 1985. In 1968 the family was able to move from Charter Oak Terrace to a home on Hebron Street in the Blue Hills section of Hartford. The accomplishments of the Copes-Bailey family represent a compelling testament to Mamie Bailey's dedication, strength, and adherence to a set of core principles for her children upon which she refused to compromise, such as possessing good manners, practicing excellent hygiene, and trying to put maximum effort into every endeavor. The observance of the values instilled in Norman Bailey by his mother and modeled by his siblings informed his upbringing and guided him in becoming an elite basketball player as well as an outstanding person.

Norman Bailey first became involved in basketball before the age of ten when he started playing in the driveways and backyards of friends like Alfred Grady and Marcus Brown, future teammates at Northwest Catholic, as well as at the homes of neighbors like Dr. Richard Cobb and Barris Cunningham. Some of his friends were students at St. Justin School on Blue Hills Avenue, and Norman Bailey was able to play on the St. Justin's CYO team by attending catechism at the school. He also played for his own school, Fox Middle, where one of the teachers, J.C. Walker, gave Norman and a select group of students an opportunity to play at the school on Saturday mornings, where Mr. Walker taught them fundamentals and provided individual instruction. Norman was coached at Fox Middle by Allan Pratt and Steve Waterman, and the team's strong play led to opportunities to play in tournaments throughout the state. Norman Bailey's rapidly improving play drew the attention of the Loomis-Chaffee School in Windsor, and he was offered a scholarship. He stayed at Loomis-Chaffee for a year, but the private school's rigorous academic environment and highly competitive student body did not appeal to him. His parents encouraged him to enroll at Northwest Catholic High School, where Norman would be reunited with neighborhood friends that had attended St. Justin. His decision to start over at Northwest Catholic would seriously impact the high school basketball landscape within the greater Hartford area.

When Norman Bailey arrived at Northwest Catholic in the fall of 1976, he was already considered a basketball prodigy. In the summer he had played in Keney Park, the launching pad for all serious hoop prospects in the North End. With a lean 6'-3" frame and explosive leaping ability, he was being tabbed as the next great Hartford basketball sensation. In his freshman year at Northwest, he did nothing to dispel the impression of impending basketball stardom. He wasn't sure he was going to start as a freshman, but in a preseason scrimmage against Torrington High at Northwest Catholic, Coach Larson told him to take the floor with the other four starters to begin the game. The Northwest fans on hand to watch the scrimmage began chanting Norman Bailey's name. The era of Bailey-mania at Northwest Catholic was underway.

In the 1976-77 basketball season, Norman Bailey's freshman year, the Northwest Catholic program was going through a challenging rebuilding phase. The team struggled against rivals in the highly competitive Hartford County Conference. In a conference game against South Catholic at the end of January, John Pinone scored 20 points, Steve Ayers 19, Paul Mercak 12, Rudi Alvarez 12, and Steve Granato 11 to defeat Northwest Catholic in West Hartford 87-69. South Catholic remained unbeaten in the conference at 6-0, while the team's overall record improved to 13-1. Northwest Catholic, which was led by Jim McKinney's 23 points and Norman Bailey's 16, fell to 0-5 in conference play and 3-8 overall. Although the Northwest Catholic game against East Catholic less than two weeks later was closer, the Rebels dropped a 70-65 decision. Norman Bailey led Northwest with 17 points, as the team fell to 4-10 overall and 1-7 in the HCC. East Catholic improved to 13-5 overall and 6-2 in the conference. But Norman Bailey continued to improve as the losing season progressed, and the experience he gained was transforming him into one of the conference's most dominant players.

Norman Bailey averaged 17 points and 11 rebounds as a freshman. He was named the team's MVP and was selected second-team All-Hartford County Conference. He had shown he was already one of the premier players in the state. But the team finished with a 6-12 record and the question lingered if he was capable of leading a team on a deep run in the state tournament, the criteria upon which all elite players from Hartford were ultimately judged. Over the next three seasons, Northwest Catholic captured three consecutive conference championships, made two semi-final state tournament appearances, and reached the state title finals, removing all doubts concerning Norman Bailey's leadership skills. His high school legacy would have been even more impressive if Northwest had not run up against two historically dominant programs, Wilbur Cross High School and Middletown High School.

Northwest Catholic showed marked improvement in Norman Bailey's sophomore year. In a non-conference game against New Britain, the Indians prevailed 47-40. Norman Bailey scored eight of his fifteen points in the first quarter to help Northwest Catholic get off to a quick start. But the Indians still struggled against the stronger teams on the schedule.

Against an undefeated Middletown team that featured the imposing future UConn Huskie Cornelius Thompson, Northwest Catholic was soundly beaten by a score of 68-46. Cornelius Thompson scored 24 points and pulled down 15 rebounds to lead Middletown to its eighth straight win of the season and 57th in a row over a two-and-a-half year period. In a game against conference opponent St. Thomas Aquinas in West Hartford, lightning-quick guard Rod Foster helped Aquinas stay undefeated at 4-0 in the conference and 6-0 overall by scoring 23 points. Norman Bailey paced Northwest Catholic with 19 points as the Indians fell to 1-1 in the conference and 6-3 overall. In the rematch against Middletown, Cornelius Thompson tied a career high with 41 points as the Tigers from Middletown edged Northwest Catholic 72-65 to notch their 59th win in a row. Tom Bisson led the Indians with 21 points, Mike Morris scored 16, and Norman Bailey 11. Northwest Catholic's inability to beat Middletown, a problem that confronted every Tigers' opponent over a historic three-year span, would come back to haunt the Indians in their final game of the season.

As the state tournament approached, Northwest Catholic pulled off a quality win against arch rival South Catholic. Hitting 17-of-18 free throws, including the final six points of the game, Northwest Catholic handed the Rebels their first conference loss, 67-64. Northwest's 5'-10" guard Tom Bisson led the Indians with 21 points, putting him over 1,000 for his career. South's 6'-8" junior center John Pinone, led the Rebels' attack with 26 points, but Norman Bailey and Marcus Brown, both 6'-5" sophomores, helped neutralize Pinone on the backboards and kept him scoreless during a critical third quarter. Norman Bailey hit on a three-point play late in a see-saw fourth quarter that put Northwest ahead to stay. He finished with 19 points as the Indians won their third straight game, providing much needed momentum heading into the tournament.

Northwest Catholic lost to Xavier in the final game of the regular season to finish third in the rugged Hartford Country Conference. But in the conference playoffs, the Indians defeated South Catholic in the semifinals and upset St. Thomas Aquinas in the finals to capture the HCC championship. In the second round of the CIAC Class M Region III state tournament, Northwest had to face Middletown, the team that had beaten the Indians twice during the regular season and was riding a 72 game winning streak, second all-time in state history to East Haven's record 77 straight wins, established between 1953-55. Northwest was playing its best basketball of the season when it counted the most – tournament time – and the Indians hoped that the lineup that was meshing so effectively, could upset mighty Middletown. Northwest Catholic featured Tom Bisson and Mike Morris as the guards and Dan Lynch, Marcus Brown, and Norman Bailey along the front line, with key reserve Paul Bisson (Tom's brother) offering strong support off the bench. But Cornelius Thompson proved too much to handle for the Indians once again, scoring 18 points and pulling down 22 rebounds to lead Middletown to a 72-55 victory in front of 2,100 fans in a packed Plainville High School gym. Norman Bailey played well, scoring 19 of his 21 points in the second half as he battled Cornelius Thompson evenly until the end of the game. Middletown would go on to win the Class M state title by defeating St. Joseph of Trumbull 71-57 at Central Connecticut State College. For Northwest Catholic, the future looked promising, with Norman Bailey and three other starters returning and brash guard Ulysses Garcia waiting in the wings to provide a jolt of excitement to the Northwest lineup.

Much was expected of Norman Bailey in his junior year. He had averaged 17 points a game as a sophomore and had been named first team All-Hartford County Conference. Coach Charlie Larson told Tom Yantz of *The Hartford Courant*, "Norman is our team leader and the most improved. He can hit that 15-foot jumper with more confidence now. Both Marcus [Brown] and Norman can only get better with two more full seasons to play."

In an early season game against non-conference opponent Springfield Commerce, the Northwest players gave an indication they were prepared to live up to the preseason hype that had installed them as one of the favorites, along with South Catholic and St. Thomas Aquinas, to win the HCC. Ulysses Garcia scored 28 points and Norman Bailey netted 22 points and grabbed 16 rebounds to lead Northwest to an 80-65 win. But Northwest's co-favorites in the conference were not inclined to concede the HCC championship without a fight. In early January, St. Thomas Aquinas beat Northwest 76-59 behind Rod Foster's game high 27 points, well below his 37 points per game average that had propelled Aquinas to an 8-0 start to the season and a 4-0 conference record. In late January, South Catholic beat Northwest 66-59 at the University of Hartford to improve to 10-2 on the season. John Pinone managed to score a game high 23 points before fouling out. Norman Bailey led Northwest with 18 points, while Ulysses Garcia scored 15 and Marcus Brown 13, as the Indians fell to 10-3 on the season and 3-2 in the conference. With exceptionally talented players to contend with on a nightly basis, like Norman Bailey, Marcus Brown, and Ulysses Garcia from Northwest Catholic, Rod Foster from Aquinas, John Pinone and Mark Parrotta from South Catholic, and Mark Murphy, Pete Kiro, and Bob Venora from East Catholic, nothing came easy in the resurgent HCC.

For the second year in a row, Northwest Catholic captured the HCC playoff championship after finishing third in the conference during the regular season. In the semi-final game, Northwest Catholic defeated South Catholic 70-56 in front of a capacity crowd at the University of Hartford behind Norman Bailey's 26 points, 10 rebounds, and three steals. John Pinone scored 21 points and recorded 14 rebounds and Mark Parrotta hit for 18 points for South Catholic in a losing effort. Northwest beat East Catholic in the finals to repeat as the conference champion.

In the Class LL Region III tournament, Northwest Catholic built a 20 point lead against New Britain, then had to hold on to win 72-66 after Norman Bailey picked up his fourth foul in the third quarter and was forced to the bench. Norman Bailey had 19 points and Ulysses Garcia 18 to pace the Indians. In the Class LL Region III finals in the Kaiser Gymnasium on the campus of Central Connecticut State College, Northwest Catholic defeated Holy Cross of Waterbury 77-58. Norman Bailey scored 17 points and grabbed 14 rebounds as the Indians improved to 21-4. In the quarterfinals of the CIAC Class LL state tournament, Northwest Catholic defeated Penney High School 52-33 at Bulkeley High School as Norman Bailey led all scorers with 17 points on 8-of-15 shooting to go along with 12 rebounds. In a thrilling semi-final game against Westhill High of Stamford, Marcus Brown hit a jump shot from the foul line as time expired to give Northwest Catholic a 66-65 victory. Norman Bailey scored 20 points, and the Indians improved to 23-4, the best record in Northwest Catholic's history. The win gave the Indians a shot at the Class LL state title against Wilbur Cross.

The Wilbur Cross team that Northwest Catholic faced in the CIAC Class LL finals had struggled to even make the tournament. The team had started the season with a 2-7 record and finished the regular season at 10-10 before losing the championship game in the regional playoffs. But over the years the Governors had demonstrated their resiliency by winning 11 state titles in fourteen years, and had won six championships under legendary coach Bob Saulsbury. In the 1979 title game against Northwest Catholic, played in front of 1,981 fans at Central Connecticut State College, Wilbur Cross once again lived up to its championship heritage. The game was tied at 71 with only a few ticks left on the clock, when senior Bernard Draughn hit a shot in the lane and was fouled. He drained the foul shot, giving Wilbur Cross a three-point lead and making Norman Bailey's long jump shot at the buzzer superfluous. Norman Bailey was named the game's Most Valuable Player on the basis of his 25 points and 12 rebounds. He had been the HCC tournament MVP as well, and for the second year in a row he was a first-team All-Hartford Country Conference selection. He was also a first-team All-State pick. In a game against New Britain High School he surpassed the 1,000 point mark. It had been a remarkable season for him personally, diminished only by the 74-73 loss to Wilbur Cross in the championship game. Yet he still had one year remaining to claim a title, and with eight of the top 11 players returning for the Indians, the prospects for a championship appeared promising.

In his senior year Norman Bailey was considered the top player in the state of Connecticut. The recognition was not conferred lightly in a particularly strong year for high school basketball players in the state. On Norman Bailey's own team, Marcus Brown and Ulysses Garcia were established players with star-quality credentials, and across the state, players like Rich Leonard from New Britain High, Monroe Trout from New Canaan, Reggie Thorne from Bridgeport Central, Al Frederick from Westhill in Stamford, Jay Murphy from Maloney, Jim Bates from Bristol Eastern, and Harold Pressley from St. Bernard in Uncasville had all emerged as elite scorers and legitimate major college prospects. What distinguished Norman Bailey was his versatility and athleticism. At 6'- 5", he could dominate on the inside or step away from the basket to utilize his quickness, ball-handling ability, and mid-range shooting touch to finesse opponents. But perhaps his most distinctive attribute on the basketball court was his ability to send down some of the most memorable dunks ever witnessed in the state, or the country. In a nationally televised game against Villanova in Norman Bailey's freshman year at UConn, he took a pass at midcourt, elevated in the lane to slam, then brought the ball back down to his waist before sending it home to finish off what the commentators on ESPN called "the dunk of the year". Mamie Bailey's calm, unassuming son

Norman could put on a show that captivated a nation.

Northwest Catholic jumped out to a quick start to the 1979-80 basketball season. In an early season game against conference rival East Catholic, Marcus Brown scored the winning basket on a feed from Ulysses Garcia with 10 seconds left on the clock to give the Indians a 57-55 win. In the following game Norman Bailey scored 23 points and pulled down a game high 14 rebounds in an 82-62 win against Bloomfield that gave the Indians a 4-0 record. East Catholic won the second game against Northwest Catholic, 77-73, overcoming 24 points each from Norman Bailey and Ulysses Garcia and handing the Indians their first loss in the conference after seven victories. Northwest Catholic's overall record dropped to 14-2, with the only other loss coming at the hands of New Britain by a score of 55-54. The Indians returned the favor, beating New Britain by the identical 55-54 score to go 16-2 on the season as the tournament approached. Northwest Catholic beat South Catholic 48-37 in the finals of the Hartford County Conference tournament for the team's third consecutive HCC championship. Norman Bailey scored 17 points and was named MVP of the conference tournament, and Northwest Catholic improved to 19-3 heading into the CIAC Class LL Region III playoffs. The Indians beat Hamden 64-57 in the first round of the playoffs, with Norman Bailey scoring 30 points on 10-of-12 shooting from the field and 10-of-12 from the foul line. Northwest faced New Britain next, the third matchup of the season between the teams that had split the two regular season games by the same 55-54 score. Northwest Catholic beat New Britain 74-66 to go 21-2 on the season and advance to the Region III title game against Southington.

The Indians defeated Southington 68-66 on a put-back rebound by Marcus Brown with 13 seconds to play to clinch the Region III championship and set up a CIAC Class LL quarter-final game against Weaver at Bloomfield High. Norman Bailey scored 21 points and Marcus Brown struck for 15 to give Northwest a 64-50 victory. The win against Weaver put the Indians in the semi-finals of the state tournament for a game against Wilbur Cross, the team that had eliminated Northwest Catholic from the tournament the previous year. It was the third year in a row during the Norman Bailey and Marcus Brown era that Northwest Catholic had advanced to the semi-final round of the state tournament. Fred Collins, a slender 5'- 7" junior co-captain, scored 17 points to lead the Academics past Northwest Catholic 67-61, ending Norman Bailey's illustrious high school career.

Norman Bailey had averaged 18.8 points for his high school career and scored 1,699 points. He was named to the New Haven Register All-State first-team for the second year in a row and he received All-American recognition. He attracted offers from multiple college programs, but he decided to stay close to home and his large family and play for his state university. He joined a talented freshman class that included Karl Hobbs and Vern Giscombe. His first start for UConn came in the NIT against South Florida in his freshman season, and although he only recorded 4 points, 3 assists, and a rebound in 28 minutes in his initial starting assignment, he impressed the coaches sufficiently to start 41 consecutive games and score 552 career points.

When his UConn career ended, he played in the Irish pro league, where he averaged 35 points a game. He later played in the Portuguese League, averaging 27 points per game. He returned to the United States after six years and held positions for Community Solutions, the Connecticut Job Corp, and the State of Connecticut.

In his sophomore year at UConn, as part of a course in educational psychology, he and several of his teammates worked with at-risk inner city teenagers between the ages of fourteen and sixteen in two branches of Hartford Neighborhood Centers, Mitchell House on Lawrence Street and Clay Hill House on Bedford Street. The teenagers were in awe of the opportunity to get to know a local basketball legend, especially someone who had faced similar challenges growing up in Hartford. Norman Bailey encouraged the young people to direct their energies towards positive goals, just as his siblings and his parents had steered him in the right direction. His message was similar to the one Mamie Bailey had delivered to him many years ago – keep trying. Following his mother's sage advice had given Norman Bailey the strength and the resolve to emerge as an outstanding basketball player and exemplary role model.

Michael Adams
Hartford Public High School 1981

When Villanova University upset the defending champion Georgetown University Hoyas to win the 1985 NCAA Division I Men's Basketball Championship, excitement over the Big East Conference was at a fever pitch. For the first time in NCAA history, the Final Four consisted of three teams from the same conference, with St. John's University emerging from the West Regional in Denver, Colorado to join Villanova and Georgetown in the semi-final round. Only Boston College's 59-57 loss to Memphis State in the Midwest Regional in Dallas, Texas prevented an all-Big East Final Four. Memphis State's Final Four appearance was later vacated by the NCAA for the use of ineligible players, further enhancing the Big East's unprecedented dominance in the 1985 tournament. The list of the top players in the Big East that historic season read like a Who's-Who of college basketball nobility: Patrick Ewing, Michael Jackson, and David Wingate from Georgetown; Ed Pinckney and Dwayne McClain from Villanova; Andre McCloud from Seton Hall; Chris Mullin and Walter Berry from St. John's; Pearl Washington, Rafael Addison, and Rony Seikaly from Syracuse; Earl Kelly from UConn; and Billy Donovan from Providence. The Boston College addition to the list of elite conference players was Michael Adams, a 5'-10" point guard from Hartford Public High School and a legitimate All-Big East and All-American candidate.

Unlike the other notable players in the Big East, however, Michael Adams had not been heavily recruited coming out of high school. Boston College was the only Division I school to offer him a scholarship, and his signing was expected to have negligible impact on a league brimming with talented recruits. It was widely believed that he was too small, too unpredictable, too undisciplined, and too inconsistent an outside shooter to have any chance of becoming an impactful major college player. Yet he led the Boston College Eagles to post-season appearances in each of his four years at the school, including an Elite Eight appearance in 1982 and a Sweet Sixteen appearance in 1985. He served as team captain as a sophomore, junior, and senior and was selected All-Big East during the three years of his captaincy. His 1,650 career points rank eighth on Boston

College's scoring list, and his 475 career assists place him fourth on the school's all-time list. His 275 career steals remain a school record and second all-time in the Big East. Michael Adams made a habit of proving his critics wrong. Not only would he become a dominant force in the Big East, he would go on to have a stellar career in the NBA as well. His unlikely rise to the pinnacle of the basketball world made him one of Hartford's greatest success stories.

Michael Adams grew up in the Bellevue Square housing project, the eighth of nine children. His mother, Willie Grace, labored in tobacco fields to earn money. Oliver, his father, worked nights as a janitor and parts inspector. By the time he was eight years of age, Michael Adams gravitated to the basketball court, mainly as a way of staying out of trouble and avoiding the disapproval of his siblings. As he told staff writer Bob Sudyk of *The Hartford Courant*, "There was trouble at every corner at the projects if you wanted it. My older brothers and sisters would knock my head off if I dared get in trouble. When the lights came on, I came home. We watched out for each other. It was the only way to survive."

His two closest friends growing up were Mike Davis, a future basketball teammate at Hartford Public, and Marlon Starling, his first cousin. Mike Davis eventually became a program analyst at Aetna Life & Casualty Co. and earned a degree in computer science from Columbia University. Marlon Starling went on to beat Mark Breland to claim the World Boxing Association welterweight title. Mike Davis told the *Courant's* Bob Sudyk, "Michael could have been a boxer. His hands were so quick, he could hold his own against Moochie [Starling] when they were kids." In an interesting sidebar to Michael Adams' inspirational personal history, the three childhood friends each emerged from the austere backdrop of Bellevue Square to achieve remarkable success in their adult lives. It was the kind of awe-inspiring story seldom told in the projects.

Word of Michael Adams' exceptional basketball talent quickly spread beyond the confines of Bellevue Square. By the time he was in the eighth grade at Quirk Middle School, he had developed a reputation as one of the most promising young players in the city. His renown carried over to the summer, when he was given the rare opportunity for a junior high school student to compete in the open division of the Greater Hartford Summer League. Yet his small stature belied the extent of his talent. When he arrived at Hartford Public High School, he was assigned to the freshman basketball team. After he averaged thirty points over the first five games, he was quickly elevated to the junior varsity, where he supplanted his good buddy Mike Davis as the starting point guard. There were no hard feelings created; the two remain friends to this day. It was apparent from the very beginning of his high school career that Michael Adams was on a fast-track to greatness and his friends and teammates felt privileged to be along for the ride.

As a sophomore, Michael Adams joined his brother Joe in the starting lineup for the Hartford Public varsity team. In an early season game against Capital District Conference rival New Britain, Michael Adams scored 23 points in the Owls' 71-58 victory. With Hartford Public leading 45-44 after three quarters, Michael Adams hit three straight baskets at the start of the fourth quarter to break the game open. Tony Camby added 15 points for the Owls, while Joe Adams contributed 13. Joe Adams was a defensive-minded player who took pride in his ability to shut down an opponent. Joe's intensity as a defender rubbed off on his younger brother, and Michael's knack for disrupting offenses with his uncanny ability to intercept passes and pick the pocket of ball-handlers became two of his most distinguishing weapons on the basketball court, not only in high school, but in college and the NBA as well.

In addition to his ball-hawking skills, another aspect of Michael Adams' game that became manifest in his sophomore year at Hartford Public was his ability to come through in the clutch. In a game against Wilbur Cross, the Owls trailed by two points when Michael Adams hit a shot at the buzzer to send the game into overtime. He scored a career high 30 points in the 97-93 win over the Governors, the first of multiple 30-point games in his illustrious career, while Joe Adams pitched in with 19 points. Michael Adams was never a one-dimensional player, intent on scoring the basketball at the expense of playing a team-oriented game. His proficiency as a scorer was augmented by his ball-handling, passing, rebounding, and defensive skills, making him a complete basketball player, capable of impacting a game in a number of different ways.

In his junior year at Hartford Public, the basketball program was racked by controversy. The team forfeited five games for using an ineligible player, 6'- 4" senior Tony Camby. As a result of the forfeitures, the Owls' record dropped to 3-10 with four games remaining in the regular season. Yet since only four of Region I's eleven teams had a winning record, Hartford

Public remained in contention to qualify for the state tournament. In the first round of the CIAC Class LL Region I tournament, Michael Adams scored 25 points and 6"- 1" senior forward Vincente Ithier and 6"- 7" senior center Chris Canty both contributed 11 points as Hartford Public defeated Norwich Free Academy 68-53 at Glastonbury High School. In the second round of the Region I tournament, Michael Adams scored 28 points on 13 of 22 shooting from the field and recorded seven steals and five assists as Hartford Public turned back Manchester 63-54 at the University of Hartford. In typical Michael Adams fashion, he went off on one of his patented shooting streaks, hitting four straight shots in the second quarter to shift the momentum in the Owls' favor. The win gave Hartford Public an 8-11 record and the right to meet Weaver in the tournament finals.

After he had scored 25 and 28 points in the first two games of the Region I tournament, Hartford Public fans were anxious to see what Michael Adams would do for an encore in the finals against Weaver. In a stunning display of dominance rarely witnessed in the Weaver/Hartford Public historic rivalry, Michael Adams erupted for 39 points, a season and career high, in an 84-65 win that gave the Owls the regional championship. After the game, Owls' coach Stan Piorkowski spoke to Bodham Kolinsky of *The Hartford Courant* about Michael Adams' performance, "That was simply unbelievable. One thing's for sure, he didn't pick up any of those moves from me."

Michael Adams scored only 11 points in the first half, but he put on a shooting clinic in the second half, hitting on scintillating drives to the basket as well as long-range heaves with his distinctive push shot that never quite looked on target until the ball settled into the bottom of the net. There were only 800 spectators on hand to witness Michael Adams' epic performance on Thursday night, March 6, 1980 at Glastonbury High School. But as the Michael Adams' legend grew, many more fans would lay claim to a first-hand viewing of the memorable victory. Michael Adams had strong support from his teammates that night; Chris Canty scored 16 points, Vincente Ithier added 13, and George Amos chipped in with 10. But in the recapping of the game by enthusiastic supporters, it was the Michael Adams' show, pure and simple. There was a new sheriff in town, and he wore his star proudly.

By his senior year, Michael Adams was drawing comparisons to the best point guards in the city's history, evoking names like Johnny Egan,

Eddie Griffin, Pooch Tolliver, and Shorty Davis. He certainly possessed similar attributes to the great point guards from Hartford's past, the ability to blow past defenders to penetrate to the basket, to hit from outside when game situations called for a long range threat, to make clever passes to open teammates, to inspire confidence through sheer determination and indomitable will to win, and to apply intense defensive pressure that created turnovers and uncertainty. In a city known for outstanding point guard play, Michael Adams was establishing himself as one of the best of all time.

In his senior year he was able to mesh his diverse skill set to become one of the top players in the state. He averaged 29.9 points per game, and he led the team to the Class LL state tournament semi-finals in both his junior and senior years. In the quarter-final game of the state tournament his senior year, the Owls faced Rippowam of Stamford. Michael Adams scored 33 points, including 13 of 14 free throws, and he added seven rebounds, five steals, and seven assists in a brilliant all-around performance that led to a 73-54 win. His cousin Destry Starling, the younger brother of Marlon Starling, contributed a career best 24 points to go along with six rebounds and three steals.

The victory set up a semi-final matchup against a Holy Cross of Waterbury team that was enjoying one of the best seasons in the school's history. The Crusaders of Holy Cross had lost their season opening game to Bishop McNamara in Forestville, Maryland, and proceeded to win 23 games in a row, a school record. All five Holy Cross starters averaged in double figures, led by 6'-4" center Jeff Wiener with 16 points per game. The Owls stayed close, pulling to within two points late in the third quarter, until Holy Cross ran off 12 straight points in the fourth quarter to secure a 98-81 win. Michael Adams scored 33 points in his final game for Hartford Public, shooting 14 for 32 from the floor and making all five of his foul shots. The Owls finished the season with a 16-7 record and Michael Adams turned his attention to formalizing plans for his future.

Central Connecticut State was one of the very few schools that showed any interest in recruiting Michael Adams. He most likely would have ended up at Central if not for Boston College assistant coach Kevin Mackey. Kevin Mackey explained to staff writer C.L. Smith Muniz of *The Hartford Courant* how he discovered Michael Adams:

"We were recruiting another guard in Connecticut and we got word that there was a better guard at Hartford High School. They said this kid was the best guard in Connecticut.

"The next night I called the coach, Stan Piorkowski, who said his team lost in the state semifinals and was finished playing, but there was a good chance he would play in an all-star game.

"I saw him a week later at the Bridgeport Jewish Community Center Classic. Michael stole the whole show … He was all over the place, stealing, scoring. It was the Michael Adams' act.

"I went to his coach and asked who was recruiting him. He said no one. I asked what was wrong. Did he have a problem? Were his grades bad? Stan said he was a nice kid. We checked out the grades and they were fine.

"A week later I went down to the YMCA in Hartford to see him play. He played so well that I said, 'Come on.' I put him into the car and said you are not getting away. We are going to see your mom.

"His mother was thrilled. She thought it was the greatest thing in the world. He said he wanted to go in the worst way. That was it. We signed him right on the spot and took him to BC for a visit that night.

"When I got to BC, I told (then coach Tom) Davis that I thought I had recruited the best player ever after Bagley."

His recruitment by Boston College and the subsequent offer of a full athletic scholarship could not have happened without the involvement of a Hartford Public High School English teacher who was interested in Michael Adams as a student rather than a basketball player. Ed Clarke served as a tutor and academic mentor for Michael Adams through the High Horizons Program, a platform in the Hartford school system (since discontinued) that helped underachieving students develop the skills and study habits needed to succeed in high school and beyond. With the help of Ed Clarke, Michael Adams was able to attain the academic credentials that would make him a credible candidate for a quality institution like Boston College. But Ed Clarke's involvement with Michael Adams did not end with Michael's admittance to college. He actually drove Michael from Hartford to his first day of classes at Boston College, and he kept in frequent contact throughout his four years of college, helping to ease the difficult transition from Bellevue Square to the affluent suburban setting of Chestnut Hill, Massachusetts. Michael Adams was able to graduate from Boston College on time with a C+ average and a degree in Communications, surpassing the academic accomplishments of many of his Eagles' teammates and fellow Big East competitors. He was the first African American basketball player to graduate from BC in a decade. Michael recognized his debt to Ed Clarke in comments made to Owen Canfield of *The Hartford Courant*, "[Ed Clarke] has had a great influence on my life. I owe the progress I have made to him." But Ed Clarke's commitment could only take Michael Adams so far. In the end it was his own tenacious pursuit of an education and a better life that motivated his success.

Michael Adams was inserted in the starting lineup at Boston College as a freshman, and he remained there all four years of his collegiate career. In his freshman year at Boston College he averaged 5.3 points in 14.6 minutes per game. His career really took off in his sophomore year, when he averaged 16.2 points per game and led the Eagles to a 25-7 record, the most wins in the program's history as the team advanced to the Elite Eight. He was the only Big East player to finish in the top ten in the conference in points and assists, as well as field goal and free throw percentage. In his junior season, Michael Adams emerged as one of the most feared scorers in the Big East. He averaged 21.3 points over the first 12 games of the season, and he was the leading scorer in five of the 12 games, including a 34 point game in a 74-63 victory at Villanova. But the team was not winning games at the same rate it had the previous year, and Michael Adams adjusted his game, intentionally dialing back his scoring to focus more on his playmaking responsibilities. The team responded and finished with an 18-12 record. Michael Adams still averaged 17.3 points a game, the highest average of his four years at Boston College. He also averaged 3.4 rebounds, 3.5 assists, and 2.9 steals per game. In his senior year he led the team in scoring with a 15.3 points per game average, while recording 3.3 rebounds, 5.2 assists, and 2.3 steals per game. The team finished 20-11 on the season, losing in the regional semifinals of the NCAA tournament. His four seasons at Boston College had come to an end, but his eleven year career as a professional basketball player was about to begin.

Michael Adams was selected by the Sacramento Kings in the third round of the NBA draft. He played 18 games with the Kings, averaging 2.2 points per game, when he was cut from the team. He spent the remainder of the 1985-86 season with the Bay State Bombardiers of the Continental

Basketball Association, where he was named Rookie-of-the-Year and selected as a second team All-Star. He was signed by the Washington Bullets the following year, cut during preseason, and then resigned when Frank Johnson was injured. He appeared in 63 games for Washington, averaging 7.2 points per game in a reserve role. He was traded to the Denver Nuggets, where he became a legitimate NBA star during a productive four year stint. His coach at Denver, Doug Moe, recognized that Michael was a perfect fit for the up-tempo, playground style of basketball he wanted his team to utilize. It was the kind of rapid-fire, fast-break system under which Michael Adams had thrived at Hartford Public and Boston College. Doug Moe gave Michael Adams' natural creativity free reign, and the impact on the league was stunning. Michael and his teammates started hoisting three-point attempts at a record-setting pace. With Michael in the lineup, the team became a serious contender in the Midwest Division. In his best season with the Nuggets, 1990-91, he averaged a staggering 26.5 points, 10.5 assists, 3.9 rebounds, and 2.2 steals per game. He was 27 years old and on top of the basketball world.

After his breakout season with the Nuggets, Michael Adams was traded back to the Washington Bullets, who realized the team had made a serious mistake in letting him get away four years earlier. While he had enjoyed incredible success in Denver, he did not mind returning to Washington. He was married to a woman from D.C. and they lived close to the Capital Centre, where the Bullets played their home games. He realized at that point in his career that the NBA was a business, and he did not take trades personally. His first year back in Washington was a memorable one for him. He made the All-Star team, validating his status as one of the NBA's elite players. In a game in the Capital Centre on November 2, 1991, he played one of the best games of his NBA career, competing against the mighty Boston Celtics, the team he had followed closely while a student at Boston College. Michael Adams scored 40 points, handed out 11 assists, and made four steals in a 126-118 overtime win. He either scored or assisted on all 14 of his team's points in overtime. One night earlier he had torched Indiana for 23 points, 13 assists, and 9 steals in a Bullets' road victory, but he was even more dominant on the second night of the back-to-back games. The Celtics team included some of the greatest NBA players of all-time in Larry Bird, Robert Parish, Kevin McHale, and Reggie Lewis, but on this night Michael Adams stood above all the other stars.

The opposing point guard on the Celtics was John Bagley, the former Warren Harding of Bridgeport standout who had been a Big East Player of the Year at Boston College. Just as John Bagley had once passed the baton to Michael Adams as the team leader and star player of the Boston College Eagles, he was again giving way to Michael's ascendancy as one of the NBA's best.

But even at the height of his career, Michael Adams never lost sight of where he came from. When he was in Denver, he called home to Hartford almost every night. He returned to Hartford during the summers, and for several years he ran a free basketball camp for kids from Hartford sponsored by the South Arsenal Neighborhood Development Corporation. John Wilson, the Executive Director of SAND, remarked to Tom Condon of *The Hartford Courant* on the importance of Michael Adams' participation in the camp, "We'd like to have the youngsters understand that there is an opportunity for success coming out of the neighborhood, not just in athletics. Michael Adams is living proof of it."

For his part, Michael Adams welcomed the opportunity to help young people growing up in his old neighborhood. He told George Smith of *The Hartford Courant*, "I was very happy to do this when they asked me. You've got to give something back, right? They [the kids] know I made it from this neighborhood. It instills hope in everybody." In talking to the youngsters at the Michael Adams Basketball Camp, he warned against the danger of putting too much faith in athletics as a means of creating a better life. He spoke to Tom Condon of *The Hartford Courant* about the message he tried to impress upon the campers, "There are two ways out of the ghetto, school and sports. If you get injured, then there's only one way out. I tell the kids they've got to stay in school and get that education. You can still work at a desk with a bad ankle ... I think the kids relate to me because I'm from Hartford, I grew up in the projects. I want them to think if I can do it, they can do it ... I used basketball, it didn't use me. I worked harder in school so I could have basketball. Making the NBA, that's just icing on the cake." Michael Adams was not only one of Hartford's greatest basketball players of all time, he was also one of the city's most influential role models.

Steven Blocker
Weaver High School 1982

When Northwest Catholic High School and Weaver High School met in the 1980 CIAC Class LL tournament quarter-finals at Bloomfield High School, Norman Bailey and Steven Blocker led their respective teams in scoring for the game, Norman with 21 points and Steven with 16. Northwest Catholic prevailed to advance to the semi-finals. Although Norman was a highly publicized senior and Steven a relatively unknown sophomore at the time, the two outstanding basketball players had much in common. They grew up in the same neighborhood in the Blue Hills section of Hartford, Norman on Hebron Street and Steven on Naham Drive. They were the youngest children in very large, athletic families; Norman had twelve siblings and Steven had nine, and they almost all played sports. They were both devoted to their mothers, Norman to Mamie and Steven to Eva. And they both had created a buzz in their neighborhoods as promising basketball players before they entered high school.

Like most young and talented basketball players in the city, they spent considerable time honing their skills in Hartford's parks and on recreation centers' courts. They knew each other casually, not necessarily as friends, but rather as potential rivals. Under different circumstances, they might have become teammates at Weaver, but their paths diverged, with Norman going to a suburban parochial school and Steven attending his neighborhood public high school. But they both bore the unique imprint of Hartford basketball, the passion for the game, the coolness under pressure, the gravity-defying feats of athletic grace, and the stubborn refusal to give in on the basketball court or in life. The toughness and the flair that they brought to their games evoked memories of the great Hartford players that had come before them.

Steven Blocker was attracted to basketball at an early age. He watched his older siblings thrive in a variety of sports. His sister Patricia, a nurse, was a tennis and track-and-field star at Northwest Catholic. His brother Osale, a police detective, was a record-setting running back at Weaver. Richard, who worked at Colt's Manufacturing Company, was an outstanding golfer. Fred, an all-around athlete, excelled at baseball. But young Steven showed an affinity for basketball. When he was 13 years old, he won a one-on-one competition at half-time of a Boston Celtics game at the Hartford Civic Center, representing the Northwest Boys & Girls Club. He sought out older players, local legends like Wayne Jones, Duffy Jernigan, and Shorty Davis, who mentored his development. He dominated youth leagues when playing against kids in his own age group. Even before he entered Weaver, he was considered a "can't-miss" future star.

Yet basketball consumed all of Steven Blocker's time and energy. He was ineligible to play during his freshman year at Weaver, his high school basketball career in jeopardy before it even started. He resolved to buckle down, focus on classroom responsibilities, and regain his eligibility. As a sophomore, he played on an undefeated JV team that included Earle Scott, Levelle Stewart, Greg Merrick, and Mike Copeland. His outstanding performance on the JV team earned him a promotion to the varsity, where he led Weaver's surge to the state tournament. His first varsity game came against arch-rival Hartford Public in a City Series match-up. Steven Blocker scored 18 points to pace the Beavers, but Michael Adams, on his way to a typical 23-point, nine-assist game, took control early to lead the Owls to a 57-41 victory. At that point in the season, the teams were headed in opposite directions. Hartford Public improved to 6-3 overall and 3-0 in the Capital District Conference, while Weaver fell to 3-5 overall and remained winless in the conference at 0-2. But Steven Blocker's presence in the Weaver lineup had added a spark to the offense, and the Beavers immediately became a much more formidable opponent.

In Weaver's next game, the team rode Steven Blocker's torrid fourth quarter to a 74-67 City Series win over Bulkeley. He scored 14 points in the final period, including eight of nine foul shots, to help Weaver overcome an eight point deficit. He finished with 25 points, while junior guard Levelle Stewart chipped in with 20 points. Bulkeley's 6'- 7" senior center, John Dyson, led the Bulldogs with 22 points. The win ended a four-game losing streak for the Beavers, improving the team's record to 4-5 overall and 1-2 in the CDC. The team continued to build momentum, beating visiting Springfield Classic, 82-75, as Earle Scott and Steven Blocker fueled another fourth quarter rally. Earle Scott finished with 22 points and Steven Blocker added 19 in his third varsity appearance. Five players scored in double figures for the Beavers, and suddenly the team looked very much like a contender for a coveted berth in the state tournament.

In spite of the team's improved production since Steve Blocker was inserted in the lineup, Weaver continued to struggle against the elite teams on the schedule. Against an always dangerous Wilbur Cross team, the Governors' 6'-7" center Jeff Hoffler torched the Beavers for 38 points and Weaver went down to a 117-103 defeat. Steve Blocker led Weaver with 24 points and Levelle Stewart and Earle Scott tallied 21 points each as the Beavers fell to 5-6 on the season. Weaver edged over the .500 mark with a 75-64 win over Prince Tech to improve to 7-6. Steven Blocker scored 26 points and Gladstone Devonish contributed 18. But the Beavers fell to Hartford Public 62-51 in the second meeting of the regular season between the city rivals. Michael Adams scored a game high 26 points and Chris Canty had 15 points and 15 rebounds for the Owls. Steven Blocker was held to two points in his first disappointing game for Weaver, while Earle Scott led the Beavers with 17 points.

Weaver ended the regular season on a high note, placing five men in double figures in defeating CDC rival New Britain 78-72. Earle Scott scored 19, Levelle Stewart 18, Steve Blocker 15, Greg Davis 13, and Kevin Jones 13. The balanced scoring attack demonstrated that Weaver could beat a quality opponent by playing a team-oriented, fast-breaking style that emphasized ball movement and pressure defense. It was an important lesson to absorb heading into the tournament. In the CIAC Class LL Region I tournament, Weaver defeated Rockville 81-74. Kevin Jones, Weaver's 6'-4" senior center, scored 22 points and dominated the backboards in his best game of the season. Greg Davis led Weaver in scoring with 23 points and Steven Blocker added 19.

But in the Region I title game, Michael Adams scored a career high 39 points as Hartford Public beat Weaver for the third time in the season, 84-65. Weaver was led by 6'-3" forward Greg Davis with 16 points. Under the CIAC format, the regional championships were non-elimination games, and both teams advanced to the quarter-final round of the Class LL state tournament. The Beavers faced Northwest Catholic at Crosby High School in Waterbury, where, ironically, two sons of Hartford's North End, Norman Bailey (21 points) and Marcus Brown (15 points) played key roles in ending Weaver's season. Steven Blocker scored 16 points to lead Weaver in a game that was closer than the final score indicated. Weaver had led at the half, despite playing two juniors and two sophomores most of the game, and the Beavers were within two points in the third quarter before the Owls pulled away. After a 2-7 start to the season, Weaver had finished with a 13-11 record, offering hope that the team could make a strong showing the following year.

But instead of the breakout year the team was anticipating in Steven Blocker's junior year, the 1980-81 season was one of the most chaotic in the program's history. The season started slowly, with the team going 1-3 after four games. In a conference game against New Britain, the Beavers mounted a fourth-quarter comeback to win 61-49 behind Steven Blocker's 18 points and 13 by Levelle Stewart to improve to 2-3. In a City Series contest at home against Bulkeley, Weaver jumped out to a 14-0 lead and held a 22-9 advantage after one quarter. The Beavers led Bulkeley at the half, 38-28, before the Bulldogs mounted a stirring comeback to hand Weaver a crushing 64-63 defeat. After the gut-wrenching loss to Bulkeley, the season began to spiral out of control. Weaver lost badly to Hillhouse, 83-62, and dropped a close game to Wilbur Cross, 63-61. At the beginning of February, disaster struck. Weaver lost more than half the team because of academic and disciplinary issues. When the team was overwhelmed by Bulkeley 96-62 in mid-February, the end of the season could not come fast enough for the 3-12 Beavers. Weaver lost the final three games to finish with a dismal 3-15 record, easily one of the most disappointing basketball seasons in the school's history.

Weaver coach John Lambert did not return for the 1981-82 basketball season. He resigned his teaching and coaching positions at Weaver to work at Workplaces, a vocational program in the Hartford school system. He was replaced by Dwight Tolliver, who had tormented the Weaver basketball team when he was an All-American and All-State point guard for Hartford Public High School from 1963-1967. Dwight Tolliver was an inspired choice to try to revive the struggling Weaver basketball program. He had grown up in Bellevue Square to become a playground and high school legend at Hartford Public. He had taken a difficult path to earning a degree from the University of Rhode Island, making stops at Winston Salem State University and St. Gregory's Junior College in Shawnee, Oklahoma, all while dealing with personal issues back in Hartford. He had immediate credibility with the Weaver players because he had lived through the same challenges they confronted in their daily lives. He had played basketball in Hartford. He understood the tradition, the pride, and the pressure that came with coaching in the city. He was uniquely qualified to accept the challenge of restoring Weaver basketball to a position of prominence in the state.

Over the course of a long and distinguished history, the Weaver High School basketball program had gone through a number of peaks and valleys. Before Charlie Horvath became the coach in the early 1950s, the team had endured a 24 game losing streak. The 1978-79 Weaver team was 1-17 as the season slogged to an end in late February. Through the decades, a number of losing seasons were interspersed with a New England title, eight state championships, and seven state runner-up finishes. If there was one characteristic that epitomized Weaver basketball through the highs and the lows, the jubilation and the upheaval, it was resiliency. Like the city of Hartford itself, Weaver High School always seemed to bounce back from adversity to scale unimagined heights of accomplishment. Under the leadership of Dwight Tolliver, Weaver basketball would rise yet again.

The 1981-82 Weaver team that Dwight Tolliver inherited had little in common with the team that had struggled mightily the previous season, particularly in terms of commitment, attitude, and team-unity. In his senior year Steven Blocker emerged as one of the state's most dominant players, a legitimate triple-double threat as a scorer, rebounder, and assist-maker every time he stepped on the court. He had a strong supporting cast around him, including Jerome Smith, Marvin Mink, Anthony Adams, Charles Terry, and Mike Copeland. Working together as a cohesive unit under a coach that inspired their confidence, these eager Beavers would help lead Weaver back to relevance in the city and the state.

The rejuvenated spirit on the team and within the school was evident in the first meeting of the season with arch-rival Hartford Public. Weaver had not beaten Hartford Public since the 1977-78 season, but Steven Blocker and his teammates were primed to put the extended losing streak behind them as they took the floor in their own gym in front of an enthusiastic home crowd. With Stephen Blocker scoring 24 points in the first half, the Beavers jumped out to a 49-41 lead at halftime. But the Owls mounted a strong third-quarter comeback, led by Angel Verdejo, Marcel Thomas, Alan Davis, and Ernie Canty. Steven Blocker was held to two foul shots in the quarter, stymied by the tenacious defense of Marcel Thomas. Hartford Public took a 71-66 lead in the fourth quarter after forward Alan Davis scored seven straight points. It was the kind of momentum reversal that would have frustrated the players a year earlier and taken them out of their game. But the 1981-82 Weaver team refused to buckle. The Beavers went on a 9-1 run to take a 75-72 lead with less than two minutes to play. With 30 seconds remaining in the game, Steven Blocker rebounded a Charles Terry miss and put back the game-clinching basket. The Weaver fans reacted with elation to the 80-79 victory, cheering wildly as though the team had won a state championship. Weaver was back!

Steven Blocker finished with a game-high 34 points in a superb all-around performance. Weaver improved to 3-0 with the win, while Hartford Public fell to 2-4 on the season. After the game, Dwight Tolliver told Bohdan Kolinsky of *The Hartford Courant*, "Our main plan was to go inside to Steve (Blocker) and we did that in the first two quarters. We stopped going to him in the third quarter and started playing individual basketball. We started jelling again, playing team ball, just in time."

And to show that the one-point win over the Owls was not a fluke, Weaver cruised to a 67-45 victory over Bulkeley on the Bulldogs' home floor in the teams' first meeting of the season. Bulkeley entered the game 6-0 on the season and ranked eighth in the state. Steven Blocker scored 15 of his 25 points as Weaver took a 32-26 halftime lead after trailing in the first quarter. Weaver dominated the second half, with the Beavers controlling the backboards and Charles Terry adding 16 points and Demetrius Dillard 11. Bulkeley had been shooting at a 55 percent clip from the floor in the team's first six games, but Weaver's stingy defense help the Bulldogs to 33 percent shooting. The win gave Weaver a 2-0 record in the City Series and inspired confidence that the team could compete for city and conference titles.

In the second meeting between Bulkeley and Weaver, the Beavers prevailed once again. Weaver, playing at home, trailed 33-31 in the third quarter, when Steven Blocker slammed home a dunk that shifted the game's momentum. He was called for a technical foul for hanging on the rim, but the home crowd erupted in excitement. In the fourth quarter Tony Adams blocked an Owls' shot and Steven Blocker picked up the loose ball at mid-court and drove to the basket for another explosive dunk that electrified the Weaver fans once again. After the game, Bulkeley Coach Joe DiChiara talked to Bohdan Kolinsky of *The Hartford Courant* about the impact of Steven Blocker's second slam, "We neglected to get back on defense on that dunk and it gave them a little spark that they needed." Weaver won the game 64-54 to improve to 9-3 on the season and 3-0 in the City Series. Bulkeley fell to 8-3 overall, with all three losses coming against Weaver and Hartford Public. Sharp shooting Mike Copeland led the Beavers in scoring with 18 points. Steven Blocker scored 16, Tony Adams 10, and Jerome Smith 10, in the kind of balanced, team-focused offensive attack and pressure defense that Coach Dwight Tolliver had emphasized throughout his first season at the helm.

When Weaver and Hartford met for the second time, the Owls needed to win to qualify for the Class LL state tournament and secure the Capital District Conference championship. It was an old-school type of Weaver-Hartford Public game, with multiple titles at stake, not the least of which was the City Series championship for bragging rights in Hartford. Tony Martin scored 21 points and Angel Verdejo added 17 to lead Hartford Public to an 89-81 victory. Recapping the game the next day in *The Hartford Courant*, Bohdan Kolinsky reflected on the vintage nature of the rivalry:

"The names are different but the game is still the same. It's been fifteen years since the Tollivers, Watermans, Adgers, Mahorns, Nashs, Tisdols and Browns dominated the Hartford-Weaver basketball series. Now, there are the Verdejos, Cantys, Martins, Blockers, Terrys and Copelands, and they put on quite a display Tuesday afternoon. It was vintage city basketball and the crowd of nearly 1,000 fans loved it."

The Owls captured the CDC title with a 5-1 record, qualified for the state tournament with an 8-10 record, and tied for the City Series with Weaver at 2-1. Steven Blocker scored 28 points for Weaver, which fell to 10-6 on the season, with two of the losses the result of forfeits for using an ineligible transfer student. But in spite of the additional losses, Weaver qualified for the tournament, and the players were excited about extending their season.

The first round of the CIAC Class LL Region I tournament featured a double header at Manchester High School, with Weaver meeting Norwich in the preliminary game and Hartford Public facing Penney in the second game. In a game that was close throughout, Weaver beat a tough Norwich team 63-59 behind Steven Blocker's twenty points, while Hartford Public beat Penney 51-41. Three nights later, Weaver and Hartford Public took part in another double header at Manchester High School, with Weaver facing Fermi and Hartford Public meeting Windham. Mike Copeland poured in 21 points for Weaver, including the last five points of the first quarter as Weaver took a 20-11 lead. He added seven points in the second quarter to give Weaver a 37-32 lead at the half. In the second half, the Beavers went 9 for 13 from the foul line in the last two minutes of the game to seal a 66-60 victory. Steven Blocker scored 19 points and Charles Terry contributed 18 in the win. In the second game, Hartford Public placed five players in double figures, led by 24 points from Alan Davis, to defeat Windham 92-73.

As a result of the victories, the two city high schools earned the right to play for the Region I title. The third meeting of the season between the rivals took place at Bloomfield High School. At the start of the game, Dwight Tolliver kept the team's two high scorers, Steven Blocker and Charles Terry, on the bench for the entire first quarter. After the game Coach Tolliver discussed the benching with Bruce Berlet of *The Hartford Courant*, "It was something I had to do to make sure they held my respect. It could have cost me the game, but that's the chance I had to take." But Dwight Tolliver had his team play a control style game, and Weaver came away with a 52-49 win to capture the CIAC Class LL Region I championship. Steven Blocker scored 14 points and grabbed 11 rebounds for the Beavers, and Charles Terry hit two free throws with 33 seconds remaining in the game to seal the victory

Both teams advanced to the quarter-finals of the Class LL state tournament. Weaver played Lee High School at Kennedy High in Waterbury. With Weaver up by one point in a hard-fought game, Willie Mills scored on a lay-up with two seconds left in the game to give Lee a 62-61 win. Mike Copeland had kept Weave close in the first half, scoring nine points, including a long jump shot at the first-half horn to give the Beavers a 29-28 lead. Weaver missed some key foul shots at the end of the game to open the door for Willie Mills' game winning shot on a feed from Frank Massey. Weaver finished the season with a 13-8 record. The stinging loss to Lee dampened a season in which the team had returned to respectability behind a new coach, the all-around superlative play of Steven Blocker, and a determined group of teammates.

After graduating from Weaver, Steven Blocker attended St. Thomas More School in Oakdale, Connecticut, along with his Weaver teammate Mike Copeland. After St. Thomas More he enrolled at Middlesex Community College in Middletown. He had an outstanding year at

Middlesex, averaging a triple-double with 17 points, 13 rebounds, and 11 assists per game, showcasing the versatility that defined his outstanding career.

Stephen Blocker became a devoted husband and father and a respected case manager for the Boys & Girls Club, the setting where he first began to distinguish himself as one of the city's elite basketball players.

Greg Davis
Weaver High School/Loomis Chaffee School 1982

When Weaver High School defeated Rockville High School 81-74 in the 1980 Connecticut Interscholastic Athletic Conference Class LL Region I basketball tournament, the Beavers were led in scoring by a relatively unheralded 6'- 4" forward named Greg Davis with 23 points. In the semifinal round, Weaver edged Penney High School of East Hartford 44-40, and Greg Davis' 11 points were high for the Beavers in the low-scoring contest. The Weaver victories in the preliminary rounds set up an all-Hartford championship game against intense rival Hartford Public High School. In the title game the Owls jumped out to an 8-0 lead and cruised to an 84-65 win. The only time in the entire game the outcome was in doubt came late in the first quarter when Weaver took a 15-13 lead on a three-point play by Greg Davis. It would be Weaver's last lead in a game remembered primarily for Owls' junior captain Michael Adams' 39-point scoring outburst, a performance that Hartford Public head coach Stan Piorkowski described as "simply unbelievable". Weaver once again was led in scoring by Greg Davis, who finished the game with 16 points. In the regional tournament format, both Hartford Public and Weaver advanced to the quarterfinal round of the CIAC Class LL state tournament. Weaver was eliminated 64-50 by a strong Northwest Catholic team led by two players from Hartford, Norman Bailey and Marcus Brown, ending the Beavers' season. It was Greg Davis' final game for Weaver. He wasn't graduating, moving, dropping out of school, or quitting basketball. Instead, he was heading to Windsor to attend the prestigious private school Loomis Chaffee, where his exceptional athletic and academic talent would become increasingly evident.

Greg Davis grew up in Bowles Park, the youngest of Mr. and Mrs. Arlette Jones Davis' three sons. One of his brothers was Wayne Jones, an outstanding basketball player for Weaver from 1963-1967. Wayne Jones was a unique and influential player in his era. At 6'- 4" and blessed with tremendous leaping ability, he was the prototypical high school center, capable of punishing opponents in the low post by jumping over or pivoting around defenders for uncontested shots around the basket. He was a deadly finisher on the fast break, soaring to the hoop for mind-numbing dunks that left spectators shaking their heads in disbelief. But Wayne Jones had an added dimension to his game that separated him from virtually all the frontcourt players of his era. He had unlimited range on his jump shot, enabling him to pull up almost anywhere inside the midcourt line to unleash his high-arcing, deliciously sweet stroke that seemed to leave the ball floating endlessly in the air before snuggling in the net. Wayne Jones was a jump shot artist; the perimeter reaches of the basketball court framed his canvass. After he graduated from Weaver, Wayne Jones went to Pratt Community College in Kansas, before transferring to Niagara University, where he was a teammate of the incomparable Calvin Murphy. His coach at Niagara, Frank Layden, a former NBA Coach-of-the Year with the New Orleans Jazz and thus an astute judge of NBA talent, said of Wayne Jones, "He's a very fine shooter and has pro range." If Greg Davis needed a role model to serve as inspiration for his own development as a basketball player, he had one of the very best in his brother, the late, great Wayne Jones.

Greg Davis began playing basketball while he was a student at Mark Twain School. He also played at the Bowles Park Boys & Girls Club for Coach "Teach" Collier, who often took the players for ice cream after games, giving Greg Davis and his friends even more reason to enjoy playing basketball. When he was entering the fourth grade, Greg Davis transferred to St. Justin School, where his parents hoped he would be challenged academically. He played on the school's CYO basketball team with Norman Bailey and Marcus Brown, the same players that would eventually help cut short his brief career at Weaver when Northwest Catholic eliminated the Beavers from the 1980 state tournament. In retrospect, it is interesting to speculate about the team that might have resulted had the three young St. Justin players remained teammates through high school. It would have been an oddity in Hartford to have three such gifted players, all in the 6'-5" range in height, playing together on the same team, and if you added Steven Blocker in the mix, another promising youngster from the same general neighborhood, you could easily envision future championships. St. Justin School did not prove the solution to engaging Greg Davis' academic potential. Hoping a change of environment might stimulate her son to perform better in school, Greg Davis' mother arranged for him to live with his uncle in Windsor and attend L.P. Wilson Junior High School. But Greg Davis missed his friends in Hartford, and he moved back in with his mother. He would try to follow in his brother Wayne's sizable footsteps and attend Weaver High School. To prepare for the challenge of playing basketball at Weaver, the summer prior to his freshman year he attended basketball camps, including one run by Calvin Murphy, Wayne Jones' teammate at Niagara University. In his first year at Weaver Greg Davis played on a talented freshman team that included his friends Daryl Thames and Earle Scott. He averaged 12 points per game as a freshman, displaying promise that he would contribute to Coach John Lamberts' varsity team as a sophomore. Although he did find success on the varsity and enjoyed playing with teammates like Steven Blocker, Tony Allison, Gladstone Devonish, Jeff Johnson, Keith Jones, and Earle Scott, he felt dissatisfied with his educational experience at Weaver. He lost interest in his classes and started hanging out at the Bowles Park Boys & Girls Club, where a concerned recreation director helped him get on track.

Joe Lapenta's career with the Boys & Girls Club of Hartford spanned more than sixty years. He used the Boys Club frequently in his youth, then started to work part time as a counselor when he was seventeen. He became the youngest Unit Director in the country, before eventually being named the organization's Executive Director. He was the director of the Bowles Park Boys & Girls Club when he met Greg Davis, and he recognized Greg's potential as an athlete and a student. He arranged for Greg to visit the Loomis Chaffee School campus and receive an interview with the Admissions' Office. Greg Davis was admitted to the prep school and became an immediate force on the Loomis Chaffee basketball team.

In Greg Davis' first game he led the team back from a 37-30 halftime deficit at Avon Old Farms School to a 69-60 victory by scoring 35 points. Throughout the season he was consistently the team's leading scorer and rebounder. He scored 23 points and grabbed 13 rebounds in a 73-70 win over Suffield Academy as Loomis improved to 8-2 on the season. He led all scorers with 17 points and added 14 rebounds as Loomis Chaffee defeated Kingswood, 67-44. In a double overtime win against Avon Old Farms in the quarterfinals of the New England Class B Prep School basketball tournament, Greg Davis scored 37 points and pulled down 21 points. Clearly, he had found his groove at the prep school, and he was taking full advantage of the opportunity to lead a team.

His success at Loomis Chafee spilled over into his senior season as well. In the opening round of the Hill Invitational tournament in Pottstown, Pennsylvania, Greg Davis scored 30 points and grabbed 14 rebounds in a 75-59 win over Lawrenceville Academy. He continued his outstanding play throughout the entire season, leading Loomis Chaffee into the New England Class B tournament by scoring a game-high 23 points in a 59-40 win over Hotchkiss. Loomis Chaffee advanced to the tournament finals before losing to Hyde School 80-74 in the title game. Greg Davis scored 19 points in his final game and Loomis Chaffee finished the season with a 16-4 record. He had enjoyed an extremely productive two years at Loomis Chaffee, and now he had to decide where he was going to spend the next four years.

The choice turned out to be Tufts University in Medford, Massachusetts, a top-tier academic institution that competed in the New England Small College Athletic Conference (NESCAC) at the NCAA Division III level. It might have seemed an odd pick for someone with Greg Davis' ability and physical attributes. It seemed he could have attracted scholarship offers from Division I and Division II basketball programs, except that his priorities were aligned with the NESCAC concept of placing academics above athletics. Greg Davis was under no illusions that he was preparing for a career in the NBA, and he wanted to put himself in the best possible position for a fulfilling life after college. A pipeline between Hartford's North End and Tufts University had already been established through Dennis Mink, a key member of the 1971 Weaver High School Class LL state championship team. Dennis Mink rewrote the record book while he played on the Tufts University basketball team from 1972-1975. In following Dennis Mink to Tufts, Greg Davis was poised to make his own assault on the university's scoring, rebounding, and shot-blocking records.

Over his four year college career, Greg Davis became one of the most dominant players in the history of Tufts University and the NESCAC conference. He scored a total of 1,785 points and averaged 19.2 points per game over his career, both school records at the time. In his sophomore year he averaged 21.2 points and 10.6 rebounds per game. As a junior, he averaged 23.8 points per game, still the second highest single season scoring average in school history. He remains the university's sixth all-time leading rebounder, with a career average of 8.9 boards per game. He was one of the best shot-blockers in Tufts' history. On January 16, 1985, Greg Davis broke the Tufts' single-game scoring mark, erupting for 43 points in a 106-77 win over Curry College. He hit 19 of 29 shots from the field and all five of his foul shots in his record-shattering performance. And to prove that he was totally invested in the student side of the student-athlete equation, he accomplished his historic run on the school's basketball records while maintaining a 3.06 grade point average, majoring in Pre-Law. Greg Davis would go on to earn his law degree from Georgetown University.

On Saturday night, January 26, 1985, ten days after Greg Davis had scored 43 points to set Tufts University's single-game scoring record, his team came to Hartford to play against Trinity College in the Ferris Athletic Center. Trinity won the game 95-75 for the team's fifth win in a row, and Ken Abere scored 27 points to go over the 1,000-point mark in his career. Bill Pfohl, Mike Donovan, and Jon Morehouse all played well for Trinity, and the night seemed to belong to the Bantams. But the game was memorable for another reason as well. A Tufts' player who had grown up several miles away from the Trinity campus in the Bowles Park housing project also surpassed the 1,000-point mark in his college career that night. Greg Davis' milestone achievement probably did not draw very much attention from the Trinity fans, but his success was nevertheless a triumph for Hartford basketball, just as his appointment as counsel for Travelers Insurance Company would be a few years later. Hartford could take pride in one of the city's most accomplished sons.

Tyrone Canino
Bulkeley High School 1983

During their highly productive years at Bulkeley High School, Kevin and Kenney Hightower helped return a struggling Bulldogs' basketball program to respectability. Bulkeley finished the 1978-79 basketball season with a record of 11-9, losing to Bristol Central by a score of 59-55 in the quarterfinals of the CIAC Class L Region III tournament. Bristol Central was led by 6'- 8" senior center Bruce Kuczenski, who would go on to play at UConn and then in the NBA for the New Jersey Nets, Philadelphia 76ers, and the Indiana Pacers. The Bulldogs did not have anyone on the team to counter a big man with Bruce Kuzenski's skill and size.

The 1980-81 Bulkeley team lost in the semifinals of the Class L tournament to St. Bernard, the eventual state champion. St. Bernard was led by 6'- 7" Harold Pressley, who was a member of the 1985 Villanova University team that won the National Championship, defeating Georgetown 66-64. Harold Pressley went on to play four seasons in the NBA for the Sacramento Kings. Once again, Bulkeley did not have anyone on the team that was capable of offsetting the production of an elite big man like Harold Pressley. Yet the answer to Bulkeley's need for a quality big man was already enrolled in the school. Over the next two years 6'- 7" Tyrone Canino would emerge as one of the premier players in the state.

Like the Hightower brothers, Tyrone Canino grew up in Charter Oak Terrace in Hartford, where he and his four brothers and a sister were raised by their mother. His mother would eventually return to school to earn her high school diploma, and she worked at Travelers Insurance Company for many years. She tried to keep close tabs on her children, and she preferred when the neighborhood kids used the Canino home as the place to hang out. Although the Canino kids played a variety of sports, Tyrone was drawn to basketball at an early age.

As a fourth grader at Mary Hooker School with above average height, Tyrone Canino showed he had a knack for rebounding. He realized that if he wanted the basketball in his hands, he needed to grab it when it bounced off the backboard or rim. From the time he started playing basketball, rebounding was the centerpiece of his game.

He was influenced at Mary Hooker School by Mr. Vinnie Mahoney, a popular fifth and sixth grade teacher who also served as the basketball coach. Tyrone Canino recalled that Mr. Mahoney took notice of his students' birthdays by buying two cakes, one that was eaten in the classroom and the other sent home for the family. As the Mary Hooker School basketball coach, Mr. Mahoney recognized Tyrone Canino's potential and made him the only fourth grader on a team with fifth and sixth graders. Tyrone Canino credited Vinnie Mahoney for helping him understand the fundamentals of basketball and enabling him to get off to a good start learning how to play as part of a team.

Another early positive influence in Tyrone Canino's life was Clarence "Sonny" Thomas, the Director of the Southwest Boys & Girls Club. Sonny Thomas served as a mentor, counselor, and advocate for Tyrone Canino, just as he had for the Hightower twins and countless other young people in the neighborhood. Tyrone remembered striving to win the Youth-of-the-Month award that Sonny Thomas implemented at the club. Sonny Thomas had enjoyed tremendous success as an athlete at Hartford Public, and he continued to serve young people in the community through an exemplary 30-year career with the Boys & Girls Club of Hartford.

Tyrone Canino did not play basketball at Bulkeley as a freshman. In an interview with Bruce Berlet of *The Hartford Courant* when he was at Central Connecticut State College, Tyrone stated, "I had to work and couldn't play my freshman year. But when I became a sophomore, I began to take the game seriously." He also suffered from asthma and was having problems adjusting to high school after attending Michael D. Fox Junior High School, two factors that may have contributed to his basketball inactivity his freshman year. As a sophomore he became a starter on an undefeated JV team. The Bulldogs were eliminated by eventual champion St. Bernard in the semifinals of the Class L state tournament. When Bulkeley coach Joe DiChiara approached Tyrone Canino weeks later and told him the team needed him to become a key contributor, he was encouraged to work hard in preparation for his junior year. He was determined to show Coach DiChiara he could be counted on to help the team succeed.

Tyrone Canino played well his junior year, averaging 14 points and 13 rebounds per game. He was named to the All-Capital District Conference first team. But although the Bulldogs had a winning record and qualified for the state tournament, the team struggled against the better teams on the schedule. If Bulkeley hoped to have any chance of winning a state championship, Tyrone Canino would have to show considerable improvement. He knew he needed to get stronger and to become a more explosive leaper in order to absorb contact around the basket and still dunk with authority. He began to train seriously with weights, adding strength to his lean 6'-7" frame. Within three months of starting a weight training and conditioning regimen, he made significant strides in transforming his body by adding muscle and improving his endurance

Tyrone Canino returned to school in the fall with renewed determination, and the Bulldogs jumped out to a strong start to the 1982-83 basketball season. In a preseason controlled scrimmage against Capital Community College, he scored 30 points and pulled down 30 rebounds, convincing him he was ready to have a dominant senior year at Bulkeley. In a CDC matchup against New Britain High School, Tyrone Canino scored 22 points and pulled down 17 rebounds in a 63-47 victory. Bulkeley improved to 4-1 on the season while handling New Britain its first loss. In Bulkeley's first City Series game of the season against Hartford Public, the Bulldogs displayed improved depth when Tyrone Canino was forced to the bench with early foul trouble. Two sophomore reserves, Ivan Powell and Anthony Bagley, not only helped keep Bulkeley in the game, they also combined for the winning basket. Anthony Bagley found Ivan Powell under the basket with 13 seconds remaining in the game to give Bulkeley a 60-59 win. In spite of foul problems, Tyrone Canino still managed to score 18 points and grab 20 rebounds. Guard Russell Shorter, a clutch Bulkeley performer all season long, added 17 points and five assists as the Bulldogs improved to 5-1. Bulkeley moved to 6-1 on the season with a 73-53 win over Maloney behind strong games by Tyrone Canino and Russell Shorter. It was exactly the kind of start Bulkeley needed to show that the team was once again in the mix to contend for a state title.

But in Hartford it was never easy for a team to gain separation from its city rivals. In a game at the Weaver Fieldhouse, the Beavers slowed Bulkeley's momentum with a 75-63 win. Weaver coach Dwight Tolliver used 6'-5" junior center Kevin Fredericks, a defensive specialist, to focus on holding down Tyrone Canino. Tyrone still managed 19 points and 17 rebounds, but the Bulkeley loss showed that good coaches like Dwight Tolliver were determined to try to keep the dangerous Canino in check. Over the course of the season, Tyrone Canino would face multiple defensive strategies designed to limit his effectiveness. On a nightly basis he would confront constant double-teams, box-and-ones, collapsing zones, and quick traps, yet he still managed to score and rebound at a consistent clip. In spite of the mongrel defenses thrown at him, he was averaging 20 points and 17 rebounds per game, while shooting 65 percent from the floor and 75 percent from the foul line. After Bulkeley's 20-point win over Maloney, Coach Norb Fahey of Maloney told Terese Karmel of *The Hartford Courant*, "Our players were intimidated by Canino. He intimidates you on defense, and he triggers their whole offense. He gets that outlet pass to half-court before you can blink." Tyrone Canino was playing with confidence and focus, and that was bad news for opposing coaches.

In a game against Bloomfield Tyrone Canino erupted for 36 points and 21 rebounds. And in the rematch against Weaver, Frank Shorter hit a layup with two seconds left in regulation to send the game into overtime, and he converted two foul shots in the extra session to give Bulkeley a 62-60 win. For Bulkeley it was the first time since the 1959-60 season that the team won the City Series title outright. When Bulkeley beat New Britain 74-54 behind Tyrone Canino's 24 points and 24 rebounds, the team captured the CDC title as well. As the Bulldogs headed into the state tournament, the team was riding a strong wave of momentum.

In the semifinals of the CIAC Class L Region III tournament, Bulkeley faced a strong East Catholic team. With East Catholic concentrating on stopping Tyrone Canino and Russell Shorter, 5'- 7" Bulldogs guard Fred Gerena broke loose for a career high 18 points, including the game-winning basket with 17 seconds left on the clock, leading Bulkeley to a 60-59 win in a game played at Conard High School. Tyrone Canino was held to nine points, but he contributed 18 rebounds and three steals to the victory. Russell Shorter added 14 points. It was Bulkeley's second one-point win of the season over East Catholic and gave the Bulldogs a 16-3 record going into the regional final against dangerous local rival South Catholic High School.

During the regular season, South Catholic had handed Bulkeley one of its three losses, beating the Bulldogs 68-65. Tyrone Canino had scored 26 points in the loss before fouling out. South Catholic had advanced to the Region III final by beating Bristol Eastern 65-59 in the semifinals behind a 36-point outburst from Doug McCrory. In the regional final game at Bloomfield High School, Russell Shorter hit a jump shot with 30 seconds remaining in the fourth quarter to send the game into overtime.

Forward Pablo Ortiz scored five of his game-total seven points in overtime to give Bulkeley the 54-51 win. Tyrone Canino was held to nine points by the excellent defensive work of South's Pat Burke and Dave Widell. Doug McCrory led South with 19 points. In the regional format, both Hartford teams advanced to the quarterfinals of the Class L state tournament, with Bulkeley facing Ledyard and South playing Hand of Madison.

Against a tough Ledyard team, Tyrone Canino had to battle 6'- 7" John Reynolds and 6- 4" Ken Nordgren under the boards. The game came down to the final seconds, with Russell Shorter hitting a 14-foot jump shot with 33 seconds left in the game that proved to be the winning basket in a 48-47 Bulkeley win. Both John Reynolds and Tyrone Canino scored 17 points, but Tyrone was held to a season low 10 rebounds. With the win, Bulkeley advanced to the semifinal round of the Class L state tournament to face Wilby High of Waterbury. Similar to Ledyard High, Wilby's height along the frontline presented Bulkeley with a formidable challenge. Wilby was led by 6'- 8" James Saunders and 6'- 4" Martin Hayre, and in the end Wilby was able to eliminate Bulkeley from the tournament. The Bulldogs finished the season 18-4, one of the best records in Bulkeley's history.

Tyrone Canino averaged 19 points and 20 rebounds in his senior year at Bulkeley High and led the team to the semifinals of the Class L state tournament. He was named All-City, All-CDC, and All-State. He had received numerous letters from Division I and Division II colleges, with UConn and Boston College showing particular interest in him. He decided to attend Central Connecticut State University, in part because of his familiarity with the Hightower twins and their success at Central. He told Tom Yantz of *The Hartford Courant*, "I played with Kevin and Kenny Hightower before. They told me about Central and the type of basketball played there." In choosing Central, Tyrone Canino was joining an illustrious list of Bulkeley graduates that opted to play for Coach Bill Detrick, including Gene Reilly, Jim Muraski, and the Hightower brothers. Bill Detrick recognized Tyrone Canino's excellent potential, telling Courant staff writer Tom Yantz, "Canino is a basketball player. He can run and fill the lane." It did not take long for Tyrone to justify his coach's confidence in him. In one of his first games at Central, he made two foul shots with seven seconds remaining in the game to seal a 70-67 win over Stonehill College. He averaged 8.9 points and 8.6 rebounds per game as a freshman, helping the team compile a 26-6 record, establishing a school record for wins in a season.

As a sophomore, Tyrone Canino was slowed by injury for a portion of the season, but he continued to develop as a reliable scorer and he led Central in rebounding. In the second game of the annual Connecticut Travel Service Classic at Kaiser Hall, Tyrone Canino had 21 points and 18 rebounds, both game highs, in a 92-78 victory over Keane State. In the tourney finals against a tough Springfield College team, Tyrone scored 24 points, including two foul shots with five seconds remaining to give Central a 57-55 win.

In his junior year at Central, Tyrone Camino emerged as an elite college player. In the eleventh annual Walter "Doc" Hurley Classic, Tyrone recorded game highs of 24 points and 14 rebounds in a 103-95 victory over Virginia State, Doc's alma mater. He scored 26 points and grabbed 15 rebounds in a 95-89 win over the University of New Haven. For the season Tyrone Camino averaged 14.4 points per game, second best average on the team, and he averaged 13.1 rebounds per game, good for fourth in the nation in Division II. The team finished the season with a 15-13 record, the Blue Devils final year as a Division II school. Tyrone Camino was poised to lead the program into Division I in his senior year.

But he was declared academically ineligible at the end of his junior year, and he would sit out Central's first full year as a Division I program. The Blue Devils struggled mightily without Tyrone Camino in the lineup during the transition to Division I, finishing the season with a 6-23 record. Tyrone returned to the team for the 1987-88 season. He was named team captain, following in the footsteps of John Pazda, Gene Reilly, Jimmy Muraski, Kevin Hightower, and Kenney Hightower as former Bulkeley players that served as captains at Central. It was a challenging season for Tyrone Canino. He suffered torn ligaments in a finger on his shooting hand in an early season 91-77 loss to Marathon Oil. There was a coaching change when Bill Detrick resigned for health reasons and was replaced by C.J. Jones. Several players were suspended for disciplinary reasons, and at one point in the season the team lost 11 of 13 games. Yet Tyrone Canino showed pride and maturity by striving to make the most of his final season at Central. New head coach C.J. Jones told Roy Hasty of *The Hartford Courant*, "Tyrone has been a leader for us on and off the court the last portion of the season. He took it upon himself that he wanted to go out a winner. This was it for him. He got into the spirit of things, began to develop and mature and took over in a leadership role."

In a 75-74 win against Hofstra that halted a five-game losing streak, Tyrone Canino scored 34 points on 15 of 21 shooting from the floor, and he added 11 rebounds, three blocked shots, 3 assists, and two steals. He scored 27 points, grabbed 23 rebounds, and blocked four shots in an 89-79 win over Maryland-Baltimore County. His 23 rebounds was one off his career high of 24 set in his junior year against Salem State. In his senior year he averaged 14.3 points, tied for the team lead with Bryan Heron, and he led the team in rebounding for the third time in his career with an average of 11.5 boards per game. His 31 blocks also led the team. He finished his career as Central's all-time leading rebounder with over 1,200 boards, and fifth in all-time scoring with more than 1,400 points. Through his relentless effort and indomitable spirit, Tyrone Canino developed into one of Hartford's premier basketball players of all time.

Peter Astwood

A.I. Prince Technical High School 1983

The Hartford Trade School was originally founded in 1915 and was located at 110 Washington Street. When the school moved to 400 Brookfield Street in 1960, it was renamed the Albert I. Prince Technical High School in honor of the former managing editor of The Hartford Times newspaper and a twelve-year chairman of the State Board of Education. The purpose of the school was to prepare students for college while providing instruction in trades and technology, and it drew students from all parts of Hartford and the surrounding towns. The school also had a basketball program, and career-minded students had the opportunity to compete against other high schools in the area. The basketball program operated in the shadows of the more renowned city high schools – Hartford Public, Weaver, Bulkeley, and South Catholic – that had all established reputations in the state as elite teams at one point or another between the decades of the fifties and the eighties. Yet the school, known familiarly as Prince Tech, produced some fine teams and truly outstanding basketball players, including one named Peter Astwood.

Peter Astwood was raised by his mother in Stowe Village, a hotbed of basketball talent in Hartford. He had six siblings, many of them athletes. One brother was a star running back on the Weaver football team and another excelled in track and field at Prince Tech. Peter Astwood began playing competitive basketball at Fred D. Wish Elementary School, where he was also an honor roll student. He recalled a class trip to Washington D.C. to visit historic landmarks that made a strong impression on him. He continued to develop as a basketball player at Lewis Fox Middle School, where his team won a league championship. He also played organized football, and he wanted to follow in his brother's footsteps as a high school football player. When he decided to attend Prince Tech, the issue of which sports to play in high school was resolved. Since Prince Tech did not have a football program, Peter Atwood could focus on basketball.

As a 5'-11" freshman, Peter Astwood averaged 20.4 points per game on the Prince Tech JV team and saw limited action on the varsity team. If he needed a role model for the type of student-athlete he hoped to become at Prince Tech, Fred Davis, the 6'-3" senior captain of the varsity team, was the ideal person to emulate. Fred Davis was a superb basketball player. He started for Prince Tech since his freshman year, and as a senior he led the team to a 16-9 record, averaging 21.9 points, 10.2 rebounds, and five assists per game while shooting an incredible 68 percent from the field. He was the school's all-time leading scorer with 1,609 career points. He was named to The Courant's All-City Basketball Team along with John Pinone from South Catholic, Ken Smith from Hartford Public, Ken Mink from Weaver, and Kevin Conneely from Bulkeley. But his academic performance was equally as impressive as his accomplishments on the basketball court. He was one of Prince Tech's top students, a potential valedictorian of his class with a solid 'A' average. His goal after he graduated from Prince Tech was to attend college to pursue a degree in business and prepare for a fulfilling career when he was through playing basketball. He provided insights into his maturity in comments he made to Ginny Apple of *The Hartford Courant*, "It's been great to be the best player on the team, but I don't want to be like a lot of guys you see hanging around. They talk about the past and how they used to be the best in their school. I've got to be the best every moment in whatever I do. There's a time when you can't play basketball anymore and nobody wants to listen. When that time comes, I'll be ready." Fred Davis set the bar extraordinarily high for players like Peter Astwood that followed after him.

In Peter Astwood's freshman year, Prince Tech advanced to the CIAC Class M tournament semifinals, losing to eventual champion Pomperaug High School, 73-72, in overtime. Fred Davis played a remarkable game, hitting on 14 of his 15 shot attempts from the floor and scoring 31 points. Peter Astwood did not get to play in the exciting tournament game, but it served as a valuable learning experience for him as he prepared to assume a more prominent role for Prince Tech as a sophomore in the absence of key graduating seniors Fred Davis and 6'- 2" Corky Scruse (yet another classic name in Hartford basketball lore). Gary Thomas, a 6'- 5" center, was the lone returning starter from the team that was eliminated in the semifinals of the Class M tournament. Gary Thomas had averaged 14.6 points and 13.5 rebounds as a junior, and he would be joined by a solid core group of players that included 6'- 2" Ricky Johnson, 6'- 6" Anthony Little, 5'- 9" Vinnie Ruff, 5'- 8" Duane Marks, and Peter Astwood.

But the team struggled to make up for the loss of Fred Davis and Corky Scruse. Prince Tech lost the first two games of the season to St. Paul and New London and had difficulty getting back on track. The first win of the season came at city rival Bulkeley's expense. Gary Thomas paced Prince Tech with 16 points and 23 rebounds in a 56-55 win on the team's home court. Duane Mack added 14 points, including a foul shot with 47 seconds remaining in the game that proved to be the winning margin. Rick Johnson and Peter Astwood chipped in with 10 points each. Peter Astwood was gradually settling into his new role as one of Prince Tech's primary offensive weapons.

Prince Tech improved to 3-3 on the season with a 56-49 win over Berlin High School behind 19 points by Glen Miller, 14 by Gary Thomas, and 8 by Peter Astwood. The momentum was short-lived, however, and Prince Tech lost the next three games in a row, including a 59-53 defeat to St. Thomas Aquinas. But Peter Astwood scored 21 points in the loss to Aquinas, and he continued to emerge as a reliable scoring threat. He had grown to 6' tall and he weighed 165 pounds, and with his outstanding leaping ability, large hands, and smooth jump shot, he could hurt opponents inside and outside. The team finished with an 8-11 record, losing to Farmington, 53-51, in the opening round of the CIAC Class M tournament. Peter Astwood still had two years remaining to try to duplicate the 1979-80 team's deep run in the state tournament.

In his junior year Peter Astwood continued to improve, but once again the graduation of key seniors, like co-captains Gary Thomas and Ricky Johnson, slowed Prince Tech's progress. The team finished the season with an 8-12 record and was eliminated early in the Region I tournament. As a senior, Peter Astwood was determined for Prince Tech to have the kind of winning season he had experienced as a freshman. The team started quickly, winning four of the first six games of the season. In a game against Inter-County Athletic Conference rival O'Brien Tech, Peter Astwood erupted for 40 points and 23 rebounds in a 93-42 win. Proving that the 40 point effort was not a fluke, he scored a career-high 44 points in a 99-66 victory over Whitney Tech. He became the third player in school history to break the 1,000 point barrier when he scored 26 points and grabbed 13 rebounds in a 66-55 win over Bristol Central. He trailed only Fred Davis with 1609 points and Gary Thomas with 1,170 points on Prince Tech's all-time scoring list and he was still going strong. In a season in which Tyrone Canino of Bulkeley and Doug McCrory of South Catholic were putting up big numbers on a nightly basis, Peter Astwood was at the top of the city's scoring leaders.

But Peter Astwood was focused on the team winning the conference championship, making the state tournament, and finishing with a winning record. He scored 24 points and grabbed 13 rebounds in an 88-65 win over Kaynor Tech as Prince Tech clinched at least a tie for the Inter-County Athletic Conference title. Guard Kendall May contributed 16 points and six assists to the win, and Darrell Forte chipped in with 14 points. Prince Tech fell to 10-8 on the season after a crushing 76-75 loss to St. Paul. Peter Astwood scored 22 points and Kendall May scored 20 in the defeat. In the next game of the season against Bulkeley, Peter Astwood scored a game-high 24 points, but it was not enough to overcome Ivan Powell's 18 points and 15 from Tyrone Canino as the Bulldogs beat the Prince Tech Falcons, 69-54. But with the goal of a winning season slipping away, Prince Tech defeated O'Brien Tech 110-57 to win the Inter-County Athletic Conference championship with a 5-1 record. Peter Astwood led the Falcons in scoring with 24 points, and Prince Tech finished the regular season with an 11-9 record, assuring the team of a winning record. In the first round of the Class L Region III tournament, East Catholic defeated Prince Tech, 81-61. Peter Astwood scored 29 points in his final game for Prince Tech.

Peter Astwood played one more game in his high school career. He was chosen for the East team in the Connecticut High School Coaches Association Basketball Festival All-Star Game, joining Tyrone Canino of Bulkeley, Mike Thomas of South Catholic, and Troy Collier of Weaver as the Hartford representatives. Playing against a West team that included some of the best players in Class LL-L in the state, like Fred Brown of Hillhouse and Anthony Moye of Wilbur Cross, Peter Astwood scored 19 points to lead the East team to a 77-70 victory at Kennedy High School in Waterbury. Peter won the MVP award for the game, demonstrating that he was not only one of the premier players in the city, but in the entire state as well.

After he graduated from Prince Tech, Peter Astwood played for Mattatuck Community College in Waterbury on one of the strongest Junior College teams in the New England region. His teammates included Kendall May, who played with Peter at Prince Tech, and Ivan Powell, who played at Bulkeley. Kendall May went on to play at Westfield State and Ivan Powell played at Maryland. After two years at Mattatuck, Peter Astwood attended Central Connecticut State University. When he completed his education, he was employed as a youth services worker for the State of Connecticut and he worked for many years at the Connecticut Juvenile Training School. He and his wife have five children. Peter Astwood was one of Prince Tech and Hartford's finest basketball players of his era.

Doug McCrory
South Catholic High School 1984

In Tyrone Canino's senior year at Bulkeley High School, his team played two epic battles against South End rival South Catholic High School. In the first meeting early in the 1982-83 season, Tyrone Canino had a monster game, finishing with a game-high 26 points, 23 rebounds, and four blocked shots before fouling out late in the fourth quarter. After the game South coach Joe Reilly spoke to Bohdan Kolinsky of *The Hartford Courant* about Tyrone Canino's outstanding performance, "He dominated the game. He was so dominant inside that we couldn't get a second shot in that second quarter." But Tyrone Canino's heroic effort was not enough to overcome South's balanced scoring and composure under pressure down the stretch. South fought back from a 38-33 halftime deficit to win the game 68-65. The rematch between the two teams occurred in the finals of the CIAC Class L Region III tournament, and Bulkeley turned the tables on South, winning in overtime by the same three-point margin, 54-51. It was Bulkeley's first win in six tries over the Rebels, and it came against a very strong South team that included Mike Thomas, Steve Pinone, David Montanaro, David Widell, and Peter Strudwick. There was another member of the South Catholic team who had emerged as one of the top players in the state, and he still had another season ahead of him before he graduated. His name was Doug McCrory, and he would become one of the most recognizable figures in Hartford for years to come.

Doug McCrory grew up on Granby Street in Hartford, the youngest of four children. His parents, Issac and Mary, had moved to Hartford from Columbus, Georgia in 1963. His mother worked nights at United Technologies. His father owned a variety of businesses in Hartford over the years. Doug McCrory's two older brothers and a sister all went to college. One of his brothers, Kenny, worked for Jesse Jackson's Operation PUSH (People United to Save Humanity), a non-profit organization intended to advance social justice, civil rights, and political activism. Doug McCrory attended Annie Fisher Elementary School, where he started on the sixth grade basketball team as a fifth grader. At Lewis Fox Middle School, he excelled in the classroom as well as on the basketball court. His math teacher, Mr. Walker, encouraged his parents to send Doug to

South Catholic. His parents agreed, and instead of attending Weaver High School, Doug McCrory commuted to South Street each day.

As a freshman at South Catholic, Doug McCrory started on the JV team and averaged 16 points per game. In his sophomore season Doug McCrory emerged as a key contributor on a strong South Catholic varsity team that included 5'- 11" senior captain John Mirabella, the explosive All-State junior guard Mike Thomas, and 6'- 5" junior center Pat Burke. In a late-season game against Northwest Catholic in West Hartford, Doug McCrory led South Catholic in scoring with 19 points, including 11 of the team's 14 third-quarter points when the Rebels pulled ahead on the way to a 65-55 win. Northwest Catholic was led in scoring by Charlie Simmons with 21 points and ball-hawking guard Jamie Cosgrove with 17 points. Jamie Cosgrove would go on to score 1,088 points at Saint Anselm College from 1983-87 and become the school's all-time leader in steals with 267 picks for his career. Jamie Cosgrove would serve as an assistant coach for Jack Phelan at the University of Hartford and is currently the successful head coach at Trinity College.

The 1981-82 South Catholic team defeated St. Joseph of Trumbull 71-60 at Quinnipiac College to advance to the semifinal game of the CIAC Class L state basketball tournament, where the Rebels lost to eventual champion St. Bernard. South Catholic finished the season with a 21-6 record. Although it was the furthest South Catholic had progressed in the tournament in three years, the loss to St. Bernard and its star player Harold Pressley stung. But with a strong core of returning players, Doug McCrory and his South Catholic teammates were hopeful that a state championship was still within their grasp.

The South Catholic Rebels began the 1982-83 season as though the team was on a mission to claim the state title that had eluded the players the previous year. In the season opening game at home against Bloomfield High School, South Catholic set a school scoring record in a 115-80 win. The school's previous high total occurred in 1968 in a 112-52 win over Eli Whitney of New Haven. Doug McCrory paced the Rebels with 28 points, but South Catholic displayed the kind of balanced scoring attack that would become representative of the team's unselfish style throughout the season. Mike Thomas added 21 points, Pete Strudwick contributed 14 points and 16 rebounds, Steve Pinone scored 13 points, and Brian Walmsley chipped in with 10 points. South Catholic opened the season with nine straight wins, including impressive victories over Bulkeley, Newington, St. Thomas Aquinas, and Xavier, leading to a showdown with undefeated and number one ranked Wilbur Cross in New Haven.

Heading into the Wilbur Cross game, Doug McCrory was averaging 21.4 points per game for 9-0 South Catholic. Perennial Class LL championship contender Wilbur Cross was 8-0, and the team was led by 6'-2" forward Anthony "Big Jim" Moye, a lethal jump shooter who was averaging 29 points per game. Before the game, legendary Wilbur Cross coach Bob Saulsbury, who won nine state championships during his 28-year coaching career, spoke to Courant staff writer Bohdan Kolinsky about Anthony Moye's shooting stroke, "He's a very smooth, very graceful shooter." Anthony Moye would go on to play at the University of Connecticut, but frustrated by a lack of playing time, he transferred to the University of Hartford at the same time that Doug McCrory was transferring from Holy Cross to the University of Hartford. The two dynamic players would eventually team-up to help make the University of Hartford a formidable Division I team, but they met as determined opponents in New Haven on January 19, 1983, intent on staking out a claim for their respective school's as the state's premier high school team.

Wilbur Cross jumped out to a 5-0 lead and kept putting pressure on South Catholic the entire game on the way to an 83-69 victory. The Rebels were so focused on slowing down Anthony Moye, who still managed to score 23 points, they did not pay sufficient attention to 5'-11" sophomore Randy Hargett, who erupted for a career-high 35 points that included a streak of hitting 14 shots in a row. Doug McCrory led South Catholic with 22 points, while Brian Walmsley added 12 points and Mike Thomas 10. South Catholic dropped to 9-1 on the season, and the team had to face the realization that the players needed to continue to improve if they hoped to beat the elite teams in the state.

South Catholic quickly bounced back from the Wilbur Cross defeat with an 80-73 win over St. Thomas Aquinas behind 24 points by Doug McCrory and 14 points by Brian Walmsley. The Rebels rattled off six wins in a row to improve to 15-1 on the season, before losing to Hartford Public, 79-75, proving once again the uncertainty that accompanied any game against a city rival, regardless of the teams' records. South Catholic went into the post-season with an 18-2 record. The team defeated St. Paul 71-69 in the semifinals of the Hartford Country Conference tournament at the University of Hartford. Doug McCrory scored 29 points and grabbed eight rebounds to pace the Rebels. Brian Walmsley hit a layup with five seconds remaining in regulation time for the winning margin. In the finals of the HCC tournament, Brian Walmsley struck again, hitting a 17-foot jump shot with three seconds on the clock to defeat St. Thomas Aquinas, 57-55. Doug McCrory scored 14 points in the fourth quarter to enable South Catholic to come from behind for the victory. The Rebels completed a perfect 12-0 season in the HCC, recording their fifth conference title in the nine-year history of the HCC playoffs. But in the finals of the CIAC Class L Region III tournament, South Catholic lost to Bulkeley in overtime, 54-51. Bulkeley's Russell Shorter hit a jump shot with 30 seconds left in the fourth quarter to send the game into overtime, and Pablo Ortiz scored five points in overtime to seal the victory.

Under the CIAC regional format, even with the loss to Bulkeley, South Catholic advanced to the quarterfinals of the Class L state tournament to face Hand High School of Madison. After beating Hand High, South Catholic faced its stiffest challenge of the season, meeting 26-0 Warren Harding of Bridgeport in the semifinals at the Crosby High field house in Waterbury in front of a crowd of 1,500 spectators. Warren Harding was led by 6'-10" Charles Smith, a future Big East Player-of-the Year at the University of Pittsburg, the third overall pick in the 1988 NBA draft, and a productive NBA player over a nine-season career. But like South Catholic, Warren Harding was hardly a one-man show. The team also featured 6'-6" Bill McBroom (a terrific name for a shot blocker) and 6'-5" Michael Gaines. Yet South Catholic was not overwhelmed in the height department, with 6'-8" Dave Widell, 6'-5" Pat Burke, 6'-5" Steve Pinone, 6'-4" Doug McCrory, 6'-4" Brian Walmsley, and 6'-3" Pete Strudwick to complement Mike Thomas' blistering quickness. All season long South Catholic had shown outstanding depth, often using nine players as part of the team's regular rotation. South Catholic would need every bit of its exceptional length and depth to defeat an imposing Warren Harding team.

The hard fought game came down to the final 42 seconds, when Warren Harding scored seven of the game's final nine points to come away with a 54-49 win. Charles Smith scored 20 points for the eventual state champions, and Pat Burke was high man for South Catholic with 16 points, while Doug McCrory contributed 14 points and 5 assists. The Rebels finished the season with a 23-4 record. Doug McCrory had enjoyed a truly outstanding season. He had averaged 22.4 points per game. He scored a career high 36 points in a 65-59 win over Bristol Central, and he led his team to a conference championship and the semifinals of the Class L state tournament. And he still had one more chance to try to win an elusive state title.

In the second game of the 1983-84 season, Joe Reilly recorded the 350th victory of his illustrious career as South Catholic defeated South Windsor, 76-38, in Hartford. Co-captains Doug McCrory and Brian Walmsley, who Coach Reilly called "the best one-two punch in the area", each scored 20 points to pace the Rebels. Against South End rival Bulkeley High School, Doug McCrory scored 34 points in a 95-83 South Catholic victory. Brian Walmsley added 27 points, relying heavily on an improved out-side shot that he had worked on during the off-season. Brian Walmsley was a versatile 6'- 4" swingman who was an adept ball-handler, passer, and shooter who capably complemented Doug McCrory's strong inside game. Brian was an honor roll student from Wethersfield, where he was following in the footsteps of two other outstanding Wethersfield residents that had chosen to attend South Catholic, Steve Ayers and John Pinone. Doug McCrory and Brian Walmsley played together for three years, and in their senior year they formed a devastating inside-outside threat that drew the attention of every South Catholic opponent.

The Rebels 5-0 winning streak to start the season was interrupted by a 90-76 loss to HCC rival St. Thomas Aquinas, in spite of 26 points from Doug McCrory and 12 points each from Brian Walmsley, Pop Fountain (another classic name), and Shelley Pace. But South Catholic avenged the team's lone defeat by beating St. Thomas Aquinas 71-53 in New Britain, led by Doug McCrory's 22 points. In a 97-63 win over Northwest Catholic, Doug McCrory scored 25 points to move into second place behind John Pinone on South Catholic's all-time scoring list. In the Rebels biggest game of the season, the team defeated Wilbur Cross, 67-65, in front of 1,000 fans in a packed South Catholic gym. Doug McCrory's basket with 13 seconds left on the clock gave South a 66-63 lead, and he hit a foul shot with two seconds remaining to seal the victory. He scored 27 points in South Catholic's first-ever win against Wilbur Cross, giving the team confidence it could compete with the very best the state had to offer.

In the same week South Catholic defeated Wilbur Cross, Doug McCrory scored 21 points and pulled down 10 rebounds in a 76-69 win over city rival Hartford Public, further enhancing the team's confidence heading into the post-season. South Catholic defeated St. Bernard of Montville, 71-61, to capture the CIAC Class L Region I title and advance to the quarterfinals of the state tournament. The Rebels beat Windham High School, 63-54, at Glastonbury High to advance to play Bassick of Bridgeport in the semifinals. Doug McCrory scored 24 points and handed out 10 assists while Mike Strudwick added14 points and Paul Williams 13 in the 66-60 win at Quinnipiac College. The victory over Windham set up a meeting between 23-3 South Catholic and 26-1Warren Harding for the Class L state championship in front of 2,200 spectators in Kaiser Hall on the campus of Central Connecticut State University. Six-foot ten-inch All-American Charles Smith scored 17 points and blocked five shots, and 5'- 6" guard Davis Brown scored 19 points and made four steals to lead Warren Harding to a 55-43 victory. Brian Walmsley led South with 18 points, while Doug McCrory, Mike Strudwick, and Paul Williams all scored eight points.

The disappointment over the loss to Warren Harding in the finals could not obscure the brilliance of Doug McCrory's career at South Catholic. He led the HCC in scoring the last two years. He averaged 23.6 points, 10 rebounds, and six assists per game as a senior. He amassed 1,517 career points and was named first team All-State. His versatility, intensity, and leadership qualities, in combination with his solid academic performance at South Catholic, made him an exceptional college prospect. He received numerous recruiting inquiries, and he narrowed his choices to Northeastern, the University of Hartford, Fairfield, and Holy Cross. After considerable deliberation, he chose Holy Cross.

His stay at Holy Cross was brief. He left the school after eight games and transferred to the University of Hartford, located only about a mile from his home on Granby Street. Back in the familiar surroundings of Hartford, Doug McCrory thrived as a basketball player and a student. His coach at the University of Hartford, the former Northwest Catholic standout Jack Phelan, spoke to Ginny Apple of *The Hartford Courant* about the positive impact Doug McCrory would have on the basketball program, "He's a winner. He's not coming out on the court to lose."

Ironically, Doug McCrory's first game as a Hartford Hawk after sitting out a year came against Holy Cross in the Hartford Civic Center. He came off the bench to score 15 points in a 69-65 win. After the game Doug

McCrory hugged Holy Cross head coach George Blaney and several of the Crusader players that he knew, showing he held no animosity towards his former team. As he told George Smith of *The Hartford Courant* about his brief time at Holy Cross, "It was a learning experience."

He moved on with his life and became a solid Division I player at the University of Hartford. As a sophomore he averaged 7.9 points and 5 rebounds per game and as a junior he produced very similar numbers, averaging 7.5 points and 5.4 rebounds per game. As a senior, he averaged 11.4 points and 4.5 rebounds per game and was tied for the team lead in steals with 40. In his senior year he had a 25-point, six rebound effort in a 69-62 upset of a rugged Wichita State team in the Hartford Civic Center. After beating UConn 49-48 in the 1986 Connecticut Mutual Classic, the Hawks had the Huskies on the ropes in 1987 for the second year in a row before losing in double overtime, 96-94. He had a career high 29 points against Canisius College.

But Doug McCrory's personal statistics told only a part of the story of his value to the Hawks during his college career. He was a standout defensive player who often drew the opponent's primary offensive threat. Coach Jack Phelan spoke to George Smith, *Courant* staff writer, about Doug McCrory's importance to the team, "He's been our most consistent player all year. He's a coach's type of player. He does all the little things that fans in the stands don't see or understand." At South Catholic offense had been his calling card, but at the University of Hartford, it was his defense that made Doug McCrory an elite player. According to Jack Phelan in remarks to George Smith of *The Hartford Courant*, "If there are four guys around a loose ball, he's usually the one that ends up taking it. He has great hands and a great heart. Without question he's the best defensive player we've had here."

Doug McCrory graduated from the University of Hartford with a BA and a Master's Degree in Business Administration. He also earned a Master's Degree in Elementary Administration from Sacred Heart University. He taught at Rawson Elementary School before serving as Vice Principal at both Fox Middle School and the Capitol Region Education Council. He worked with Sadiq Ali to establish the Benjamin E. Mays Institute to develop a curriculum promoting self-esteem and African American history. He served six terms as a Representative in the Connecticut General Assembly. He currently serves as a Senator for the 2nd district in the Connecticut

State Senate. He lives in the Blue Hills neighborhood of Hartford with his wife Foye Smith, Hartford Judge of Probate Court, and their children. Doug McCrory has been a life-long resident of the city where he became known as one of Hartford's most outstanding basketball players.

Tony Judkins
Hartford Public High School 1985

Through the decades, the lure of a championship motivated the elite basketball players from Hartford. It began with the quest for titles in elementary school, CYO leagues, Park Department, and junior high school, and carried over to the pursuit of supremacy at the high school level in the city, conference, and state. Only the chosen few in any era ever experienced the elation of winning a City Series or conference title or, better yet, cutting down the nets after winning a state or New England championship. All players recognized that even highly successful seasons and careers usually concluded with a crushing defeat that seared the memory long after the thrill of random victories had faded. The desire to be recognized as champions – to achieve the goal that every team strove for but only the very best could ever accomplish – motivated exceptional players at every stage of their development to give everything they had to the game of basketball. And when they did, win or lose, they could walk away from the court with their heads held high.

Tony Judkins was one player from Hartford to scale the heights of his chosen sport. His basketball journey began in Stowe Village, where he was raised by his mother along with his three siblings. He attended Barbour Elementary School and Fox Middle School. With the help of a concerned teacher at Fox Middle, he was able to participate in a middle school enrichment program at the Loomis Chaffee School in Windsor that exposed him to the academic skills required for success in high school and college. He stayed in the program for two years, and returned as a staff member in his senior year of high school, laying the groundwork for his eventual pursuit of a college education.

When he finished Lewis Fox Middle School, Tony Judkins moved in with his aunt in Ellington, Connecticut because his mother was anxious that he have a safe environment and attend good schools. The attempt to transition into the Ellington school system did not go well, however, and he returned to the city to attend Hartford Public High School. His mother knew how important playing basketball was to him, and she made his participation on a team contingent on good grades and proper behavior, a deal he was willing to strike.

From a very early age, he grasped some of the essential truths that led to success on the basketball court. He played on a team with his friends Kevin Ward and the three Clarke brothers, Kevin, Kyle, and Brian. Years later, when he was a student-athlete at Sacred Heart University, he spoke to Roy Hasty of *The Hartford Courant* about the keys that made the youthful team successful, "We were a small team, but we played the team concept. Everyone was always looking, and we pressed, too. I thought that was amazing because in street ball I don't think everyone is too conscious about defense. But we did that. We played a lot of defense." The commitment to team play and defensive intensity that he acquired on the asphalt courts of Hartford neighborhoods stuck with him throughout his career. One of his earliest coaches, the former Hartford Public and Springfield College star Steve Waterman, reinforced in Tony Judkins the concept of how to play the game the right way. It was a lesson he learned well and applied diligently in high school and college.

Tony Judkins spent his first two years at Hartford Public getting acclimated to the demands of an elite high school basketball program. At 6'-4" and 165-pounds with explosive leaping ability, he had the size, athleticism and court vision to make an immediate contribution, but he may have lacked the strength and know-how to uncover his true potential in his early high school years. As his coach on the JV team in Tony's sophomore season, Steve Waterman helped him develop his natural instincts and unselfish mindset in preparation for his dramatic evolution as one of the most complete players in the state.

In his junior year Tony Judkins emerged as a solid, all-purpose forward for Hartford Public, capable of scoring from inside and outside, rebounding with authority, and playing outstanding defense. Coach Stan Piorkowski spoke to Bohdan Kolisky of *The Hartford Courant* about Tony's value to the team, "Tony Judkins, in my belief, is one of the better players in the state. He plays the game quietly, takes high-percentage shots and gets the job done very well." The Owls had a strong team, featuring talented players in addition to Tony Judkins, like Daryl Lindsey, Kevin Clarke, Ken Lester, and Tony Mayo, but the tough competition on a demanding schedule left little room for error in trying to qualify for the state tournament.

The Owls started the season slowly, struggling to settle into a comfortable rhythm. The team lost twice to powerful Hillhouse, by 29 points the first game and by four points in the second meeting. The Owls also lost to Wilbur Cross, 73-71. But there were satisfying victories as well. In a game against Lee High School, Tony Judkins scored the tie-breaking basket and added two free throws with four seconds to play to seal a 57-55 win. In the rematch against Wilbur Cross, Hartford Public won 86-84 behind Tony Judkins 24 points, 22 by Daryl Lindsey, and 16 by Kevin Clarke. It was Wilbur Cross' second two-point defeat in Hartford in three days, after suffering a 67-65 loss to South Catholic earlier in the week. When South Catholic and Hartford Public met a few days later, South Catholic was led by Doug McCrory's 21 points and 10 rebounds in a 76-69 win. In the Class LL East Region II quarterfinal match-up against Norwich, Tony Judkins scored 27 points, hitting 11 of 15 field goal attempts to lead Hartford Public to a 64-57 win. But in the semifinal game at Kennedy High School in Waterbury, Wilbur Cross beat Hartford Public 82-62. The Owls went on to play Hillhouse in the quarterfinals of the CIAC Class LL state tournament and were defeated 85-49, ending their season with a record of 11-11. It was not the kind of season the Owls had hoped to put together.

The Hartford Public players started out in a much more aggressive posture in the 1984-85 season, determined to reverse the slow start that had hindered the team the previous year. The Owls began the season with a 65-64 win over Weaver. Hartford Public followed up the season opening City Series victory with a 71-62 win over East Hartford High School. Tony Judkins scored 23 points and pulled down 14 rebounds, drawing praise from his coach. Stan Piorkowski told Roy Hasty of *The Hartford Courant*, "Tony Judkins surprises you with his stats. He's not flashy, but he works hard and usually his man doesn't score many points." Daryl Lindsey, a 6'-3" center, contributed 19 points and 10 rebounds for the Owls. Hartford Public ran off nine straight wins to open the season, before losing to Penney High School of East Hartford. Daryl Lindsey scored 21 points and Tony Judkins contributed 18 in the Owls' first loss of the season.

As usual, some of the stiffest competition Hartford Public faced all season came within the city limits. After winning the first City Series game against Bulkeley 77-66, the Owls dropped the rematch 71-69 to fall to 11-2 on the season. The win improved Bulkeley's record to 12-2, and showed once again the unpredictability of the results of games played between city rivals. Bulkeley players like guard Hamilton Garcia, who scored 24 points, and rugged Ivan Powell, were not intimidated by the Owls number four ranking in the state. City Series contests were about bragging rights during the off-season and brought out the best in players that had played against each other most of their lives. Tony Judkins had scored 25 points, Daryl Lindsey 22, and the quick Hartford Public guards Shase Ricks and Glen Smith had pressured the Bulldogs the entire game. Yet after a spirited second half rally by the Owls erased a 15-point third quarter deficit, Bulkeley walked off their home court as winners, providing the players a sense of pride and accomplishment they would carry over into the summer and for many years to come.

After the loss to Bulkeley, Hartford Public went right back to work piling up victories, several coming against their fiercest rivals. On their home court on Forest Street, the Owls literally fought their way to a 54-46 victory over Wilbur Cross. Bohdan Kolinsky described the ending of the game in *The Hartford Courant*, "The game had an abrupt, near-riotous ending. With 3 seconds left, tempers flared at the HPHS foul line, both benches emptied and, when fans closest to the fight began to pour onto the court, officials Gerry McGrath and Skip Griffin decided it was best to end it right there."

If city rivalries were intense, games against the New Haven schools were even more passionate, and lacked the camaraderie bred from years of familiarity. Through the years Wilbur Cross had wrecked the dreams of too many Hartford teams to earn any goodwill within the city. Against a talented Governors' lineup that included Wilbert Frazier, a bruising 6'- 7" 240-pound center, and skilled guards Troy Bradford and Ron Moye, Tony Judkins and his teammates knew they had to bring all the competitive fire they could muster to match Wilbur Cross' intensity. The animosity between the rivals was built on respect, but it did not allow either team to back down or relent. Glenn Smith led the 17-2 Owls in scoring with 16 points, Tony Judkins and Kevin Clarke added 13 points each, and Wilbert Frazier paced 14-5 Wilbur Cross with 21 points. The hostilities at the end of the game were unfortunate, but they fueled expectations for the next showdown between the two powerful teams.

In an exciting City Series game against Weaver, it required two overtime periods for Hartford Public to subdue the Beavers, 75-73. Tony Judkins hit a shot as time expired in regulation that was ruled to have left his hand too late by official John Fontana, sending the game into the first overtime. The game remained tied after the first overtime when Weaver's Greg Mills' last second shot missed the mark. In the second overtime, Tony Judkins stole the ball at mid-court and threw down a resounding dunk to give Weaver a four-point lead it would not relinquish. Tony Judkins scored 22 points, Daryl Lindsey 18, and Glenn Smith 14 for Hartford Public, overcoming a 35-point effort from Weaver's Curtis Wilson. It was the last home game of his high school career for Tony Judkins, and he had helped make it one of the most memorable. But the two teams would meet again a week later in the first round of the CIAC Class LL East Region tournament.

Hartford Public and Weaver met for the third time in the season at Plainville High School. The first two games had been decided by one and two points, but the third game lacked the dramatic quality of the previous two. Tony Judkins scored 27 points and grabbed 14 rebounds to power the Owls to a 70-55 win, ending Weaver's season with an 8-13 record. Hartford Public improved to 19-2. The Owls won the Class LL East Region tournament and advanced to face Bridgeport Central in the Class LL state tournament. Daryl Lindsey scored 23 points and Tony Judkins 19, including two foul shots with eight seconds remaining in the game to secure a 72-68 win. In the semifinals of the state tournament against Newington High School, Tony Judkins had a team-high 21 points and Daryl Lindsey added 19 in a 74-66 win, setting up a climactic meeting between heated rivals Hartford Public and Wilbur Cross in the finals of the Class LL state tournament at Central Connecticut State University.

It had been 23 years since the Owls of Hartford Public last won the state championship. The team had beaten Wilbur Cross in the next to the last game of the regular season in the fight-marred game, but the Governors were gunning for their ninth state title under Coach Bob Saulsbury, and the team featured a tournament tested "Big Three" in Wilbert Frazier, Ron Moye, and Terry Bradford. But Hartford Public had a veteran team as well, led by Daryl Lindsey, Glenn Smith, Kevin Clarke, and Tony Judkins. Hartford Public coach Stan Piorkowski praised Tony Judkins' outstanding play to Bodhan Kolinsky of *The Hartford Courant*, "He's as close to a complete player that we have. He rebounds, shoots very well, plays the inside, and can handle the ball, too, if he has to." But Hartford Public's long championship drought was not over. Wilbur Cross won the title with a 71-65 victory, fueled by tournament MVP Troy Bradford's 25 points.

It was a disappointing game for Tony Judkins. He picked up three fouls with barely a minute gone in the first quarter, forcing him to sit out for the rest of the first half and to play tentatively when he returned. But in one respect, his uncharacteristic uneven performance had a very positive impact on his future. One of the spectators in the stands for the finals was Dave Bike, the head basketball coach at Sacred Heart University in Bridgeport. He had come to the previous game to get a closer look at Daryl Lindsey, a potential recruit, and he came away from the game extremely impressed with Tony Judkins. It did not bother Dave Bike that Tony had an off game in the finals. He had seen enough the prior game to know he was going to offer Tony a scholarship, and he felt Tony's under-performance against Wilbur Cross enhanced his chances of landing a prized recruit. As it turned out, Dave Bike's competition for Tony Judkins was limited to other Division II and Division III schools. Tony had led the Owls in scoring his senior year with 18 points a game. He was named second team All-State as a junior and first team All-State as a senior. But he did not attract the attention of Division I programs. His decision to accept Dave Bike's scholarship offer turned out to be a win-win for Tony Judkins and Sacred Heart University.

In his freshman year at Sacred Heart, Tony Judkins started all 32 games, averaged 10.4 points and 6.2 rebounds per game, and helped the team win the NCAA Division II National Championship. Before Sacred Heart faced Florida Southern University in a Final Four semifinal match-up in the Springfield Civic Center, Dave Bike spoke to Owen Campfield of *The Hartford Courant* about his valuable freshman forward, Tony Judkins, "Maybe Keith Bennett scored more points as a freshman for us, but overall, no freshman I've had ever had a finer year." On March 22, 1986, Sacred Heart University defeated Southeast Missouri State 93-87 to win the Division II National Championship. It only took Tony Judkins one year in college to win the championship he had been denied in high school.

Tony Judkins had a brilliant career at Sacred Heart. His teams averaged 22 victories a season over his four years at the university. Sacred Heart appeared in three NCAA Division II tournaments, winning two New England championships and an NCAA title. Tony averaged 18.5 points and 7.9 rebounds per game in his senior year. He was a Division II third-team All-American in 1988 and a Division II second-team All-American in 1989. His name is scattered all over the Sacred Heart record book. He is eighth in career scoring at the university with 2,009 points, a 15.9 points per game average. He is second all-time in foul shots made with 467, fourth in blocked shots with 119, and seventh in rebounds with 909. He had a career high 45 points in a game at Franklin Pierce.

As his career was drawing to a close, Tony Judkins spoke to Tom Yantz of *The Hartford Courant* about the team's pursuit of another title in his senior year, "When we won the title in '86, my roommate in Springfield was Roger Younger [former Middletown High star]. He told me I had the talent and character to be a team leader after he and the other seniors left. Now my career is almost over. It started with the NCAAs my first year. Now we're there again … Not bad for this skinny kid, not too bad at all."

His career at Sacred Heart ended with a 58-57 loss to North Carolina Central in the Division II Elite Eight. He walked off the court in the Springfield Civic Center in disappointment, as almost all great players eventually do, but no one could ever say that Tony Judkins was not a champion.

More Hartford Legends
Appendix

Ronnie Harris / Weaver High School 1954
Ronnie Harris was the burly 6'- 3" center for Weaver's 1954 state championship team. This first team All-State performer was a tough rebounder and a gifted outside shooter. He was the MVP of the state tournament finals and the top vote getter on the 1954 New Haven Register All-State team. He was a forerunner of many of the great players that came after him.

Frank Keitt / Weaver High School 1954
This lefty was one of the great guards of his era and a major contributor to Weaver's 1954 State Championship team. Frank Keitt was super quick and a skilled ball handler. He was a member of the Hartford Capitols professional basketball team and a founding organizer of the Greater Hartford Summer league.

Ron Jefferson / Weaver High School 1955
Ron Jefferson was perhaps the fastest player in Hartford during his era. Jefferson participated in a track meet and won several events. He was a pivotal player on the 1954 state championship team.

Bill Schmitt / Bulkeley High School 1955
This 6'- 5" wide-body was one of Lou Bazzano's first great players. Bill Schmitt earned first team All-CDC and first team All-State honors in 1955. He went on to play basketball at the University of Connecticut. He earned a starting spot at UConn as a sophomore and earned MVP honors in a prestigious tournament that featured Seattle University and NBA great Elgin Baylor.

Clarence "Sonny" Thomas / Hartford Public High School 1955

Clarence "Sonny" Thomas, a baseball and basketball legend at Hartford Public, was one of the school's first African American superstars. He was a first team All-State performer in basketball in 1955. He played professionally for the Harlem Magicians Traveling Team, Scranton Miners of the Eastern Basketball League, and the Milford Chiefs. Through his 30 year association with the Boys & Girls Club of Hartford, he became a inspirational mentor for many of Hartford's youth.

John Sullivan / Weaver High School 1957

John Sullivan arrived in Hartford from Louisiana as a tenth grader and had an immediate impact on the Weaver basketball program. A three year starter at center, the 6'- 2" Sullivan was a fierce shot blocker and rebounder. During the undefeated 1957 State and New England dream season, John Sullivan averaged 15 points and 15 rebounds per game. He was selected first team All-State in 1957, along with his teammate Johnny Egan.

Russell Carter / Weaver High 1958

Russell Carter was one of the elite talents of the 1950s. An aggressive defender, Russell Carter utilized an unorthodox high dribble, but he was a superb ball-handler who possessed the poise and command of a consummate floor general. As a sophomore and junior, he helped Weaver win a New England championship and back-to-back state titles.

Stan Egnat / Hartford Public High School 1958

Stan Egnat was a two-sport star at Hartford Public in baseball and basketball during the 1950s. In basketball he led the Owls to a 15-4 record and co-City and CDC championships in his senior year. He was named first team All-State and he made the All-Tournament team in the CIAC state tourney. After graduating from Hartford Public, he served in the U.S. Army and worked for 18 years with the New Britain Boys & Girls Club.

Gene Jenkins / Hartford Public High School 1958

Gene Jenkins was a multi-sport athlete who starred in basketball, football, and track and field. As a basketball player, he was co-captain of the 1957-58 team and earned All-CDC honors. He had a distinguished military career and retired from the United States Post Office.

Carmen Perrone / Bulkeley High School 1958

Carmen Perrone was Mr. Basketball in Connecticut, earning first team All-State and All-American honors in 1958. Known as a prolific jump shooter, Carmen Perrone led the Bulldogs to the New England championship game in 1958. He had five 30 point games during his senior year, as well as a 44 point game against New London High School, a school record at the time.

Charles "Corky" Terry / Hartford Public High School 1958

Charles "Corky" Terry was a dynamic offensive guard with the ability to carve out space on drives to the hoop. He was an All-Capital District Conference selection in 1958 and a prominent player in Hartford's famed Industrial League.

Ron Copes / Hartford Public High School 1959

Ron Copes was a two-way football star at HPHS who brought his leadership and competitive spirit to the hardwood. After graduating from Lincoln University, where he is a member of the Athletic Hall of Fame, he served for 27 years in the United States Army, attaining the rank of colonel. He is a recipient of the Silver Star. He received an M.B.A. from Atlanta University and served as vice president of Community Relations at MassMutual Financial Group.

Pat Burke / Hartford Public High School 1961

Pat Burke was instrumental in Hartford Public's first New England Championship, scoring 14 points and grabbing eight rebounds while playing stellar defense against Wilbur Cross star Dave Hicks in the 68-62 Owls' victory. He was in the midst of a tremendous career at Fairfield University when he died in a tragic accident in 1966. He was inducted into both the Hartford Public and Fairfield University Athletic Hall of Fame.

Otis Woods / Hartford Public High School 1961

Otis Woods was a standout on the 1961 New England Championship team that included Pat Burke, Eddie Griffin, Bruce Maddox, and Stanley Poole. He was an exceptional long range shooter and a creative ball-handler. Otis Woods attended Virginia State University.

Jimmy Belfiore / Bulkeley High School 1962

Jimmy Belfiore was a 2nd team All-State selection for the 1962 Bulkeley High School team that lost four games during the season, all to Hartford Public, including the state and New England title games. The left-handed sharpshooting Jim Belfiore went on to become a two-time captain at Trinity College, where he established the school's career scoring record at the time with 1,368 points. He averaged 24.5 points per game and set the single game scoring record with 47 points. He is regarded as perhaps the best pure shooter ever to play at Trinity. He was inducted into the inaugural class of the Trinity College Basketball Hall of Fame. Jim Belfiore passed away in 2003 at the age of 59.

Joe Hourihan / Bulkeley High School 1962

Joe Hourihan was a three-sport athlete at Bulkeley High School, where he earned seven varsity letters while excelling in football, baseball, and basketball. He was the catcher on the baseball team for two of the best pitchers in Bulkeley's history, Bob Raffalo and Gene Reilly. He co-captained the baseball and football teams in his senior year, earning second team All-CDC honors in both sports. Joe Hourihan was the point guard on the 1962 Bulkeley basketball team that was the runner up in the state and New England championship tournaments. He received the Casey Athletic Medal as Bulkeley's outstanding senior athlete. He excelled academically at Bulkeley as well, where he was ranked third in his class. Joe Hourihan continued his stellar three-sport athletic career at Trinity College. He was the captain of the undefeated Trinity freshman basketball team and the co-captain of the freshman baseball team. During his career at Trinity, he established school records for most assists in a single game, season, and career. He was presented the McCook Award, given to the outstanding senior athlete at Trinity College. He was inducted into the Trinity College Basketball Hall of Fame, where he joined his high school and college teammate and lifelong friend Jim Belfiore.

Len Kostek / Hartford Public High School 1962

Len Kostek earned a total of seven letters at HPHS, three for basketball and four in baseball. Len was a major contributor on the 1961-1962 HPHS basketball teams that won a State Championship and two New England titles. He was honorable mention All-State as a basketball player. Len also was captain of the 1962 basketball team.

Ted Kwash / Bulkeley High School 1962

Ted Kwash was co-captain of the Bulkeley basketball team that reached the state and New England finals in 1962, before losing to Hartford Public. He had the distinction of being a 5'- 11" starting center, where his crafty play helped spearhead one of the great Bulkeley teams of all time. Ted Kwash also captained the University of Hartford Hawks' basketball team.

Bruce Maddox / Hartford Public High School 1962

Bruce Maddox was a product of Bellevue Square and Brackett Northeast Junior High School, where he earned a reputation as one of Hartford's most promising young basketball players. His text-book jump shot helped the Owls win a state title and two New England championships. Bruce Maddox died in a tragic automobile accident in 1965.

Gene Reilly / Bulkeley High School 1962

Gene Reilly was one of Bulkeley High School and Central Connecticut State College's greatest athletes. In his senior year at Bulkeley he was selected first team All-State and All-New England while leading the Bulldogs to the finals in both tournaments. He set the CIAC tournament record by making 30 straight free throws. He was also an outstanding pitcher on Bulkeley's baseball team. He went on to play basketball and baseball at Central Connecticut. He scored 1,597 career points at Central, and he led the nation in free throw percentage, earning All-American honors. He was a pitcher in the San Francisco Giants organization for two years before serving in the United States Army during the war in Viet Nam. He pitched briefly with the Giants' Double A team in Armarillo, Texas before returning to Hartford as an assistant to his brother Joe at South Catholic High School. He went on to a successful basketball and baseball coaching career at Portland High School, where he also served as the director of athletics.

Gene Nelson / Weaver High School 1963
At 6'- 5" Gene Nelson was an elite center for Weaver. He was an All-CDC performer and went on to have a fine basketball career at Virginia State University.

John Joiner / Hartford Public High School 1964
John Joiner possessed blazing quickness and great leaping ability. As a sophomore, he was a key contributor on the 1962 team that won the State and New England Championships. In 1964 Joiner's undersized Owls team made it to the State Championship game before losing to Hillhouse.

Maurice Williams / Weaver High School 1964
Maurice Williams was a dangerous outside shooter for Weaver. He co-captained the 1964 team with Ben Billie. He was a familiar presence at Keney Park over the years.

Art Blackwell / Weaver High & Hartford Public High 1965
Art Blackwell starred at Weaver High School before transferring to arch rival HPHS for his senior year. A true gym rat, Art Blackwell was a devastating jump-shooter with a smooth all-around game. He played in multiple leagues in the area after graduating from Hartford Public.

Nate "Shotgun" Adger / Hartford Public High School 1966
Nate "Shotgun" Adger was a valuable member of Hartford Public's outstanding teams in the mid-sixties. He was a fluid and multi-dimensional player who was an effective scorer, rebounder, and defensive stalwart. He was a junior college All-American at Johnson & Wales, where he led the team in scoring and rebounding during his two years at the school. He earned All-Yankee Conference honors at the University of Rhode Island, where he reunited with his former Hartford Public teammate Dwight Tolliver. Nate Adger served as Dwight Tolliver's assistant coach at Weaver, where they won a state championship.

Mike Sadowski / South Catholic High School 1966

Mike Sadowski was Joe Reilly's first one thousand point scorer at South Catholic. A 6'- 2", 195-pound center, he earned All-Hartford County Conference honors twice, and he was a second team All-State performer as a senior. Mike Sadowski played two years at Saint Anselm College as a shooting guard, and he graduated from the University of Hartford with a degree in Economics.

Greg Harrell / Hartford Public High School 1967

Greg Harrell was a ball-handling wizard who could also shoot the ball extremely well. He teamed up with Dwight "Pooch" Tolliver to form one of the most explosive backcourts in Hartford basketball history.

Wayne Jones / Weaver High School 1967

Wayne Jones was a first team All-City performer in his senior year, averaging 18.8 points per game while helping Weaver to a 17-3 record. As a junior, he led the Beavers to the finals of the CIAC Class LL State Tournament, before losing to Wilbur Cross by two points. He was extremely athletic, capable of rebounding and blocking shots against the best big men in the state. He possessed one of the purest long-range jump shots Hartford has ever known. He teamed with Norwalk's Calvin Murphy at Niagara University. He was drafted by the Detroit Pistons and played professionally overseas for several years.

Ben Mathews / Weaver High School 1967

Ben Matthews was one of Weaver's most outstanding frontcourt players of all time. He led the Beavers in scoring as a senior, averaging 19.4 points per game, while often drawing the toughest defensive assignment on the floor, regardless of position. At 6'- 4" he was an extremely versatile player who could rebound, shoot, pass, and handle the ball. He teamed up with Wayne Jones and Jewett Newkirk to give Weaver a dominant frontcourt. Ben was the older brother of another Weaver standout, Fred "Dee-Dee" Mathews.

Donald Chaffin / Hartford Public High School 1968
Donald Chaffin was a 6'- 5" 205-pound player who dominated in the low post and excelled at playing fundamental basketball. After he graduated from Hartford Public, he averaged over 30 points per game at Manchester Community College. He was the MVP of the 1971 Greater Hartford Basketball Summer League.

John Holiday / Weaver High School 1969
John Holiday was a talented 6'-3" front court player with a solid all-around game. He was a first team All-City and All-CDC performer who averaged 17 points and 12 rebounds per game as a senior.

Bob LaVigne / South Catholic High School 1969
Bob LaVigne was a very athletic player who combined exceptional strength and leaping ability to excel in all areas of the game. As a powerful 6'-2" swing-man at South Catholic, Bob LaVigne led his team in scoring as a senior tri-captain with 18 points per game. He was named South Catholic's Outstanding Senior Athlete. He went on to play basketball and baseball at Amherst College, where he was again named his school's Outstanding Senior Athlete.

Thomas Cummings / Hartford Public High School 1971
Thomas "Chucky" Cummings possessed a lethal mid-range jump shot. He was a valuable starter on Hartford Public's 1971 team that lost in the state finals to Weaver High School. He was a competitive player in city leagues until the age of 50.

Myron Goggins / Weaver High School 1971
Myron Goggins was a 6'- 5" player who possessed outstanding athleticism and superior instincts. He was named to the All-City in 1971. Myron Goggins made one of the biggest shots in the Beavers' basketball history when he scored the winning field goal in the state title game against Hartford Public in 1971, giving Weaver its 3rd State Championship.

Kemp Mitchell / Hartford Public High School 1971
Kemp Mitchell, a strong 5'- 10" guard, was an exceptional ball-handler and clutch shooter. He became a featured player in Hartford area leagues for many years.

Billy Tisdol / Hartford Public High School 1971
Billy Tisdol and his younger brother Doward were exceptional front court players for Hartford Public's successful teams of the early 1970s. At 6'- 5", Billy Tisdol could handle the ball like a guard and was an exceptional mid-range shooter. Billy Tisdol also played at the Robinson School in West Hartford, helping to elevate the status of the private school with his outstanding play.

Lee Otis Wilson / Weaver High School 1971
Lee Otis Wilson was one of the finest jump shooters in the history of Hartford basketball. He led Weaver in scoring during his junior and senior seasons. Lee Otis Wilson had outstanding leaping ability, which made his jump shot impossible to stop. He was a two-time All-City performer and a second team All-State selection. He was a key member of Weaver's 1971 state championship team. He continued his role as a sharpshooter at the University of Connecticut under coach Dee Rowe.

Donnie Lambert / Weaver High School & Kingwood Oxford 1972
Donnie Lambert transferred to Kingswood Oxford School from Weaver High School, where he had already established himself as a star point guard. He was exceptionally quick and elusive. He captained the football and basketball teams at Kingswood and earned All-League honors in basketball and lacrosse.

Ron LaVigne / Bulkeley High School 1972
At 6'- 4", Ron LaVigne's great leaping ability allowed him to lead his Bulkeley team in scoring, rebounding and blocked shots his senior year. He had a 31-rebound game against New Britain. He was a co-captain his senior year and made the All-City Team. Ron LaVigne played four years of basketball at Eastern Connecticut State University.

Nick Oliver / Hartford Public High School 1972

Nick Oliver earned a reputation as one of Hartford's greatest defensive players, capable of playing suffocating man-to-man defense and coming up with timely steals. He earned first team All-City honors as a senior. He organized a successful youth basketball league at Hartford's famed Keney Park in the early 1980s.

Joe Pina / Hartford Public High School 1972

At 6'- 5" and 240 pounds, Joe Pina was an incredible physical specimen. He was the prototypical power forward who enjoyed setting picks, rebounding, blocking shots, and running the floor. He participated in many physical battles with his good friend Owen Mahorn. Joe Pina earned a basketball scholarship to Palmer Junior College in Iowa.

Sam Booker / Weaver High School 1973

Sam Booker was an outstanding all-around athlete who thrived in baseball, football, and basketball. He was one of the founding stars of the Greater Hartford Summer league. He played professionally in Europe. An exciting and fiercely competitive combination guard, Booker relished competing against the best.

Peter Palermino / Bulkeley High School 1973

Peter Palermino was a first team All-City selection in 1973. He was a heady point guard and exceptional defensive player for the Bulldogs. He once helped to limit Weaver legend Owen Mahorn to seven points. Peter Palermino has been a prominent high school and college basketball official for over thirty-five years and serves as the state rules interpreter for basketball officials in Connecticut.

Doward Tisdol / Hartford Public High School 1973

Doward Tisdol was an athletic scoring and rebounding machine. He was a two-time first team All-State performer who played in three State Championship games. At Virginia State University he was All-CIAA, All-American, and a legitimate NBA prospect. He was drafted by the Los Angeles Lakers in the sixth round. He was the younger brother of Hartford Public standout Bill Tisdol.

Osee Tolliver / Hartford Public High School 1973

Osee Tolliver was one of the most dazzling passers and ball handlers of his era. In 1973 he was a first team All-City performer and a second team All-State selection. He played in three state championship games. A cerebral talent, Tolliver was a dominant player in the city.

Nick Davis / Weaver High School 1974

Nick Davis was a strong player with the ability to hang in the air and finish with acrobatic shots around the basket. He was also a fine passer and a superior defensive player. Nick Davis was the older brother of George "Shorty" Davis.

Michael Johnson / Bulkeley High School 1976

Michael Johnson: At 6'- 2", Michael Johnson excelled in the front court for Bulkeley and averaged 20 points and 12 rebounds per game as a senior. He earned All-City, All-Capital District Conference, and third team All-State honors. He played JV hoops at the University of Connecticut.

Ronnie Smith / Weaver High School 1976

At only 5'-9", Ronnie Smith was a fearless combination of speed, quickness and leaping ability. He was an excellent jump shooter on the fast break. He was named to the All-City and All-Capital District Conference teams in 1975 and 1976.

Daryl Turner / Weaver High School 1976

Daryl " Tuna" Turner was a smooth and efficient player for Weaver. Turner excelled within 15 feet of the basket with athletic tip-ins or by knocking down timely jump shots. He was an important contributor on Weaver's 1976 team that reached the finals of the Class LL state tournament before losing to Sly Williams and Lee High School.

Jerry "Rat" Ager / Hartford High School 1977

Jerry "Rat" Ager played no nonsense defense in the tradition of Owls' guards Kemp Mitchell, Nick Oliver and Darrell Brown. He was lightning quick on defense and able to come up with many key steals. Ager and his buddy Charles "Duffy" Jernigan led Hartford Public on a winning streak that enabled the Owls to qualify for the state tournament in 1977.

Robert Scott / Weaver High School 1977

Robert "Bird" Scott was an outstanding combination guard who was influenced by Weaver standouts Keith Morgan and George "Shorty" Davis. Robert Scott was the standard bearer for Rawson playground ball players to follow. At 5'- 8", he was unselfish and highly competitive. In 1977 he was a first team All-City and All-CDC performer.

Joe Tancredi / Bulkeley High School 1977

Joe Tamcredi excelled as a shooter, ball-handler, and passer. He was first team All-City and All Capital District Conference as a senior.

Allen Broughton / Weaver High School 1978

Allen "Baldy" Broughton was one of the few freshmen to play varsity basketball at Weaver. At 5'- 6", he was a tenacious competitor who used amazing speed, quickness, and a lethal pull-up jump shot to torment opponents.

Glen Maulden / Weaver High School 1978

Glen Maulden was the ultimate utility man on the hardwood.   He excelled on the defensive end of the floor.

John Meaney / Kingwood Oxford School 1978

John Meaney paired with Phil Moran to form one of the finest backcourts in New England prep school history. John Meaney was a tough point guard and floor leader. At Trinity College, John Meaney was a four-year starter, three-year captain, and first-team academic All American.

Kenny Smith / Hartford Public High School 1978

Kenny Smith was a great outside shooter who was a master bank shot artist. He averaged almost 27 points per game during his senior year while earning first team All-City and second team All-State recognition in 1978. He was one of Hartford's most dominant players of his era. Kenny Smith attended Portland Community College in the state of Oregon.

Sylvester Turner / Weaver High School 1978

As a young player, Sylvester "Sly" Turner worked tirelessly on his game. In high school Sly Turner was a valuable 5'- 7" point guard at Weaver. He went on to star at Middlesex Junior College and to became one of the most sought-after point guards in leagues throughout Connecticut and Massachusetts. He was a player who made his teammates better. He became a highly respected basketball official in central Connecticut.

Joe Adams / Hartford Public High School 1979

Joe Adams was a gifted athlete who used his defensive skills to generate offense. As a senior, he teamed with younger brother Mike Adams to form one of the best back courts in the history of Hartford basketball. He played briefly at Central Connecticut State University.

Marcus Brown / Northwest Catholic High School 1980

Together with Norman Bailey, 6'- 6" Marcus Brown was the other half of one of the best front court duos the city of Hartford ever produced. Marcus Brown won three HCC championships and he was a key member of the 1979 Northwest Catholic team that lost to Wilbur Cross in the LL title game, 74-73. Marcus Brown was an exceptionally effective offensive player, rugged rebounder, and standout defensive player. He is the younger brother of HPHS legend Sadiq Ali (Bill Brown).

Leroy Cruel / Hartford Public High School 1980

At 5'- 11", Leroy Cruel was an effective shot blocker and he was able to maneuver on the court with the grace of an elite point guard. An outstanding one-on-one player, Leroy Cruel had record-breaking scoring performances at Greater Hartford Community College.

Vincent Ithier / Hartford Public High School 1980

Vicente Ithier played only one full varsity season at HPHS but averaged a double-double and received All CDC honors. At 6'- 2" Vincent Ithier walked on the UConn basketball team during the advent of the Big East Conference. He played professional basketball overseas and represented Puerto Rico in the Seoul, Korea Olympics.

Chris Canty / Hartford Public High School 1981

Chris Canty was perhaps the most dominant big man at Hartford Public since the Bob Nash era. He turned many assists from Michael Adams into ferocious slam dunks. The 6'- 8" Canty was a team-first player and an excellent shot blocker. He was an All-CDC performer and an exceptional talent.

Ulysses Garcia / Northwest Catholic High School 1981

Ulysses Garcia was a first team All-State performer at Northwest Catholic in 1981. He went on to lead the University of Hartford Hawks in scoring all four years at the school. He is seventh in career scoring at the University of Hartford with 1,485 points, eighth in career assists with 297, and 10th in free throw percentage at .774.

Zachary Harris / Simsbury High School 1981

Zachary Harris was a four-year starter at Simsbury High School and co-captain of the basketball team in his senior year. He lived on Andover Street in Hartford and attended Simsbury High School through Project Concern. He was a solidly built 6'- 2" performer who played hard on both ends of the floor. He was the son of Weaver High School great John Lee.

Earle Scott / Weaver High School 1981

Earle Scott was an outstanding mid-range jump shooter, master ball-handler, and slick passer for Weaver. He was the younger brother of former Weaver standout Robert "Bird" Scott. At 5'- 8", he used his skill at handling the ball to create scoring opportunities.

Jerome Williams / Weaver High School 1981

Jerome Williams was a 6'- 1" lefty whose long arms and great lateral quickness made him a superb defender. He excelled at driving to the basket. Jerome Williams had a career high of 30 points against HPHS in 1981.

Russell Shorter / Bulkeley High School 1982

Russell Shorter was part of Bulkeley's dynamic one-two punch with Tyrone Canino. As a junior, Russell Shorter led the Bulldog's to an upset victory over HPHS and All-State guard Mike Adams. He was a two-time All-Conference performer as a junior and senior.

Charles Terry / Farmington High & Weaver High 1982

Charles "Lump" Terry was the son of former HPHS standout Charles Terry, Sr. The 6'- 3" point guard starred at Farmington High School before transferring to Weaver High School for his senior year in 1982. He became an All-CDC performer and helped the Beavers make a deep run in the CIAC state tournament.

Pete Simpson / Bulkeley High School 1983

Pete Simpson was a 6"- 1" gym rat and a classic streak shooter. Once he got it going, he was unstoppable. He became a popular player in numerous leagues around Greater Hartford, and he was an inspiration and a mentor to many young players. Now in his fifties, Pete Simpson still plays competitive basketball.

Ivan Powell / Bulkeley High School 1984

Ivan Powell: Powell was a first team All-State performer in 1984 at Bulkeley High School and a junior college All-American at Mattatuck Community College. He was a devastating outside shooter. He went on to play at the University of Maryland. Ivan Powell later became an accomplished gospel performer.

Curtis Wilson / Weaver High School 1984

Curtis Wilson was a slick ball handler who possessed superior body control as a scorer and passer. He was impossible to guard one-on-one or to press full court. A McDonald's All American nominee in 1984.

Acknowledgments

First and foremost I would like to thank God. Through the process of putting this book together I realized the power of the written word. The Almighty has given me the inspiration to believe in my passion and pursue my dreams. I could never have done this without the faith I have in you, the Almighty.

I would also like to express my gratitude to the many people who saw me through this book; to all those who provided support, talked things over, read, wrote, offered comments, which allowed me to grow in the process of writing this book.

I would also like to thank Howie Greenblatt and Dean Greenblatt- You guys were a Godsend. Without your partnership, I can't imagine this book being published. You both took this project to another level. I will never forget you both. You guys are the best!

I would like to thank Dorothy Helfrick. You are a special person. You helped ignite a fire in me for writing that I never thought existed. You were more than a fine editor. You became a friend.

I would like to thank Carson Kenney for designing the book-cover. You are very gifted and talented. It was great working with you.

I would like to thank my family, who has always supported and encouraged me to do my best. I love my family. I'm so proud to be a Copeland!

I would like to thank Kevin Johnson and the staff of the Connecticut State Library. They were always there with willing hearts to assist me with my research. If you love history, you should visit the Connecticut State Library.

Special thanks to Annetta Green and Carol Vincuilla for scanning hundreds of photos of the many players who are highlighted in the book. You are two of the classiest ladies ever. You guys were always there in the clutch.

Thanks to Joe Hourihan and Garrett Hourihan. You guys were helpful in some of my most challenging moments. Thanks again.

Special thanks to my teachers and mentors who, like my family, inspired me to be the best that I could be. Every one of you is very much a part of me.

Special shout out to Dave Ferguson and the staff of Adelbrook

Behavioral & Developmental Services. Each of you encouraged me from the very beginning. Your words fueled me to the very end. It's great to work with such good people.

Special shout out to the basketball players and coaches from 1954-1984. Thanks for allowing me to interview you. It was the thrill of a life time. You guys are a credit to your family, friends and the City of Hartford. Hopefully this book will enlighten a broad audience about the greatness of Hartford basketball.

I would also like to thank Randy LaVigne, Tia Woods, Andrew Williams, Norman Bailey, Kyle Anderson, Kevin Budds, Howie Greenblatt and Peter Egan for being a tower of support and strength. Whatever I needed, you guys were always there.

Last but not least: I beg forgiveness of all those who have been with me over the course of the years and whose names I have failed to mention. Blame it on my head and not my heart.

Mike Copeland

About the Authors

Mike Copeland is a 1982 graduate of Weaver High School, where he was a proud member of the basketball team. As a senior playing for new coach Dwight "Pooch" Tolliver, Mike Copeland averaged 14 points a game and earned All-Capital District Conference honors. The highlight of his Weaver basketball career was a 33-point effort against Hillhouse that included the game-winning basket in an 85-84 victory. He also played basketball at St. Thomas More School in Oakdale, Connecticut. He holds a Bachelor's degree in Human Services from Springfield College. In 1995 he was the co-founder and Executive Director of The Sons of Thunder Coalition, an organization committed to bettering the lives of young people through scholarships and college programs. This is his first book.

Howie Greenblatt graduated from Weaver High School in 1967, where he played basketball for Coach Frank Scelza. He continued his basketball career at Trinity College in Hartford, serving as captain of the 1970-71 team. He was inducted into the Trinity College Basketball Hall of Fame and the New England Basketball Hall of Fame. He has an M.A. and Ph.D. in English and American Literature from Brandeis University. He serves as vice president of the Richard M. Keane Foundation, a nonprofit organization that provides athletic and academic enrichment programs for Wethersfield youth, and he is a member of the Wethersfield Hunger Action Team.